Accounting and Financial Reporting Challenges for Government, Non-Profits, and the Private Sector

Fábio Albuquerque
Instituto Politécnico de Lisboa, Portugal

Paula Gomes dos Santos
Instituto Politécnico de Lisboa, Portugal

IGI Global
PUBLISHER of TIMELY KNOWLEDGE

A volume in the Advances in Finance, Accounting, and Economics (AFAE) Book Series

Published in the United States of America by
IGI Global
Business Science Reference (an imprint of IGI Global)
701 E. Chocolate Avenue
Hershey PA, USA 17033
Tel: 717-533-8845
Fax: 717-533-8661
E-mail: cust@igi-global.com
Web site: http://www.igi-global.com

Library of Congress Cataloging-in-Publication Data

Names: Albuquerque, Fábio, 1980- editor. | Gomes dos Santos, Paula, 1972- editor.
Title: Accounting and financial reporting challenges for government, non-profits, and the private sector / Fábio Albuquerque, Paula Gomes dos Santos, editors.
Description: Hershey, PA : Business Science Reference, [2023] | Includes bibliographical references and index. | Summary: "Accounting and Financial Reporting Challenges for Government, Non-Profits, and the Private Sector addresses the latest accounting topics and their practical and educational relations with local and international regulations, standards, and practices. It deals with new challenges and trends in accounting and reporting for organizations from different institutional sectors, including the private, public, and non-profit ones. Covering topics such as creative accounting, financial reporting, and stakeholder participation, this premier reference source is an excellent resource for accountants, government officials, business leaders, managers, policymakers, students and educators of higher education, librarians, researchers, and academicians"-- Provided by publisher.
Identifiers: LCCN 2022057786 (print) | LCCN 2022057787 (ebook) | ISBN 9781668472934 (hardcover) | ISBN 9781668472941 (paperback) | ISBN 9781668472958 (ebook)
Subjects: LCSH: Financial statements--Standards. | Accounting. | Nonprofit organizations--Accounting.
Classification: LCC HF5681.B2 A323 2023 (print) | LCC HF5681.B2 (ebook) | DDC 657/.3--dc23/eng/20221201
LC record available at https://lccn.loc.gov/2022057786
LC ebook record available at https://lccn.loc.gov/2022057787

This book is published in the IGI Global book series Advances in Finance, Accounting, and Economics (AFAE) (ISSN: 2327-5677; eISSN: 2327-5685)

British Cataloguing in Publication Data
A Cataloguing in Publication record for this book is available from the British Library.
All work contributed to this book is new, previously-unpublished material. The views expressed in this book are those of the authors, but not necessarily of the publisher.
For electronic access to this publication, please contact: eresources@igi-global.com.

Advances in Finance, Accounting, and Economics (AFAE) Book Series

Ahmed Driouchi
Al Akhawayn University, Morocco

ISSN:2327-5677
EISSN:2327-5685

Mission

In our changing economic and business environment, it is important to consider the financial changes occurring internationally as well as within individual organizations and business environments. Understanding these changes as well as the factors that influence them is crucial in preparing for our financial future and ensuring economic sustainability and growth.

The **Advances in Finance, Accounting, and Economics (AFAE)** book series aims to publish comprehensive and informative titles in all areas of economics and economic theory, finance, and accounting to assist in advancing the available knowledge and providing for further research development in these dynamic fields.

Coverage

- Bankruptcy
- Macroeconomics
- Economics Geography
- Economics of Migration and Spatial Mobility
- Stock Market
- Development Economics
- International Trade
- Corporate Finance
- Risk Analysis and Management
- Field Research

IGI Global is currently accepting manuscripts for publication within this series. To submit a proposal for a volume in this series, please contact our Acquisition Editors at Acquisitions@igi-global.com or visit: http://www.igi-global.com/publish/.

The Advances in Finance, Accounting, and Economics (AFAE) Book Series (ISSN 2327-5677) is published by IGI Global, 701 E. Chocolate Avenue, Hershey, PA 17033-1240, USA, www.igi-global.com. This series is composed of titles available for purchase individually; each title is edited to be contextually exclusive from any other title within the series. For pricing and ordering information please visit http://www.igi-global.com/book-series/advances-finance-accounting-economics/73685. Postmaster: Send all address changes to above address.

Titles in this Series

For a list of additional titles in this series, please visit: http://www.igi-global.com/book-series/advances-finance-accounting-economics/73685

Perspectives on Blockchain Technology and Responsible Investing
Sonal Trivedi (Chitkara Business School, Chitkara University, India) Rashmi Aggarwal (Chitkara Business School, Chitkara University, India) and Gurmeet Singh (The University of the South Pacific, Fiji)
Business Science Reference • © 2023 • 317pp • H/C (ISBN: 9781668483619) • US $250.00

Mainstreaming Cryptocurrency and the Future of Digital Finance
Hamed Taherdoost (University Canada West, Canada)
Business Science Reference • © 2023 • 330pp • H/C (ISBN: 9781668483688) • US $250.00

Handbook of Research on Designing Sustainable Supply Chains to Achieve a Circular Economy
Yanamandra Ramakrishna (Skyline University College, UAE) and Siti Norida Wahab (Universiti Teknologi MARA, Malaysia)
Business Science Reference • © 2023 • 697pp • H/C (ISBN: 9781668476642) • US $295.00

Emerging Insights on the Relationship Between Cryptocurrencies and Decentralized Economic Models
Dhanapal Kesavan (SRM Institute of Science and Technology, India) and N. Mari Anand (Department of Business Studies, University of Technology and Applied Sciences, Salalah, Oman)
Business Science Reference • © 2023 • 256pp • H/C (ISBN: 9781668456910) • US $250.00

Exploring Business Ecosystems and Innovation Capacity Building in Global Economics
Mihir Joshi (Banasthali Vidyapith University, India) Mohsen Brahmi (University of Sfax, Tunisia) Luigi Aldieri (University of Salerno, Italy) and Concetto Paolo Vinci (University of Salerno, Italy)
Business Science Reference • © 2023 • 393pp • H/C (ISBN: 9781668467664) • US $250.00

Handbook of Research on Changing World Economic Order in the Post-Pandemic Period
Sushanta Kumar Mahapatra (IBS Hyderabad, The ICFAI Foundation for Higher Education, India) and Vishal Sarin (Lovely Professional University, India)
Business Science Reference • © 2023 • 470pp • H/C (ISBN: 9781799868965) • US $325.00

Concepts, Cases, and Regulations in Financial Fraud and Corruption
Abdul Rafay (University of Management and Technology, Pakistan)
Business Science Reference • © 2023 • 419pp • H/C (ISBN: 9781668450079) • US $250.00

IGI Global
PUBLISHER of TIMELY KNOWLEDGE

701 East Chocolate Avenue, Hershey, PA 17033, USA
Tel: 717-533-8845 x100 • Fax: 717-533-8661
E-Mail: cust@igi-global.com • www.igi-global.com

Table of Contents

Detailed Table of Contents

Accounting has been evolving to follow the latest developments in economic, political, social, and technological matters. Therefore, there is a need for researchers to also include in their research agenda the emerging topics in the accounting area. This chapter uses archival research as a method and content analysis as a technique to review the literature in accounting research. A top journal in accounting (The Journal of Accounting Research) is used as the source of information from 2000 to 2022, aiming to cover more generalist research topics in this area. The findings indicate that this journal is accessible to the newest discussions and topics. Notwithstanding, their emergence as a research matter seems to be slower or less evident than their apparent development in the accounting environment. Despite being limited to a single journal, the proposed analysis in this chapter may contribute to professionals, academia, and the scientific community overall, enabling the identification of the state of the art in the accounting research area.

This study intends to provide additional evidence regarding practices of reporting based on the recommendations of the Task Force on Climate-Related Financial Disclosures, and to relate it with performance scores of reporting based on corporate social responsibility indicators. Despite the announcements of the adoption of those recommendations, the level of compliance is relatively low. Additionally, the relation with corporate social responsibility exists, but only when the comparison is with environmental disclosures. The contribution of this study is to provide evidence that the adoption of the recommendations of the Task Force on Climate-Related Financial Disclosures is challenging because there are two perspectives for corporate reporting as the disclosure performance based on indicators of corporate social responsibility (inside-out) differs from the recommendations of the Task Force on Climate-Related Financial Disclosures (outside-in). The results may support understanding the

Transparency is a key factor in ensuring family firms' commercial success and establishing and nurturing trust among stakeholders, including managers and teams. However, transparency appears to depend on business contexts and, more specifically, on family members' involvement in these companies, which helps explain researchers' growing interest in corporate transparency in family firms. This chapter examines the most relevant literature on this topic to provide an integrative overview of studies of transparency practices in family businesses and identify the main research gaps that comprise paths for future investigations. To this end, a non-systematic compilation and review was conducted of 50 related articles published in journals included in the Academic Journal Guide 2021. Content analysis revealed that the majority are based on empirical research focusing on the quality of information disclosed via earnings management. The most significant findings are discussed in this chapter, including research questions to be answered in further studies of this topic.

Accounting communication has attracted substantial attention in the last decade since several regulators issued guidelines that aim to increase financial reporting quality. In this chapter, the authors aim to study the association between the issuance of the technical guidance 07 (OCPC 07) by the Brazilian Accounting Standard Committee (CPC) and the readability of notes to the financial statements of Brazilian public firms. The authors use a multiple linear regression of panel data, controlling by industry and year fixed effect. The results suggest that there is no significant change in the average readability of financial notes after the issuance of OCPC 07. The authors contribute with additional disclosure to accounting literature by collecting empirical evidence on the relationship between the publication of normative guidance and accounting evidence. Moreover, these results may contribute to regulatory decisions made by regulatory agencies, which are certainly among the main stakeholders in the impacts caused by the issuance of norms and guiding the preparation and disclosure of economic-financial information.

The theme of governance has occupied the spaces of debate and practice in public administration. The evaluation of good examples of institutional management, in the current scenario, is always linked to the implementation of governance principles and their guidelines. In this sense, this chapter aims to indicate an initial step to increase risk management in Brazilian educational institutions. To this end, the authors present the historical path of the concept of governance until its adoption by public management in Brazil, seeking to understand the current political-economic-social; then, in order to show that good practices lead to good results, the authors list some Brazilian educational institutions that present a high Government Management Index, pointing out some of their actions that contributed to the excellence status. Finally, in the last chapter, the authors describe the initial stages of implementation of risk management, using the Swot Matrix as a useful tool for the systematic knowledge of the institution, which enables decision making more consistent with the reality of the context.

Despite being an international reference, the majority of countries did not fully adopt international public sector accounting standards (IPSAS). Given the importance of due processes to the IPSAS Board (IPSASB) legitimation, this chapter uses the comment letters sent by different stakeholders within its due processes to assess their level of participation and agreement with the IPSASB position concerning their distinctive characteristics. For this purpose, seven ongoing projects in August 2021 are used as a source of information, and contingency tables and the chi-square test as statistical analysis techniques. The findings show, as matters of constraint to the IPSASB legitimacy, a low level of responses overall, as well as a lower level of agreement by government entities and national standards setters. The study provides inputs to the understanding of the limited implementation of IPSAS, proposing as a future avenue the inclusion of some elements that can be particularly useful to explain stakeholders' engagement and interests in IPSASB public consultation processes.

One of the measures that emerged within the scope of the European audit reform was the report of key audit matters (KAM) with the objective of providing greater transparency in the auditor's reports. In 2015 the International Auditing and Assurance Standards Board (IAASB) approved the international standard on auditing (ISA) 701- Communicating KAM in the independent auditor's report. This chapter aims to analyse the evolution of the KAM report, in companies listed on Euronext Lisbon, from 2016 to 2019, and the impact of auditor rotation on that report. For this purpose, a mixed methodology was used with the KAM categorization followed by descriptive statistics. Through the research developed about the evolution of the report, it has been concluded that there was a decrease in the number of KAM reported during the period and that the majority of KAM reported each year are reported again in the following year. Regarding the impact that the audit firm change may have on KAM report, it was not possible to make a direct relationship between the audit firm change and KAM report.

In an increasingly global information society, public disclosure of corruption cases has been frequent, making us question the conduct of those involved. In order to avoid social alarmism and to safeguard the identification of those involved, a system of reporting channels, also known as the whistleblowing system, has been developed throughout the world. In turn, the evolution in the way financial reports are produced and analysed has caused new demands for social scrutiny to be incorporated such as those relating to the whistleblowing system. This text will address the impact of whistleblowing system on financial reporting, speaking on the recent legal diplomas approved in Portugal, largely influenced by situations that occurred in the USA, within the financial markets, more specifically relating the auditors' work. Compliance, which used to be understood as the best voluntary practices of integrity and organisational transparency, is now legally obligatory and institutionalised in public and private entities, and the content of financial reports is given new prominence.

Preface

ABOUT THIS BOOK

To follow the macroeconomic scenario in which the entities are inserted, financial reporting is constantly evolving. In addition to the topics that need to be considered, there is also an evolution in how the report itself is produced and analyzed where technological developments exert a permanent influence on the process. Several of the trending topics do not fall within the jurisdiction of the competent authorities. The needs of the users of the report also influence the form and content of the report as an element that also changes over time.

Accounting and Financial Reporting Challenges for Government, Non-Profits, and the Private Sector addresses the latest accounting topics and their practical and educational relations with local and international regulations, standards, and practices. It deals with new challenges and trends in auditing, accounting, and reporting for organizations from different institutional sectors, including private, public, and non-profit ones.

EXPECTATIONS

With an emphasis on financial reporting, this book covers several themes of interest for professionals in several industries, researchers, academicians, managers, instructors, and students. Although the authors are predominantly from Europe (Portugal, Spain, and Greece) and America (Brazil and Mexico), they have experienced researchers who discuss international topics, even when local perspectives are the object of analysis. The many topics, objects and fields covered in this publication include, but are not limited to:

- Accounting Harmonization
- Accounting Research
- Auditing
- Climate-Related Matters
- Corporate Social Responsibility
- Disclosures Analyses
- Educational Institutions
- Emerging Technologies
- External Auditors
- Family Businesses

- Financial Reporting
- Government
- Listed Companies
- Local and International Regulatory Issues
- Non-Profit Organizations
- Reporting of Cash-flows
- Stakeholders' Perspectives
- Whistleblowing

ORGANIZATION OF THIS BOOK

Chapter 1, "Recent Trends in Accounting Research: A Literature Review," uses archival research as a method and content analysis as a technique to review the literature in accounting research. A top journal in accounting (The Journal of Accounting Research) is used as the source of information from 2000 to 2022.

Chapter 2, "Climate-related Financial Disclosures and Corporate Social Responsibility: Evidence from European Companies," provides evidence regarding practices of European companies reporting according to the recommendations of the Task Force on Climate-related Financial Disclosures and relate it with performance scores of reporting based on corporate social responsibility indicators.

Chapter 3, "Accounting Systems with Smart Contracts: Building Accounting Records in Blockchain Step by Step," proposes a practical solution for its implementation and use in a generalized way. We present two new Proofs of Concept, which are part of an ongoing work process to obtain the development of the Portuguese Accounting System using Blockchain.

Chapter 4, "Assessing the Comparability and the Understandability of the Information on Cash Flows by European Listed Entities," assess the comparability and understandability of information on cash flows through the choices by European entities in the presentation of the statement of cash flows and the disclosure of non-generally accepted accounting principles measures related to cash flow information, respectively.

Chapter 5, "An integrative View of Corporate Transparency in the Family Businesses," examines the most relevant literature on corporate transparency in the family businesses to provide an integrative overview of studies of those practices and identify the main research gaps that comprise paths for future investigations. A non-systematic compilation and review was conducted of 50 related articles published in journals included in the Academic Journal Guide 2021.

Chapter 6, "Normative Guidelines and Financial Disclosure: Relationship between OCPC07 and Readability of Notes," studies the association between the issuance of the technical guidance 07 by the Brazilian Accounting Standard Committee and the readability of notes to the financial statements of Brazilian public firms.

Chapter 7, "The Secret of the Best: The Practice of Risk Management in Brazilian Educational Institutions," presents the historical path of the concept of governance until its adoption by public management in Brazil, assesses some Brazilian educational institutions and describes the initial stages of implementation of risk management in those institutions.

Chapter 8, "An Assessment of the Stakeholders' Participation and view in IPSASB Due Process," uses the comment letters sent by different stakeholders within its due process to assess their level of participation and agreement with the IPSASB position concerning their distinctive characteristics.

Chapter 9, "Developing a Social Accounting System for European Social Enterprises based on Public Accounting," proposes an operational accounting system based on the relationship between social enterprises and public organizations in the broader context of accounting, social finance and public accounting, with both theoretical and practical contributions by developing a common accounting language and practices between them.

Chapter 10, "External Auditors Discover Management Breach of Trust: Evidence from Mexico," uses a Mexican case study to highlight the relevance of external auditors and provide a fresh perspective about the breach of trust in the accounting professional ethical code and its criminal implications.

Chapter 11, "The Impact of Auditor Rotation on Key Audit Matters (KAM): Evidence from the Listed Portuguese Companies," analyses the impact of auditor rotation on the evolution of the KAM report, using data from companies listed on Euronext Lisbon between 2016 and 2019.

Chapter 12, "The Impact of Whistleblowing System on Financial Reporting," addresses the impact of the Whistleblowing System on financial reporting, based on the recent legal diplomas approved in Portugal, largely influenced by situations that occurred within the financial markets in the USA, impacting the audit profession.

Fábio Albuquerque
Instituto Politécnico de Lisboa, Portugal

Paula Gomes dos Santos
Instituto Politécnico de Lisboa, Portugal

Chapter 1
Recent Trends in Accounting Research:
A Literature Review

Fábio Albuquerque
https://orcid.org/0000-0001-8877-9634
Instituto Politécnico de Lisboa, Portugal

Paula Gomes dos Santos
https://orcid.org/0000-0003-2192-8855
Instituto Politécnico de Lisboa, Portugal

ABSTRACT

Accounting has been evolving to follow the latest developments in economic, political, social, and technological matters. Therefore, there is a need for researchers to also include in their research agenda the emerging topics in the accounting area. This chapter uses archival research as a method and content analysis as a technique to review the literature in accounting research. A top journal in accounting (The Journal of Accounting Research) is used as the source of information from 2000 to 2022, aiming to cover more generalist research topics in this area. The findings indicate that this journal is accessible to the newest discussions and topics. Notwithstanding, their emergence as a research matter seems to be slower or less evident than their apparent development in the accounting environment. Despite being limited to a single journal, the proposed analysis in this chapter may contribute to professionals, academia, and the scientific community overall, enabling the identification of the state of the art in the accounting research area.

DOI: 10.4018/978-1-6684-7293-4.ch001

INTRODUCTION

The literature review has identified the difficulty of adequacy and monitoring the developments associated with the advent of new technologies by educational institutions (Islam, 2017). It has been also demonstrated that research in accounting needs to evolve and follow contemporary trends that are present not only in the technological environment but also in other themes, including those related to other scientific fields (Christensen, 2018). According to Kaplan (2011), accounting research has neglected topics of interest, being too rigid, cautious, and conservative. Additionally, scholars have identified a greater difficulty in publishing in this area, compared to other areas of business in general (Al-Adeem, 2019).

Although the definition of accounting has evolved, this is not reflected in the understanding of accounting as a social and moral practice, but only as a technical one, despite the efforts of academics in this regard over the last four decades (Carnegie et al., 2021). Research is thus an essential element for understanding the new forms of management in the so-called digital economy, as well as identifying the new skills and instruments that professionals need to have to remain relevant and be able to add value to the work they develop (Moll & Yigitbasioglu, 2019).

This chapter aims to identify, through a literature review (bibliometric analysis), the papers published in a generalist top journal in accounting since 2000, providing an evolutionary analysis of the recent trends in different areas of accounting research. Textual analysis will be used as a complementary tool to identify the most frequent terms (words and expressions) from the gathered research, providing an overview of the central themes and topics from those investigations. Through this analysis, topics considered as research opportunities in different fields of education and professional practice in accounting will be discussed and, consequently, this chapter intends to contribute to professionals, academia, and the scientific community overall, enabling the identification of the state of the art in the accounting research area.

Bibliometric studies on recent trends in accounting research overall have not yet been identified at this stage, despite the significant number of studies that assesses specific topics of accounting, methods used, or even regions, as the examples provided in the suggested readings section in the end of this chapter. The same is applied to the research on accounting information systems, which has dedicated reviews to specific topics within this field, such as the so-called emerging technologies, for instance, the research by Chiu et al. (2019). Therefore, considering this gap and the newest challenges in the accounting profession and education, it seems relevant to evaluate what issues surround accounting research and what topics are being accepted by a top accounting journal.

The structure of this chapter is as follows. The next section presents a background as regards the newest topics underlying the accounting profession and education. The third section is divided into two subsections, the first presenting the objectives and the selected methodology and the second one dedicated to reviewing the literature as proposed for this chapter. The fourth section provides future avenues for researchers in accounting. Finally, the last section presents the conclusion of this research.

BACKGROUND

Accounting, as an applied social science, requires a constant analysis of the threats and opportunities that emerge, among others, in the political, social, environmental, economic, and legal contexts, which, in turn, are interconnected. Islam (2017), in an International Federation of Accountants (IFAC) Business Reporting released five years ago, already highlighted some challenges that relate to three essential subjects: digital and intelligent technology, globalization, and new forms of regulation. Within the first topic, the author included the development of increasingly intelligent soft than in other areas of business ware, particularly from the growth of artificial intelligence-based technologies, which include not only the technologies that make use of machine learning processes, and the new paths of sophisticated Enterprises Resources Plannings (ERP), which replace the traditional approach to work, but also cloud computing, which leads to an increase in the trend of outsourcing services across borders.

Furthermore, there is a need for more intensive use of social networks for communication and providing financial reporting, which makes the entity closer to its different stakeholders and, thus, promotes greater transparency and increased accountability (Islam, 2017). This last aspect arises specifically from the need to utilize big data tools to interpret new forms of reporting, not only by entities but also by the stakeholders themselves. More recently, aligned with the concerns identified by the author, the relevance of blockchain-based technologies, as suggested by Schmitz and Leoni (2019), could be also added to this list. Regarding globalization, the author identified the opportunities and threats to professionals arising from processes of harmonization of financial reporting and auditing. Other aspects of globalisation include increased global flows of goods and capital transfer and outsourcing activities, leading to challenges related to the existence of clashes amongst different cultures, and financial and tax systems that need to be addressed.

Finally, concerning the challenges associated with regulation, Islam (2017) highlights the need to avoid fraudulent activities related to international flows of goods and capital, such as tax evasion, money laundering, and transfer prices, because of the previous point (globalization). Additionally, the increased visibility of the entities' reports and pressure from stakeholders are expected to strengthen regulation in the areas of social and environmental responsibility. More recently, another current theme to add to the author's concerns relates to the regulation of whistleblower protection and strengthening of whistleblowing channels, having the European Union (EU) an example in this matter, through the issuing of Directive 2019/1937/EU of the European Parliament and the Council of 23 October 2019.

The link between globalisation and regulation has been also evolving towards an ever-widening scope of entities obliged to disseminate non-financial information, as well as attempts to define non-financial reporting standards for a subsequent harmonisation. In this context, the recent developments in the EU can also be mentioned, through the directives 2013/34/EU and 2014/95/EU of the European Parliament and the Council of 26 June 2013 and 22 October 2014, respectively, and subsequent proposals to amend the existing sustainability reporting legislation (European Commission, 2021).

Furthermore, some entities previously dedicated exclusively to financial reporting based on the International Accounting Standards (IAS) and the International Financial Reporting Standards (IFRS) have also begun some development work in this regard, such as the IFRS Foundation and the European Financial Reporting Advisory Group (EFRAG, 2021), as an advisory body of the EU. Thus, these entities were added to the traditional standard-setter bodies that developed standards and guidelines in these matters, such as the Global Reporting Initiative (GRI) and, more recently, the International Integrated Reporting Council (IIRC), which is the one that developed the so-called report that integrates financial and non-financial information (integrated reporting). More recently, the concerns about compliance with the so-called Sustainable Development Goals (SDG) under the United Nations (UN) 2030 agenda are also a topic of interest. Those developments are aligned with the perspective of Carnegie et al. (2021, p. 67), who state that "appeals for broadening the contribution of accounting in corporate accountability to stakeholders and sustainability has been called by scholars across many years". In this sense, those authors proposed incorporating those aspects in a comprehensive definition of accounting, also discussing why sustainability reporting has not been still mandated around the world.

Despite these challenges, Islam (2017) highlights the difficulty that remains in universities to adapt curricula to the needs that occur in the professional environment, especially in terms of the introduction of new technologies. In the same sense, it also identifies gaps in scientific research, which has not been able to keep up with such changes, thus suggesting a greater network of collaboration between companies and academia, especially with larger companies and audit multinationals, which have a greater capacity for investment and adaptation.

In a vision that goes beyond new technologies, however, Barth (2018, p. 384) defended the need for a deeper connection between academia and professionals, so that they see themselves as "part of the same profession". In other words, the academy must meet the needs of professionals, as they should see the academy as the channel for obtaining the necessary knowledge for solving their problems, which leads to the objective of reporting as a useful source of information for decision-making aiming at the development of prosperous societies. To achieve this objective, the academy should seek to develop fundamental and applied research, communicate better inside and outside its fronts, and interact with professionals and different stakeholders of accounting information.

In a different perspective, although in line with the previous one, Christensen (2018) recognized the difficulty that the academy presents in following the evolution that is observed in professional practice, arguing that accounting is still taught as it has been for 40 years. The author suggests, then, a deeper integration between teaching and research, integrating the research findings within the teaching to motivate students towards the benefits and usefulness of research for the advancement of accounting, for example, through the integration of those results in the scholar books. In addition, he also advocates the need for greater integration of accounting research not only with other areas of business sciences but also with other areas of knowledge, particularly social sciences, and humanities, with interdisciplinary links to accounting that enhance findings about how accounting influences and is influenced, among others, by the environment and political context, social, environmental, economic, and legal situation where it is included.

The suggestion by Christensen (2018) for strengthening the interdisciplinary in accounting also relates to the previous discussion on the regulation and globalization issues and the currently reviewed importance of non-financial information. Therefore, new topics also emerge as an object of debate and social discussion in accounting research. Several issues are addressed in this field, including gender equality, ethnic diversity, and social inclusion, as well as the social role of accounting and reporting. Furthermore, new paths of education and work in the post-pandemic world appear relevant, thus pushing the boundaries of traditional themes in accounting research, mainly reporting and its impacts from the perspective of capital providers (European Parliament, 2022; Bebbington & Unerman, 2020; Tweedie & Hazelton, 2019).

In a recent long-term call for papers, for instance, the editor of the Accounting & Finance Review [*Revista Contabilidade & Finanças* (*RC&F*)] indicate a set of topics that the journal's editorial board has identified as relevant to be considered by researchers since some criticisms indicated that accounting research has usually been looking to the past, or, in other words, "taking a look at what was already published" (Frezatti, 2021). The criticisms pointed out by him comprised the following aspects:

i. a frequent discontent about the distance of research concerning the organisations' realities;
ii. as a consequence of the previous item, frequent questioning about the papers' usefulness;

iii. occurrence of disruptive changes in the organizational environment, such as the dimension of digital transformation, with enormous space for research and publication; and
iv. research replication on the same topics with a low level of innovation.

Amongst the topics proposed as innovative, the following can be found (Frezatti, 2021):

i. use of innovative data sources, digital transformation, and the use of new technologies in accounting, auditing, and educational environments, as well as the new methods for implementing management control systems (e.g. the use of data from social networks big data and relevant tools to collect and assess the data, such as innovative dashboards, data analytics, artificial intelligence, blockchain, dematerialization of processes and accounting information);
ii. innovative ways of reporting (e.g. new formats and channels for financial and non-financial reporting, also including social networks);
iii. new methods of labour relationships, especially after the covid-19 pandemic (e.g. remote work, discussion of precariousness, and outsourcing);
iv. recent regulatory issues (e.g. new mechanisms of governance, and whistleblowing implementation and effectiveness);
v. the social relevance of accounting (e.g, proposing links between governance and external regulatory issues, or the discussion on the social influence of accounting);
vi. sustainability matters (e.g. including the topics on the environmental, social, and governance (ESG), SDG initiatives, and climate change);
vii. social, ethnic-racial, and gender inclusion (e.g. assessing the different perspectives regarding the profession and financial education concerning ethnic, social, racial, as well as gender, sexual orientation, and religiosity issues);
viii. innovations in accounting theory (e.g. materiality, relevance, individual and consolidated financial statements, and the recognition and measurement of specific elements of financial statements under discussion, such as cryptocurrencies);
ix. critical analysis of IAS and IFRS (e.g. practical and social implications of external regulation and the issues on international accounting harmonisation);
x. new paths for balance sheet analysis (eg, improvement of risk management and analysis models, integrated valuation models, etc.).

Following the previous discussions, the next section presents the literature analysis proposed for this chapter.

LITERATURE ANALYSIS

This section summarizes the accounting papers published in the selected journal. It is divided into two subsections. An overview of the basic methodological issues surrounding the analysis is presented in the first subsection, including the scope of the study and the textual analysis proposed for it. The next subsection reports the findings of the analysis, which are focused on the themes found in the papers reviewed.

Methodological Notes

The findings from this chapter are based on the assessment of papers gathered from the Scopus database by 30 September 2022. Papers released from 2000 onwards were selected from a single top journal in accounting, providing an overview of the last 22 years of accounting research covering three different areas of analysis. The Journal of Accounting Research (JAR) was selected to make it feasible to manage a significant dataset to cover research on accounting fields dedicated to no specific (general) subjects. Further reasons for selecting this journal include its complete coverage for the proposed period (since 2000 from 2022), as well as its comparatively higher Scopus ranking among journals not containing any other terms besides accounting.

Based on the information available on the Scopus website, JAR is defined as a general-interest accounting journal. It publishes original research in all areas of accounting and related fields that utilizes tools from basic disciplines such as economics, statistics, psychology, and sociology. This research typically uses analytical, empirical archival, experimental, and field study methods and addresses economic questions, external and internal, in accounting, auditing, disclosure, financial reporting, taxation, and information as well as related fields such as corporate finance, investments, capital markets, law, contracting, and information economics. It is classified as a Q1 journal in 2021, with an impressive SCImago Journal Rank (SJR) of 5.92, based on the Scopus criteria for best quartile classification in accounting. It has been published since 1996 by Wiley-Blackwell Publishing Ltd, based in the United Kingdom.

Besides the papers' data releases and the journal proposed, the searching process in Scopus was only restricted to papers with available abstracts. No additional criteria were applied and then, no terms or expressions were used as the key searching term in the abstracts of the papers selected. At the end of this process, 730 papers were gathered for assessment from JA. The analysis will provide a breakdown for three distinct periods: from 2000 to 2009, from 2010 to 2019, and, finally, from 2020 to 2022. The first two periods were selected to identify the differences (a comparative analysis) between the topics proposed by researchers in the journals under assessment during the two initial decades of this century. The last period, despite being shorter than the previous ones, was particularly proposed to identify the trending topics on accounting from the same source.

Textual analysis tools, available free of charge on the Internet (the CountWordsFree and {L}exos), are also used as complementary information for this purpose, particularly to identify the most frequent words found in the abstract of the papers gathered. As usual in these processes, some of those words have no meaning for research purposes and, consequently, must be removed from the analysis (the "stop words").

The CountWordsFree uses a set of predefined stop words according to a given language (in this case, English). Therefore, there is no option to include or remove stop words based on user criteria. The list provided, which can be found on the website where this tool is available, includes the most usual prepositions, particles, interjections, unions, adverbs, pronouns, introductory words, numbers from 0 to 9 (unambiguous), another frequently used official, independent parts of speech, symbols, punctuation, modal verbs, as well as the different forms of the most common verbs, such as the verbs to be, to go, to have, to ask, and similar. Finally, commonly sequences of symbols used on the Internet, such as "www", ".com", and "http" are also stop words. The word "information" is also a stop word considered by this tool. Then, given the analysis proposed for this chapter, this relevant absence should be taken into account. This tool is also used to identify the number of times in which a given word appeared in the abstracts published by each journal under assessment by period. The findings from this tool are presented in tables.

On the other hand, the {L}exos has no automatic process, requesting users to identify those stop words. Therefore, a judgment must be made to exclude them. Then, for a more in-depth analysis, besides the before mentioned stop words, it was added additional words frequently used in research papers with no interest for the analysis proposed for this chapter, as they are only "linking words", such as "paper", "study", "work", "sample", "focus", "aim", "purpose", "contribution", "relevance", "objective", "propose", "study", "effects", impacts", "evidence", "higher", "lower", "significant", and similar ones. An image of two consecutive and random interactions is presented as a figure (word cloud). Finally, the information regarding the number of citations by each paper is used, particularly for the first periods, as a proxy for their impact on the literature, despite the comparison should consider the disadvantages of the most recent papers in this matter.

Table 1 presents a summary of the papers selected by period and their textual characteristics.

Table 1. Summary of the textual characteristics of papers selected by period

Journal	Period	Number of papers	Number of terms occurring once	Total number of terms	Distinct number of terms	Vocabulary Density
JAR (N=730)	2000-2009	296	1 784	21 900	4 124	0.188
	2010-2019	317	1 841	22 758	4 352	0.191
	2020-2022	117	1 341	8 527	2 677	0.314

It can be seen from those figures a trend for an increasing number regarding the indicators provided, which is also valid even for the last three-year period since it already indicates about or more than one-third of the figures for the same indicators published in the previous one. The vocabulary density has also increased over the period. Notwithstanding, it is worthwhile to notice that the figures for the distinct number of terms and vocabulary density as regards the last (shortest) period cannot be compared with the previous ones.

A review of the papers selected is presented in the following subsection.

Literature Overview

This subsection is dedicated to the analysis of the papers published in the journal selected for this study, also considering the three comparative periods proposed.

Journal of Accounting Research (JAR)

Figure 1 shows the number of papers (NoP) and citations (NoC) published in the JAR over the three periods of analysis. It can be concluded from these data and considering the first two most comparable periods (2000 to 2009 and 2010 to 2019), that citations dropped by more than half (from about 48,000 to about 21,000, respectively), despite a rise in the number of papers (from 296 to 317, respectively). Therefore, the average number of citations per paper also decreased, from 162 to 66. Notwithstanding, and despite the discernible distance between the two periods assessed, it is worth noting that the most recent periods may have a relative disadvantage when it comes to citations.

Figure 1. Summary of the number of papers and citations by periods in the JAR

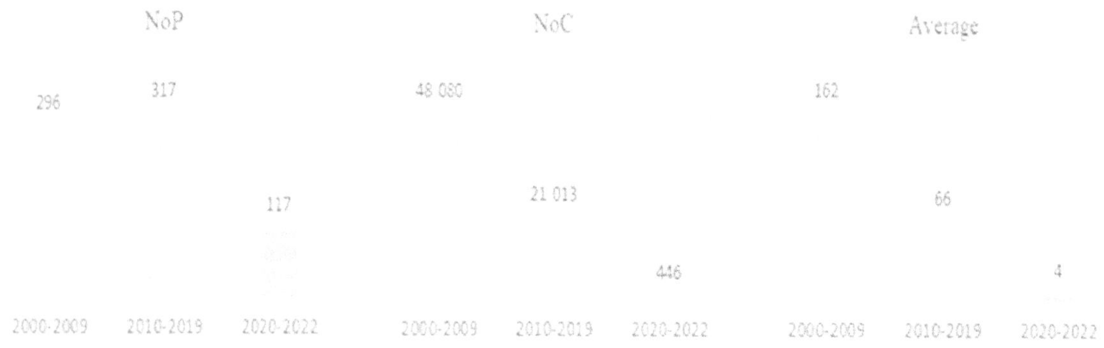

Papers published in the JAR over the first decade demonstrate the previously identified discrepancy. Specifically, 23 papers reached over 500 citations in the first period, compared with only one in the second period, namely the study by Loughran and Mcdonald (2016) on textual analysis in accounting and finance research. As of the first period, three papers have already received more than 1,000 citations (Leuz & Verrecchia, 2000; Barth et al., 2008; Lambert et al., 2007), with a maximum of 1,349 citations identified for the first referenced study on capital cost, published at the beginning of the analysis period. Also co-authored by Leuz and Verrecchia are studies on the same topic identified in the three most cited studies mentioned above (particularly Lambert et al., 2007), while Barth et al. (2008) assess the quality of the reports according to IAS and IFRS.

Despite being less cited, the most relevant studies for the second period find more diverse themes. Aside from the study by Loughran and Mcdonald (2016), it is also possible to locate studies on a variety of topics, such as audit quality, with 491 citations (Reichelt & Wang, 2010), the information content of forward-looking statements using machine learning, with 463 citations (Li, 2010), or the relationship between disclosures and financial reporting regulations, with 447 citations (Leuz & Wysocki, 2016).

Significant attention was paid to financial information in the papers identified during the first period (2000 to 2009), assessing the reliability, quality, and transparency of disclosures, including impression management strategies and the relevance of the information (e.g. Hope, 2003; Bushman et al., 2004; Barth et al., 2008; Daske et al., 2008) but also their consequences or impacts to the cost of capital (majority), profitabilities or return on shares (e.g. Bushee & Noe, 2000; Leuz & Verrecchia, 2000; Gebhardt et al., 2001; Botosan & Plumlee, 2001, 2002; Lambert et al., 2007).

It is also common to discuss earnings analysis issues, particularly strategies and incentives related to accounting conservatism practices, earnings management, or accruals quality, occasionally related to profitability prediction (Hribar & Collins, 2002; Karamanou & Vafeas, 2005; Ajinkya et al., 2005; Narayanamoorthy, 2006; Wang, 2006). In the study by Francis et al. (2008), for instance, the implications associated with voluntary disclosures, earnings quality, and capital costs sometimes appear interconnected. Previous research has also used future cash flow information to support such analyses (for example, Hribar & Collins, 2002; Lambert et al., 2007).

Lastly, whether or not associated with the above themes, studies of this period also addressed aspects related to external audit and the role of audit committees in the detection of fraud, including the first analysis on the Sarbanes-Oxley Act (SOX) impacts, which continued in subsequent periods (e.g. DeFond et al., 2002, 2005; Fan & Wong, 2005; Karamanou & Vafeas, 2005; Srinivasan & Richardson, 2005; Ashbaugh-Skaife et al., 2009; Piotroski & Srinivasan, 2008; Gao et al., 2009; Hochberg et al., 2009).

During a decade associated with a profusion of major financial scandals, political connections and capital market regulation also play a significant role (e.g. Gul, 2006; Ball, 2009). In addition, the first studies have been conducted on the economic effects and relevance of information prepared or reconciled under IAS and IFRS (e.g. Barth et al., 2008; Daske et al., 2008; Christensen et al., 2009).

To sum up, the importance of the quality of financial information and its impact on issues of a more financial nature, such as future profitability, cash flows, and returns on shares, can be summarized by pointing out that these aspects deserved greater attention in this period.

Following, Table 2 summarizes the most common words found in the abstracts of papers published during this first period in the JAR, using the CountWordsFree tool.

Table 2. Summary of the most common words from the papers in the JAR (from 2000 to 2009)

Word	N	Word	N	Word	N	Word	N	Word	N
earnings	442	audit	123	higher	99	news	76	costs	64
firms	394	investors	119	forecast	98	disclosures	74	model	64
accounting	226	evidence	118	quality	93	auditors	73	sample	64
firm	185	risk	112	study	93	provide	73	incentives	63
market	165	cost	111	equity	81	capital	72	investment	60
financial	152	consistent	104	examine	81	future	71	positive	60
disclosure	143	performance	103	managers	81	greater	71	negative	59
management	139	returns	103	analyst	78	reporting	70	relative	54
analysts	136	paper	102	measures	77	cash	68	decisions	52
stock	131	forecasts	99	Price	77	increase	67	investigate	52

Reinforcing the previous evidence, among the most relevant terms are the terms associated with these topics, such as "earnings", "performance", "management" or "managers", "disclosure" or "disclosures" or "financial" and "reporting", "quality", "stock", "market", "investment", "forecast" or "forecasts", "capital", "stock", "market", "price", "equity", "returns", "risk", "investors", "analyst" or "analysts", "news", "decisions" "cost" or "costs", "cash", "audit" or "auditors".

Figure 2 indicates the most common words found in the abstracts of papers published during this period, using the {L}exos.

From Figure 2, similar terms related to the lines of investigation beforementioned also appear. Examples of such cases include the terms "income"; "accruals", "changes", "flows", "trading", "securities", "announcements", "time", "valuation", "incentives", "debt", "valuation", "bias", "accuracy" and "governance".

For the second review period (from 2010 to 2019), a greater diversity of topics can be observed for the most frequently cited topics when compared to the previous period, although not predominantly and in many cases related to the topics of the previous period. In particular, it includes the issues related to the dissemination of information in its various aspects of analysis (such as quality, transparency, usefulness, and its impact on the cost of capital), the analysis of current and prospective earnings (e.g. accounting conservatism practices, earnings management, accrual quality, and their related predictive models), as well as the role of external and internal audit and market regulations to mitigate the fraud events, also including the measures related to the SOX implementation.

Figure 2. Word clouds from the papers in the JAR (from 2000 to 2009)

Studies on the role of political connections or incentives continue in the same period. However, these studies not only address issues related to the context of the audit but also its impact on previously mentioned issues such as the cost of capital and the quality of accruals (e.g. Ramanna & Roychowdhury, 2010; Ben-Nasr et al., 2012; Guedhami et al., 2014; Houston et al., 2014; Piotroski et al., 2015). Examples of new topics being researched include gender issues in explaining misreporting (e.g. Jia et al., 2014), the analysis of investor sentiment (e.g. Brown et al., 2012), the impact of ideological positioning on legal decisions (e.g. Huang et al., 2019) or more sophisticated studies on the objectives underlying companies disclosures through various discourse analysis techniques (e.g. Hobson et al., 2012; Tan et al., 2014; Loughran & Mcdonald, 2016).

Research related to the disclosure of non-financial information, while also present in the previous period, seems to play a more significant role in this second one (e.g. Hasan et al., 2017; Manchiraju & Rajgopal,2017). Similarly, studies that focus particularly on aggressive tax behaviour seem to gain prominence in this period stemming from issues such as fraud and disclosure decisions, including new approaches to assess, for instance, the effect of public pressure on this matter (e.g. Klassen & Laplante, 2012; Rego & Wilson, 2012; Lennox et al., 2013; Lisowsky et al., 2013; Dyreng et al., 2016; Hasan et al., 2017). Due to the ever-increasing international harmonisation of financial reporting, studies also continued to be conducted assessing the impact of the adoption of local convergence to IFRS in different areas (e.g. Byard et al., 2011; Tan et al., 2011; Daske et al., 2013; Ball et al., 2015). Later in the decade, new debates emerge, namely those on the predictive utility and meaningfulness of so-called Non-Generally Accepted Accounting Principles (non-GAAP) measures.

Finally, it should be stated that the first study found on the topic of emerging technologies was found at the beginning of this period, which proposed the use of machine learning for assessing the content analysis of disclosed information (Li, 2010). In the middle of the period, it can be found the first study that used social media as a source of information, namely the market impact from the manifesting consumer satisfaction (Lee et al., 2015). Finally, in the last years of this period, studies on the whistleblowing issue in the context of fraud detection also emerged (Call et al., 2018; Heese et. al., 2019).

Table 3 identifies the most common terms for the 2010-2019 period, using CountWordsFree.

Table 3. Summary of the most common words from the papers in the JAR (from 2010 to 2019)

Word	N	Word	N	Word	N	Word	N	Word	N
firms	337	analysts	118	corporate	90	investment	74	incentives	62
earnings	280	reporting	116	capital	89	future	72	auditors	60
accounting	202	audit	114	examine	89	provide	71	greater	60
financial	195	higher	111	stock	86	news	70	date	59
firm	192	quality	108	banks	81	decisions	69	findings	59
disclosure	156	investors	107	public	81	equity	69	private	59
managers	142	risk	107	disclosures	79	price	68	economic	58
evidence	136	management	104	cost	77	increases	65	forecasts	58
market	134	consistent	101	paper	77	returns	64	debt	57
performance	131	study	95	effects	76	prior	63	increase	55

Despite the previous highlights, it should be noted that there is no novelty regarding the term that indicates a significant change in the recurring themes for this new period. The exception is due to new terms such as "banks", "public" and "private", which are likely associated with the industry and/or nature of the entities under assessment. Notwithstanding, and compared to the findings from the same source assessed in the previous period (from 2000 to 2009), the relative importance or frequency of some terms has also slightly changed.

Figure 3, in turn, using {L}exos, also provides the most frequent terms for this new period, after excluding those terms that are not relevant to the aims of the content analysis proposed in this chapter.

Based on the identified terms in Figure 3, it can be observed the maintenance and similar relative importance of the preceding terms. However, in line with the previous analysis, the figure also highlights, in this new period, the increase of research related to the adoption of international standards (based on terms such as "IFRS" and "adoption") as well as the topics related to tax issues (from the term "tax") associated with either new sources of analysis or new lines of research.

The most recent period (2020 to 2022) continues the greater diversity of topics and perspectives of analysis initiated in the previous period, with more prominent use of machine learning tools, artificial intelligence, or mobile devices included in more traditional topics, such as detecting fraud and misreporting, predicting future incomes, analysts' perceptions of reported information and their behaviour in investment or debt decisions, and also for assessing newest topics such as predicting terrorist attacks through the use of blockchain-based systems (e.g. Bao et al., 2020; Brown et al., 2020; Grant, 2020; Amiram et al., 2022; Chen et al., 2022; Commerford et al., 2022; Liu, 2022). Differentiated analysis proposals involving the use of novel technologies can also be found in the study of topics as diverse as the use of satellites to determine vehicle circulation and its impacts on the competitive advantage and, consequently, the level of turnover in the retail trade (Kang et al., 2021).

Figure 3. Word clouds from the papers in the JAR (from 2010 to 2019)

Following, this latest period has also new studies on social media, with more nuanced approaches compared to those identified in the previous one. More specifically, this period includes studies that assess, for instance, the labour relations policies from the disciplinary effects of the use of new social media by employees (Dube & Zhu, 2021) or the analysis of LinkedIn profiles to identify analyst characteristics (Aslan, 2022). It also identifies a study that combines those topics using new technologies (machine learning) based on LinkedIn profiles as a source of information, assessing a similar area to the previous one, namely the analyst characteristics and behaviours from the impact of the regulatory environment and gender differences (Peng et al., 2022).

The use of new sources of information is also relevant as a research opportunity, although not as exclusive to this period, such as the analysis of the relationship of transparency and attributed credit ratings to local governments (Gillette et al., 2020) or the analysis of the impact of customer complaints on the implementation of internal policies developed in response to these events by the banking sector (Hayes et al., 2021). Cultural issues, in addition to gender, were also a topic explored in these last years, although not necessarily more prolific than the findings in this matter from the previous periods (e.g. Barrios et al., 2022).

Studies on the impact of political connections or forces also continue, with more diverse proposals in terms of approaches and their potential effects, such as ideological issues related to regulation, influence on governments, or definitions of antitrust actions in the context of mergers and acquisitions (e.g. Bischof et al., 2020; Cuny et al., 2020; Mehta et al., 2020). In addition, whistleblowing as a mechanism for detecting or avoiding fraud also emerges during this period, becoming also more differentiated regarding the proposed approaches to this issue, for instance, its effectiveness based on the different communication channels (e.g. Stubben & Welch, 2020; Soltes, 2020; Dey et al., 2021; Berger & Lee, 2022). Finally, this period includes, and is even more diverse, the continuity of studies on the disclosure and impacts of non-GAAP financial measures, which were initiated at the end of the last decade (e.g. Chen et al., 2021; Hribar et al., 2022; Hallman et al., 2022; Guggenmos et al., 2022).

Although not a novelty in thematic terms, it is observed the maintenance of the opportunity for further studies and discussions of a more qualitative nature, such as those related to the reproducibility of accounting research (Bourveau et al., 2020). It is worth mentioning, on the other hand, the absence in this period of studies focusing, specifically, on sustainability reports, integrated reporting, or other types of reports of non-financial information, considering the latest developments in this area in recent years. In addition, and as a theme specifically associated with this period, a single study on the effects of the Covid-19 pandemic is also identified, although dedicated, in this case, to a more traditional theme, namely its impact on the stock market (Dechow et al., 2021).

Following the previous discussion, Table 4 provides, using CountWordsFree, the most common terms from the papers published in this last period in the JAR.

Table 4. Summary of the most common words from the papers in the JAR (from 2020 to 2022)

Word	N	Word	N	Word	N	Word	N	Word	N
firms	150	examine	48	reporting	33	model	23	costs	20
disclosure	84	effects	45	provide	32	paper	23	foreign	20
audit	64	higher	45	disclosures	31	price	23	increases	20
financial	62	consistent	44	managers	31	equity	22	negative	20
earnings	58	quality	43	greater	29	forecasts	22	prices	20
evidence	57	market	39	risk	27	regulation	22	private	20
firm	57	study	37	increase	26	stock	22	returns	20
Investors	54	auditors	36	corporate	24	document	21	credit	19
performance	50	public	36	incentives	24	enforcement	21	management	19
accounting	49	findings	35	auditor	23	measure	21	markets	19

As evidenced by Table 4, it can be seen, once again, a set of similar terms to those found in the previous periods, evidencing not only the permanence but the prevalence of the more traditional themes. Despite this, some exceptions arise from differences that can be identified as evidence of a potential greater diversity of addressed topics or the use of either new approaches or new data sources, namely:

i. the lower relative preponderance of more traditional studies on capital costs (for the first time, the term "capital" does not appear amongst the most common on this list);
ii. the lower relative influence of studies on earnings management or accounting conservatism strategies, considering the latest relative positioning of the terms such as "earnings", "accounting" and "management"; or
iii. the absence of terms such as "news" or "future" in the set of words, evidencing a smaller number of studies, in relative terms, on the analysis of the type or nature of the information disclosed.

Finally, and as a difference found for this period it should also be highlighted the greater presence of the term "audit", replacing the relative position in the top 3 for the term "accounting". Also, it emerges, for the first time, the terms "regulation" and "enforcement", which indicate a superior presence of studies in the field of audit and on regulatory issues, having the implementation and the performance assessment of measures in whistleblowing as an example in this matter.

Figure 4 identifies the results of a similar analysis performed using {L}exos, which removes additional terms not relevant to the proposed content analysis.

Figure 4. Word clouds from the papers in JAR (from 2020 to 2022)

Terms such as "capital" and "news" appear in Figure 4, albeit with less relative importance compared to earlier periods. Despite the different methodologies used to identify the most frequent terms, the figure globally corroborates the previous conclusions but also highlights new aspects, namely the increase in research related to non-GAAP measures (linked to the emergence of the term previous "GAAP"). In addition, the emergence of new terms such as "social" seems to indicate the opening of this period to new thematic lines. Overall, however, and despite the still limited number of years in this period for the proposed analysis, there appears to be scope for further diversification of topics in the accounting research.

The next section provides future research directions.

FUTURE RESEARCH DIRECTIONS

In the first decade of this millennium, the more generalist literature in accounting research seemed to be focused on the reliability and relevance of financial information from the initial stages to the final report, which includes the assessment of its quality, bias, fraud detection, usefulness, constraints, and benefits. During this period, those studies were mostly focused on financial measures included as dependent or independent variables, such as current and future earnings, cost of capital, cash flows, and stock prices, although they retained their relevance afterwards. The prominence of a global and more interconnected business environment also played an important role, influencing accounting research from the analysis of their effects on reporting and regulatory issues, including, for instance, the IAS and IFRS adoption and dissemination, the reporting using XBRL or the implementation of whistleblowing mechanisms and processes. Over this century, despite the maintenance of those topics, literature has evolved to also incorporate new trends under discussion, which has a more consensual perspective of accounting as an applied social science with diverse political, social, economic, and environmental impacts.

Therefore, despite a more favourable evolution in the field of accounting research and profession, there is still ample room for the development of research, particularly in emerging technologies, in comparison to the evolution observed in the educational field. From the literature, such gaps can be identified either in terms of the lack of professional experience and/or inadequate updating of accounting teachers on these topics or of the accounting books published in the last five years, which are usually too traditional and, therefore, there is lack as regards the content related to information systems and technologies.

Currently, innovative research has been developed combining the newest available data sources for data collection, technological methods for data assessment, and the so-called trending topics in accounting, which include a social and sustainable accounting perspective but also new methods and channels for different types of accounting reporting. This seems to be a path to be followed as an avenue for future research in accounting.

As an avenue to develop a literature review on accounting research, it is suggested the use of innovative tools to diversify the set of journals under assessment to include, for instance, accounting journals dedicated to the educational field or non-financial reporting.

CONCLUSION

This chapter has selected a top generalist journal in accounting to assess the research topics published and their evolution over this century (from 2000 to 2022). For this purpose, the analysis compares three distinct periods, namely the first two decades and the last three years. The latest period is particularly used as a proxy for the recent trends in accounting research.

Professionals, academics, and researchers have highlighted the difficulty of adequacy and monitoring the developments in the accounting profession and education due to new topics and technological advancements. They argue that accounting research needs to evolve and follow contemporary trends in reporting, regulation, work methods, social and political trends, as well as the technological environment, with a stronger connection between professionals, academia, and researchers. Therefore, following such challenges, and keeping up with the needs and demands of the professional environment that surrounds them, is a relevant matter.

Despite the relative openness of literature to new topics, the findings indicate a certain resilience of traditional themes, even when new methodologies and trending topics are applied. As a reference, the most cited papers from the first period seem to indicate that the underlying research themes remain. Furthermore, accounting research tends to incorporate new topics at relatively slow rates or in later stages than day-to-day practice, technical discussions, technological impacts, or regulation issues. The incipient research as regards the emergence of the covid-19 pandemic, and the dissemination of non-financial reporting requirements worldwide can be mentioned as examples of this finding. This can be potentially explained by the necessary time to collect and assess data that underlies the different research methods in accounting. Notwithstanding, this might contribute to the feeling that accounting research has not been following the recent advances seen in the accounting profession.

The challenges professionals face needs to be monitored by researchers and educational institutions since it is crucial to include information technologies as a basic subject of curricula content for professional success. Additionally, professional associations can be of great usefulness whenever deficiencies or constraints are identified, as they possess the resources or can exert political pressure to overcome them.

Therefore, the analysis performed in this chapter, despite covering a relevant period, is limited. Therefore, this limitation must be considered in the context of those conclusions, given that journals may have a particular editorial policy that can bias the proposed analysis.

Notwithstanding, this research may provide a relevant contribution to different interested parties in the accounting area, including academic members and professionals, as it identifies an overall perspective of the evolution trends and recent topics under discussion in this field. The issues identified as trending topics can be seen as new sources of themes for researchers, and the results of these investigations can be reverted to benefits for academia and, consequently, professionals in the accounting area.

ACKNOWLEDGMENT

This research was supported by the Instituto Politécnico de Lisboa (IPL/2022/REPUKRAINE_ISCAL).

REFERENCES

Ajinkya, B., Bhojraj, S., & Sengupta, P. (2005). The association between outside directors, institutional investors and the properties of management earnings forecasts. *Journal of Accounting Research*, *43*(3), 343–376. doi:10.1111/j.1475-679x.2005.00174.x

Al-Adeem, K. R. (2019). Who decides what is publishable? Empirical study on the influence of a journal's editorial board on the observed paradigm shift in US academic accounting research. *The North American Accounting Studies*, *2*(1), 1-21. https://papers.ssrn.com/sol3/papers.cfm?abstract_id=4127109

Amiram, D., Jørgensen, B. N., & Rabetti, D. (2022). Coins for bombs: The predictive ability of on-chain transfers for terrorist attacks. *Journal of Accounting Research*, *60*(2), 427–466. doi:10.1111/1475-679X.12430

Ashbaugh-Skaife, H., Collins, D. W., Kinney, W. R. Jr, & Lafond, R. (2009). The effect of SOX internal control deficiencies on firm risk and cost of equity. *Journal of Accounting Research*, *47*(1), 1–43. doi:10.1111/j.1475-679X.2008.00315.x

Aslan, H. (2022). Personal financial distress, limited attention. *Journal of Accounting Research*, *60*(1), 97–128. doi:10.1111/1475-679X.12409

Ball, R. (2009). Market and political/regulatory perspectives on the recent accounting scandals. *Journal of Accounting Research*, *47*(2), 277–323. doi:10.1111/j.1475-679X.2009.00325.x

Ball, R., Li, X., & Shivakumar, L. (2015). Contractibility and transparency of financial statement information prepared under IFRS: Evidence from debt contracts around IFRS adoption. *Journal of Accounting Research*, *53*(5), 915–963. doi:10.1111/1475-679X.12095

Bao, Y., Ke, B., Li, B., Yu, Y. J., & Zhang, J. (2020). Detecting accounting fraud in publicly traded U.S. firms using a machine learning approach. *Journal of Accounting Research*, *58*(1), 199–235. doi:10.1111/1475-679X.12292

Barrios, J. M., Bianchi, P. A., Isidro, H., & Nanda, D. (2022). Boards of a feather: Homophily in foreign director appointments around the world. *Journal of Accounting Research*, *60*(4), 1293–1335. doi:10.1111/1475-679X.12416

Barth, M. (2018). Accounting in 2036: A learned profession. *The Accounting Review*, *93*(6), 383–385. doi:10.2308/accr-10627

Barth, M. E., Landsman, W. R., & Lang, M. H. (2008). International accounting standards and accounting quality. *Journal of Accounting Research*, *46*(3), 467–498. doi:10.1111/j.1475-679X.2008.00287.x

Bebbington, J., & Unerman, J. (2020, October 20). Advancing research into accounting and the UN Sustainable Development Goals. *Accounting, Auditing & Accountability Journal*, *33*(7), 1657–1670. doi:10.1108/AAAJ-05-2020-4556

Ben-Nasr, H., Boubakri, N., & Cosset, J. (2012). The political determinants of the cost of equity: Evidence from newly privatized firms. *Journal of Accounting Research*, *50*(3), 605–646. doi:10.1111/j.1475-679X.2011.00435.x

Berger, P. G., & Lee, H. (2022). Did the Dodd–Frank whistleblower provision deter accounting fraud? *Journal of Accounting Research*, *60*(4), 1337–1378. doi:10.1111/1475-679X.12421

Bischof, J., Daske, H., & Sextroh, C. J. (2020). Why do politicians intervene in accounting regulation? the role of ideology and special interests. *Journal of Accounting Research*, *58*(3), 589–642. doi:10.1111/1475-679X.12300

Botosan, C. A., & Plumlee, M. A. (2002). A re-examination of disclosure level and the expected cost of equity capital. *Journal of Accounting Research, 40*(1), 21–40. doi:10.1111/1475-679X.00037

Bourveau, T., She, G., & Žaldokas, A. (2020). Corporate disclosure as a tacit coordination mechanism: Evidence from cartel enforcement regulations. *Journal of Accounting Research, 58*(2), 295–332. doi:10.1111/1475-679X.12301

Brown, N. C., Christensen, T. E., Elliott, W. B., & Mergenthaler, R. D. (2012). Investor sentiment and pro forma earnings disclosures. *Journal of Accounting Research, 50*(1), 1–40. doi:10.1111/j.1475-679X.2011.00427.x

Brown, N. C., Crowley, R. M., & Elliott, W. B. (2020). What are you saying? using topic to detect financial misreporting. *Journal of Accounting Research, 58*(1), 237–291. doi:10.1111/1475-679X.12294

Bushee, B. J., & Noe, C. F. (2000). Corporate disclosure practices, institutional investors, and stock return volatility. *Journal of Accounting Research, 38*(SUPPL.), 171–202. doi:10.2307/2672914

Bushman, R. M., Piotroski, J. D., & Smith, A. J. (2004). What determines corporate transparency? *Journal of Accounting Research, 42*(2), 207–252. doi:10.1111/j.1475-679X.2004.00136.x

Byard, D., Li, Y., & Yu, Y. (2011). The effect of mandatory IFRS adoption on financial analysts' information environment. *Journal of Accounting Research, 49*(1), 69–96. doi:10.1111/j.1475-679X.2010.00390.x

Call, A. C., Martin, G. S., Sharp, N. Y., & Wilde, J. H. (2018). Whistleblowers and outcomes of financial misrepresentation enforcement actions. *Journal of Accounting Research, 56*(1), 123–171. doi:10.1111/1475-679X.12177

Carnegie, G., Parker, L., & Tsahuridu, E. (2021). It's 2020: What is accounting today? *Australian Accounting Review, 31*(1), 65–73. doi:10.1111/auar.12325

Chen, J. V., Gee, K. H., & Neilson, J. J. (2021). Disclosure prominence and the quality of non-GAAP earnings. *Journal of Accounting Research, 59*(1), 163–213. doi:10.1111/1475-679X.12344

Chen, K. C. W., Chen, T., Han, W., & Yuan, H. (2022). Auditors under fire: The association between audit errors and the career setbacks of individual auditors. *Journal of Accounting Research, 60*(3), 853–900. doi:10.1111/1475-679X.12399

Christensen, H. B., Lee, E., & Walker, M. (2009). Do IFRS reconciliations convey information? the effect of debt contracting. *Journal of Accounting Research, 47*(5), 1167–1199. doi:10.1111/j.1475-679X.2009.00345.x

Christensen, J. (2018). Accounting in 2036: A learned profession. *The Accounting Review, 93*(6), 387–390. doi:10.2308/accr-10628

Commerford, B. P., Dennis, S. A., Joe, J. R., & Ulla, J. W. (2022). Man versus machine: Complex estimates and auditor reliance on artificial intelligence. *Journal of Accounting Research, 60*(1), 171–201. doi:10.1111/1475-679X.12407

Cuny, C., Kim, J., & Mehta, M. N. (2020). Politically connected governments. *Journal of Accounting Research, 58*(4), 915–952. doi:10.1111/1475-679X.12325

Daske, H., Hail, L., Leuz, C., & Verdi, R. (2008). Mandatory IFRS reporting around the world: Early evidence on the economic consequences. *Journal of Accounting Research, 46*(5), 1085–1142. doi:10.1111/j.1475-679X.2008.00306.x

Daske, H., Hail, L., Leuz, C., & Verdi, R. (2013). Adopting a label: Heterogeneity in the economic consequences around IAS/IFRS adoptions. *Journal of Accounting Research, 51*(3), 495–547. doi:10.1111/1475-679X.12005

Dechow, P. M., Erhard, R. D., Sloan, R. G., & Soliman, M. T. (2021). Implied equity duration: A measure of pandemic shutdown risk. *Journal of Accounting Research, 59*(1), 243–281. doi:10.1111/1475-679X.12348

DeFond, M. L., Raghunandan, K., & Subramanyam, K. R. (2002). Do non-audit service fees impair auditor independence? evidence from going concern audit opinions. *Journal of Accounting Research, 40*(4), 1247–1274. doi:10.1111/1475-679X.00088

Dey, A., Heese, J., & Pérez-Cavazos, G. (2021). Cash-for-information whistleblower programs: Effects on whistleblowing and consequences for whistleblowers. *Journal of Accounting Research*, 59(5), 1689-1740. doi:10.1111/1475-679X.12370

Dube, S., & Zhu, C. (2021). The disciplinary effect of social media: Evidence from firms' responses to Glassdoor reviews. *Journal of Accounting Research, 59*(5), 1783–1825. doi:10.1111/1475-679X.12393

Dyreng, S. D., Hoopes, J. L., & Wilde, J. H. (2016). Public pressure and corporate tax behavior. *Journal of Accounting Research, 54*(1), 147–186. doi:10.1111/1475-679X.12101

European Commission. (2021). Proposal for a directive of the European Parliament and of the Council amending Directive 2013/34/EU, Directive 2004/109/EC, Directive 2006/43/EC and Regulation (EU) No 537/2014, as regards corporate sustainability reporting. https://eur-lex.europa.eu/legal-content/EN/TXT/?uri=CELEX:52021PC0189

European Financial Reporting Advisory Group. (2021). *Proposals for a Relevant and Dynamic EU Sustainability Reporting Standard-Setting,* 228. EFRAG. https://www.efrag.org/Assets/Download?assetUrl=%2Fsites%2Fwebpublishing%2FSiteAssets%2FEFRAG%2520PTF-NFRS_MAIN_REPORT.pdf

European Parliament. (2022). Proposal for a Directive of the European Parliament and of the Council amending Directive 2013/34/EU, Directive 2004/109/EC, Directive 2006/43/EC and Regulation (EU) No 537/2014, as corporate sustainability reporting. https://www.consilium.europa.eu/media/57644/st10835-xx22.pdf

Fan, J. P. H., & Wong, T. J. (2005). Do external auditors perform a corporate governance role in emerging markets? evidence from east Asia. *Journal of Accounting Research, 43*(1), 35–72. doi:10.1111/j.1475-679x.2004.00162.x

Francis, J., Nanda, D., & Olsson, P. (2008). Voluntary disclosure, earnings quality, and cost of capital. *Journal of Accounting Research, 46*(1), 53–99. doi:10.1111/j.1475-679X.2008.00267.x

Frezatti, F. (2021). *Calls for paper*. FEA. http://rcf.fea.usp.br/index.php/news/

Gao, F., Wu, J. S., & Zimmerman, J. (2009). Unintended consequences of granting small firms exemptions from securities regulation: Evidence from the Sarbanes Oxley act. *Journal of Accounting Research*, *47*(2), 459–506. doi:10.1111/j.1475-679X.2009.00319.x

Gebhardt, W. R., Lee, C. M. C., & Swaminathan, B. (2001). Toward an implied cost of capital. *Journal of Accounting Research*, *39*(1), 135–176. doi:10.1111/1475-679X.00007

Gillette, J. R., Samuels, D., & Zhou, F. S. (2020). The effect of credit ratings on disclosure: Evidence from the recalibration of Moody's municipal ratings. *Journal of Accounting Research*, *58*(3), 693–739. doi:10.1111/1475-679X.12307

Grant, S. M. (2020). How does using a mobile device change investors' reactions to firm disclosures? *Journal of Accounting Research*, *58*(3), 741–775. doi:10.1111/1475-679X.12299

Guedhami, O., Pittman, J. A., & Saffar, W. (2014). Auditor choice in politically connected firms. *Journal of Accounting Research*, *52*(1), 107–162. doi:10.1111/1475-679X.12032

Guggenmos, R. D., Rennekamp, K., Rupar, K., & Wang, S. (2022). The relationship between non-GAAP earnings and aggressive estimates in reported GAAP numbers. *Journal of Accounting Research*, *60*(5), 1915–1945. doi:10.1111/1475-679X.12434

Gul, F. A. (2006). Auditors' response to political connections and cronyism in Malaysia. *Journal of Accounting Research*, *44*(5), 931–963. doi:10.1111/j.1475-679X.2006.00220.x

Hallman, N. J., Schmidt, J. J., & Thompson, A. M. (2022). Audit implications of non-GAAP reporting. *Journal of Accounting Research*, *60*(5), 1947–1989. doi:10.1111/1475-679X.12433

Hasan, I., Hoi, C.-S., Wu, Q., & Zhang, H. (2017). Does social capital matter in corporate decisions? evidence from corporate tax avoidance. *Journal of Accounting Research*, *55*(3), 629–668. doi:10.1111/1475-679X.12159

Hayes, R. M., Jiang, F., & Pan, Y. (2021). Voice of the customers: Local trust culture and consumer complaints to the CFPB. *Journal of Accounting Research*, *59*(3), 1077–1121. doi:10.1111/1475-679X.12364

Heese, J., & Pérez-Cavazos, G. (2019). Fraud allegations and government contracting. *Journal of Accounting Research*, *57*(3), 675–719. doi:10.1111/1475-679X.12258

Hobson, J. L., Mayew, W. J., & Venkatachalam, M. (2012). Analyzing speech to detect financial misreporting. *Journal of Accounting Research*, *50*(2), 349–392. doi:10.1111/j.1475-679X.2011.00433.x

Hochberg, Y. V., Sapienza, P., & Vissing-JØrgensen, A. (2009). A lobbying approach to evaluating the Sarbanes Oxley act of 2002. *Journal of Accounting Research*, *47*(2), 519–583. doi:10.1111/j.1475-679X.2009.00321.x

Hope, O. (2003). Disclosure practices, enforcement of accounting standards, and analysts' forecast accuracy: An international study. *Journal of Accounting Research*, *41*(2), 235–272. doi:10.1111/1475-679X.00102

Houston, J. F., Jiang, L., Lin, C., & Ma, Y. (2014). Political connections and the cost of bank loans. *Journal of Accounting Research*, *52*(1), 193–243. doi:10.1111/1475-679X.12038

Hribar, P., & Collins, D. W. (2002). Errors in estimating accruals: Implications for empirical research. *Journal of Accounting Research*, *40*(1), 105–134. doi:10.1111/1475-679X.00041

Hribar, P., Mergenthaler, R., Roeschley, A., Young, S., & Zhao, C. X. (2022). Do managers issue more voluntary disclosure when GAAP limits their reporting discretion in financial statements? *Journal of Accounting Research*, *60*(1), 299–351. doi:10.1111/1475-679X.12401

Huang, A., Hui, K. W., & Li, R. Z. (2019). Federal judge ideology: A new measure of ex ante litigation risk. *Journal of Accounting Research*, *57*(2), 431–489. doi:10.1111/1475-679X.12260

Islam, M. A. (2017). *Future of accounting profession: Three major changes and implications for teaching and research.* International Federation of Accountants (IFAC). https://eprints.qut.edu.au/104070/

Jia, Y., Lent, L. V., & Zeng, Y. (2014). Masculinity, testosterone, and financial misreporting. *Journal of Accounting Research*, *52*(5), 1195–1246. doi:10.1111/1475-679X.12065

Kang, J. K., Stice-Lawrence, L., & Wong, Y. T. F. (2021). The firm next door: Using satellite images to study local information advantage. *Journal of Accounting Research*, *59*(2), 713–750. doi:10.1111/1475-679X.12360

Kaplan, R. S. (2011). Accounting scholarship that advances professional knowledge and practice. *The Accounting Review*, *86*(2), 367–383. doi:10.2308/accr.00000031

Karamanou, I., & Vafeas, N. (2005). The association between corporate boards, audit committees, and management earnings forecasts: An empirical analysis. *Journal of Accounting Research*, *43*(3), 453–486. doi:10.1111/j.1475-679X.2005.00177.x

Klassen, K. J., & Laplante, S. K. (2012). Are U.S. multinational corporations becoming more aggressive income shifters? *Journal of Accounting Research*, *50*(5), 1245–1285. doi:10.1111/j.1475-679X.2012.00463.x

Lambert, R., Leuz, C., & Verrecchia, R. E. (2007). Accounting information, disclosure, and the cost of capital. *Journal of Accounting Research*, *45*(2), 385–420. doi:10.1111/j.1475-679X.2007.00238.x

Lee, L. F., Hutton, A. P., & Shu, S. (2015). The role of social media in the capital market: Evidence from consumer product recalls. *Journal of Accounting Research*, *53*(2), 367–404. doi:10.1111/1475-679X.12074

Lennox, C., Lisowsky, P., & Pittman, J. (2013). Tax aggressiveness and accounting fraud. *Journal of Accounting Research*, *51*(4), 739–778. doi:10.1111/joar.12002

Leuz, C., & Verrecchia, R. E. (2000). The economic consequences of increased disclosure. *Journal of Accounting Research*, *38*(SUPPL.), 91–124. doi:10.2307/2672910

Leuz, C., & Wysocki, P. D. (2016). The economics of disclosure and financial reporting regulation: Evidence and suggestions for future research. *Journal of Accounting Research*, *54*(2), 525–622. doi:10.1111/1475-679X.12115

Li, F. (2010). The information content of forward-looking statements in corporate filings-A naïve bayesian machine learning approach. *Journal of Accounting Research*, *48*(5), 1049–1102. doi:10.1111/j.1475-679X.2010.00382.x

Lisowsky, P., Robinson, L., & Schmidt, A. (2013). Do publicly disclosed tax reserves tell us about privately disclosed tax shelter activity? *Journal of Accounting Research*, *51*(3), 583–629. doi:10.1111/joar.12003

Liu, M. (2022). Assessing human information processing in lending decisions: A machine learning approach. *Journal of Accounting Research, 60*(2), 607–651. doi:10.1111/1475-679X.12427

Loughran, T., & Mcdonald, B. (2016). Textual analysis in accounting and finance: A survey. *Journal of Accounting Research, 54*(4), 1187–1230. doi:10.1111/1475-679X.12123

Manchiraju, H., & Rajgopal, S. (2017). Does corporate social responsibility (CSR) create shareholder value? evidence from the Indian companies act 2013. *Journal of Accounting Research, 55*(5), 1257–1300. doi:10.1111/1475-679X.12174

Mehta, M. N., Srinivasan, S., & Zhao, W. (2020). The politics of M&A antitrust. *Journal of Accounting Research, 58*(1), 5–53. doi:10.1111/1475-679X.12291

Moll, J., & Yigitbasioglu, O. (2019). The role of internet-related technologies in shaping the work of accountants: New directions for accounting research. *The British Accounting Review, 51*(6), 100833. doi:10.1016/j.bar.2019.04.002

Narayanamoorthy, G. (2006). Conservatism and cross-sectional variation in the post-earnings announcement drift. *Journal of Accounting Research, 44*(4), 763–789. doi:10.1111/j.1475-679X.2006.00218.x

Peng, L., Teoh, S. H., Wang, Y., & Yan, J. (2022). Face value: Trait impressions, performance characteristics, and market outcomes for financial analysts. *Journal of Accounting Research, 60*(2), 653–705. doi:10.1111/1475-679X.12428

Piotroski, J. D., & Srinivasan, S. (2008). Regulation and bonding: The sarbanes-oxley act and the flow of international listings. *Journal of Accounting Research, 46*(2), 383–425. doi:10.1111/j.1475-679X.2008.00279.x

Piotroski, J. D., Wong, T. J., & Zhang, T. (2015). Political incentives to suppress negative information: Evidence from chinese listed firms. *Journal of Accounting Research, 53*(2), 405–459. doi:10.1111/1475-679X.12071

Ramanna, K., & Roychowdhury, S. (2010). Elections and discretionary accruals: Evidence from 2004. *Journal of Accounting Research, 48*(2), 445–475. doi:10.1111/j.1475-679X.2010.00373.x

Rego, S. O., & Wilson, R. (2012). Equity risk incentives and corporate tax aggressiveness. *Journal of Accounting Research, 50*(3), 775–810. doi:10.1111/j.1475-679X.2012.00438.x

Reichelt, K. J., & Wang, D. (2010). National and office-specific measures of auditor industry expertise and effects on audit quality. *Journal of Accounting Research, 48*(3), 647–686. doi:10.1111/j.1475-679X.2009.00363.x

Schmitz, J., & Leoni, G. (2019). Accounting and auditing at the time of blockchain technology: A research agenda. *Australian Accounting Review, 29*(2), 331–342. doi:10.1111/auar.12286

Soltes, E. (2020). Paper versus practice: A field investigation of integrity hotlines. *Journal of Accounting Research, 58*(2), 429–472. doi:10.1111/1475-679X.12302

Srinivasan, S., & Richardson, S. A. (2005). Consequences of financial reporting failure for outside directors: Evidence from accounting restatements and audit committee members. *Journal of Accounting Research, 43*(2), 291–334. doi:10.1111/j.1475-679x.2005.00172.x

Stubben, S. R., & Welch, K. T. (2020). Evidence on the use and efficacy of internal whistleblowing systems. *Journal of Accounting Research, 58*(2), 473–518. doi:10.1111/1475-679X.12303

Tan, H., Wang, S., & Welker, M. (2011). Analyst following and forecast accuracy after mandated IFRS adoptions. *Journal of Accounting Research, 49*(5), 1307–1357. doi:10.1111/j.1475-679X.2011.00422.x

Tan, H., Ying Wang, E., & Zhou, B. (2014). When the use of positive language backfires: The joint effect of tone, readability, and investor sophistication on earnings judgments. *Journal of Accounting Research, 52*(1), 273–302. doi:10.1111/1475-679X.12039

Tweedie, D., & Hazelton, J. (2019). Economic inequality: Problems and perspectives for interdisciplinary accounting research. *Accounting, Auditing & Accountability Journal, 32*(7), 1982–2003. doi:10.1108/AAAJ-09-2018-3649

Wang, D. (2006). Founding family ownership and earnings quality. *Journal of Accounting Research, 44*(3), 619–656. doi:10.1111/j.1475-679X.2006.00213.x

ADDITIONAL READING

Armstrong, C., Kepler, J. D., Samuels, D., & Taylor, D. (2022). Causality redux: The evolution of empirical methods in accounting research and the growth of quasi-experiments. *Journal of Accounting and Economics, 101521*(2-3), 101521. Advance online publication. doi:10.1016/j.jacceco.2022.101521

Chalmers, K., Hay, D., & Khlif, H. (2018). Internal control in accounting research: A review. *Journal of Accounting Literature, 42*(1), 80–103. doi:10.1016/j.acclit.2018.03.002

de Villiers, C., & Hsiao, P. C. K. (2018). A review of accounting research in Australasia. *Accounting & Finance, 58*(4), 993-1026. htpps:// doi:10.1111/acfi.12424

Gulluscio, C., Puntillo, P., Luciani, V., & Huisingh, D. (2020). Climate change accounting and reporting: A systematic literature review. *Sustainability (Basel), 12*(13), 5455. doi:10.3390u12135455

He, R., Luo, L., Shamsuddin, A., & Tang, Q. (2022). Corporate carbon accounting: A literature review of carbon accounting research from the Kyoto Protocol to the Paris Agreement. *Accounting and Finance, 62*(1), 261–298. doi:10.1111/acfi.12789

Lennox, C., & Wu, J. S. (2022). A review of China-related accounting research in the past 25 years. *Journal of Accounting and Economics, 101539*(2-3), 101539. doi:10.1016/j.jacceco.2022.101539

Marrone, M., & Hazelton, J. (2019). The disruptive and transformative potential of new technologies for accounting, accountants, and accountability: A review of current literature and call for further research. *Meditari Accountancy Research, 27*(5), 677–694. doi:10.1108/MEDAR-06-2019-0508

Schmidthuber, L., Hilgers, D., & Hofmann, S. (2022). International Public Sector Accounting Standards (IPSASs): A systematic literature review and future research agenda. *Financial Accountability & Management, 38*(1), 119–142. doi:10.1111/faam.12265

Chapter 2

Climate-Related Financial Disclosures and Corporate Social Responsibility:
Evidence From European ompanies

Ana Isabel Dias
https://orcid.org/0000-0002-6503-4792
Instituto Politécnico de Lisboa, Portugal

Sónia Raquel Baptista Fernandes
https://orcid.org/0000-0001-6858-1049
Instituto Politécnico de Lisboa, Portugal

Pedro Pinheiro
https://orcid.org/0000-0003-3210-3963
Instituto Politécnico de Lisboa, Portugal

ABSTRACT

This study intends to provide additional evidence regarding practices of reporting based on the recommendations of the Task Force on Climate-Related Financial Disclosures, and to relate it with performance scores of reporting based on corporate social responsibility indicators. Despite the announcements of the adoption of those recommendations, the level of compliance is relatively low. Additionally, the relation with corporate social responsibility exists, but only when the comparison is with environmental disclosures. The contribution of this study is to provide evidence that the adoption of the recommendations of the Task Force on Climate-Related Financial Disclosures is challenging because there are two perspectives for corporate reporting as the disclosure performance based on indicators of corporate social responsibility (inside-out) differs from the recommendations of the Task Force on Climate-Related Financial Disclosures (outside-in). The results may support understanding the companies' challenges in the practical implementation of the existing guidelines.

DOI: 10.4018/978-1-6684-7293-4.ch002

INTRODUCTION

As corporate reporting is a concept in development that is transforming the economic paradigm with the influence of the concept of social responsibility (Bychkova, Karelskaia, Abdalova & Zhidkova, 2021; Christensen, Floyd, Liu & Maffett,2017; Wang, Cao & Ye, 2018), the concern about reporting both financial and non-financial information on Environmental, Social, and Governance (ESG) has increased (Chouaibi, Rossi, Siggia & Chouaibi, 2022; Kinderman, 2020; Xu & Liu, 2018).

Climate-related information is commonly presented by companies as part of corporate non-financial reporting (Lombardi, Schimperna, Paoloni & Galeotti, 2022; Santos & Rodrigues, 2021). The expression "non-financial reporting" frequently includes notions such as ESG information, climate risks, and opportunities, or key performance indicators of climate-related matters, depending on the stakeholders and the specific business characteristics (Haller, Link & Grob, 2017; Kashyap, Menisy, Caiazzo & Samuel, 2020).

As the awareness of non-financial reporting grows, more attention is being paid to corporate social responsibility (CSR) activities, affecting the interests of investors (Xu & Liu, 2018). Traditionally, in CSR, producing a non-financial statement is an orientation to provide information to all types of stakeholders (Breijer & Orij, 2022) and not mainly investors and creditors like financial information. Cox and Wicks (2011) argued that investors concerned with long-term profits consider CSR disclosure an effective way to obtain CSR information and an important decision-making factor in evaluating the value of a company. A more contemporary view on CSR is given by Wang and Juslin (2012) that present the concept associated with the notion of business ethics, i.e., the importance of social and ethical dimensions conversely to the focus on a CSR economic-based perspective that prevailed during the XX century. Giannarakis (2014) also stated that CSR should be understood as a key issue in modern management with a broader scope. Hence, non-financial reporting has become more popular and has been used by companies similarly to financial reporting sometimes reported alongside financial reports (Cawkwell, 2021). The link between financial reports and non-financial reporting was generically understood as non-financial reporting depends on context (Erkens, Paugam & Stolowy, 2015; Haller, Link & Grob, 2017).

In what concerns the development of non-financial reporting, in the European Union the recent Corporate Sustainability Reporting Directive (CSRD) 2022/2464, requires undertakings to report both on the impacts of the activities on people and the environment, a so-called inside-out perspective, and on how sustainability matters affect the undertakings, an outside-in perspective. This was the clarification of the concept of "double materiality" and a requirement for corporate reporting to incorporate those two perspectives.

The generalized growing interest in non-financial reporting, much due to the pressure related to climate change to create low-carbon economies (UNCTAD, 2021), created a propitious scenario where organizations that were, until now, dedicated to the harmonization of financial reporting, have extended their scope of action to another type of reporting, nowadays commonly known as sustainability reporting.

This is the case of the International Financial Reporting Standards (IFRS) Foundation, with the creation of the International Sustainability Standards Board (ISSB), which will work alongside the International Accounting Standards Board (IASB) to develop the IFRS Sustainability Disclosure Standards. This is one of the major developments in international standard-setting (UNCTAD, 2021). The IFRS Foundation named representatives of the following investor-focus reporting initiatives to work on prototypes of the sustainability standards: the Climate Disclosures Standard Board (CDSB), the Task Force on Climate-related Financial Disclosures (TCFD), the Value Reporting Foundation (VRF) Integrated Reporting

Framework as well as industry-based Sustainability Accounting Standards Board (SASB) standards, and the World Economic Forum's stakeholder capitalism metrics, supported by the International Organization of Securities Commissions (IOSCO). The proposed requirements in the Exposure Draft IFRS S2 Climate-related Disclosures are built upon the recommendations of the TCFD and on requirements derived from SASB standards.

Within the European Union with the CSRD, another organization expanded its mission from financial reporting to non-financial reporting: the European Financial Reporting Advisory Group (EFRAG), that now is working on those two pillars. The EFRAG was asked to develop European Sustainability Reporting Standards (ESRS). Climate-related reporting is, therefore, within the scope of such standards and EFRAGs had as its primary focus the identification of good reporting practices and assessment of the level of maturity in the implementation of the TCFD recommendations, while also taking into consideration the climate-related reporting elements of the Non-Financial Reporting Directive (EFRAG, 2020).

According to Demaria and Rigot (2021), the TCFD framework tries to link financial and non-financial information, requiring companies to present the financial impact of climate risks and opportunities on their business plan and financing plan in the financial report, understood as the outside-in perspective. The TCFD framework functions as a mean for disclosing to investors CSR-related information and establishes the main ESG factors which affect the capability to distribute shareholder values (Halkos & Nomikos, 2021).

Wang, Cao, and Ye (2018) conclude that mandatory CSR disclosure mitigates information asymmetry by improving financial reporting quality. This may be attributed to the efforts of the Global Reporting Initiative (GRI) organization that elevated sustainability reporting to be on par with that financial reporting. The TCFD framework is in contrast with the GRI Standards, which present an inside-out perspective, and takes a broader stakeholder focus encouraging disclosure of management approach, strategy, and governance oversight, in addition to specific indicators (Abhayawansa & Adams, 2022).

Hence, this study aims to verify if the TCFD framework is being adopted by companies, as part of financial or non-financial reporting. It is intended to compare the level of the TCFD disclosures with indexes of CSR reporting, as the first ones represent the impact of climate change on the company, an improvement in the quality of CSR reporting (Efimova & Rozhnova, 2020) as the latter represents the impact that the company has on climate change in the past and does not allow to forecast its resolutions for a sustainable company facing climate risks. More specifically, the purpose of this chapter is to analyze and compare the climate-related disclosures, to compare the indexes of disclosure following frameworks with different backgrounds. As such, the specific purposes of this study are to:

- Perform a content analysis of the corporate reports that disclose information following the recommendations of the TCFD and formulate an index of compliance; and
- Compare the self-formulated TCFD index with existing CSR reporting indexes.

The sample of this study includes companies that are part of the Refinitiv Global Europe index between the period 2017 and 2021. However, as climate-related topics are those in focus in the recommendations of the TCFD, the sample includes only three sensitive industries: electricity, oil, coal and gas, water, and alternative energy. The sample was limited to those companies with available information in English, Portuguese, and Spanish. After applying the mentioned criteria, it was obtained a sample of 28 companies in 14 European countries.

The main contribution of this study is to assess the relation between well-established practices of CSR reporting under the inside-out perspective with more recent practices of reporting, such as the TCFD framework, that underline the outside-in perspective. This study highlights the development of the guidelines of corporate reporting, particularly the companies' adherence to increasing disclosures on the risk of climate-related matters as an encouragement to achieve knowledge of the challenges created by climate change. This type of study also introduces the relation between the disclosures under the concept of "double materiality".

This chapter is structured as follows: section 2 presents the literature review, section 3 the methodology, section 4 the results of the empirical study and the subsequent discussion, and section 5 the concluding remarks.

LITERATURE REVIEW

The Reporting of Climate-Related Financial Disclosures

The 2015 Paris Agreement has in its base that climate change is a planetary problem that has motivated pressures toward low-carbon economies. Reporting how business activities are facing that problem is the driver to accelerate the achievement of that goal (UNCTAD, 2021).

IFRS Foundation (2020) stated that climate-related matters are of interest because of their potential material effect on companies' business models, cash flows, financial position, and financial performance. Anderson (2019), as an individual IASB member, pointed out that while the expression "climate change" is not used in IFRS Standards, the topics that relate to material environmental and societal issues, complement the information in financial statements prepared accordingly by the IFRS. Thus, there is a need to promote high-quality reporting on climate-related matters.

Climate-related matters are traditionally part of non-financial reporting (Cho & Lee, 2020), which has, since the 1980s been primarily voluntary, and not mandatory (Jackson et al., 2020; Kinderman, 2020; Zhou, 2022). Since the beginning of CSR voluntary disclosure, much research has focused on its purpose (Landrum & Ohsowski, 2018) with the corporate reports differing in terms of specificity, guidance provided, target audience, and the type and extent of ESG topics covered, and focused (Abhayawansa & Adams, 2022).

Thus, the interpretation of the term "non-financial reporting" or CSR reporting has depended on the perception of the preparer of the information and its stakeholder as well as their contexts (Eccles & Serafeim, 2015).

In the European Union, the CSRD states that many stakeholders consider that the term "non-financial" may imply that the information in question has no financial relevance, but the literature frequently points out to the contrary (Clarkson, Fang, Li & Richardson, 2013; Iatridis, 2013; Krasodomska, Michalak & Świetla, 2020; O'Dwyer & Unerman, 2016). The CSRD expresses its preference to use the term "sustainability information" rather than "non-financial information" as many organizations, initiatives, and practitioners in the area already do so.

In terms of guidance, the frameworks for non-financial reporting or sustainability reporting may be listed as mentioned by Breijer and Orij (2022): SASB, International Integrated Reporting Council (IIRC), Economic Co-operation and Development (OECD), European Federation of Financial Analysts Societies (EFFAS), GRI, United Nations Global Compact (UNGC), International Organization for Standardization (ISO), AccountAbility (AA), formerly the Carbon Disclosure Project (CDP). Nevertheless, the GRI reporting framework has been the dominant standard until recently (Lozano, Nummert, & Ceulemans, 2016), with companies now also reporting using frameworks such as the United Nations Sustainable Development Goals (SDGs), the TCFD, and the SASB standards (Zhou, 2022).

Petersen, Herbert, and Daniels (2022) indicate that the available frameworks and guidelines can be either investor-focused, such as TCFD, SASB standards, or Integrated Reporting (IR) from the IIRC or multistakeholder-focused, like GRI standards, the 17 Sustainable Development Goals (SDGs) of the 2030 Agenda for Sustainable Development from UNGC or CDP. The authors state that as investors are likely to demand relevant "non-financial information" other stakeholders may seek for sustainability-related information to evaluate value creation for society. For this purpose, UNCTAD (2021) refer that at the 37th session of the Intergovernmental Working Group of Experts on International Standards of Accounting and Reporting was recognized that climate-related financial disclosures are critical to understanding the exposure of companies' activities to the effects of climate change, as well as their impacts on society. Adams and Abhayawansa (2022) argue that using financial materiality to determine which sustainability disclosures are to be provided contradicts the GRI's view that sustainability reporting provides critical information informing the decisions of a wide range of stakeholders including employees, policymakers, and investors. Nevertheless, the IFRS Foundation seems to have evolved the concept from financial relevance to a broad impact on society (UNCTAD, 2021), and the European Union accompanied that tendency.

The previously mentioned typology by stakeholder is complemented with the clarification made in the CSRD (note 29) regarding the concept of "double materiality", which is intended to provide information on two perspectives:

(…) information to the extent necessary for an understanding of the undertaking's development, performance and position, but also on information necessary for an understanding of the impact of the undertaking's activities on environmental, social and employee matters, respect for human rights, anti-corruption and bribery matters.

Therefore, the CSRD exposes the need for companies to transparently disclose information on the impact of activities on the environment and people, the inside-out perspective of reporting, but also how sustainability matters, such as climate-related, affect the company, the outside-in perspective. The CSRD also states that the companies must disclose material information from both perspectives and if the materiality is only assessed from one perspective.

Whatever the characteristics of the guidelines and frameworks, over the years, the literature points out that the disclosed non-financial information is imprecise and too descriptive (Beck, Campbell & Shrives, 2010; Melloni, Caglio & Perego, 2017), which led to arguments that disclosure of information requirements is a key part of market discipline - the influence that investors and other stakeholders have on an institution's behavior and risk profile (Christensen, Floyd, Liu & Maffett, 2017; Rigot, Amar & Demaria, 2022).

Christensen, Floyd, Liu, and Maffett (2017) conclude that the reporting of CSR information in financial reports can have real effects, even if this information is already publicly available. Kinderman (2020) states that by providing more complete and higher quality information about companies' social and environmental impacts, mandatory non-financial reporting can influence internal decision-making (Eccles & Serafeim 2015) and help external stakeholders, such as investors and civil society organizations, to push companies in a more sustainable direction. This is also applicable to climate-related matters (IFRS Foundation, 2020), for which regulators that were mainly dedicated to financial reporting, have extended their scope of action to non-financial reporting. This is the case of the IFRS Foundation, with the creation of the ISSB that will work alongside the IASB to develop the IFRS Sustainability Disclosure Standards; and also the case of EFRAG now with EFRAG Financial Reporting Board and the EFRAG Sustainability Reporting Board.

IFRS Foundation (2021a) indicates the representatives of the joint work that resulted in exposure drafts of the requirements for climate and general disclosures: the TCFD, the VRF – that have integrated the IIRC framework and the SASB standards, the CDSB and the World Economic Forum. EFRAG's activities are organized into two pillars, a financial reporting pillar, and a sustainability reporting pillar, with the latter providing technical advice to the European Commission in the form of draft ESRS and/or respective amendments. These initiatives are intended to create a global sustainability disclosure standard-setter that the financial markets lack (EFRAG, 2020; IFRS Foundation, 2021b; Zhou, 2022).

Marsh (2022) states that the strength of an international agreement that relies on reporting climate-related financial disclosures according to the TCFD is taking place, with the United Nations, IFRS Foundation, and G20 calling for the adoption of the framework. This adoption could lead to a standard that would allow for an understanding of how the effects of climate change are being addressed and to responsibly manage those impacts, risks, and opportunities, including the efficient allocation of capital supporting a transition to a more sustainable, low-carbon economy (UNCTAD, 2021). Notwithstanding, EFRAG (2020) argues that it has observed a wide variation in the approaches taken by companies to adopt the TCFD recommendations and the requirements of the Non-Financial Reporting Directive (EFRAG, 2020). This led EFRAGs to propose drafts of the ESRS based on those two guidelines after identifying the good climate-related reporting practices, and those to be avoided.

The Task Force on Climate-Related Financial Disclosures (TCFD)

The TCFD was created by the Financial Stability Board (FSB) to improve and increase reporting of climate-related financial information, and to date, is composed of 31 members from across the G20, representing both preparers and users of financial disclosures.

In June 2017, the TCFD released its final recommendations (TCFD, 2017), providing a framework for companies to voluntarily disclose information about the financial risks of climate change. The TCFD (2017) recommendations are structured into four core areas: governance, strategy, risk management, and metrics and targets. These areas are supported by eleven recommended disclosures that have as purpose to understand how reporting organizations think about and assess climate-related risks and opportunities.

Demaria and Rigot (2021) state that these disclosures are one of the means to enhance financial transparency via the market discipline mechanism and Abhayawansa and Adams (2022) affirm that it is the most authoritative framework on climate-related risk reporting. Elshandidy, Shrives, Bamber, and Abraham (2018) state that risk reporting on financial matters is spread among a wide range of accounting standards, which is a challenge for an accurate interpretation, and suggest a stand-alone risk-reporting accounting standard.

At this point, it is important to underline that the Exposure Draft IFRS S2 Climate-Related Disclosures (Climate Exposure Draft) from ISSB builds on the recommendations from the TCFD and incorporates industry-based disclosure requirements derived from the SASB Standards.

Furthermore, on the presentation of financial risks of climate change, the TCFD proposes that the recommended disclosures should be included in the company's mainstream "annual financial filings", thus complementing financial reporting. Nevertheless, Eccles and Krzus (2019) observed that companies provided more information relevant to the TCFD recommendations in their voluntary sustainability reports than in the SEC Forms 10-K or 20-F. Comparable results were obtained by EFRAG (2020).

Regarding the adoption of the TCFD recommendations, Abhayawansa and Adams (2022) or Amar, Rigot, and Demaria (2022) call TCFD recommendations a global reference, although not binding, but underline its success by referring to the inclusion in recent legislative proposals in jurisdictions such as the European Union, the United Kingdom, and the United States of America. Marsh (2022) clarify that, at that point, 13 countries have endorsed the TCFD framework or similar, and 9 are in the process of making it mandatory. In this regard, Zhou (2022) points out that the United Kingdom and New Zealand were the first countries to require their largest listed companies to disclose climate-related financial information from 2022-2023 and that the Securities and Exchange Commission (SEC) in the United States of America has recently released a proposal that would require companies to disclose climate-related disclosures for investors. The European Union, with its 2021 CSRD proposal, showed its support for the TCFD. This was expected as the TCFD recommendations were, in 2019, integrated into Directive 2014/95/EU, the Non-Financial Reporting Directive, through the official Guidelines on Climate-Related Information (European Commission, 2019). Those guidelines are intended to increase awareness and understanding of climate-related risks and opportunities within the company and improve dialogue with all stakeholders. TCFD (2021) states that the 2021 CSRD proposal led to TCFD-aligned reporting for nearly 50.000 large companies with a presence in the European Union. The recent CSRD reinforce that support and stated the alignment with disclosures included in international frameworks (such as GRI, IIRC, SASB, CDSB, and CDP), including the recommendations of the TCFD. The CSRD extended the scope to all large companies and all companies listed on regulated markets (except listed micro-enterprises), requires the audit (assurance) of reported information, introduces more detailed reporting requirements, and a requirement to report according to mandatory EU sustainability reporting standards, the ESRS. It is assumed that these standards include business strategy and the resilience of the business model and strategy about risks related to sustainability matters, compatible with the transition to a sustainable economy and with the objectives of limiting global warming.

Demaria and Rigot (2021) expose that the framework of the TCFD has some characteristics that differentiate it from the existing standards: (1) it adopts an approach that focuses on the impact of climate change on the company, rather than the risks the company creates (Johnston, 2018), the outside-in perspective; (2) it especially focuses on climate risks and opportunities and not on CSR, which is a detachment from how the company is affecting the environment; and (3) it tries to link the financial and non-financial information, requiring firms to present the financial impact of climate risks and opportunities on their business plan and their financing plan in the financial report.

Despite this, in 2019, only 42% of companies with a market capitalization greater than $10 billion disclosed information in line with the TCFD to some extent (TCFD, 2022). Achenbach (2021), in an analysis of the determinants of disclosure, concludes that those companies who already implement the recommendations of TCFD progressed further in identifying, managing, and mitigating climate-related risks than those companies who do not report in line with TCFD.

Although the TCFD annually reviews the alignment of companies' reporting with its recommendations and its most recent status report (TCFD, 2022) shows that the number of companies reporting has increased in the latest years, the report does not assess the quality of companies' climate-related disclosure. Additionally, their adoption of automated content analysis methods impedes locating interesting patterns in disclosure. Notwithstanding, studies such as Eccles and Krzus (2019) or UNCTAD (2021) are providing additional evidence to assess experiences and good practices in the reporting of climate-related matters, such as the TCFD recommendations.

Hence, for a good understanding of the phenomenon – the adoption of the recent TCFD framework, which relies on the concept of climate-related financial disclosures, the company's perspective on how climate change is affecting it, and its response, one has to consider how does it bring a new perspective and what is its relationship with existing models of reporting, namely CSR disclosures.

Climate-Related Disclosures and CSR Indexes

Climate-related disclosures may be classified into two perspectives (Abhayawansa & Adams, 2022): (1) the outside-in perspective, reporting the impact of climate change on the company, thus affecting value creation (Adams, 2017); and (2) the inside-out perspective, disclosing the impact of the company's operations on the climate, impacting sustainable development, particularly as climate change has an impact on the achievement of other SDGs. In the European Union, the CSRD incorporates such duality requiring reports both on the impacts of the activities on people and the environment and on how sustainability matters affect the companies' activities.

The TCFD recommendations, focused on the investor as the stakeholder (Petersen, Herbert & Daniels, 2022), clearly are positioned to disclose the impact of climate change on the company (Demaria & Rigot, 2021) and the GRI standards or the UNGC framework, for instance, as multi-stakeholders guidelines (Petersen, Herbert & Daniels, 2022) are meant to disclose the impact of the company's operations on the climate (Halkos & Nomikos, 2021).

Although companies have been accused of being responsible for many negative impacts on the environment where they operate (Lozano, Nummert & Ceulemans, 2016) which made the focus of debate on reporting of ESG topics, Adams (2017) demonstrates that it is the requirement to disclose strategy and management approach with governance oversight (TCFD, 2017) that gets organizations thinking about what they do and how they do it.

Nevertheless, physical climate-change risks, for example, while difficult to translate into financial statement impacts, are relevant to investors in that they have implications for long-term value creation (Abhayawansa & Adams, 2022; Cox & Wicks, 2011). Within the long-term value creation, Sarfraz, Qun, Hui, and Abdullah (2018) argue that a company with stronger CSR ratings, particularly in the environmental concerns, has higher debt financing and, therefore, it improves investment decisions and social communication, and better CSR performance.

Halkos and Nomikos (2021) also argue that a higher level of CSR-related information disclosure leads to greater forecast accuracy by analysts and is thus associated with more positive recommendations from analysts. Hence, the company's reporting has increased its importance based on a relatively novel framework, the TCFD recommendations that consider companies as the vectors of a more sustainable economy, but that incorporate part of the concept of CSR reporting (Amar, Rigot & Demaria, 2022).

Eccles and Krzus (2019) asked to what extent were oil and gas companies already following the TCFD recommendations using existing guidance from the SEC, GRI, and SASB and concluded that there was no company reporting on all recommendations, but at least one was doing it, showing that the implementation of that type of reporting could be done in the industry. But the recommendations of the TCFD seem to include a more qualitative step in the development of non-financial reporting, (Efimova

& Rozhnova, 2020). Bychkova, Karelskaia, Abdalova, and Zhidkova (2021) agree as they state that the development vector of non-financial reporting is determined by the requirement for the company to disclose its climate risks. Eccles and Krzus (2018) state that companies have several reasons to start implementing this type of disclosure: investor pressure and lack of motivation when the climate-risk disclosures are not made, and the possibility to develop better strategies.

Lozano, Nummert, and Ceulemans (2016) state that to make companies more sustainability-oriented, it is necessary to understand the links between the technical, managerial, and organizational processes and sustainability reports, and to change organizational issues, including values, visions, philosophies, policies, employee empowerment, and change management practices.

This vision is in line with Cho and Lee (2020) that argue that this recent movement toward integrated reporting may be an indication that current financial reporting has limitations and is a clear example of the increasing demand for non-financial disclosures.

However, it is a possibility for reporting to go beyond what has the company done to impact the environment and improve reporting on their strategies and risk management (Marsh, 2022). Efimova and Rozhnova (2020) state that harmonizing financial and non-financial reporting will improve the relevance, reliability (quality), and consistency of information for its users about the development of a company in the context of climatic risks.

This study aims to compare indexes of performance on CSR communication with a self-formulated index for compliance with the TCFD recommendations. This will allow obtaining evidence of whether companies that are good performers are communicating their CSR activities under the existing frameworks are adapting their form of communication to this perspective – the requirements of the TCFD. Nevertheless, although the relationship may be hypothesized, due to the lack of previous literature, it is not presented as a hypothesis.

METHODOLOGY

Sample and Data

Measuring non-financial reporting or sustainability reporting is not easy to implement, either due to the ambiguity of its definition or to the heterogeneity of existing elements and dimensions of analysis (Galant & Cadez, 2017). Among the various approaches that are usually used to measure non-financial reporting disclosure, it is possible to highlight the use of content analysis and compliance or performance indexes. Previous studies have used either content analysis and/or an index to measure the level of transparency of climate-related topics (Black, 2013; Liu, Zhou, Yang & Hoepner, 2016; Lovell, Aguiar, Bebbington & Larrinaga-Gonzalez, 2010; Matsumura, Prakash & Vera-Muñoz, 2014; Steenkamp, Rahman & Kashyap, 2011; Warwick & Ng, 2012).

Content analysis has high levels of subjectivity when a qualitative approach is intended. Whether by counting words, pages, or sentences, several authors point out numerous limitations to be considered (Guthrie & Abeysekera, 2006; Turzo, Marzi, Favino & Terzani, 2022). Galant and Cadez (2017) also highlight that those limitations stem from the fact that in the preparation of reports are used different font types, sizes, spacing, pagination, and the heterogeneous use of tables, graphs, and images (Aras, Aybars, & Kutlu, 2010; Haniffa & Cooke,2005). Additionally, some corporate reports may present different readabilities, conciseness, and tones (Melloni, Caglio & Perego, 2017).

Performance or compliance indexes not only eliminate the subjectivity that may arise from content analysis but also guarantees a clear reduction of the bias that the researcher can bring in the collection, cataloging, and indexing process of the collected data.

The present study considers both methods since it performed a content analysis on the annual reports and sustainability reports that included disclosures based on the TCFD recommendations and afterward, with the results of that content analysis, it was developed a self-formulated index to assess the performance of disclosure under the requirements.

The are two types of performance indexes of disclosure in this study: one that is self-formulated, based on content analysis of the corporate reports, and the other type chosen were those provided by Refinitiv Global Europe, reflecting the performance of CSR disclosures.

The population defined takes into consideration that it was intended to analyze the largest companies in Europe since the companies' size is frequently mentioned as having a significant and positive influence on disclosures (Archambault & Archambault, 2003; Nakayama & Salotti, 2014; Glaum, Schmidt & Street, 2013; Lucas & Lourenço, 2014). Hence, the population of this study is composed of companies that are part of the Refinitiv Global Europe index. Refinitiv's ESG index is considered relevant as a proxy for CSR performance as stated by De Villiers, Jian, and Li (2022) that have identified 285 studies in 74 journals and 135 of them published during 2019 and 2020, demonstrating the growing importance of the index. De Villiers, Jian, and Li (2022) also stated that the indicators included in Refinitiv´s ESG index show greater potential to measure constructs with novel theoretical meanings.

In addition, as one of the objectives of the study is to compare the disclosures made under the TCFD recommendations with an ESG index, Refinitiv Global Europe provides separate data regarding environmental, social, and governance topics.

Therefore, the sample of this study comprises the European companies included in the abovementioned index that according to the International Classification Benchmark (ICB) belong to the industries of energy and utilities since those are the sectors with the highest environmental impact (Jackson et al., 2020).

Afterward, it was assessed whether those companies reported and complied with the TCFD recommendations according to the information available on the TCFD website. On this website, it is possible to verify which companies are nowadays declaring to report using the TCFD's recommendations and since when.

The annual reports (location recommended by the TCFD for the disclosures) or sustainability reports were collected from the company's website, namely the available reports that were in English, Spanish, or Portuguese that specifically refer to a disclosure based on those recommendations.

Of a total of 81 companies included in the energy and utilities industries, 28 disclose information accordingly to the TCFD recommendations (Table 1), approximately 35%. This result is similar to the one obtained by Zhou (2022) regarding Australian companies.

For a better understanding of the characteristics of the sample, it is also relevant to consider the sector to which they belong, the location of the company, and the initial year that it has applied the TCFD recommendations. Table 1 evidence these characteristics.

Table 1. Company list

Company	Sector	Location	Application Date
OMV	Oil, Gas, and Coal	Austria	2019
CEZ Group	Electricity	Czech Republic	2021
Fortum Corporation	Electricity	Finland	2019
Neste Corporation	Oil, Gas, and Coal	Finland	2021
Total S.A.	Oil, Gas, and Coal	France	2021
E.ON SE	Gas, Water, and Multi-utilities	Germany	2019
RWE AG	Gas, Water, and Multi-utilities	Germany	2021
MOTOR OIL GROUP	Oil, Gas, and Coal	Greece	2021
A2A SpA	Electricity	Italy	2020
Eni SpA	Oil, Gas, and Coal	Italy	2017
Gruppo Hera	Gas, Water, and Multi-utilities	Italy	2020
SBM Offshore NV	Oil, Gas, and Coal	Netherlands	2019
TGS ASA	Oil, Gas, and Coal	Norway	2021
Polski Koncern Naftowy ORLEN	Oil, Gas, and Coal	Poland	2021
EDP	Electricity	Portugal	2018
Galp	Oil, Gas, and Coal	Portugal	2019
Enagas	Oil, Gas, and Coal	Spain	2017
Repsol	Oil, Gas, and Coal	Spain	2018
Lundin Energy	Oil, Gas, and Coal	Sweden	2020
BP	Oil, Gas, and Coal	United Kingdom	2020
Centrica plc	Gas, Water, and Multi-utilities	United Kingdom	2021
Drax Group plc	Electricity	United Kingdom	2020
National Grid	Gas, Water, and Multi-utilities	United Kingdom	2017
Pennon Group	Gas, Water, and Multi-utilities	United Kingdom	2020
Severn Trent	Gas, Water, and Multi-utilities	United Kingdom	2019
SSE	Electricity	United Kingdom	2020
Tullow Oil	Oil, Gas, and Coal	United Kingdom	2019
United Utilities	Gas, Water, and Multi-utilities	United Kingdom	2019

Summarily, table 2 presents the sample representation per industry. The industry with higher representation in the sample is Oil, gas, and coal sector, with 50% of the companies operating in such sector, followed by companies in Gas, water, and multi-utilities with 29%, and finally, Electricity with 21%.

Table 2. Industry

Industry	Number of companies	%
Oil, Gas, and Coal	14	50
Electricity	6	21
Gas, Water, and Multi-utilities	8	29
Total	**28**	**100**

To assess the geographical diversity, Table 3 shows that the country with more companies disclosing accordingly to the TCFD recommendation is the United Kingdom with 9 companies (32,14%) followed by Italy with 3 companies (10,71%), and then Finland, Germany, Portugal, and Spain with only 2 companies each (7,14%).

Table 3. Location

Location	Number of companies	%
Austria	1	3,57%
Czech Republic	1	3,57%
Finland	2	7,14%
France	1	3,57%
Germany	2	7,14%
Greece	1	3,57%
Italy	3	10,71%
Netherlands	1	3,57%
Norway	1	3,57%
Poland	1	3,57%
Portugal	2	7,14%
Spain	2	7,14%
Sweden	1	3,57%
United Kingdom	9	32,14%
Total	**28**	**100%**

Regarding the financial year that reflects the beginning of the adoption of the TCFD recommendations, it is possible to assess that 2019 is a turning point for its adoption (Table 4). At this point, it is important to underline that the recommendations were first implemented for annual periods that began in 2017 (TCFD, 2017), but continuous work has been made providing further guidance and supporting materials (TCFD, 2022).

Table 4. Application data

Application Date	Number of companies
2017	3
2018	2
2019	8
2020	7
2021	8
Total	**28**

In summary, the sample comprises 28 companies located in 14 countries and operating in 3 environmentally sensitive sectors.

Variables

In this section, the variables will be presented and their importance to the present research will be enlightened. There are mainly two types of variables to evaluate the disclosure of non-financial information: the TCFD self-formulated index and the CSR indexes obtained from the Refinitiv database.

The TCFD Index

The TCFD index of disclosure was self-formulated using a content analysis technique. This index intends to measure the level of compliance with the TCFD recommendations, and it represents the level of compliance with the eleven recommendations from the TCFD, in the four quadrants: governance, strategy, risks, and metrics and targets.

For this purpose, the data was hand-collected from annual reports or sustainability reports for the financial years comprehended between 2017 and 2021. The year 2017 was chosen as the initial year because it was the first year for the voluntary adoption of the TCFD recommendations.

From a total of 28 companies (for 2021), it was obtained 68 observations since 2017 until 2021. It should be noted that not all companies included in the sample complied with the TCFD recommendations since 2017, as there are companies that only comply it in the following years.

Table 5 summarizes the 11 general disclosures recommended, regardless of the industry in which the company operates.

Table 5. Recommendations and Supporting Recommended Disclosures

Governance	Strategy	Risk Management	Metrics and Targets
Disclose the organization's governance around climate-related risks and opportunities.	**Disclose the actual and potential impacts of climate-related risks and opportunities on the organization's businesses, strategy, and financial planning where such information is material.**	**Disclose how the organization identifies, assesses, and manages climate-related risks.**	**Disclose the metrics and targets used to assess and manage relevant climate-related risks and opportunities where such information is material.**
a) Describe the board's oversight of climate-related risks and opportunities.	a) Describe the climate-related risks and opportunities the organization has identified over the short, medium, and long term.	a) Describe the organization's processes for identifying and assessing climate-related risks.	a) Disclose the metrics used by the organization to assess climate-related risks and opportunities in line with its strategy and risk management process.
b) Describe management's role in assessing and managing climate-related r	b) Describe the impact of climate-related risks and opportunities on the organization's businesses, strategy, and financial planning.	b) Describe the organization's processes for managing climate-related risks.	b) Disclose Scope 1, Scope 2, and, if appropriate, Scope 3 greenhouse gas (GHG) emissions, and the related risks.
	c) Describe the resilience of the organization's strategy, taking into consideration different climate-related scenarios, including a 2°C or lower scenario.	c) Describe how processes for identifying, assessing, and managing climate-related risks are integrated into the organization's overall risk management.	c) Describe the targets used by the organization to manage climate-related risks and opportunities and performance against targets.

Source: TCFD (2017)

To properly understand the items included under each of the four quadrants of the TCFD recommendations and to formulate the individual index of disclosure for each quadrant to assess the companies' compliance, it was used the general recommendations, and the specific recommendations for non-financial groups, namely in what concerns the quadrants of strategy and metrics, and targets.

Regarding the industry-specific recommendations, concerning item b) of the quadrant "Strategy", the additional disclosure recommended is regarding a discussion on how climate-related risks and opportunities are integrated with their current decision-making and in its formulation of strategy. The TCFD (2017) states regarding the supplemental Guidance for Non-Financial Groups: "Organizations should consider discussing how climate-related risks and opportunities are integrated into their (1) current decision making and (2) strategy formulation, including planning assumptions and objectives around climate change mitigation, adaptation, or opportunities.".

For the quadrant "Metrics and targets", additional information is also required regarding item a). It should be noted that the illustrative examples of metrics of the four non-financial groups are aligned with the GRI standards, CDP and SASB. Once again, regarding the supplemental Guidance for Non-Financial Groups, the TCFD (2017) recommend that "organizations should consider providing historical trends and forward-looking projections (by relevant country and/or jurisdiction, business line, or asset type). Organizations should also consider disclosing metrics that support their scenario analysis and strategic planning process and that are used to monitor the organization's business environment from a strategic and risk management perspective. Organizations should consider providing key metrics related to GHG emissions, energy, water, land use, and, if relevant, investments in climate adaptation and mitigation that address potential financial aspects of shifting demand, expenditures, asset valuation, and cost of financing."

Through the information collected from the companies' reports regarding each item of the four quadrants, general and industry-specific, a compliance index was composed for each recommendation using a weighted average. The process of collecting the information for each item of the TCFD recommendations was initially based on assigning "0" when companies do not disclose the information and "1" when they do. However, during that process, it was considered relevant to assign a value between "0" and "1" if the companies partially disclose information concerning a certain item.

After having the index for each of the four quadrants, a general INDEX was calculated through the average of the results obtained for each quadrant.

The INDEX was calculated according to the formula (1) presented below:

$$\textbf{Index} = \left[\sum_{i=l}^{n} di \right] / \mathbf{n} \tag{1}$$

where d_i is the disclosed information for each recommendation and n is the total number of items of disclosure for the quadrant.

Companies that obtain a result of "1" disclose information regarding all the recommendations of the TCFD, and those with a result of "0" do not disclose any of the requirements.

CSR Reporting: Environmental and Governance

The data regarding the environmental performance score (ENV) is based on a score collected from Refinitiv Global Europe in which the environmental pillar brings together three categories (emissions, innovation, and resource use), 10 themes, and 68 indicators.

According to Refinitiv (2022) the emission category score "measures the commitment and effectiveness towards reducing environmental emissions in its production and operational processes" and it is divided into four different themes: emissions, waste, biodiversity, and environmental management systems.

Refinitiv (2022) states that the innovation category score reflects "a company's capacity to reduce the environmental costs and burdens for its customers, thereby creating new market opportunities through new environmental technologies and processes, or eco-designed products" and is divided into two different themes: product innovation and R&D and Capital Expenditures (Capex).

Finally, Refinitiv (2022) states that the resource category score reflects the "performance and capacity to reduce the use of materials, energy or water, and to find more eco-efficient solutions by improving supply chain management" and is divided into four themes: water, energy, sustainable packaging, and environmental supply chain.

The environmental pillar measures a company's impact on the environment, including air, land, and water, as well as entire ecosystems. This reflects how well a company uses best management practices to avoid environmental risks and capitalize on environmental opportunities (Refinitiv, 2022).

This pillar is calculated using a weighted sum using the three different category scores which means that the emission score has a relative weight of 0,35, the resource use scores a relative weight of 0,35, and finally, the innovation score has a relative weight of 0,30.

The data regarding the governance performance score (GOV) is based on a score that brings together also three categories (management, shareholders, and CSR strategy), 6 themes, and 59 indicators.

According to Refinitiv (2022), the management category score "measures a company's commitment and effectiveness towards following best practice corporate governance principles"; the shareholders' category score "measures a company's effectiveness towards equal treatment of shareholders and the use of anti-takeover devices"; and the strategy category score reflects "a company's practices to communicate that it integrates economic (financial), social and environmental dimensions into its day-to-day decision-making processes".

This pillar is calculated using a weighted sum using the three different category scores which means that the management score has a relative weight of 0,67, the shareholders score a relative weight of 0,20 and finally, the CSR strategy score has a relative weight of 0,13.

Both scores, environmental and governance, ranged from 0 to 100. The minimum value represents that no information is disclosed related to the pillar, and the maximum represents that the companies disclose all the relevant information regarding the pillar.

The methodological approach regarding the ESG scores data collection is in line with recent studies (Constantinescu, Caraiani, Lungu & Mititean, 2021; Cristea et al., 2022; Duque-Grisales & Aguilera-Caracuel, 2021; Gull et al., 2022; Kuo, Chen & Meng, 2021) and allows to eliminate the subjectivity that may result from content analysis and, simultaneously, measure the CSR performance.

Statistical Techniques

Taking into consideration that the main variable is the self-constructed index based on the level of disclosure regarding the recommendations of the TCFD a univariate analysis was performed and discussed with evidence found in the literature.

Notwithstanding, to compare the variable INDEX with the variables of CSR from Refinitive and assess the relationship between the two indexes, it was followed the techniques used by Pivac, Vuko, and Cular (2017) regarding the quality of the information in annual reports. First, it was performed Kruskal-Wallis's test, as the assumptions of normality were not verified nor the assumptions of homoscedasticity. The Kruskal-Wallis tests for differences between several samples, and it's the non-parametric test analog the one-way analysis of variance (ANOVA), and an extension of the Mann-Whitney U test to allow the comparison of more than two independent groups. As such, it will report the median and interquartile range of each group. Hence, the non-parametric Kruskal-Wallis's test is used to find the differences in ranks between companies in all countries measured by the INDEX and the indicators of performance disclosure by Refinitive: the environmental performance score (ENV) and the governance performance score (GOV).

Further, binary logistic regression is also estimated for each company to investigate if there is a dependence between the INDEX and companies' indicators of performance disclosure. Once again, as the sample does not follow a normal distribution, it was used Spearman's rank-order correlation as it is the nonparametric version of the Pearson product-moment correlation. Spearman's rank order measures the strength and direction of association between the INDEX, the environmental performance score (ENV), and the governance performance score (GOV).

RESULTS AND DISCUSSION

Descriptive Statistics

The TCFD Index

The following results are meant to verify the adoption of the TCFD requirements from 2017 to 2021. It is to be noted that at the beginning of this period, the number of companies that comply with the TCFD requirement is smaller than in the latest years, making this panel unbalanced. Hence, apart from table 8, tables 6 to 11 are regarding the panel of 68 observations that occurred between 2017 and 2021; table 8 expresses the number of observations obtained per year.

Table 6 presents the results regarding descriptive statistics for the variable INDEX. On one hand, it is possible to assess that the minimum disclosure level is 0.035 and that company-year results show a very low level of compliance with the TCFD recommendations. On the other hand, a maximum of 1 is obtained for at least one company-year observation which represents a full disclosure level. The average of 0.584 indicates that the level of compliance with the TCFD recommendations between the period 2017-2021 is not as desirable as if there was a scenario of "full compliance" with each requirement. On average companies disclose only half of the items that they should. The average is particularly affected when the standard deviation is considered (0.259), meaning that between company-year there are significant differences in the disclosure provided throughout the period 2017-2021.

Table 6. Descriptive Statistics

Variables	Mean	SD	Median	Min	Max
INDEX	0.584	0.259	0.632	0.035	1

Grouping the companies according to the results obtained for the INDEX (Table 7) evidence that most of the companies comply with the TCFD recommendations above the average (63.23%) with a significant number of them (26.47%) complying above 75%. Nevertheless, almost 20% of the observations represent a low level of disclosure. Nonetheless, it is relevant to remind that these companies are stated as adopters of the TCFD recommendations. One possible explanation for these initial results may be related to the fact that the pressure to disclose this kind of information is still recent (Eccles & Krzus, 2018), and for this specific sample, it was voluntary.

Table 7. Distribution of the INDEX

INDEX distribution	Number of observations	%	Accumulated %
0 – 0.250	13	19.12	19.12
0.251 – 0.500	12	17.65	36.77
0.501 – 0.750	25	36.76	73.53
0.751 – 1	18	26.47	100
Total	**68**	**100**	

As the recommendations of the TCFD were reported in 2017, and consequently adopted in periods that begin in or after 2017, it was also considered relevant to analyze the average of the INDEX over time (Table 8). Through the analysis of the INDEX per year, it was assessed that compliance with the TCFD recommendations has continuously been increasing from 2017 until 2021. The number of observations and, consequently, of companies that adopt these recommendations has also increased.

Table 8. Average disclosure index per year

	2017	2018	2019	2020	2021	Total
INDEX mean	0.269	0.631	0.549	0.598	0.628	0.584
N	3	5	13	19	28	68

The country where companies are located is also an interesting issue to analyze (Table 9) as Anglo-Saxon countries may be keener to encourage the disclosure of information focused on the investor. The United Kingdom is the country with more observations, which is due to an incentive by the market regulator to listed companies, to disclose information based on the recommendations of the TCFD. However, there are countries with very few observations, such as Czechia, France, Greece, Norway, Poland, and Sweden. Between the countries with more than one observation, Austria presents a high average and the Netherlands a very low average.

Table 9. Average disclosure index per country

Country	INDEX mean	N
Austria	0.888	3
Czechia	0.343	1
Finland	0.652	4
France	0.815	1
Germany	0.234	4
Greece	0.219	1
Italy	0.733	8
Netherlands	0.140	3
Norway	0.549	1
Poland	0.733	1
Portugal	0.496	7
Spain	0.573	9
Sweden	0.301	2
United Kingdom	0.667	23
Total	**0.584**	**68**

Table 10 presents the results for each quadrant of the recommendations of the TCFD. The results show that in all quadrants there is at least one recommendation that is not disclosed throughout the period 2017-2021, but there are observations where the recommendation is fully disclosed. Overall, it can be assessed that there is not a company-year observation that fully complies with all the 11 recommendations. UNCTAD (2021) pointed out that there are some leader-companies in specific aspects of climate reporting, but it is challenging to find companies that show a high level of sophistication in all aspects of climate reporting.

The quadrant that, on average, companies mostly comply with the TCFD recommendations is "Governance" and the quadrant which they least comply with is "Strategy". The result obtained for "Strategy" is in line with Demaria and Rigot (2021) and Rigot, Amar, and Demaria (2022) but not for what "Risk Management" concerns. The low level of compliance for "Strategy" may be explained either by a lack of preparation for the implementation of the different climate-related scenarios regarding the resilience of the companies' strategy, (which includes a 2°C or lower), or by a lack of transparency regarding the recommendations on that quadrant. It is to be noted that Demaria and Rigot (2021) found a weak disclosure level for the "Governance", "Risk Management", and "Metrics and Targets", which, in what concerns "Governance" is not accordingly to the results of this study. The results obtained for "Strategy" are also not in line with Eccles and Krzus (2019) that concluded "Strategy" disclosures in both SEC filings and sustainability reports to be high. This may indicate that there are different types of difficulties that companies are facing in the preparation of the *reporting*. FSB (2022), based on a TCFD survey of the preparers of the reporting, concludes that three of the major challenges are related to the resilience of strategy, scope 3 GHG emissions, and the need for standardized climate-related metrics. Overall, it is possible to assess that improvement is necessary on all quadrants regardless of the recommended disclosures, in line with UNCTAD (2021).

Table 10. Detailed information per quadrant of the disclosure index of the TCFD

Quadrant	N	Mean	SD	Median	Min	Max
Governance	68	0.745	0.287	0.833	0	1
Strategy	68	0.488	0.297	0.476	0	1
Risk Management	68	0.603	0.388	0.694	0	1
Metrics and Targets	68	0.501	0.314	0.556	0	1

Table 11 presents the average results per quadrant and per country of the TCFD recommendations. The results obtained for France are equivalent to those obtained by Demaria and Rigot (2021), with the observations of the French company fully complying with the recommendations for disclosures on "Risk management" and Metrics and targets". Companies located in Austria, France, Italy, and Poland are those that show full compliance with "Risk management" recommendations. Austria stands out concerning 3 of the 4 quadrants ("Governance", "Risk management" and "Metrics and targets") showing a high level of disclosure. Companies located in Italy and Poland obtained very good results concerning the level of information disclosed regarding the "Governance" and "Risk management" quadrants. However, companies located in Czechia, Germany, Greece, and the Netherlands present a very low level of disclosure regarding "Strategy", "Risk management" and "Metrics and targets". Finally, regarding the

"Strategy" quadrant, the country with the highest value is the United Kingdom. From another perspective, the disclosures for the quadrant may be analyzed regarding full compliance: "Governance" aspects are fully disclosed by companies of Austria, Czechia, Italy, and Poland, with French companies obtaining a high index; "Strategy" recommendations are not fully or almost fully disclosed in any country; "Risk Management" recommendations are fully disclosed by companies of Austria, France, Italy, and Poland; and "Metrics and targets" topics are fully disclosed by companies of Austria and France. Therefore, the quadrant "Strategy" seems to be a challenge to achieve either transparency of reporting or capability of reporting, followed by "Metrics and targets". Notwithstanding it is to be noted that there may be companies, Austrian, French, Italian, and Polish that are taking the lead in the reporting of climate-related financial topics.

Table 11. Average per TCFD quadrant and country

Country	Governance Mean	Strategy Mean	Risk Management Mean	Metrics and targets mean
Austria	1,000	0,550	1,000	1,000
Czechia	1,000	0,000	0,222	0,148
Finland	0,760	0,363	0,847	0,639
France	0,875	0,383	1,000	1,000
Germany	0,646	0,125	0,083	0,083
Greece	0,375	0,167	0,222	0,111
Italy	1,000	0,600	1,000	0,333
Netherlands	0,375	0,072	0,000	0,111
Norway	0,750	0,167	0,611	0,667
Poland	1,000	0,600	1,000	0,333
Portugal	0,560	0,407	0,357	0,659
Spain	0,694	0,507	0,617	0,472
Sweden	0,208	0,525	0,278	0,194
United Kingdom	0,796	0,644	0,634	0,595

Figure 1 also presents the average results per quadrant and per country of the TCFD recommendations, but it serves to assess more visually that companies located in Austria, Finland, France, Italy, Norway, Poland, and the United Kingdom are disclosing more information accordingly to the recommendations from the TCFD.

Figure 1. Average per TCFD quadrant and country

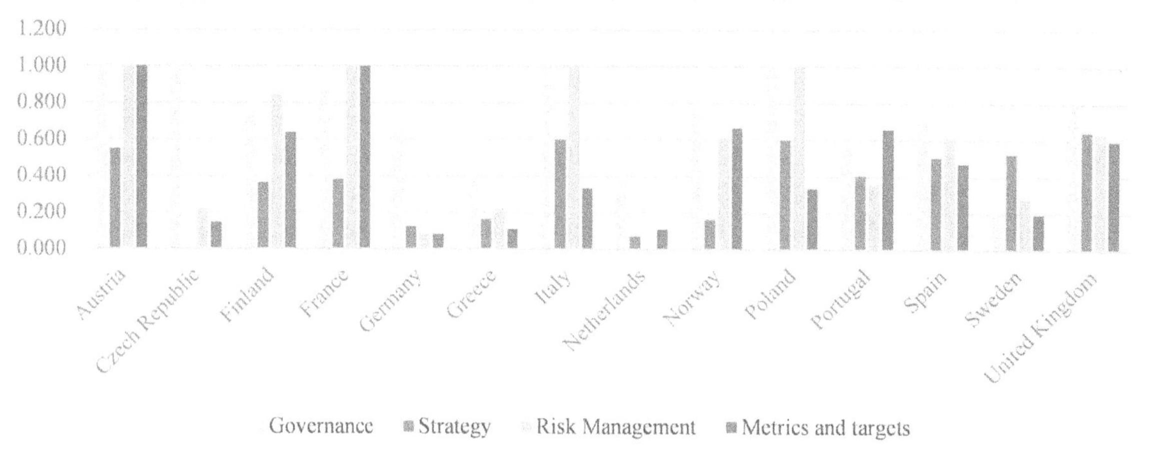

Regarding the level of compliance with TCFD recommendations, it is proper to affirm that it was over the last 3 years (2019 to 2021) that companies most complied. These results lead to arguing that companies are improving disclosure from year to year, or at least disclosing more information focusing on the investors' need for system-level data (Eccles & Krzus, 2019).

A concluding note that is worth mentioning at this point, is that despite having a population of 81 European companies, only 28 (35%) were part of the sample representing 14 countries, which means that there are still many companies that don't consider those recommendations as relevant (TCFD, 2020). Additionally, even those that state to adopt those recommendations, are only partially complying, as there is a significant lack of information in the reports.

The United Kingdom is the country with most of the observations, noting that it is a country with an Anglo-Saxon reality, and this could be the origin of being the European country with the most observations. Another reason for the abovementioned result is the fact that for the companies located in the United Kingdom, the TCFD requirements will be mandatory, and an earlier adoption could be a preparation for it.

Another issue to highlight regarding the adoption of the TCFD recommendations is that companies are still at the beginning of the path and there is still a long way to improve climate-related financial disclosures (Demaria & Rigot, 2021; Eccles & Krzus, 2019).

CSR Reporting: Environmental and Governance

The following results are meant to verify the scores of disclosures of CSR reporting, using Refinitiv scores, from 2017 to 2021. It is to be noted that, unlike the TCFD index, the number of observations is constant throughout that period, making this panel balanced. Hence, the panel of 140 observations that occurred from 2017 through 2021 are presented in tables 12 to 19.

Environmental Pillar Score (ENV)

Table 12 presents the descriptive statistics regarding the performance index related to the Environmental Pillar Score. It can be verified that the minimum value is 0.236, which means that there is at least one company with poor disclosures on environmental practices. A maximum of 0.941 reflects that there is at least one company with excellent disclosure practices at this level. Regarding the average value (0.682) it highlights that companies present a moderated level of environmental performance.

Table 12. Descriptive Statistics

Variables	Mean	SD	Median	Min	Max
ENV	0.682	0.168	0.706	0.236	0.941

When the observations are grouped according to the results obtained for the ENV score (Table 13) it can be verified that most companies have good disclosure practices at the environmental level because about 80% of the obtained results for this score are above 0.501. Consequently, a minority find themselves in the opposite situation, since only about 20% of the companies are below average.

Table 13. Distribution of the ENVSCORE

ENV distribution	Number of observations	%	Accumulated %
0 – 0.250	1	0.71	0.71
0.251 – 0.500	26	18.57	19.28
0.501 – 0.750	55	39.29	58.57
0.751 – 1	58	41.43	100
Total	**140**	**100**	

Table 14 presents the average disclosure of the ENV score per year. The results show that over the last 5 years, the score remains constant. So, it is possible to assess that this type of reporting is more constant throughout the period of study. Although voluntary, the existing reporting frameworks such as GRI are more consolidated from the perspective of the information preparers (Lozano, Nummert, & Ceulemans, 2016).

Table 14. Average ENV per year

	2017	2018	2019	2020	2021	Total
ENV mean	0.675	0.678	0.676	0.681	0.702	0.682
N	28	28	28	28	28	140

The average score by country (Table 15) shows that the country where companies have the best ENV is France, followed by Spain and Italy. However, it should be highlighted that France only has information regarding only 1 company (for 5 years), in Spain 2 companies and in Italy for 5 companies. The countries in which companies have the lowest values for ENV are Sweden and Norway. Finally, the country with the most observations is the United Kingdom, where the ENV score is above average (0.606).

Table 15. Average ENV per country

Country	ENV mean	N
Austria	0.677	5
Czech Republic	0.714	5
Finland	0.775	10
France	0.922	5
Germany	0.735	10
Greece	0.592	5
Italy	0.826	15
Netherlands	0.553	5
Norway	0.422	5
Poland	0.660	5
Portugal	0.765	10
Spain	0.854	10
Sweden	0.378	5
United Kingdom	0.606	45
Total	**0.682**	**140**

Governance Pillar Score (GOV)

Table 16 presents descriptive statistics regarding the performance index related to the Governance Pillar Score. It can be verified that the minimum value is 0.198, which means that there is at least one company with poor disclosures on governance practices and a maximum of 0.975 reflects that there is at least one company with excellent disclosures on governance practices. The average value (0.673) indicated that companies present a moderated level of disclosures on governance performance.

Table 16. Descriptive Statistics

Variables	Mean	SD	Median	Min	Max
GOV	0.673	0.190	0.713	0.198	0.975

When the observations are grouped according to the results obtained for the GOV score (Table 17) it can be assessed that most of them have good disclosure practices at the governance level because about 80% of the obtained results for this score are above 0.501. Consequently, a minority find themselves in the opposite situation, since only about 20% of the companies are below the average.

Table 17. Distribution of the GOV

GOV distribution	Number of observations	%	Accumulated %
0 – 0.250	5	3.57	3.57
0.251 – 0.500	24	17.14	20.71
0.501 – 0.750	52	37.14	57.85
0.751 – 1	59	42.14	100
Total	**140**	**100**	

Table 18 presents the average disclosure of the GOV score per year. Similarly with the ENV score, the results show that over the last 5 years the score has been increasing, indicating improvement in the disclosure practices regarding governance issues.

Table 18. Average GOV per year

	2017	2018	2019	2020	2021	Total
GOV mean	0.609	0.622	0.670	0.711	0.751	0.673
N	28	28	28	28	28	140

The average score by country (Table 19) shows that the countries where companies have the best performance on governance disclosures are Sweden and Norway. However, it should be highlighted the fact that for both countries there is information regarding only 1 company each (for 5 years). The country in which companies have the lowest values for the GOV variable is Greece. Finally, the country with the most observations is the United Kingdom, where the GOV score is above average (0.654).

Table 19. Average GOV per country

Country	GOV mean	N
Austria	0.862	5
Czech Republic	0.545	5
Finland	0.804	10
France	0.789	5
Germany	0.676	10
Greece	0.248	5
Italy	0.686	15
Netherlands	0.640	5
Norway	0.902	5
Poland	0.706	5
Portugal	0.501	10
Spain	0.640	10
Sweden	0.953	5
United Kingdom	0.654	45
Total	**0.673**	**140**

INDEX, ENV, and GOV Variables

This subsection intends to assess the relationship between the 3 variables: INDEX, ENV, and GOV. First, it was followed Kruskal-Wallis's test for the analysis of the variances between the several samples. The test of normality, using a Kolmogorov-Smirnov test (Table 20) indicates that the sample does not follow a normal distribution.

Table 20. Kolmogorov-Smirnov Test

	Statistic	Gl	Sig.
ENV	,109	140	<,001
GOV	,085	140	,014
INDEX	,310	140	<,001

a. Lilliefors Significance Correlation

The analysis of the variances following the Kruskal-Wallis test (Table 21) indicates that there is no significant evidence for the rank between samples regarding the INDEX and the score of ENV as the p-value is higher than 5%. This suggests that the level of compliance for the disclosures made under the TCFD recommendations does not significantly differ from the score of performance in disclosing environmental issues under CSR reporting. A distinct result is obtained for the relation between INDEX and GOV. Although the recommendations from the TCFD (2017) include governance topics on climate-related issues, when the comparison is made with the governance topics under CSR reporting, the ranks differ, indicating that there are differences in the levels of disclosures.

Table 21. Summary of test hypothesis

	Null Hypothesis	Test	Sig.[a,b]	Decision
1	The distribution of ENV is the same across categories of INDEX.	Independent-Samples Kruskal-Wallis test	,160	Retain the null hypothesis.
2	The distribution of GOV is the same across categories of INDEX.	Independent-Samples Kruskal-Wallis test	,047	Reject the null hypothesis.
a. The significance level is, 050.				
b. Asymptotic significances are displayed.				

Further, it complemented the study to verify if there was a relation between the variables. As the variables do not have a normal distribution, it was used Spearman's coefficient. The results are presented in Table 22.

In the correlation matrix, it is assessed that the only significant correlation and positive is between the variable INDEX and ENV, despite the low value obtained. This reveals that as environmental performance disclosures improve according to CSR scores, there is better compliance with the TCFD recommendations. This relation proposes that companies with better performance regarding environmental disclosures are more prepared to successfully comply with the recommendations of the TCFD. However, due to the descriptive analysis, it is argued that this relation is possible due to the disclosures in the quadrants of governance and metrics and targets.

Amar, Demaria, and Rigot (2022) also conclude an improvement in voluntary disclosures of climate-related information particularly for CO2-intensive companies, thus indicating that these companies are more prepared to disclose environmental information.

Table 22. Correlation matrix

			ENV	GOV	INDEX
Spearman	ENV	**Correlation coefficient**	1,000	-,165	,296**
		Sig. (2 extremities)	.	,051	<,001
		N	140	140	140
	GOV	**Correlation coefficient**	-,165	1,000	,116
		Sig. (2 extremities)	,051	.	,171
		N	140	140	140
	INDEX	**Correlation coefficient**	,296**	,116	1,000
		Sig. (2 extremities)	<,001	,171	.
		N	140	140	140
**. The correlation is significant at the 0.01 level (2 extremities).					

As a concluding remark for discussion of the analysis made, it is to be noted that the comparison between the disclosures made accordingly with the recommendations of the TCFD (2017) with the scores of disclosures based on CSR reporting exists but seems to be weak. This may be because those recommendations include the disclosure of metrics that are included in CSR reports that companies prepare on standards or frameworks that are more consolidated from the point of view of preparers (Lozano, Nummert, & Ceulemans, 2016).

Notwithstanding, the recommendations of the TCFD (2017) are based on the perspective of outside-in, thus requiring information more focused on the needs of the investors, which is distinct from other existing frameworks or standards, multi-stakeholder and based on the inside-out perspective (Abhayawansa & Adams, 2022). The obtained results could also point out the difficulty in the adoption of the concept of "double materiality" included in the recent CSRD in the European Union, as the systems of information that are implemented in the companies may not be prepared for these new requirements. Even if the companies are now seen as "good" performers in what concerns CSR reporting, as the relation suggested is weak, it can be argued that those can continue to be seen as such.

Notwithstanding, Eccles and Krzus (2019) provided evidence that it was possible for companies that already adopted standards or frameworks within the concept of CSR (the inside-out perspective) to implement reporting based on the recommendations of the TCFD. Hence, it seems that there are significant changes to be made to include both perspectives – the TCFD and the CSR – in one report and that companies that are "good" CSR reporters may already be on the path to doing it.

CONCLUSION

The recent developments in corporate reporting of non-financial information, affecting the interests of investors, raised arguments that CSR must be an effective way of obtaining information that is important for decision-making. CSR reporting has presented a significant improvement throughout the 21st century and become an instrument used by companies similarly to financial reporting, to provide information, nowadays based on three pillars: environmental, social, and governance.

In 2022, the harmonization for sustainability reporting was marked with important steps: the creation of the ISSB which issued two proposals for sustainability standards based on the joint work with TCFD, the VRF, the CDSB, and the World Economic Forum, supported by the IOSCO; and the emission of the CSRD in the European Union in line with the re-definition of EFRAGs mission, and consequently emission of the first set of draft ESRS.

The alignment with the recommendations published by the TCFD in 2017, is an important step in increasing the quality of climate-related information published, more transparent, and more related to the concept of sustainable companies as they implement strategies and governance policies that will comply with a global resolution – to achieve low carbon economies.

Nevertheless, it is important to point out that, out of the possible 81 companies that could adopt such reporting recommendations, only 28 representing 35%, did it throughout the period of study. Moreover, the existing literature and the evidence provided by this research concludes with a process of implementation of the TCFD recommendations that still have several issues to be solved regarding the preparation of the reporting, although compliance has increased particularly since 2019. The United Kingdom's incentive by the market regulator to listed companies and the preparation for mandatory adoption are explanations for why the increase in such disclosures. More specifically, recommendations on "Governance" are at the top of the companies' preferences for disclosure, maybe because those are the ones that they are better prepared to disclose; on the other end recommendations regarding "Strategy" lack reporting, which may be for reasons of (un)preparation, mainly in what concerns the resilience of the strategy, when different scenarios related with the global average temperature are taken into account or deliberately lack of transparency.

Additionally, this study provided some insights into climate-related disclosure practices and their relation to CSR reporting, concluding that there is a relation, although weak, between the TCFD recommendations with the scores of disclosures based on CSR reporting. From these results, it may be concluded that even the companies that reported CSR information based on consolidated frameworks or standards, such as GRI, may present some difficulties in implementing reporting systems that result in information on climate risks and opportunities. This is also indicating the difficulties that European companies may have in the adoption of the concept of double materiality included in the recent CSRD.

There were some limitations in developing this study, and some may represent an opportunity for further research. The number of companies that were reporting climate risks according to the TCFD recommendations was lower than expected. However, the mandatory requirements for these recommendations are becoming a reality in some European countries and the United States of America, which may facilitate the development of this analysis. Moreover, the exposure draft IFRS S2, built on the recommendations of the TCFD and requirements of SASB standards is expected to be issued around the end of the second quarter of 2023, which will increase disclosures. This study was also more focused on the quantity of information on climate risks that companies are disclosing, but another type of methodology may provide more insights on the subject.

Future research could study its quality and assess the difficulties that companies are facing to implement reporting according to the TCFD recommendations, thus providing practical advice on how to improve the implementation process. After further developing the possible TCFD indexes it would be logical to relate them to short, medium, and long-term returns.

REFERENCES

Abhayawansa, S., & Adams, S. A. (2022). Towards a conceptual framework for non-financial reporting inclusive of pandemic and climate risk reporting. *Meditari Accountancy Research*, *30*(2), 710–738. doi:10.1108/MEDAR-11-2020-1097

Achenbach, M. (2021). Transparency of Climate-Related Risks and Opportunities: Determinants Influencing the Disclosure in Line with the Task Force on Climate-Related Financial Disclosures. *Globality*, *4*(1), 1–20. doi:10.5334/glo.32

Adams, C. (2017). Conceptualizing the contemporary corporate value creation process. *Accounting, Auditing & Accountability Journal*, *30*(4), 906–931. https://doi.org/https://doi.org/10.1108/AAAJ-04-2016-2529. doi:10.1108/AAAJ-04-2016-2529

Adams, C. A., & Abhayawansa, S. (2022). Connecting the COVID-19 pandemic, environmental, social, and governance (ESG) investing and calls for 'harmonisation' of sustainability reporting. *Critical Perspectives on Accounting*, *82*, 102309. doi:10.1016/j.cpa.2021.102309

Amar, J., Rigot, S., & Demaria, S. (2022). *What are the drivers of Corporates' climate transparency? Evidence from S.* Index.

Anderson, N. (2019). IFRS Standards and climate-related disclosures. In *Brief Climate-related and other emerging risks disclosures: Assessing financial statement materiality.* https://www.ifrs.org/content/dam/ifrs/news/2019/november/in-brief-climate-change-nick-anderson.pdf

Aras, G., Aybars, A., & Kutlu, O. (2010). Managing corporate performance: Investigating the relationship between corporate social responsibility and financial performance in emerging markets. *International Journal of Productivity and Performance Management, 59*(3), 229–254. doi:10.1108/17410401011023573

Beck, A. C., Campbell, D., & Shrives, P. J. (2010). Content Analysis in Environmental Reporting Research: Enrichment and Rehearsal of the Method in a British-German Context. *The British Accounting Review, 42*(3), 207–222. doi:10.1016/j.bar.2010.05.002

Black, C. M. (2013). Accounting for Carbon Emission Allowances in the European Union: In Search of Consistency. Accounting in Europe, 10(2), 223–239. doi:10.1080/17449480.2013.834730

Breijer, R., & Orij, R. P. (2022). The Comparability of Non-Financial Information: An Exploration of the Impact of the Non-Financial Reporting Directive (NFRD, 2014/95/EU). *Accounting in Europe, 19*(May), 332–361. doi:10.1080/17449480.2022.2065645

Bychkova, S. M., Karelskaia, S. N., Abdalova, E. B., & Zhidkova, E. A. (2021). Social responsibility as the dominant driver of the evolution of reporting from financial to non-financial: Theory and methodology. *Foods and Raw Materials, 9*(1), 135–145. doi:10.21603/2308-4057-2021-1-135-145

Cawkwell, S. (2021). *Mandatory Corporate Social Responsibility Reporting; The way forward for more Sustainable Companies? LAWS521: Organisational Law.* Victoria University of Wellington.

Cho, S., & Lee, C. (2020). Financial Reporting Conservatism and Voluntary CSR Disclosure. *Accounting Horizons, 34*(March), 63–82. doi:10.2308/horizons-17-093

Chouaibi, S., Rossi, M., Siggia, D., & Chouaibi, J. (2022). Exploring the moderating role of social and ethical practices in the relationship between environmental disclosure and financial performance: Evidence from esg companies. *Sustainability (Basel), 14*(1), 209. doi:10.3390u14010209

Christensen, H. B., Floyd, E., Liu, L. Y., & Maffett, M. (2017). The real effects of mandated information on social responsibility in financial reports: Evidence from mine-safety records. *Journal of Accounting and Economics, 64*(2–3), 284–304. doi:10.1016/j.jacceco.2017.08.001

Clarkson, P. M., Fang, X., Li, Y., & Richardson, G. (2013). The Relevance of Environmental Disclosures: Are Such Disclosures Incrementally Informative? *Journal of Accounting and Public Policy, 32*(5), 410–431. doi:10.1016/j.jaccpubpol.2013.06.008

Constantinescu, D., Caraianim, C., Lungu, C., & Mititean, P. (2021). Environmental, social and governance disclosure associated with the firm value. Evidence from energy industry. *Accounting and Management Information Systems, 20*(1), 56–75. doi:10.24818/jamis.2021.01003

Cox, P., & Wicks, P. G. (2011). Institutional Interest in Corporate Responsibility: Portfolio Evidence and Ethical Explanation. *Journal of Business Ethics*, *103*(1), 143–165. doi:10.100710551-011-0859-0

Cristea, M., Noja, G., Thalassinos, E., Circiumaru, D., Ponea, C., & Duaru, C. (2022). Environmental, Social and Governance Credentials of Agricultural Companies—The Interplay with Company Size. *Resources*, *11*(3), 30. doi:10.3390/resources11030030

De Villiers, C., Jia, J., & Li, Z. (2022). Corporate social responsibility: A review of empirical research using Thomson Reuters ASSET4 data. *Accounting and Finance*, *00*(4), 1–46. doi:10.1111/acfi.13004

Demaria, S., & Rigot, S. (2021). Corporate environmental reporting: Are French firms compliant with the Task Force on Climate Financial Disclosures' recommendations? *Business Strategy and the Environment*, *30*(1), 721–738. doi:10.1002/bse.2651

Directive (EU) 2014/95. *Directive (EU) 2014/95 of the European Parliament and of the Council* Non-financial Reporting Directive. https://eur-lex.europa.eu/legal-content/EN/TXT/PDF/?uri=CELEX:32014L0095&from=EN

Directive (EU) 2022/2464. *Directive (EU) 2022/2464 of the European Parliament and of the Council.* Corporate Sustainability Reporting Directive. EUR-Lex - 32022L2464 - EN - EUR-Lex (europa.eu)

Duque-Grisales, E., & Aguilera-Caracuel, J. (2021). Environmental, Social and Governance (ESG) Scores and Financial Performance of Multilatinas: Moderating Efects of Geographic International Diversifcation and Financial Slack. *Journal of Business Ethics*, *168*(2), 315–334. doi:10.100710551-019-04177-w

Eccles, R. G., & Krzus, M. P. (2018). Why Companies Should Report Financial Risks From Climate Change. *MIT Sloan Management Review*, *9*(3), 1–6.

Eccles, R. G., & Krzus, M. P. (2019). Implementing the Task Force on Climate-related Financial Disclosures Recommendations: An Assessment of Corporate Readiness. *Schmalenbach Business Review*, *71*(2), 287–293. doi:10.100741464-018-0060-4

Eccles, R. G., & Serafeim, G. (2015). Corporate and integrated reporting: A functional perspective. In E. Lawler, S. Mohrman, & J. O'Toole (Eds.), *Corporate Stewardship: Achieving Sustainable Effectiveness* (pp. 156–171). Greenleaf. doi:10.9774/GLEAF.9781783532605_10

Efimova, O.V., & Rozhnova, O.V. (2020). The Strategy for Harmonizing Financial and Non-financial Reporting on Climate Risk Disclosures. *Accounting. Analysis. Auditing.* *7*(3):18-25. (In Russ.) doi:10.26794/2408-9303-2020-7-3-18-25

EFRAG [European Financial Reporting Advisory Group] (2020). How to improve climate-related reporting. *Project Task Force on Climate-related Reporting*. European Reporting Lab. https://www.efrag.org/Lab1

Elshandidy, T., Shrives, P. J., Bamber, M., & Abraham, S. (2018). Risk Reporting : A Review of the Literature and Implications for Future Research. *Journal of Accounting Literature*, *40*(1), 54–82. doi:10.1016/j.acclit.2017.12.001

Erkens, M., Paugam, L., & Stolowy, H. (2015). Non-financial information: State of the art and research perspectives based on a bibliometric study. In Accounting Auditing Control, 21(3), 15–92. doi:10.3917/cca.213.0015

Galant, A., & Cadez, S. (2017). Corporate social responsibility and financial performance relationship: A review of measurement approaches. *Ekonomska Istrazivanja, 30*(1), 676–693. doi:10.1080/1331677X.2017.1313122

Giannarakis, G. (2014). Corporate governance and financial characteristic effects the extent of corporate social responsibility disclosures. *Social Responsibility Journal, 10*(4), 569–590. doi:10.1108/SRJ-02-2013-0008

Gull, A. A., Hussain, N., Khan, S. A., Khan, Z., & Saeed, A. (2022). Governing Corporate Social Responsibility Decoupling: The Efect of the Governance Committee on Corporate Social Responsibility Decoupling. *Journal of Business Ethics*. doi:10.100710551-022-05181-3

Guthrie, J., & Abeysekera, I. (2006). Content analysis of social, environmental reporting: What is new? *Journal of Human Resource Costing & Accounting, 10*(2), 114–126. doi:10.1108/14013380610703120

Halkos, G., & Nomikos, S. (2021). Corporate social responsibility: Trends in global reporting initiative standards. *Economic Analysis and Policy, 69*, 106–117. doi:10.1016/j.eap.2020.11.008

Haller, A., Link, M., & Groß, T. (2017). The Term 'Non-financial Information'–A Semantic Analysis of a Key Feature of Current and Future Corporate Reporting. *Accounting in Europe, 14*(3), 407–429. doi:10.1080/17449480.2017.1374548

Haniffa, R. M., & Cooke, T. E. (2005). The impact of culture and governance on corporate social reporting. *Journal of Accounting and Public Policy, 24*(5), 391–430. doi:10.1016/j.jaccpubpol.2005.06.001

Iatridis, G. E. (2013). Environmental Disclosure Quality: Evidence on Environmental Performance, Corporate Governance and Value Relevance. *Emerging Markets Review, 14*(1), 55–75. doi:10.1016/j.ememar.2012.11.003

IFRS Foundation. (2020*). Effects of climate-related matters on financial statements (November),* 1–6. IFRS. https://www.ifrs.org/content/dam/ifrs/supporting-implementation/documents/effects-of-climate-related-matters-on-financial-statements.pdf

IFRS Foundation. (2021a). *IFRS Foundation announces International Sustainability Standards Board, consolidation with CDSB and VRF, and publication of prototype disclosure requirements*. IFRS. https://www.ifrs.org/news-and-events/news/2021/11/ifrs-foundation-announces-issb-consolidation-with-cdsb-vrf-publication-of-prototypes/

IFRS Foundation. (2021b). *Global sustainability disclosure standards for the financial markets*. IFRS. https://www.ifrs.org/news-and-events/news/2021/11/global-sustainability-disclosure-standards-for-the-financial-markets/

Jackson, G., Bartosch, J., Avetisyan, E., Kinderman, D., & Knudsen, J. S. (2020). Mandatory Non-financial Disclosure and Its Influence on CSR: An International Comparison. *Journal of Business Ethics, 162*(2), 323–342. doi:10.100710551-019-04200-0

Johnston, A. (2018). Climate-Related Financial Disclosures: What Next for Environmental Sustainability? *Research Paper Series 2018–02*. University of Oslo Faculty of Law Legal Studies.

Kinderman, D. (2020). The challenges of upward regulatory harmonization : The case of sustainability reporting in the European Union. *Regulation & Governance*, *14*(4), 674–697. doi:10.1111/rego.12240

Krasodomska, J., Michalak, J., & Świetla, K. (2020). Directive 2014/95/EU: Accountants ' Understanding and Attitude towards Mandatory Non-Financial Disclosures in Corporate Reporting Directive 2014 / 95 / EU Disclosures Incorporate Reporting. *Meditari Account. Res.*, *28*(5), 751–779. doi:10.1108/MEDAR-06-2019-0504

Kuo, T., Chen, H., & Meng, H. (2021). Do corporate social responsibility practices improve financial performance? A case study of airline companies. *Journal of Cleaner Production*, *310*, 127380. doi:10.1016/j.jclepro.2021.127380

Landrum, N. E., & Ohsowski, B. (2018). Identifying Worldviews on Corporate Sustainability: A Content Analysis of Corporate Sustainability Reports. *Business Strategy and the Environment*, *27*(1), 128–151. doi:10.1002/bse.1989

Lee, C.-C., Kuo, S.-Y., Hsu, H.-H., Mo, T.-L., Chang, E.-Y., & Huang, K.-C. (2022). How does the research community contribute to corporate climate-related risk disclosures? The gap between ideals and reality. In Corporate Social Responsibility and Environmental Management. Wiley. doi:10.1002/csr.2397

Liu, Y. S., Zhou, X., Yang, J. H., & Hoepner, A. G. F. (2016). Corporate Carbon Emission and Financial Performance: Does Carbon Disclosure Mediate the Relationship in the UK? *Henley Discussion Paper Series*. ICM.

Lombardi, R., Schimperna, F., Paoloni, P., & Galeotti, M. (2022). The climate-related information in the changing EU directive on non-financial reporting and disclosure: First evidence by Italian large companies. *Journal of Applied Accounting Research*, *23*(1), 250–273. doi:10.1108/JAAR-04-2021-0117

Lovell, H., de Aguiar, T. S., Bebbington, J., & Larrinaga-Gonzalez, C. (2010). Accounting for Carbon. In *Accounting for Carbon*. Monitoring, Reporting and Verifying Emissions in the Climate Economy. doi:10.1017/CBO9781316162262

Lozano, R., Nummert, B., & Ceulemans, K. (2016). Elucidating the relationship between Sustainability Reporting and Organisational Change Management for Sustainability. *Journal of Cleaner Production*, *125*, 168–188. doi:10.1016/j.jclepro.2016.03.021

Marsh. (2022). Reporting Climate Change Risk. Preparing for compulsory disclosure. *Marsh*. https://www.marsh.com/tr/en/risks/climate-change-sustainability/insights/reporting-climate-change-risk-preparing-for-compulsory-disclosure.html

Matsumura, E. M., Prakash, R., & Vera-Muñoz, S. C. (2014). Firm-value effects of carbon emissions and carbon disclosures. *The Accounting Review*, *89*(2), 695–724. doi:10.2308/accr-50629

Melloni, G., Caglio, A., & Perego, P. (2017). Saying More with Less? Disclosure Conciseness, Completeness and Balance in Integrated Reports. *Journal of Accounting and Public Policy*, *36*(3), 220–238. doi:10.1016/j.jaccpubpol.2017.03.001

O'Dwyer, B., & Unerman, J. (2016). Fostering Rigour in Accounting for Social Sustainability. *Accounting, Organizations and Society*, *49*, 32–40. doi:10.1016/j.aos.2015.11.003

Petersen, A., Herbert, S., & Daniels, N. (2022). The likely adoption of the IFRS Foundation's proposed sustainability reporting standards. *The Business and Management Review*, *13*(2). Advance online publication. doi:10.24052/BMR/V13NU02/ART-03

Pivac, S., Vuko, T., & Cular, M. (2017). Analysis of annual report disclosure quality for listed companies in transition countries. *Ekonomska Istrazivanja*, *30*(1), 721–731. doi:10.1080/1331677X.2017.1311231

Refinitiv. (2022). Environmental, Social and Governance (ESG) Scores from Refinitiv. Refinitiv. https://www.refinitiv.com/content/dam/marketing/en_us/documents/methodology/esg-scores-methodology.pdf

Rigot, S., Amar, J., & Demaria, S. (2022). Enhancing Financial Transparency to Mitigate Climate Change: Toward a Climate Risks and Opportunities Reporting Index. *Environmental Modeling and Assessment*, *27*(3), 425–439. doi:10.100710666-021-09800-7

Santos, A. L., & Rodrigues, L. L. (2021). Banks and climate-related information: The case of Portugal. *Sustainability (Basel)*, *13*(21), 12215. doi:10.3390u132112215

Sarfraz, M., Qun, W., Hui, L., & Abdullah, M. I. (2018). Environmental risk management strategies and the moderating role of corporate social responsibility in project financing decisions. *Sustainability (Basel)*, *10*(8), 2771. Advance online publication. doi:10.3390u10082771

Steenkamp, N., Rahman, A., & Kashyap, V. (2011). Recognition, measurement and disclosure of carbon emission allowances under the EU ETS - An exploratory study. *CSEAR 2011 Australasian Conference.*

TCFD [Task Force on Climate-related Financial Disclosures]. (2017). *Final Report: Recommendations of the Task Force on Climate-Related Financial Disclosures*. FSB. https://www.fsb-tcfd.org/recommendations/

TCFD [Task Force on Climate-related Financial Disclosures]. (2022). *Task Force on Climate-related Financial Disclosures 2022 Report Status*. FSB. https://www.fsb.org/2022/10/2022-tcfd-status-report-task-force-on-climate-related-financial-disclosures/

Turzo, T., Marzi, G., Favino, C., & Terzani, S. (2022). Non-financial reporting research and practice : Lessons from the last decade. *Journal of Cleaner Production*, *345*, 131–154. doi:10.1016/j.jclepro.2022.131154

UNCTAD [United Nations Conference on Trade and Development]. (2021). *Climate-related financial disclosures in mainstream entity reporting: Good practices and key challenges*. UNCTAD. https://unctad.org/system/files/official-document/ciiisard98_en.pdf

Wang, L., & Juslin, H. (2012). Values and corporate social responsibility perceptions of Chinese university students. *Journal of Academic Ethics*, *10*(1), 57–82. doi:10.100710805-012-9148-5

Wang, X., Cao, F., & Ye, K. (2018). Mandatory Corporate Social Responsibility (CSR) Reporting and Financial Reporting Quality: Evidence from a Quasi-Natural Experiment. *Journal of Business Ethics*, *152*(1), 253–274. doi:10.100710551-016-3296-2

Warwick, P., & Ng, C. (2012). The "Cost" of Climate Change: How Carbon Emissions Allowances are Accounted for Amongst European Union Companies. *Australian Accounting Review*, *22*(1), 54–67. doi:10.1111/j.1835-2561.2011.00158.x

Xu, S., & Liu, D. (2018). Do Financial Markets Care about Corporate Social Responsibility Disclosure? Further Evidence from China. *Australian Accounting Review*, *28*(1), 79–103. doi:10.1111/auar.12161

Zhou, S. (2022). Reporting and Assurance of Climate-Related and Other Sustainability Information: A Review of Research and Practice. *Australian Accounting Review*, *32*(102), 315–333. doi:10.1111/auar.12387

KEY TERMS AND DEFINITIONS

Climate Risks and Opportunities: the existing possibilities that climate changes create; climate risks based on an analysis of the negative consequences that climate change may generate; climate opportunities based on an analysis of the positive situations that may emerge from climate changes.

Climate-Related Reporting: the disclosure of information that is related to climate, whether it is non-financial or financial nature.

Compliance: the act of complying with the requirements, recommendations, or others.

Corporate Reporting: the disclosure of information from the company to its stakeholders.

Corporate Social Responsibility: the environmental, social, and ethical dimensions of the institutions

Indexes of Compliance: a measure or an indicator for compliance.

Non-Financial Reporting: disclosure of information that is not financial.

Chapter 3
Accounting Systems With Smart Contracts:
Building Accounting Records in Blockchain Step by Step

Helena I. B. Saraiva
https://orcid.org/0000-0003-1734-1250
Guarda's Polytechnic Institute, Portugal

Paulo A. A. Vieira
https://orcid.org/0000-0003-4692-5546
Guarda's Polytechnic Institute, Portugal

ABSTRACT

The theme of accounting in blockchain environment has been referenced and theoretically discussed over the last few years in international publications, both of academic and professional nature. However, until today, there are no other known works that pursued a path in order to perform accounting records in blockchain. In the present work the authors go beyond this, as they will demonstrate, also proposing a practical solution for its implementation and use in a generalized way. The authors present two new proofs of concept, which are part of an ongoing work process to obtain the development of the Portuguese accounting system using blockchain. The most recent of the sequential steps was designing and developing the tokenization process and a Dapp that will be used to perform and consult accounting operations through any mobile device, by developing smart contracts. In a near future, this system will allow accounting operations to be carried out, in a simple way, on the blockchain, assuming implications for the way in which accountants, users of financial information, and software houses work.

DOI: 10.4018/978-1-6684-7293-4.ch003

INTRODUCTION

The attention that has been devoted to the topic of accounting in a Blockchain environment is clearly evident in the international scientific literature. Among the various authors, who over the past few years, have dedicated themselves to the issue, we highlight, in academic publications, Kitsantas & Chytis (2022), Pascual-Pedreño et al. (2021), Arslanian & Fischer, (2019), Bonsón & Bednárová (2019), Islam et al. (2019), Dai & Vasarhelyi (2017), Grigg (2005); as well as in professional-oriented content Primavera (2022), FIPECAFI (2019), Thomson Reuters (2019), Deloitte (2016), PricewaterhouseCoopers (2016). In all these works, the potential of the Blockchain environment for the development of accounting solutions is obvious.

Most of the professional works that we identified in the previous paragraph, addresses, conceptually, to general issues such as reducing business costs, increasing the speed of transaction settlement, reducing the risk of fraud, improving the transaction audit function, and increasing the effectiveness of monitoring. Specifically, on the accounting issue, works refers to the possibility of improving next generation business processes to structurally change shared practices between customers, competitors, and suppliers (PricewaterhouseCoopers, 2016). The consultancy firm Deloitte (2016) assumes expectations that Blockchain will improve collaboration between companies and individuals, transparency of business processes and data, as well as productivity and sustainability of the economy.

All the previous referred works considered, generally, regards that the functions inherent in the Blockchain system, such as the protection of data integrity, the immediate sharing of necessary information, as well as programmable and automatic process controls, could facilitate the development of a new accounting ecosystem (Kitsantas & Chytis, 2022; Pascual-Pedreño et al., 2021; Arslanian & Fischer, 2019; Bonsón & Bednárová, 2019; Islam et al, 2019; Dai & Vasarhelyi, 2017; Grigg, 2005; Primavera, 2022; FIPECAFI 2019; Thomson Reuters 2019; Deloitte 2016; PricewaterhouseCoopers, 2016). In theory they state that this technology could also serve as the basis for enabling automated assurance and help the current audit paradigm become more agile and accurate.

However, all the potential benefits and challenges that Blockchain could bring to the accounting and auditing domains are still under-explored (Dai & Vasarhelyi, 2017). We would add that since there are no accounting solutions developed on blockchain yet known, it is difficult to predict the effects of accounting in a Blockchain environment, since these effects can only emerge departing from its practical use. Still, reinforcing our just mentioned interpretation, in the professional world (Primavera, 2022), is clearly mentioned and highlighted the need for a Proof of Concept (PoC) to emerge as soon as possible.

This chapter corresponds to a project that aims to fill this gap, by presenting two PoC, generating knowledge for both practitioners and Professional Associations, as well as for regulators in the accounting field, for software houses and also for the users of financial information, in a global way. Our project consists of developing the Portuguese Accounting System in a Blockchain environment. After this, accounting in Blockchain can be and, most surely, will be, developed for any accounting system anywhere in the world.

The following sections will explain in some detail the steps followed: first, is provided a background on the theme of accounting in Blockchain environment, then a theoretical and methodological framework is presented, after that a section on the set of accounting movements that we have considered to start the development of the system, followed by the description of the PoC processes regarding Smart Contract and the operationalization of a Dapp (Decentralized App). We finalize with future research directions and perspectives, followed by the conclusions.

BACKGROUND

Accounting and Blockchain

Despite the proclaimed enormous potential of the accounting framework in Blockchain, the extent of academic research on this topic is limited (Schmitz & Leoni, 2019; Cai, 2021). Schmitz & Leoni (2019) conducted a systematic literature review on Blockchain in accounting and auditing, published between 2008 and 2018, in which they identified sixteen papers.

Subsequently, we also considered, apart from the paper of Schmitz & Leoni (2019), a paper from Cai (2021), drawing on the work of Schmitz & Leoni (2019), which identifies three more papers on the theme published in 2019.

After 2019, based on a similar criterion to the one considered by Schmitz & Leoni (2019), we have found eight more published papers, by resorting to the B-on database. Our search was based on the expressions Blockchain and Accounting and Auditing, with the choice of English language, scientific journals, peer-reviewed and full text, and performed regarding the period between 2020 and 2022. Lastly, we considered only articles published in indexed journals with impact factor. Due to this last condition, we only considered five of the eight initially identified.

As to these twenty-five works, the papers considered are presented in table 1.

Table 1. Identified and considered published papers between 2008 and 2022

Year	Author(s)	Title	Journal/Book
2016	Fanning & Centers	Blockchain and Its Coming Impact on Financial Services	Journal of Corporate Accounting and Finance
2016	Peters & Panayi	Understanding Modern Banking Ledgers Through Blockchain Technologies: Future of Transaction Processing and Smart Contracts on the Internet of Money	Banking Beyond Banks and Money (Book - Springer)
2017	Atzori	Blockchain Technology and Decentralized Governance: Is the State Still Necessary?	Journal of Governance and Regulation
2017	Coyne & McMickle	Can Blockchains Serve an Accounting Purpose?	Journal of Emerging Technologies in Accounting
2017	Dai & Vasarhelyi	Toward Blockchain-Based Accounting and Assurance.	The Journal of Information Systems
2017	Kokina et al.	Blockchain: Emergent Industry Adoption and Implications for Accounting	Journal of Emerging Technologies in Accounting
2017	O'Leary	Configuring Blockchain Architectures for Transaction Information in Blockchain Consortiums: The Case of Accounting and Supply Chain Systems	Intelligent Systems in Accounting, Finance and Management
2017	Ølnes et al.	Blockchain in Government: Benefits and Implications of Distributed Ledger Technology for Information Sharing	Government Information Quarterly
2017	Piazza	Bitcoin and the Blockchain as Possible Corporate Governance Tools: Strengths and Weaknesses.	Penn State Journal of Law & International Affairs
2017	Rooney et al.	'Q&A'	Technology Innovation Management Review
2017	Ruckeshauser	Do We Really Want Blockchain-based Accounting? Decentralized Consensus as Enabler of Management Override of Internal Controls	Proceedings der 13. Internationalen Tagung Wirtschaftsinformatik (Book)
2017	Yermack	Corporate Governance and Blockchains	Review of Finance
2018	Carlin	Blockchain and the journey beyond double entry	Australian Accounting Review
2018	Kozlowski	An Audit Ecosystem to Support Blockchain-based Accounting and Assurance	Continuous Auditing: Theory and Application (Book -Emerald Publishing)
2018	O'Leary	Open Information Enterprise Transactions: Business Intelligence and Wash and Spoof Transactions in Blockchain and Social Commerce	Intelligent Systems in Accounting, Finance and Management
2018	Rozario & Vasarhelyi	Auditing with Smart Contracts	International Journal of Digital Accounting Research
2018	Wang & Kogan	Designing Confidentiality - preserving Blockchain-based Transaction Processing Systems	International Journal of Accounting Information Systems
2019	Karajovic et al.	Thinking outside the block: projected phases of blockchain integration in the accounting industry	Australian Accounting Review
2019	Schmitz & Leoni	Accounting and auditing at the time of blockchain technology: a research agenda	Australian Accounting Review
2019	Tan & Low	Blockchain as the database engine in the accounting system	Australian Accounting Review
2020	Appelbaum & Nehmer	Auditing cloud-based blockchain accounting systems	Journal of Information Systems – (Scopus)
2021	Cai	Triple-entry accounting with blockchain: How far have we come?	Accounting & Finance - (Scopus; WoS)
2021	Desplebin, et al.	To be or not to be: blockchain and the future of accounting and auditing	Accounting Perspectives – (Scopus; WoS)
2022	Secinaro et al.	Blockchain in the accounting, auditing and accountability fields: a bibliometric and coding analysis	Accounting, Auditing & Accountability Journal - (Scopus)
2023*	Han, et al.	Accounting and auditing with blockchain technology and artificial Intelligence: A literature review	International Journal of Accounting Information Systems - (Scopus)

Source: own, based on Schmitz & Leoni (2019), and Cai (2021).
Note (*): Available online in the year 2022

Among the identified twenty-five peer-reviewed publications, and when considering the first twenty analysed in the paper by Cai (2021), most of those considered works are limited to conceptualising Blockchain innovations in accounting and discussing possible practical implications for the accounting and auditing profession at a theoretical level (Cai, 2021).

On the other hand, Schmitz & Leoni (2019), in their previous work, refer that despite Blockchain Technology has been applied in some industries and entities, it is not still used in the accounting area "but is expected to strongly impact on the accounting and auditing profession in the future" (Schmitz & Leoni, 2019: 331).

At this point our aim is to emphasize that all the considered literature about accounting and auditing in Blockchain is based mainly on literature reviews and theoretical papers, since no one, until now has established how to do accounting entries in Blockchain.

Considering the works that we added to the previous analyses carried out by Schmitz & Leoni (2019), and Cai (2021), most of them are literature reviews on the potentialities of Blockchain relating to the accounting and auditing functions (Cai, 2021; Desplebin et al., 2021; Han, et al., 2023). Finally, Secinaro et al. (2022), present a bibliometric and coding analysis of blockchain articles published in the accounting, auditing and accountability fields.

However, we must highlight that Cai (2021) and Dai and Vasarhelyi (2017) mention the possibility that accounting in Blockchain environment will be developed following the traditional double entry system, yet complemented by a third layer of blockchain ledger. The aforementioned works, although also assuming a speculative approach, are the closest to the solution implemented by us.

Appelbaum & Nehmer (2020) considered the characteristics proposed by Nakamoto relating to blockchain and how auditors could analyse companies' transactions related to a blockchain with those general characteristics, addressing the audit domain related to such transactions.

Desplebin et al. (2021) noted that "the functions and potentialities of blockchain are still unknown in the accounting field. As such, the purpose of this article is to provide an overview of this technology, as well as to take a forward-looking approach to the challenges and perspectives it offers for the fields of accounting and auditing" (Desplebin et al., 2021 p. 746).

Secinaro et al. (2022) conducted an analysis on the characteristics of blockchain, providing indications of the definitions and technical structures most used in the literature. The analysis looks beyond blockchain and searches connections with other technologies. Finally, they explained what definitions of accounting theory are the most used.

Han et al. (2023) reviewed how blockchain technology can contribute to improve transparency and trust in accounting practice, how professionals can improve decision-making using blockchain's consensus-driven data, trying to determine how blockchain will impact accounting and auditing, particularly related to Artificial Intelligence.

In a global way, most of the papers listed above considers that conceptually, the Blockchain's ability to ensure transparency, accurate distribution, immutability, and the computer syntax of Blockchain technology can help companies overcome information asymmetry and reduce ethical risks through Smart Contracts.

It is also referred that additionally, the technology can also facilitate new forms of financial collaboration for a set of professionals in the management, accounting and auditing areas, and as well for investors, to achieve both cooperation and coordination in Blockchain environment.

Another topic is that Blockchain technology will exponentially increase the difficulty for managers to tamper accounting data because it uses Smart Contracts and thus accurately records data. The data recorded on a Blockchain is validated through the consensus of multiple stakeholders: one sets the smart contract, but another or others have to enable it by accepting it.

The claim that this makes data manipulation virtually impossible, and that the Blockchain ledger in triple-entry accounting automates reconciliation is also presented, and that payments invoice, expenses reporting, sample auditing, and compliance processes can be automated using Smart Contracts, turning easier for organizations to control and monitor accounting information.

However, all the works considered continued to present conceptual Blockchain innovations related to accounting and possible practical implications at a theoretical level. Considering this, none of the papers present proposals for putting accounting on Blockchain into operation. Because of the absence of these possibilities, the audit function in the same environment, cannot also be implemented.

Smart Contracts

According to Zheng et al. (2020), conventional contracts need to be complemented in their formalization by a trusted third party, which results in a longer execution time, as well as additional costs. In contrast to the traditional situation, in a Blockchain environment, what is referred to as *Smart Contracts* occurs. A smart contract consists of transactions that are essentially stored, replicated and updated. If a smart contract is used in a context of agreement between economic agents, the contractual clauses described in computer programs will be automatically executed when certain prerequisite conditions are met.

Following Zheng et al. (2020), the integration of Blockchain technology with Smart Contracts will make the dream of a "peer-to-peer market" a reality (Zheng et al, 2020 p. 1).

Also based on the information provided by the Ethereum platform, Smart Contracts digitize agreements, transforming the terms of an agreement into computer code that automatically executes when the terms provided in the contract are fulfilled (Ethereum, n.d.).

Considering Schmitz & Leoni (2019) accounting and auditing have so far been characterized by the involvement of human beings at all stages. However, this need for the involvement of human intervention and analysis may change with the development of the blockchain. Blockchain can not only carry real-time transaction data but can also carry a programmed version of human action. This programmed version takes the form of what is meant by *Smart Contracts*. These Smart Contracts encode relevant aspects on a Blockchain and are executed automatically when previously defined conditions are met. They consist of computer code and are executed by a computer network that uses consensus protocols to agree on the sequence of actions specified in a contract that may or may not be a formal one, but always corresponds to an agreement between parties. The smart contract only occurs if two or more parties accept the conditions proposed and posted or made available on the network by one of those parties.

Thus, based on this notion, the present work translates the realization of a set of two Proofs of Concept (Goldsack et al., 2021), and that will be described below by the acronym PoC, which initiates a tokenization process of the Accounting Normalization System (SNC), in force in Portugal, as well as the provision of a Dapp to operationalize the accounting operations accordingly with the SNC System.

Blockchains consist of nodes, which are computers or computer clusters. In its initial architecture each node is connected to all the others. This network architecture is called Peer to Peer (P2P). The network architecture of Blockchains has evolved to an architecture that is not fully P2P, but one of a distributed or decentralized network.

In the context of a distributed network, nodes are gateways that can receive, store, and send information along different routes through that network. Generally, all nodes are of equal importance in the network, which means that the eventual loss of a node does not significantly harm the network. Blockchain nodes have a ledger, which consists of the set of all accepted transactions. This ledger exists in each one of them, which makes it a distributed ledger. A node is connected to a network of nodes and can receive, send, and create information related to digital assets.

In Blockchains, asset transactions are recorded in this ledger. In each node there is a ledger, containing all validated transactions and some transactions in confirmation. The content of the ledger relative to the validated transactions is identical in all nodes. Registering a new transaction is performed by a node that then disseminates it for confirmation to the other nodes to include it in their ledger. This confirmation is subject to the demonstration of conformity of the registration with a consensus protocol.

The recorded transactions on the Blockchain correspond to asset transactions. These transactions are organized by the nodes into blocks. Each block can contain multiple transactions.

So, another interesting and important (in the context of this chapter), concept is the idea of tokenization. Hence, this chapter aims to demonstrate that it is possible to tokenize the Portuguese Accounting Standards System using Smart Contracts.

The tokenization of the Portuguese System demonstrates, in turn, that it will be possible to do the same for the accounting systems of other European or even non-European countries, since the basis of the systems is common to all EU countries, as well as to most countries, at a global level. Since the IASB standards are in use in most of the countries in the world - currently in 167 jurisdictions (IFRS Foundation, n.d.) -, we can conclude that, as the basis is the same, it is possible to replicate in any of the countries using the standards the experience here presented.

Moreover, tokenization can be applied to any public or private accounting system since both types of accounting are ruled by the double-entry principle. This principle is based on the idea that each entry assumes a counterpart, using two accounts simultaneously - thus assuming the perspective of the entity and the perspective of a third party, or counterparty, with whom a business relationship is established, or resulting from a business deal.

The transactions registered in the Blockchain correspond to asset transactions. These transactions are organized by the nodes into blocks. Each block can contain multiple transactions. These assets can be digital money or the digitalization of some aspect of real life such as: an idea, a song, a painting, a contract between parties, or many other things.

This digitalization of aspects of our life is called tokenization. Tokenization is carried out through a Blockchain formalism called Smart Contracts. Smart Contracts are executable code at a Blockchain address.

Thus, Smart Contracts are Blockchain addresses that correspond for example to records relating to a song, a document, a contract between parties, etc...

Assuming that a Smart Contract is built, with it we may perform three types of operations:

- **Creation (registration) of the Smart Contract, on the Blockchain (deploying the contract to the Blockchain)**
- **Calling an existing Smart Contract, and**
- **Querying a Smart Contract that already exists.**

In the first two operations there is a change of information in the Blockchain, in the third there is no change of information in the Blockchain. However, the third one allows the verification of the existence of the contracts, as well as their content - which is extremely important, when we are dealing with accounting records, because this allows us to consult, verify and audit them.

In order to include transactions in the blocks, a fee is required to be charged by the nodes, being registered in the Ledger; in Ethereum, this value is presented in *Gas* (a form of designation that can also be understood as fuel). The amount of *Gas* is determined by the node, but its value in *Ethers* is indicated by the proponents (bidders) of the transaction. They (the bidders) specify how much are they willing to pay for the transaction to be included in a block. The transactions are included in the block in a binary hash tree system, which means that they must be in potencies of two (2). That is, in a block there can be transactions in numbers of 1, 2, 4, 8, 16, 32, 128, etc... The possibilities now mentioned, in terms of number of transactions, are based on the following potencies of 2: 2^0, 2^1, 2^2 ^3, 2^4, 2^5, etc. This causes that those nodes, in order to close blocks, often resort to gas offers, for *Ether*, with a value of zero. These kinds of offers are the ones that are made to record accounting entries in an accounting ID number. In Ethereum a value bid in *Ether* is required, even if the value of the *Gas* (or fuel), is zero. *Gas* is represented by *GWei*.

In Ethereum, the tokenization of certain aspects is standardized in ERC (Ethereum Request Comment) specifications that indicate how and what Smart Contracts should include. Therefore, in this chapter the SNC specification will be designed in ERC and its implementation will be completed through the development of our project.

Decentralized Apps

Bitcoin is a distributed system because its public ledger, the Blockchain, resides on several computers. On the other hand, it is also a decentralized system because if one node fails, the network still has the ability to function. So, any application that uses a Blockchain along with other peer-to-peer tools can be distributed and decentralized.

The expression Dapp stands for Decentralized App. According to Raval (2016), the Dapp concept is still in an emerging phase, as there are many experimental initiatives ongoing. Quoting the same author "different developers have different opinions on what exactly a Dapp is" (Raval, 2016 p. 4).

However, it ends up defining some aspects that a decentralized app geared towards a business model whose objective is profit should ensure: being open-source, having internal currency, assuming decentralized consensus, and having no central point of failure (Raval, 2016).

Previously, Swan (2015) mentions the idea that regarding Blockchain-related technologies, they could already be subdivided into three typologies corresponding to phases: Blockchain 1.0 is currency, Blockchain 2.0 adds Smart Contracts (stocks, bonds, financial assets), and Blockchain 3.0 covers applications beyond pure finance in areas such as governance and health (Dapps). Also, Iqbal et al., reinforces the idea that the marketplace for Dapps is expected to increase substantially in the near future.

THEORETICAL FRAMEWORK

In the present chapter we try to translate to the accounting area the possibility of developing a tokenization process to complete accounting records directly in the Blockchain. In this sense we have adopted a theoretical framework and a methodological positioning.

Both of them are related to the nature of our work: in a very practical way, since our innovative work consists of the possibility of a practical solution, we have adopted a methodology that directly reflects this characteristic of the research presented in this chapter; on the other hand, our theoretical perspective is framed in the Actor Network Theory (ANT) (Callon, 1986a, 1986b; Latour 1987, 2012), since by presenting the possibility of this practical solution, we intend to obtain the adhesion of the professionals of the area, in order to test this experimental solution and transform it into a generalized and institutionalized practice.

In theoretical terms we followed the phases presented by Callon (1986a, 1986b), having as a starting point the *problematization* stage (how can accounting be carried out in a Blockchain environment), followed by the *translation* (technical solution presented by us); in order to, after that, obtaining the *inscription* of the potential users (to achieve adhesion by the professional sector, to refine the presented concept), and several other stakeholders in the process of change in accounting; finally we aim to achieve *science made*, or *completed* – a *black box* in the words of Latour (Latour, 1987).

ANT is, alongside other theories, one of the most used theoretical bases to analyze, explain and support settings of change in accounting (Robson, 1991, 1992). In the present case it is necessary to promote change, since the Blockchain, despite being often pointed out as a potential system of excellence to support accounting, there has not been presented, until this date and before this work, a proposal for the actual implementation of this possibility.

Concerning the *problematization* process, Hopwood (1987), referring to another accounting change scenario, stated that accounting should stop being *what it was not* on the way to becoming *what it should be*. This is the spirit of our work in what concerns to accounting in Blockchain, since most papers in this area only refer to the issue in a theoretical perspective. Despite all the knowledge and reflection generated by these previous works, accounting in Blockchain environment is not yet a reality (meaning that *what it was not* makes some sense also on the present scenario), but it can become one in the short term (so, our intention is providing a way in which accounting is becoming *what it should be*, concerning to the Blockchain environment).

However, on the other hand, concerning the methodological area, the chapter is inserted in an Action-Research perspective, as presented by Avison et al. (1999, 2018).

In this type of research, what is done is more relevant than the verbalization or communication of what was done. However, the situation regarding the results of these investigations can be found in numerous articles discussing the lessons learned from specific projects, sometimes described as case studies, system design, software engineering projects and more (Avison et al., 1999).

In the two PoC (Goldsack et al., 2021), carried out throughout the project, the operations of creating a Smart Contract were implemented as operations of accomplishing accounting identification addresses of an entity, in a first phase and the creation of a Dapp, in a more recent phase.

In our view, the implementation of these PoC constitutes a way of reducing the risks associated with a future investment in the development of the use of Blockchain in the performance of accounting records.

Several authors, including Kitsantas & Chytis (2022), Pascual-Pedreño et al. (2021), Islam et al. (2019), refer the possibility that through the use of Blockchain a system can be designed in which contractual positions between entities are available in a shared and accessible chain, in an environment in which agreements, processes, tasks and payments are recorded and accessible to all actors, through a digital identification, making their validation, storage and sharing possible.

In this sense, the use of Blockchain presents similarities with the functions that accounting, in any entity, should assume and ensure: making a record that is verifiable, that can be shared with all stakeholders, and that record being secure and traceable.

Thus, it seems possible and advantageous to us that any operation, whether carried out through a Blockchain or not, can be registered, in accounting terms, in the Blockchain itself. This will contribute to benefit the transparency of operations, allowing access in real time; clear use; identification of the user; as well as ensure trust in this kind of transactions.

On the other hand, it should also be considered that many practical uses have been inferred from the use of the Blockchain environment (Bonsón & Bednárová, 2019).

An example of this reality is the European Blockchain Services Infrastructure (EBSI) Initiative, implemented by the European Commission and the European Blockchain Partnership. The aim of this Initiative is to leverage Blockchain to accelerate the creation of cross-border services for public administrations and their ecosystems to verify information and make services more trustworthy. Since 2020, EBSI has been implementing a European network, supporting applications focused on selected use cases (European Commission, n.d.).

All this leads us to believe that the importance of the emergence of practical applications in the various fields of knowledge, specifically in Europe, will undergo a huge expansion in the coming years and that Accounting will have to move quickly to keep up with these developments.

To this end, we began by developing the process of registering accounting operations and entries in Blockchain. This implied a PoC with four accounting records, performed simultaneously with the respective operations: the first corresponds to the commitment to purchase or sell using a Smart Contract, followed by the movements and records related to payments and receipts that occurred not simultaneously, but sometime later.

The accounting records were made in the traditional double entry accounting system, which proves that accounting in a Blockchain environment is not just cash accounting but can be a true accounting support system because its technology allows it, due to its main features which are security, anonymity, and data integrity. This was followed by a new PoC, presented here, through the creation of a Dapp, which supports the operationalization of accounting registration activities, in a streamlined manner, by professionals.

ACCOUNTING RECORDS

In this section we present two examples of some of the most common accounting movements and the registration in the respective accounts.

Our goal is to demonstrate, based on these movements, that Blockchain is not a mere payment system, but rather a technical solution that, besides allowing the tokenisation of many aspects of real life, has potential application in many fields, including accounting. Also, the question often raised (although wrongly), that it will only serve for purposes related to Cash Flows, is here clearly overthrown.

For this we have used some of the simplest accounting record situations: a purchase and a sale of goods, with payment and receipt in a postponed manner, precisely to illustrate that the movements related to Cash Flows are treated in a similar way to those which have no impact in this area.

First Example

The first example, presented in Table 2, consists in the recording of a purchase of goods, presented in the General Ledger, subject to VAT at 23%, with payment made after the purchase, in Table 3, in the normal payment term (without interest). Stock movements or Inventory have not been considered.

At the time of purchase:

Table 2. Entry at the Moment of the purchase

Date	Description	Debit	Credit	Value
Date of purchase	Purchase of goods on credit	31		1000€
		2432		230€
			22	1230€

Source: own.

Moment of payment of the value of the purchase invoice:

Table 3. Entry at the Time of payment of the purchase value

Date	Description	Debit	Credit	Value
Date of payment	Payment of the purchase invoice amount	22	12	1230€

Source: own.

Second Example

In the second example we present the register of Sale of Goods (Table 4), in the General Ledger, with VAT at 23%, with payment received some time later after the sale (Table 5), in the normal payment term (without interest). Also, in this case, the Inventory movements have not been considered.

At the time of the sale:

Table 4. Entry at the Time of Sale

Date	Description	Debit	Credit	Value
Date of Sale	Sale of goods on credit	21		1845€
			2433	345€
			71	1500€

Source: own.

Sometime after, in the moment of the receipt of the sales invoice value:

Table 5. Entry at the Moment of Sales Receipt

Date	Description	Debit	Credit	Value
Date of receipt	Receipt of the sales invoice value	12	21	1845€

Source: own.

These were the basic operations that we used for the conceptualization of the Smart Contract that will be presented in the next section.

SMART CONTRACTS

In this section we present the process of formalizing a Smart Contract on the examples referred to in the previous section. This contract should be seen as a PoC on the possibility of tokenization of the Accounting Standards System used in Portugal (SNC) and constitutes the beginning of a project under development.

Here, rather than explaining what a smart contract is - which we effectively tried to do in section 2 -, we will present the technical solution that we have developed in order to formalize the issue of the operationalization of accounting records in Blockchain. At this point, we will present what we consider to be the greatest contribution of our work, which is a contribution of a practical nature, unlike the approach adopted by most of the works analyzed in the section 2.

Following the examples presented in the aforementioned section 2, related to the possibilities that each Smart Contract allows, we defined that the creation (or deployment) of a Smart Contract in the Blockchain that corresponds, in this case, to the setting of an account (for instance 31-Purchases), or a group of accounts (for instance the entire SNC system); then, we can do calls on an existing Smart Contract (changes in the smart contract – that means to perform accounting records or doing an adaptation of the SNC in order to adjust it to a certain organization); and finally we can query a Smart Contract (that means consulting an account or a group of accounts or even consulting all the accounts pertaining to a certain entity).

The all system was implemented in *Ethereum*, that is a blockchain platform that enables the development of decentralized applications, Smart Contracts, cryptocurrency transactions and other tokens. *Ethereum* is the most important Smart Contract platform, and it was on this platform that Smart Contracts were created and emerged for the first time.

The computing code for creating SNC Accounts in a Blockchain environment was done as follows: an <account> in SNC has the syntax of <account_number>_<account_name> but in Smart Contract it is identified as <account_name>_<account_number>. For example, account 31-Purchases in SNC, is integrated in Smart Contract as Purchases_31.

For each account two variables are defined in Smart Contract: the possibility to register a debit (D<account>), as well as the possibility to do an accounting record on credit (C<account>).

To continue the example with the account 31-Purchases: it is associated DC-Purchases_31 and CC-Purchases_31, relating respectively to the debit (D<account>), and credit (C<account>), in the corresponding bookkeeping account.

In order to establish calls to a smart contract, for accounting changes (e.g. making a registry), functions have been implemented, one for each account. The functions have the following sample syntax statement, set<account>(D<account, C<account>).

The contract is written and verified in the remix (Figure 1), which is the *Ethereum* development environment where Smart Contracts are programmed. The PoC was performed on one of *Ethereum's* test networks: the *Ethereum Ropsten Test Network*.

In the test we used the *MetaMask Wallet* in conjunction with the *remix*. All these transactions, done through a wallet, can be viewed in the Ethereum explorer of the network used. In the case of this work, the query and visualization were done in the explorer *Ethereum Ropsten Test Network* explorer and in the *Metamask Wallet*. A wallet is a virtual cryptocurrency purse that allows users to check their balance, operate between different blockchain networks and sign their own transactions, thus avoiding the involvement of intermediaries, as is the case with banks in the traditional economy.

Figure 1. Remix IDE, http://remix.ethereum.org
Source: own.

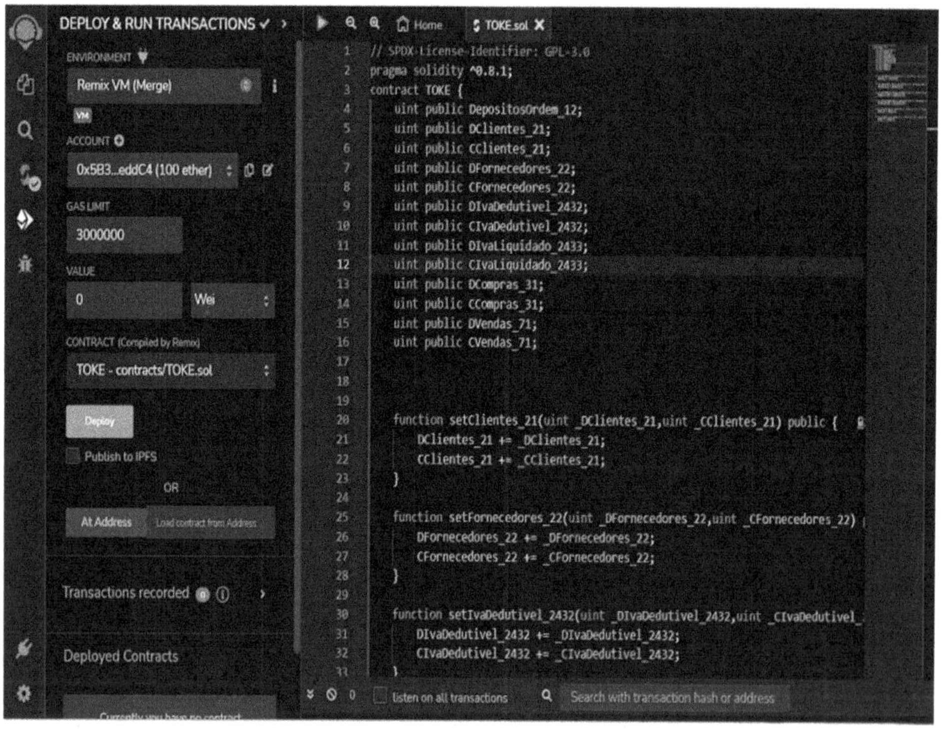

The creator of the contract is a Blockchain account. In the example it was: **0xc2612AB954A4Abda6D37dD4cC9b3F85FDfF52eD8**.

Here we must point out that we are referring to two types of accounts: one is the bookkeeping accounting accounts which we created through Smart Contracts and the other is the existence of accounts on the Blockchain platform - in other words, addresses on the blockchain.

The contract was inserted into the transaction set block: in the example it was block **12198142**.

To each contract is assigned an address on the Blockchain. The address of the contract, in the test was the address: **0xe95d160609c6b81aaec8e6d4fa4666a1e8769cb2**.

Transactions on the Blockchain are entered on-chain by the hash of the information they contain; the hash of the performed transaction was as follows:

```
0x7fa9e0006d96d86c999743f64d76e2dcdd6aa5795d3b3f16990e363243d8ad6d.
```

For this transaction - the creation of the contract - fees had to be paid in *Ether* (a cryptocurrency which is also represented by ETH.); specifically, 0.000999765650031992 48 *Ether*. In the moment that this transaction took place, the *Ether* was traded at 3$ USA, or 2,85 EUROS. This value was charged by the node that registers the block transaction.

The introduction of the contract into the Blockchain, or contract deployment, can be seen in Figure 2 - *MetaMask*. The calls to the contract allow recording the account movements and can be viewed in *MetaMask* (also Figure 2) as contract interactions.

Figure 2. MetaMask wallet
Source: own.

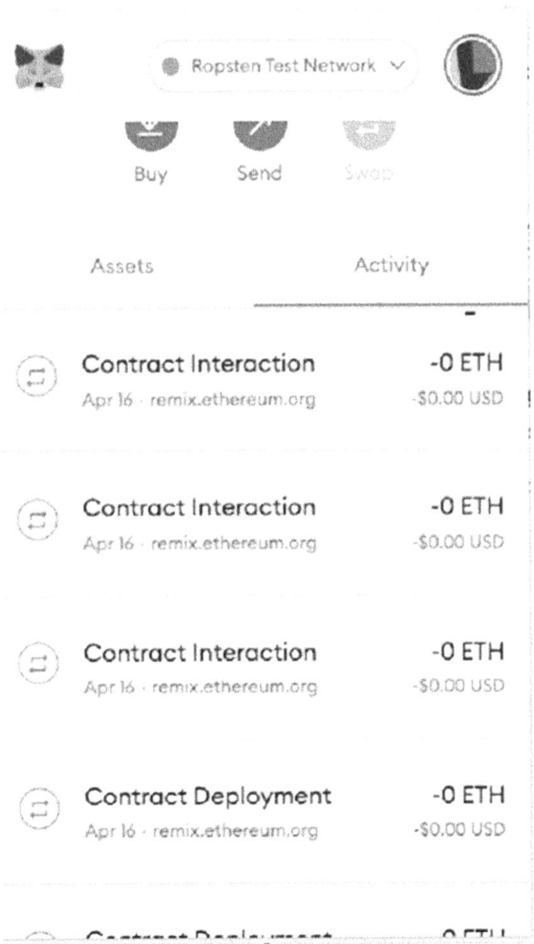

These movements were recorded in the Blockchain as transactions. In the model we developed the contract deployment is a transaction with a cost. In this case it was 0.00011672 ETH, or $0.35 USD.

However, calls to the contract that allow basic accounting operations in the bookkeeping accounts, to be performed, in the case of an existing contract, will have a cost of zero ETH. In the model we build it is done with a *gas* price of 0.0 *GWei*, which makes its cost zero.

Gas is the value charged each time a transaction or smart contract is executed on *Ethereum*, and *GWei* is the measurement unit in which *Gas* is accounted for. *Ethereum* can be divided into small units. These units are called Wei. ETH is much more divisible than other digital currencies (for example when compared to Bitcoin). By convention, each ETH is equivalent to 1,000,000,000,000,000,000 *Wei*.

The compensation of the nodes, through the gas price different from zero (i.e. with value), will be made only by the registration of the contract and eventually by function calls associated with certain special accounting movements to be defined in the ERC specification. These special movements may be, for example, capital increases, issue of shares, etc.

The interactions with the users, namely with the account and wallet user (*Wallet*) are shown in Figure 3, which will soon be available through a *Dapp* for limited testing.

Once again, in the solution we have found and presented, there are three types of contract operations: contract creation, contract calls (setters) and queries (getters), of variable value.

Ethereum nodes charge fees for the first two types, but the last one, in our model, is free. Getters are not registered operations on the Blockchain (in Figure 3, the blue commands), but creation and calls are (in Figure 3, the orange commands).

In synthesis, the orange commands are used to create entities and accounts for each entity; the blue buttons serve to move accounts, i.e., make accounting entries and records.

Figure 3. Blockchain Dapp - user's interface
Source: own.

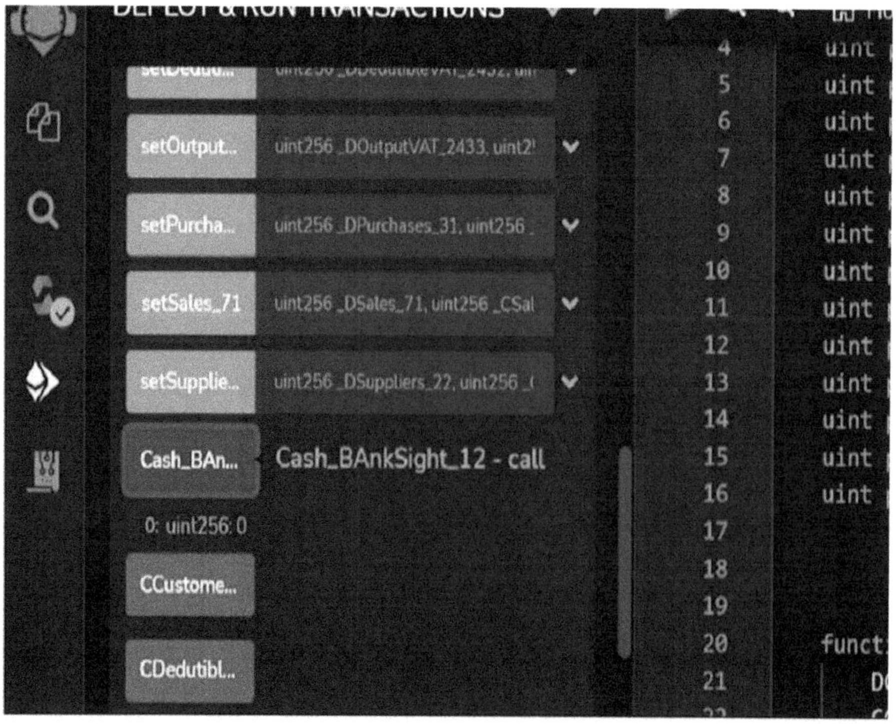

The *Dapp*, which can be installed on any mobile device, is a sequence of two screens (figures 4 and 5), where the second screen (figure 5) has several functionalities triggered through commands; to activate some of the functionalities already implemented in the PoC.

This *Dapp* corresponds to a second PoC, after the first one, which was the formalization of the Smart Contracts for the tokenization of the accounting records.

Figure 4. Blockchain Dapp – first screen
Source: own.

We have named the *Dapp* as "*Accounting on the Blockchain*", to highlight, precisely, the scope of its application.

Figure 5. Blockchain Dapp – second screen
Source: own.

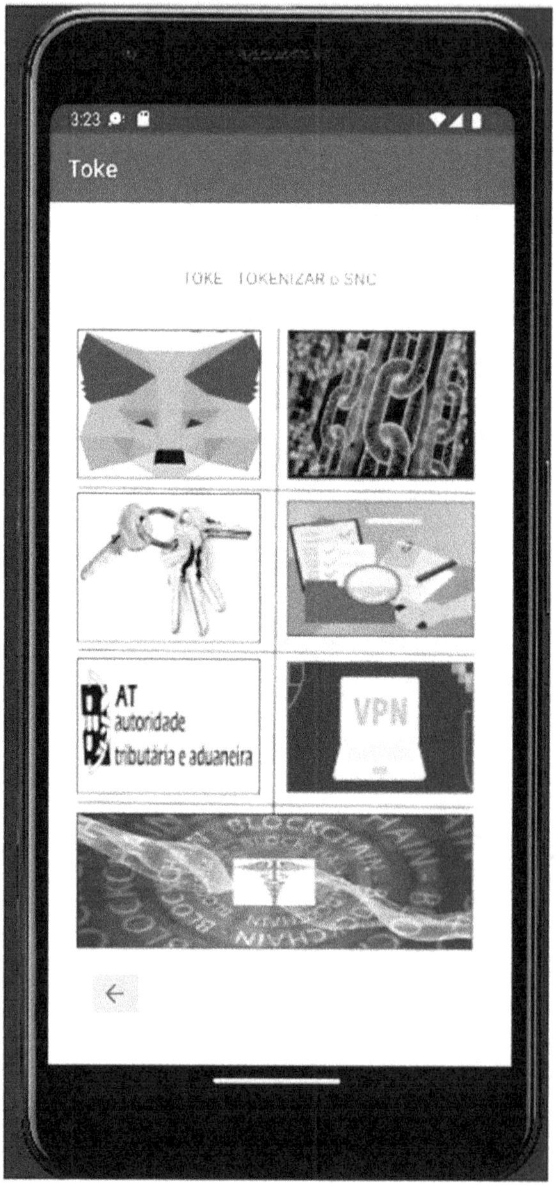

Each of the commands figuring on the second screen assumes a function, related with which of the themes identified in the figure 6.

Figure 6. Themes and Functions of the Dapp commands
Source: own.

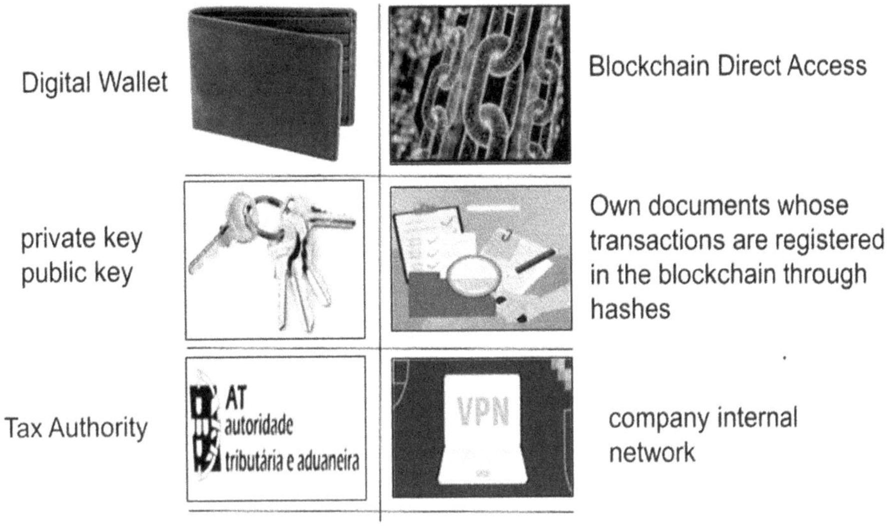

As can be noticed on figure 6, the functions of each theme are related to the currency (digital wallet), to the access to the Blockchain, to the ID of the user on the Blockchain, to the possibility of storage and consult digital documents owned by the user, and to access the tax authority and the company internal network.

Concerning the digital wallet, we have implemented on our model *MetaMask,* but, surely, another wallet could have been used. The examples on the other themes are related to the Portuguese case-study.

Thus, a very important and necessary step towards the operationalization of accounting in a Blockchain environment has now been taken, allowing an accounting technician, a Chartered Accountant, and finally an Accounting Auditor, without the need for extremely in-depth knowledge of Information Technology or Artificial Intelligence, to create accounts for entities and accounting records directly on the Blockchain, as well as to consult accounts and documents on it.

FUTURE RESEARCH DIRECTIONS

Once the initial work, whose stages have been explained here, has been fully completed, it will be necessary to implement the following steps. These next steps to be conducted will be Cases of Use, as pointed out by the European Commission (n.d.), within the scope of the applications using the Blockchain environment.

These Cases of Use, that will be performed by specific groups, will allow refining the solution and making it suitable for generalized use. These are the main tasks that will follow in a near future. So, we expect to change the way in which technology supports accounting, by resorting to the Blockchain. To do this, we should appeal to a set of entities that assume themselves as potential users of this technology and that will help us to perfect the proposed solution. This network of actors will have to be formed by accountants, auditors, professional associations, software companies, regulators, and users of financial information. On the other hand, this network is also composed by the blockchain and the technical solutions that we propose to implement the accounting systems in this environment – that is, human and non-human actors (Callon, 1986a;1986b; Latour, 1987). By considering all actors and seeking different points of view, groups and their interests will be adjusted and shaped into action, thus achieving a mobilization that leads to a compromise. Will we thus have a *black box* (Latour, 1987), i.e., a solved problem and science completed? We surely hope so!

Other possibilities are the replication of this process to other accounting standards national systems, which will necessarily confront us with other several and varied research questions and different types of practical problems (Nobes, 2020; Nobes & Parker, 2020). However, this is a very real possibility, since the set of Accounting Standards used in Portugal is based on the Accounting Standards of the European Union (EU), which, in turn, have been derived from the Standards issued by the International Accounting Standards Board (IASB), also known as international accounting standards (Saraiva et al., 2015).

CONCLUSION

This chapter is a translation (Callon, 1986a; 1986b; Latour, 1987; 2012), adjusted to the accounting theme of the beginning of a new project, for the Tokenization of the Portuguese Accounting System, which consists of a set of PoC, and shows that the project is feasible.

Throughout the use of Blockchain it is possible to design a system where contractual positions between entities are available in a shared and accessible chain, in an environment where agreements, processes, tasks and payments are recorded and accessible to all actors through a digital record and identification, making it possible to validate, store and share them (Islam et al., 2019).

In this sense, the use of Blockchain presents similarities with the functions that accounting, in any entity, should assume and ensure. This will contribute to benefit the transparency of operations, allowing access in real time; transparent use; identification of the user; as well as ensuring trust in this type of transactions, since one of the functions of accounting is to ensure trust, maintaining the public interest that accounting records allow.

To this end, we started by developing the process of registering in Blockchain four very simple operations in a previous work. This implied four accounting records, made simultaneously with the respective operations: the first ones are the purchase or sale commitment (using a smart contract), followed by the movements and records related to payments and receipts. The accounting records were made in the traditional double-entry accounting system, which proves that accounting in a Blockchain environment is not just Cash Flow accounting (Veira & Saraiva, 2023).

Next, we developed a solution intended to facilitate the use of all this process by developing a *Dapp*, that allows that any professional in the area, can conduct accounting entries and registries based on the use of the Blockchain, allowing a secure process.

The issue of trust is, in the accounting area, essential, since accounting is the basis and underpinning of the entire financial system. Here, Blockchain technology can ensure this issue due to its technical characteristics (Pascual-Pedreño et al, 2021), which allows the verifiability and accessibility of data by all those involved, as well as the possibility of identifying any changes to records.

In this sense, both the accounting and audit review functions may experience changes in relation to the practices currently developed. However, only from the operationalisation of accounting will we be able to see whether the theoretical body of knowledge currently existing can be confirmed or, on the contrary, disproved. We hope to be able to make these verifications soon and to draw conclusions from the use of this model by professionals. In this sense we consider to have made a real contribution to the literature, since the review completed in the second section of this chapter shows that all contributions to the literature until now, in the fields of accounting and auditing are merely theoretical and of a speculative nature.

In our perspective, after this PoC, the application of the Blockchain to accounting reveals that, on the one hand, the Blockchain environment is compatible with the traditional double entry system; but on the other hand, it may include the possibility mentioned by Grigg (2005), of becoming a triple entry system, however with some differences to the idea of triple entry mentioned by this author. In this sense we confirm the ideas presented by Cai (2021) and previously Dai and Vasarhelyi (2017), according to which the double entry could be maintained in Blockchain environment, complemented with a third layer of ledger provided by the Blockchain system.

In fact, by further analyzing the theme, in this case, we can consider the double entry inherent to accounting records, is always conducted taking into account two different perspectives (for example the perspective of the entity that is selling, and the perspective of those who are buying). Adding to these different perspectives the possibility of verification given by the analysis of the contracts and also the verification that becomes possible by the analysis of the wallet movements, in the Blockchain, leads us to consider that it may be stated that the system is a multiple-entry system because it is verified and assessed by all the entities in a block.

The present work constitutes a milestone, from which we move from theorization to the real possibility of practical application. Related to this fact, we consider that a full set of actors will be impacted by our work, such as accountants, auditors, professional associations, software companies, regulators, and users of financial information.

The limitations of this work are necessarily related to the fact that the project is still at an early stage having only taken the initial steps, and that there is still much work to be done to achieve the desired global tokenization process.

REFERENCES

Appelbaum, D., & Nehmer, R. A. (2020). Auditing cloud-based blockchain accounting systems. *Journal of Information Systems*, *34*(2), 5–21. doi:10.2308/isys-52660

Arslanian, H., & Fischer, F. (2019). Blockchain as an enabling technology. In *The Future of Finance* (pp. 113–121). Palgrave Macmillan., doi:10.1007/978-3-030-14533-0_10

Atzori, M. (2017). Blockchain Technology and Decentralized Governance: Is the State Still Necessary? *Journal of Governance and Regulation*, *6*(1), 45–62. doi:10.22495/jgr_v6_i1_p5

Avison, D. E., Davison, R. M., & Malaurent, J. (2018). Information systems action research: Debunking myths and overcoming barriers. *Information & Management*, *55*(2), 177-187. doi:10.1016/j.im.2017.05.004

Avison, D. E., Lau, F., Myers, M., & Nielsen, P. A. (1999). Action research. *Communications of the ACM*, *42*(1), 94–97. doi:10.1145/291469.291479

Bonsón, E., & Bednárová, M. (2019). Blockchain and its implications for accounting and auditing. *Meditari Accountancy Research*, *27*(5), 725–740. doi:10.1108/MEDAR-11-2018-0406

Cai, C. W. (2021). Triple-entry accounting with blockchain: How far have we come? *Accounting and Finance*, *61*(1), 71–93. doi:10.1111/acfi.12556

Callon, M. (1986a). ÉLÉMENTS POUR UNE SOCIOLOGIE DE LA TRADUCTION: La domestication des coquilles Saint-Jacques et des marins-pêcheurs dans la baie de Saint-Brieuc. *L'Année sociologique*, *16*, 169–208.

Callon, M. (1986b). Some elements of a sociology of translation: domestication of the scallops and the fishermen of St Brieuc Bay. In J. Law (Ed.), *Power, action and belief: a new sociology of knowledge?* (pp. 196–223). Routledge.

Carlin, T. (2018). Blockchain and the journey beyond double entry. *Australian Accounting Review*, *29*(2), 305–311. doi:10.1111/auar.12273

Coyne, J., & McMickle, P. (2017). Can Blockchains Serve an Accounting Purpose? *Journal of Emerging Technologies in Accounting*, *14*(2), 101–111. doi:10.2308/jeta-51910

Dai, J., & Vasarhelyi, M. A. (2017). Toward Blockchain-Based Accounting and Assurance. *Journal of Information Systems*, *31*(3), 5–21. doi:10.2308/isys-51804

Deloitte. (2016). *Blockchain: Enigma, Paradox, Opportunity*. DeLoitte. https://www2.deloitte.com/content/dam/Deloitte/nl/Documents/financial-services/deloitte-nl-fsi-blockchain-enigma-paradox-opportunity-report.pdf

Desplebin, O., Lux, G., & Petit, N. (2021). To be or not to be: Blockchain and the future of accounting and auditing. *Accounting Perspectives*, *20*(4), 743–769. doi:10.1111/1911-3838.12265

Ethereum. (n.d.). *Introduction to Smart Contracts*. Ethereum. https://ethereum.org/pt-br/smart-contracts/#introduction-to-smart-contracts. (Retrieved in May 2022).

European Commission. (n.d.). The European Blockchain Services Infrastructure [EBSI] - European Blockchain. https://ec.europa.eu/digital-building-blocks/wikis/display/EBSI/About+us (retrieved in September 2022)

Fanning, K., & Centers, D. (2016). Blockchain and Its Coming Impact on Financial Services. *Journal of Corporate Accounting & Finance*, *27*(5), 53–57. doi:10.1002/jcaf.22179

FIPECAFI. (2019). Blockchain e o futuro da contabilidade como fonte informacional. Fipecafi. https://blog.fipecafi.org/blockchain-e-o-futuro-da-contabilidade-como-fonte-informacional/

Goldsack, J. C., Dowling, A. V., Samuelson, D., Patrick-Lake, B., & Clay, I. (2021). Evaluation, Acceptance, and Qualification of Digital Measures: From Proof of Concept to Endpoint. *Digital Biomarkers*, *5*(1), 53–64. doi:10.1159/000514730 PMID:33977218

Grigg, I. (2005). Triple entry accounting. *Systemics Inc*. Iang. https://iang.org/papers/triple_entry.html

Han, H., Shiwakoti, R. K., Jarvis, R., Mordi, C., & Botchie, D. (2023). Accounting and auditing with blockchain technology and artificial Intelligence: A literature review. *International Journal of Accounting Information Systems*, *48*, 100598. doi:10.1016/j.accinf.2022.100598

Hopwood, A. G. (1987). The archeology of accounting systems. *Accounting, Organizations and Society*, *12*(3), 207–234. doi:10.1016/0361-3682(87)90038-9

IFRS Foundation. (n.d.). *Who uses IFRS Accounting Standards?* IFRS. https://www.ifrs.org/use-around-the-world/use-of-ifrs-standards-by-jurisdiction/

Iqbal, M. O., Obaid, A. J., Agarwal, P., Mufti, T., & Hassan, A. R. (2023). Blockchain Technology and Decentralized Applications Using Blockchain. In M. Tuba, S. Akashe, & A. Joshi (Eds.), *ICT Infrastructure and Computing. Lecture Notes in Networks and Systems* (Vol. 520, pp. 555–563). Springer. doi:10.1007/978-981-19-5331-6_57

Islam, A. K. M. N., Mantymaki, M., & Turunen, M. (2019). Why do blockchains split? An actor-network perspective on bitcoin splits. *Technological Forecasting and Social Change*, *148*, 119743. doi:10.1016/j.techfore.2019.119743

Karajovic, M., Kim, H., & Laskowski, M. (2019). Thinking outside the block: Projected phases of blockchain integration in the accounting industry. *Australian Accounting Review*, *29*(2), 319–330. doi:10.1111/auar.12280

Kitsantas, T., & Chytis, E. (2022). Blockchain Technology as an Ecosystem: Trends and Perspectives in Accounting and Management. *Journal of Theoretical and Applied Electronic Commerce Research*, *17*(3), 1143–1161. doi:10.3390/jtaer17030058

Kokina, J., Mancha, R., & Pachamanova, D. (2017). Blockchain: Emergent Industry Adoption and Implications for Accounting. *Journal of Emerging Technologies in Accounting*, *14*(2), 91–100. doi:10.2308/jeta-51911

Kozlowski, S. (2018). An Audit Ecosystem to Support Blockchain-based Accounting and Assurance. In D.Y. Chan, V.C. & M.A. Vasarhelyi (Eds.), Continuous Auditing: Theory and Application (299–313). Emerald Publishing. https://doi.org/ doi:10.1108/978-1-78743-413-420181015

Latour, B. (1987). *Science in action: How to follow scientists and engineers through society*. Harvard University Press.

Latour, B. (2012). Visualisation and cognition: Drawing things together. In H. Kuklick (Ed.), *Knowledge and Society Studies in the Sociology of Culture Past and Present* (Vol. 6, pp. 1–40). Jai Press.

Nobes, C. (2020). A half-century of Accounting and Business Research: The impact on the study of international financial reporting. *Accounting and Business Research*, *50*(7), 693–701. https://doi.org/https://doi.org/10.1080/00014788.2020.1742446. doi:10.1080/00014788.2020.1742446

Nobes, C., & Parker, R. (2020). *Comparative International Accounting* (14th ed.). Pearson.

O'Leary, D. (2017). Configuring Blockchain Architectures for Transaction Information in Blockchain Consortiums: The Case of Accounting and Supply Chain Systems. *International Journal of Intelligent Systems in Accounting Finance & Management*, *24*(1), 138–147. doi:10.1002/isaf.1417

O'Leary, D. (2018). Open Information Enterprise Transactions: Business Intelligence and Wash and Spoof Transactions in Blockchain and Social Commerce. *International Journal of Intelligent Systems in Accounting Finance & Management*, *25*(1), 148–158. doi:10.1002/isaf.1438

Ølnes, S., Ubacht, J., & Hanssen, M. (2017). Blockchain in Government: Benefits and Implications of Distributed Ledger Technology for Information Sharing. *Government Information Quarterly*, *34*(3), 355–364. doi:10.1016/j.giq.2017.09.007

Pascual-Pedreño, E., Gelashvili, V., & Pascual-Nebreda, L. (2021). Blockchain and its application to accounting. *Intangible Capital*, *17*(1), 1–16. doi:10.3926/ic.1522

Peters, G., & Panayi, E. (2016). Understanding Modern Banking Ledgers Through Blockchain Technologies: Future of Transaction Processing and Smart Contracts on the Internet of Money. In P. Tasca, T. Aste, L. Pelizzon, & N. Perony (Eds.), *Banking Beyond Banks and Money* (pp. 239–278). Springer., doi:10.1007/978-3-319-42448-4_13

Piazza, F. S. (2017). Bitcoin and the Blockchain as Possible Corporate Governance Tools: Strengths and Weaknesses. *Penn State Journal of Law & International Affairs*, *5*(2), 262–301. https://elibrary.law.psu.edu/jlia/vol5/iss2/3

PricewaterhouseCoopers. (2016). *What's Next for Blockchain in 2016?* PWC. https://www.pwc.com/us/en/financial-services/publications/viewpoints/assets/pwc-qa-whats-next-for-blockchain.pdf

Primavera. (2022). E Se A Contabilidade Fosse Em Blockchain? *Prima Vera BSS*. https://mz.primaverabss.com/pt/blog/blockchain-na-contabilidade/#:~:text=Com%20a%20blockchain%20na%20contabilidade%2C%20o%20registo%20das,um%20sistema%20interligado%20de%20registos%20de%20contabilidade%20duradouros

Raval, S. (2016). *Decentralized applications: harnessing Bitcoin's blockchain technology*. O'Reilly Media, Inc.

Robson, K. (1991). On the arenas of accounting change: The process of translation. *Accounting, Organizations and Society*, *16*(5-6), 547–570. doi:10.1016/0361-3682(91)90041-C

Robson, K. (1992). Accounting numbers as "inscription": Action at a distance and the development of accounting. *Accounting, Organizations and Society*, *17*(7), 685–708. doi:10.1016/0361-3682(92)90019-O

Rooney, H., Aiken, B., & Rooney, M. (2017). Q&A. Is Internal Audit Ready for Blockchain? *Technology Innovation Management Review*, *7*(10), 41–44. doi:10.22215/timreview/1113

Rozario, A. M., & Vasarhelyi, M. A. (2018). Auditing with Smart Contracts. *The International Journal of Digital Accounting Research*, *18*(1), 1–27. doi:10.4192/1577-8517-v18_1

Ruckeshauser, N. (2017). Do We Really Want Blockchain-based Accounting? Decentralized Consensus as Enabler of Management Override of Internal Controls. In Leimeister, J. M. & Brenner, W. (Eds.), Proceedings der 13. Internationalen Tagung Wirtschaftsinformatik (16–30). Institute of Information Management - St. Gallen University.

Saraiva, H. I. B., Alves, M.-C. G., & Gabriel, V. M. S. (2015). As raízes do processo formal de harmonização contabilística, a sua evolução e influência em Portugal. *De Computis. Spanish Journal of Accounting History*, *12*(22), 172–204. doi:10.26784/issn.1886-1881.v12i22.32

Schmitz, J., & Leoni, G. (2019). Accounting and auditing at the time of blockchain technology: A research agenda. *Australian Accounting Review*, *29*(2), 331–342. doi:10.1111/auar.12286

Secinaro, S., Dal Mas, F., Brescia, V., & Calandra, D. (2022). Blockchain in the accounting, auditing and accountability fields: A bibliometric and coding analysis. *Accounting, Auditing & Accountability Journal*, *35*(9), 168–203. doi:10.1108/AAAJ-10-2020-4987

Swan, M. (2015). *Blockchain: Blueprint for a new economy*. O'Reilly Media, Inc.

Thomson Reuters. (2019). Futuro da Contabilidade: Veja os impactos da tecnologia blockchain na contabilidade. *Domininiosistemas*. https://www.dominiosistemas.com.br/blog/veja-os-impactos-da-tecnologia-blockchain-na-contabilidade/

Vieira, P., & Saraiva, H. (2023). Tokenizing the Portuguese Accounting Standards System. In Prieto, J., Benítez-Martínez, F.L., Ferretti, S., Arroyo Guardeño, D., Tomás Nevado-Batalla, P. (Eds.). *Blockchain and Applications, 4th International Congress. BLOCKCHAIN 2022. Lecture Notes in Networks and Systems*, 595 (324-333). Springer. https://doi.org/10.1007/978-3-031-21229-1_30

Wang, Y., & Kogan, A. (2018). Designing Confidentiality-preserving Blockchain-based Transaction Processing Systems. *International Journal of Accounting Information Systems*, *30*(1), 1–18. doi:10.1016/j.accinf.2018.06.001

Yermack, D. (2017). Corporate Governance and Blockchains. *Review of Finance*, *21*(1), 7–31. doi:10.1093/rof/rfw074

Zheng, Z., Xie, S., Dai, H.-N., Chen, W., Chen, X., Weng, J., & Imran, M. (2020). An overview on Smart Contracts: Challenges, advances and platforms. *Future Generation Computer Systems*, *105*, 475–491. doi:10.1016/j.future.2019.12.019

ADDITIONAL READING

Bracci, E., Tallaki, M., Ievoli, R., & Diplotti, S. (2022). Knowledge, diffusion and interest in blockchain technology in SMEs. *Journal of Knowledge Management*, *26*(5), 1386–1407. doi:10.1108/JKM-02-2021-0099

Cai, C. W. (2021). Triple-entry accounting with blockchain: How far have we come? *Accounting and Finance*, *61*(1), 71–93. doi:10.1111/acfi.12556

Dai, J., & Vasarhelyi, M. A. (2017). Toward Blockchain-Based Accounting and Assurance. *Journal of Information Systems*, *31*(3), 5–21. doi:10.2308/isys-51804

Liu, M., Wu, K., & Xu, J. J. (2019). How will blockchain technology impact auditing and accounting: Permissionless versus permissioned blockchain. *Current Issues in Auditing*, *13*(2), A19–A29. doi:10.2308/ciia-52540

Mohanty, D., Anand, D., Aljahdali, H. M., & Villar, S. G. (2022). Blockchain Interoperability: Towards a Sustainable Payment System. *Sustainability (Basel)*, *14*(2), 913. doi:10.3390u14020913

Saraiva, H. I. B., Alves, M. C. G., & Gabriel, V. M. S. (2017). Adaptation of International Accounting Standards: Case of Portugal. In S. Gokten (Ed.), *Accounting and Corporate Reporting*. IntechOpen., doi:10.5772/intechopen.68732

Schmitz, J., & Leoni, G. (2019). Accounting and auditing at the time of blockchain technology: A research agenda. *Australian Accounting Review*, *29*(2), 331–342. doi:10.1111/auar.12286

Stockman, C., & Vieira, P. (2023). *Moral Machines: Critiquing Kantian Deontology for Blockchain Polygraphs*. International Journal of Applied Philosophy. ONLINE FIRST., doi:10.5840/ijap2023220180

Tan, B. S., & Low, K. Y. (2019). Blockchain as the database engine in the accounting system. *Australian Accounting Review*, *29*(2), 312–318. doi:10.1111/auar.12278

Vieira, P., Stockman, C., & Crocker, P. (2020). Blockchain, Facebook and a Polygraph. In F. Matos (Ed.), *Proceedings of the European Conference on the Impact of Artificial Intelligence and Robotics* (pp. 178-184).

Chapter 4
Assessing the Comparability and the Understandability of the Information on Cash Flows by European-Listed Entities

Ana Rita Velez
Instituto Politécnico de Lisboa, Portugal

Fábio Albuquerque
https://orcid.org/0000-0001-8877-9634
Instituto Politécnico de Lisboa, Portugal

Vera Pinto
Instituto Politécnico de Lisboa, Portugal

ABSTRACT

This chapter aims to assess the comparability and understandability of information on cash flows through the choices by entities in the presentation of the statement of cash flows (SCF) and the disclosure of non-generally accepted accounting principles measures (NGM) related to cash flow information, respectively. Data were obtained from 484 consolidated annual reports, between 2018 and 2021, from 121 entities listed on Euronext. The findings indicated that interest paid and received (dividends paid) were generally classified in the operating (financing) category, contrary to (aligned with) the proposed in the exposure draft (ED) issued by the International Accounting Standards Board (IASB). The findings also showed that entities often disclose NGM related to cash flows and present their formula and the possibility of reconciliation with the SCF. This research contributes to the discussion around the comparability, and understandability of information in the context of the current IASB's ED, which aims to standardise the presentation and the disclosure requirements on cash flows.

DOI: 10.4018/978-1-6684-7293-4.ch004

INTRODUCTION

The financial report plays a relevant role in the taking of internal and external decisions since it makes known the economic and financial situation of the entities (Coelho, 2016; Daga et al., 2015; Gope, 2017; Macedo et al., 2011; Magro, 2014; Oliveira, 2017). It is important to jointly assess all the information from the financial statements (Oliveira, 2017; Silva, 2020). In turn, the presentation of the financial statements must meet the qualitative characteristics defined in the Conceptual Framework issued by the International Accounting Standards Board (IASB), which includes comparability and understandability (IFRS Foundation, 2018). Cash flow information, which is mostly provided in the statement of cash flow (SCF), is essential in this matter, having the IASB a specific standard regarding the requirements of preparation and presentation of this financial statement, namely the International Accounting Standard (IAS) 7 - Statement of Cash Flows.

Nevertheless, globalization requires improvements in financial reporting preparation, since standards deficiencies can compromise the reliability and comparability of financial information (Rodrigues, 2019). Dias et al. (2004) stress some issues regarding the financial information communication process, as there may be different accounting choices, in terms of presentation and terminology adopted for some of the items within financial statements. In this sense, one of the barriers faced by the IASB is the existence of alternative criteria in matters of recognition, measurement, presentation and disclosure of financial information that negatively influence the quality of the financial information presented (Albuquerque et al., 2017; Costa et al., 2019; Guimarães & Rover, 2018; Gope, 2017; Gope & Mitra, 2015). These factors have led to the need for financial reporting harmonisation, to improve their comparability and increase their transparency at an international level. These elements are part of the set of objectives pursued by the IASB, resulting in better quality and greater usefulness of financial information for decision-making (IFRS Foundation, 2018).

The IASB is the standard-setter board that assumed the previous IAS from the International Accounting Standards Committee and issued International Financial Reporting Standards (IFRS) from 2001 onwards, intending to harmonise the financial information presented by entities and thereby ensure improvements in the transparency and comparability of financial statements, eliminating some existing accounting barriers, and contributing to the regular functioning of capital markets. The harmonisation of the financial report is materialised, in the context of the European Union (EU), through Regulation (EC) No 1606/2002 of the European Parliament and the Council of 19 July 2002. This regulation imposes the application of the IAS and IFRS, as endorsed by the EU, to certain types of entities, aiming to, among others, promote the comparability of the financial statements by the entities included in its mandatory scope, also providing an optional provision for it.

Considering IAS 7, the presentation of the SCF is divided into three categories of activity flows: operating, investing and financing activities. However, some items of the SCF, such as interest and dividends, have different classifications between those categories. In IAS 7, it is also reported that an entity can present operating cash flows (OCF) using the either direct or indirect method, and there are no concrete guidelines regarding the initial result to be used if the entities report the OCF using the indirect method.

The flexibility inherent to SCF, associated with the lack of a standardised presentation model, are factors that hinder the comparability of information by stakeholders (Macedo et al., 2011; Silva et al., 2018), which must be ensured both between different periods (consistency of presentation) or between entities (Taplin, 2011). Nevertheless, the need for greater alignment in the presentation of the SCF and the dissemination of related information is a controversial issue. Thus, from the perspective of some authors, the flexibility of some choices to present the SCF can lead to opportunistic behaviours, favouring the specific interest of each entity but, on the other hand, it can also lead to a presentation of more relevant information, since it can be adapted to the specific circumstances of each entity (e.g., Costa et al., 2019; Maciel et al., 2019).

In addition, understandability, achieved mainly through the transparency of the financial information disclosed, is a crucial element for the analysis of an entity (Oliveira et al., 2008), being recurrent in this purpose the resource to the non-generally accepted accounting principles (non-GAAP) measures (NGM) (Souza, 2020), which has been gaining prominence in recent decades (Brown, 2020). Thus, on the one hand, such measures can provide useful information that can contribute to the analysis of financial statements and the quality of the accounting report (Arena, 2021; Silva, 2020). On the other hand, NGM disclosures have subjective and discretionary characteristics, which can mitigate their comparability, between either entities or reporting periods, since there is no specific guidance on their disclosure (Neto, 2020).

Therefore, despite the benefits of the use of such indicators, there are also problems related to their disclosure, particularly in terms of the discretion of the information, since they are subject to different criteria defined by each entity, making it difficult to assess and compare them (Black, 2016; Cardeira, 2012; Neto, 2020). In this sense, inconsistencies in the calculation and presentation of such indicators can be identified, including their possible nonconformity with further information within the entities' reporting, which is an issue that has been the subject of literature (Black, 2016). Regarding free cash flow, being a widely used NGM from SCF, there are divergences among entities in its calculation, associated with transparency problems, since entities tend not to present information that allows users to understand it (Chen et al., 2021).

More recently, the need to promote improvements in matters such as the presentation of financial statements and the disclosure of related information, including NGM, led the IASB to issue the Exposure Draft (ED) - General Presentation and Disclosure, in December 2019. The opportunity of this discussion, associated with the potential impacts of this process regarding comparability and understandability of the information reported by the entities, justifies the relevance of the theme analysis.

Based on the foregoing, the exploratory study presented in this chapter proposes the following research questions (RQ):

- RQ1. As regards **comparability**, the question is "what are the presentation choices adopted by such entities concerning reported information on cash flows?"
- RQ2. As regards **understandability**, from the perspective of information transparency, "what is the level of transparency of the NGM related to cash flows"?

In more specific terms, and from the previous research questions, the following objectives have been defined:

- To assess the **comparability** of the SCF from the choices adopted by entities to present the information on cash flows, more specifically, the compliance level with the current guidelines proposed by the IASB in its ED on the subject.
- To assess the **understandability** (transparency) of the information disclosed on the NGM related to SCF, namely whether there are references to additional explanations about the NGM disclosed, based on the suggestions outlined in the IASB´s ED on this subject.

The data were gathered from the consolidated annual reports of European entities listed on EU-regulated markets as the study's target population. More specifically, the entities included in the European New Exchange Technology (Euronext) indices were selected, except for financial and insurance sector entities. Thus, data from 121 entities during the years 2018 to 2021 were assessed, totalling 484 reports. The study uses archival research as a method and content analysis as a research technique, using descriptive statistical techniques (univariate) for information analysis.

This study is timely for the academic and business universe for different reasons, differing from previous investigations by using the IASB´s ED under discussion as a reference for some of the dependent and independent variables compiled, which presents itself as an element of proposed novelty. In this sense, this study contributes to the identification of the potential impact of the changes proposed by the ED and its potential benefits within the scope of the objectives proposed in this research, namely the comparability and understandability of the information. In addition, it seeks to analyse, across the board, different aspects relating to information on cash flows, from an analysis that includes different European countries and sectors of economic activity.

As a more specific contribution, the study shows evidence of the potential impacts of the introduction of the revised standard on this subject (cash flows), as well as the relevance of the proposed amendments, particularly on comparability and understandability. It also contributes to the literature on the understandability of the NGM on cash flows, a theme still scarcely explored (Jacinto, 2019), especially from the perspective of the transparency of disclosures.

This chapter is divided into three more sections in addition to this introduction. The second section concerns the theoretical level underlying the proposed topics. The third relates to the empirical analysis, including the underlying methodology. Finally, the fourth section is dedicated to presenting the conclusions from this research and its limitations, as well as future avenues for future research on this subject.

THEORETICAL FRAMEWORK

This section provides the regulatory framework for SCF, which is divided into two subsections. The first presents the current framework on this topic, whilst the second one explores the recent ED issued by the IASB and its suggestions regarding the primary financial statements.

IAS 7: Statements of Cash Flows

To ensure the competitiveness of European capital markets and with the aim of the convergence of accounting standards used by European countries, Regulation (EC) No 1606/2002 identified entities within the scope of IAS and IFRS in this continent. That regulation covered a mandatory scope (Art. 4) and an optional scope (Art. 5), thus leaving it up to the Member States to extend the universe of entities subject to their use.

IAS 7 - Statement of Cash Flows is the existing international standard on SCF, which was adopted by the IASB in 2001, the year of the extinction of the previous International Accounting Standards Committee (IASC). It comes from the IAS 7 - Statement of Changes in Financial Position, issued by the IASC in 1977, and became, in 1992, IAS 7 - Cash Flow Statements, which entered into force on January 1, 1994. In 2007, and because of changes made to IAS 1 - Presentation of Financial Statements, IAS 7 met its current designation.

IAS 7 has undergone several changes over the years, either through direct revisions or through other standards revisions, particularly those implemented in the IAS 1, IFRS 10 - Consolidated Financial Statements, IFRS 11 - Joint Arrangements, IFRS 16 - Leases and IFRS 17 - Insurance Contracts. In 2016, finally, the IASB carried out a final revision of IAS 7 following the issue of the ED entitled Disclosure Initiative (Amendments to IAS 7), which entered into force on 1 January 2017, to improve disclosures regarding changes in liabilities arising from financing activities.

The purpose of IAS 7 is to establish how information on an entity's cash flows is presented so that users of the financial statements have information about historical changes in cash and cash equivalents (IAS 7, §10). This IAS states that cash flows presented in the SCF must be classified into one of the following three activities: operating, investing and financing (IAS 7, §10). This classification is considered useful for users of financial statements since it allows them to determine the impact of each activity on the financial position of the entity and in the amounts of cash and cash equivalents, as well as to evaluate the relationships between these activities (IAS 7, §11).

Operating activities are defined as the principal revenue-generating activities of the entity and also being a residual concept, as activities that are not classified as investing or financing (IAS 7, §6). Then, the operating cash flows (OCF) are considered a key indicator, since they allow the identification of those operations that can produce sufficient cash flows to cover the entity's expenses, pay dividends and make new investments, without recourse to external financing (IAS 7, §13). It should be noted that the information from these flows is also useful for future OCF projections (IAS 7, §13).

Investing activities, in turn, relate to the acquisition and disposal of long-term assets and other investments that are not considered cash equivalents (IAS 7, §6). It should also be noted that only expenditures that have a recognised asset in the statement of financial position can be classified as investing cash flows (ICF) (IAS 7, §16).

Financing activities, finally, are those cash flows that may cause changes in the size and/or composition of the entity's equity and financing (IAS 7, §17), hereinafter described as financing cash flows (FCF).

Figure 1 summarizes the information regarding the three activities described in IAS 7.

Figure 1. Activities described in IAS 7 to classify cash flows in the SCF

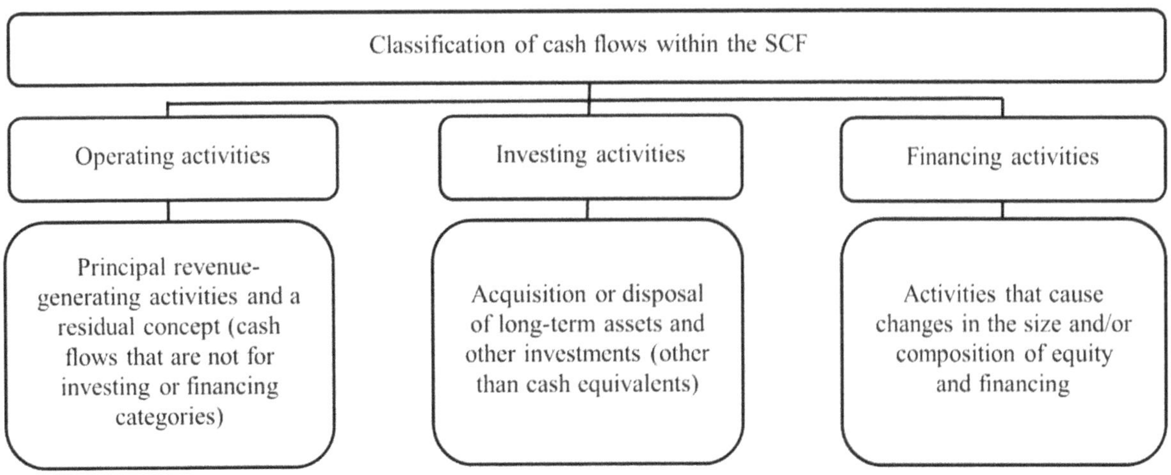

In IAS 7, it is also mentioned that an entity can report OCF using either direct or indirect methods (IAS 7, §18). In the direct method, the main categories of cash received and payments are disclosed (IAS 7, §18). Using the indirect method, the accrual basis net profit or loss is adjusted according to the effect of some transactions that occurred in the period that were not reflected in cash or cash equivalents, which include accruals and deferred, as well as income and expenses associated with activities other than operating activities (IAS 7, §18). It should be noted, however, that entities are encouraged to use the direct method, since, according to the IASB, this is the method that allows entities to estimate future cash flows using information that is not available using the indirect method (IAS 7, §19).

It should also be noted that there are transactions whose classification in terms of cash flows may differ depending on the entities. In particular, the classification of interest and dividends (paid and received) arises in this context, since the IAS 7 establishes that cash flows relating to those must be disclosed separately, but are subject to discretionary classification as an operating, investing or financing activity, depending on the type of flow (cash-inflow or cash-outflow) (IAS 7, §31). Figure 2 summarises the options proposed by IAS 7 in this regard.

Figure 2. Interest and dividend flows paid and received in the light of IAS 7

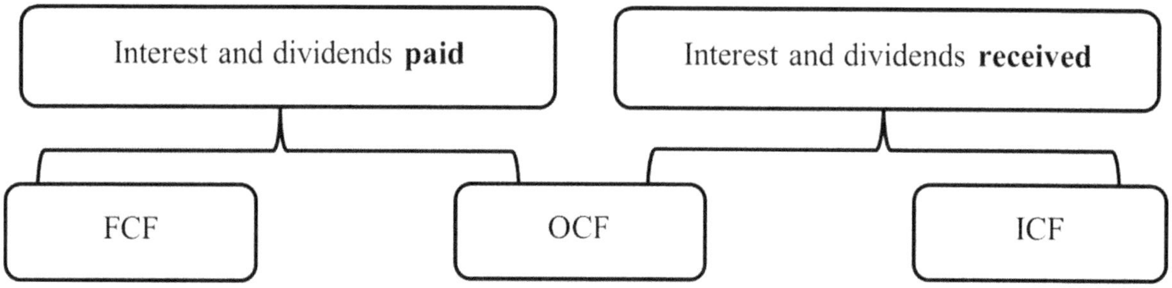

As shown in Figure 2, the OCF correspond to the activity that can be used for reporting both the interest and dividends paid or the interest and dividends received. In more specific terms, IAS 7 states that a financial institution normally classifies interest paid and interest and dividends received as OCF, however, no rule is established, especially for entities from other industries or institutional sectors. Thus, these operations can be classified as OCF, since they impact the net profit or loss (IAS 7, §33). In turn, interest paid may also be classified as FCF and interest and dividends received as ICF since they are related to expenses incurred to obtain financial resources or returns on investment, respectively (IAS 7, §33).

Following, dividends paid can be classified as OCF because they are considered as a cost of obtaining financial resources (IAS 7, §33). However, alternatively, they can be classified as FCF since they represent a cost incurred to obtain financial resources or as operating cash flow since it determines the entity's ability to pay its dividends (IAS 7, §34). Finally, cash flows relating to income taxes are also discretionary since they should be classified as OCF. However, if specifically identified with such activities, they can be classified as either FCF or ICF (IAS 7, §35).

The next subsection is dedicated to presenting the main changes proposed in the IASB's ED.

The ED: General Presentation and Disclosures

More recently, and as a response to the criticisms presented by different stakeholders, the IASB developed an ED, entitled General Presentation and Disclosures, within the ongoing project on the primary financial statements, from which some changes were proposed as future implementations to improve the information provided to stakeholders.

In this context, the role of primary financial statements is presented as providing stakeholders with a structured and comparable summary of the assets, liabilities, equity, income, and expenses as well as cash flows of a reporting entity, to obtain an overview of the entity and its strengths (IFRS Foundation, 2016). This set of information is comprised of the statement of financial position, the statement of financial performance, the statement of changes in equity, and the SCF (IFRS Foundation, 2016). Within the statement of financial performance, the IASB's ED uses the term statement of profit or loss to cover those cases in which an entity presents a single statement, with a profit or loss section (by simplification purposes, statement of profit or loss had the same meaning in this context) and another comprehensive income one, as well as the statement of profit or loss itself, for those cases in which an entity presents a statement of profit or loss and a separate statement presenting comprehensive income.

The focus on the information provided to stakeholders and the efforts to better regulation in the matter of primary financial statements arose from the identification of some subjectivity within the financial statements analysis process, with effects on the comparability among entities (IFRS Foundation, 2016). The IASB's ED proposal cover presentation and disclosure requirements, with no implications in terms of recognition and measurement (ED, BC240). Thus, the post-implementation process of the IASB's ED will directly affect those matters in a qualitative aspect, as it is not possible to accurately measure its quantitative effects.

It should be noted that the possibility of defining a standard model for the financial statements under discussion within the IASB's ED was also initially discussed (ED, BC27). However, this suggestion was initially rejected given the difficulty of implementing a global model applicable to all entities, regardless of their economic activity sectors and jurisdictions, which might introduce significant divergences with previous models used by some entities (ED, BC27). Nevertheless, the IASB provided a set of illustrative examples of the proposed changes within its ED to guide accountants over the world.

The initiative regarding changes in primary financial statements began with public discussions started in 2014, from which IASB received the first feedback from stakeholders on their concerns about the financial statements' comparability and transparency. Thus, the analysis of the comments received between 2015 and 2019 was the basis for the ED developed by the IASB, with a final version being released in December 2019. The proposed period to receive further stakeholders' comments ended in September 2020. Then, the IASB assessed the comments gathered between December 2020 and January 2021. Since then, and having those comments as a starting point, IASB has been discussing and redeliberating, during its meetings, the improvements to be made and the next steps of this project.

There is currently no set date for the implementation and entry into force of the proposed amendments. However, it was defined that there will be, at the end of this process, a transition period between 18 and 24 months for entities to reformulate the financial statements, with a retrospective application (ED, BC 181). In this transitional period, entities must adapt accounting systems as well as address possible operational challenges or barriers that hinder the adaptation to the proposed changes (ED, BC 181; BC 182). Based on the feedback received, this is a project that stakeholders aim to see implemented as soon as possible (IFRS Foundation, 2021).

In more specific terms, the ED come out of some criticisms presented by stakeholders regarding the financial statements, suggesting that the IASB prioritize projects with an impact on primary financial statements (IFRS Foundation, 2016). The objective is to improve how financial information is communicated, especially in matters related to transparency and comparability of the information reported in the statement of profit or loss: in this latter case, either among entities or in the context of the entity itself between different periods (IFRS Foundation, 2016; IFRS Foundation, 2019). Although initially focused on the statement of profit or loss, issues related to other financial statements were also discussed, especially the SCF.

In summary, the ED proposed amendments to the following matters:

i. **Presentation of new subtotals for the statement of profit or loss**

To address issues related to the statement of profit or loss analysis, the IASB aims to promote relevant information and create a more consistent presentation structure with benefits for comparability. These issues result from the fact that, currently, IAS 1 does not require or define the presentation of subtotals, allowing entities to incorporate different components (ED, BC7).

Within the ED, the IASB proposes a structured model for the statement of profit or loss presentation to be applied by all entities, also requiring the presentation of additional subtotals that incorporate the same components for all entities, improving the comparability of these financial statements (ED, BC12). In this sense, additional subtotals are presented only if they are considered relevant by the entity (ED, BC31).

Based on this guidance, and to promote the alignment between the statement of profit or loss and the SCF, it was also proposed that statement of profit or loss should be divided into the same categories or segments of incomes as those existing in the SCF, namely the operating, investing and financing ones (ED, BC 30). In addition, the project also proposes the creation of a new category for integral associates and joint ventures.

The new category follows the proposal to differentiate the classification of associates and joint ventures between integral and non-integral, to facilitate the analysis of the entities' investments (ED, BC12b, BC28). From this distinction, it is intended that the information about non-integral associates and joint ventures will be classified, in the statement of profit or loss, within the investing category, while information on integral associates and full joint ventures will be specifically presented as a new category, between the operating and investing ones (ED, BC32, BC52, BC80, BC83). Thus, and with the exceptions provided in the ED, the following lines will be presented as new subtotals in the statement of profit or loss: a) operating profit; b) operating profit and income and expenses from integral associates and joint ventures; and, finally, c) profit before financing activities and income taxes (ED, BC 29).

The ED also clarifies that the exchange rate differences should be presented within the same income and expenses categories where the items that gave rise to them were classified (ED, BC 91). Gains and losses on derivatives, in particular changes in fair value, should, in turn, be attributed to the investing category as a rule (ED, BC 93).

Furthermore, and despite the exception provided in the ED, the income, and expenses of hedging financial instruments may be classified into the operating, investing and financing categories, depending on the risks they are intended to cover, i.e., it would be classified into the same categories of the related income and expenses, with the investing category defined as the residual one (ED, BC 94). In the exceptions envisaged, the investing category is also the one proposed for the hedging instruments classification, following the recommended option for derivatives in general (ED, BC 95).

Figure 3 provides a summary of the proposed changes concerning the structure of the statement of profit or loss within the IASB's ED.

Figure 3. Changes proposed by the ED to the Statement of Profit or Loss
Source*: Adapted from IFRS Foundation (2020)*

SPL		
Revenue	x	Operating category
Other income	x	
Changes in inventories of finished goods and work in progress	(+/-)	
Cost of goods sold	(x)	
Professional fees	(x)	
Depreciation and amortization	(x)	
Inventory impairments (losses/reversals)	(+/-)	
Impairments of trade receivables	(+/-)	
Other expenses	(x)	
(...)		
Operating profit	(+/-)	
Share of profit or loss of integral associates and joint ventures	(+/-)	Category of Integral associates and joint ventures
Gains on disposal of integral associates and joint ventures	(+/-)	
Impairments of integral associates and *joint ventures* (losses/reversals)	(+/-)	
(...)		
Operating profit and income and expenses from integral associates and joint ventures	(+/-)	
Share of profit or loss of non-integral associates and joint ventures	(+/-)	Investing category
Gains/losses on disposal of non-integral associates and joint ventures	(+/-)	
Interest	x	
Dividends		
(...)		
Profit before financing and income tax	X	
Expenses from financing activities	(x)	Financing category
Cash and cash equivalent	(+/-)	
Financing Unwinding of discount on pension liabilities and provisions	(x)	
(...)		
Profit before tax	(+/-)	
Income tax	(+/-)	
Profit for the period	(+/-)	

Figure 3 shows a separate presentation of the proposed categories, including the newest integral associates and joint ventures, in addition to the operating, investing and financing ones, besides the proposed subtotals, such as the following:

i. operating profit;
ii. operating profit and income and expenses from integral associates and joint ventures;
iii. the profit before financing and income tax;
iv. the profit before income tax; and
v. the profit for the period.

The structure proposed is merely exemplificative and not exhaustive, that is, it does not contemplate all possible situations. Additionally, it does not apply to financial entities, since for these entities the income and expenses arising from financing activities are usually included in the operating category (ED, BC 31).

Considering the proposed amendments, entities may be forced to further disaggregate the statement of profit or loss, as is the case with impairment losses of financial instruments, which may be presented in different categories. The ED considers that this approach allows the achievement of a reliable and relevant representation of each category within the statement of profit or loss (ED, BC108).

Finally, it should be noted that the operating category comprises the remaining income and expenses which does not fall into other categories, such as investing, financing, integral associated and joint ventures, as well as those classified as income taxes or discontinued activities. Thus, the operating category can be seen as a residual category (ED, BC 54), although it also includes in its definition the investments that relate to the entity's main business activity (ED, BC54). This definition helps entities to distinguish the income and expenses within this category from those of the investing one, which must have different purposes (ED, BC49, BC72).

The financing category will include income and expenses from liabilities of financing activities, cash, and cash equivalents, as well as other liabilities not related to financing activities (ED, BC108). This last component includes income and expenses that reflect the effect of the time value of money, such as those arising from liabilities (or assets) of defined benefits and provisions for assets dismantling, removal or restoration.

ii. Requirements relating to the disaggregation of information with a focus on relevance

This topic includes, among others, the discussion on the principles of disaggregation in general and for specific matters, such as the presentation of operating expenses in the statement of profit or loss, either by nature or by functions, as well as the relevant balances to be provided as regards items commonly referred to as "other" or "unusual" income and expenses (ED, BC9, BC 23, BC 24).

This topic follows criticism stemming from the quality of the presentation of information in the financial statements and the notes to the financial statements, due to the lack of guidance on the aspects of aggregation or disaggregation of items, suggesting that the way some entities usually disaggregate the information in the financial statements does not provide the relevant information for analysis (ED, BC9). As such, the ED provided more comprehensive guidance on these matters, indicating specific principles and requirements to be observed, and the information that should be aggregated/disaggregated according to its characteristics.

The ED also defines the role of the primary financial statements and the notes to the financial statements, specifying what information should be included in each case and whether it should be presented separately or grouped with other similar information (ED, BC23 and BC24). In this sense, it states that the role of primary financial statements is to provide a structured and comparable summary of the financial situation of a given entity, to help users to obtain an overview of it and the possibility of comparison between reporting periods and among entities. The notes to the financial statements, in turn, must be aligned with the IAS and IFRS to provide additional relevant information to help users to understand and assess the financial statements.

It should be noted that an indicative threshold was initially proposed within the ED, to facilitate the entities' decisions regarding the process of aggregation or disaggregation of financial information, for example, amounts above 10% of revenues or total income. However, considering that the concept of materiality is decisive in this context, this proposal was rejected for the following reasons: firstly, because it is not easy to find a proper reference to be consensually used to all situations and entities; secondly, it could give rise to inconsistencies with the definition of materiality provided for in the conceptual framework, where no threshold for that concept is proposed (ED, BC26).

Considering these changes, new items emerge to be disclosed in the financial statements, namely the distinction between integral and non-integral associates and joint ventures, which may impact the statement of profit or loss, the SCF and the balance sheet. Additionally, it was proposed that the balance sheet should provide a new specific line for the goodwill since IAS 1 does not determine this requirement currently (ED, BC62; BC119; BC 257; BC 272).

iii. **Improvements in NGM disclosures**

NGM are those indicators that provide relevant additional information on the current and future performance of a given entity since they complement the information related to those based on the accounting and financial reporting standards officially used by entities to prepare their financial statements (ED, BC6c).

Despite their outstanding relevance, the NGM are alternative indicators that do not follow the IASB's guidelines, with possible changes in their presentation between reporting periods (inconsistencies) and lack of comparability among entities, which hinders their analysis and, consequently, their auditability (ED, BC 9; BC 148), as also highlighted in a wide literature on this topic (Santos et al., 2021; Neto, 2020; Albuquerque et al., 2017; Marques, 2010).

The IASB stresses the importance of those measures, arguing, however, that they must comply with the financial statements, represent the financial performance of the entity and be consistent among reporting periods (ED, BC 158). It should also be aligned with the orientation proposed in the ED on aggregation and disaggregation of financial information (ED, BC 158c).

Thus, to fill the identified gaps, the IASB proposes a definition for the NGM, framing them as management performance measures. More specifically, in the context of the statement of profit or loss, NGM was defined as subtotals of income and expenses that are presented outside this financial statement, complementing the totals or subtotals specified by IAS and IFRS to communicate the management's view on a given aspect of an entity's financial performance (ED, BC153).

The IASB also proposes that entities disclose such information in a single note within the notes to the financial statements, identifying a set of disclosures specifically aimed at this matter, including, inter alia, the need for reconciliation with the comparable subtotals of the statement of profit or loss, among other information (ED, BC152, BC163). Thus, it is intended to increase its transparency, as well as the comparability of the different NGM used by the entities (ED, BC11 and BC12d).

Associated with this orientation, it was also proposed the need for describing the NGM used, explaining why it is relevant and what it is intended to complement (ED, BC152). It should also be noted that such proposals within the ED were restricted to the subtotals of income and expenses in the statement of profit or loss, not covering other financial indicators, such as the NGM related to cash flows (BC 154, BC 171).

iv. Changes in the SCF to improve comparability by eliminating the existing options

The IASB also proposes some amendments specifically aimed at the SCF. On the structure of this financial statement, criticism stemmed from its lack of comparability, since IAS 7 allows the use of different classifications for the components of interest and dividends, as previously mentioned. Another proposed change involves the identification of the initial indicator or variable from the statement of profit or loss to be used for proving the OCF through the indirect method since there is also a lack of comparability among entities regarding this matter.

The diversity of variables used as starting point for providing the OCF using the indirect method was identified as a matter that mitigates a proper analysis and comparison of the SCF since IAS 7 currently mentions the profit or loss in a general sense or the income and expenses presented in the statement of profit or loss adjusted by the changes in inventories and operating receivables and payables. The IASB notes that entities have used, inter alia, operating profit or loss, net profit or loss or profit or loss from continuing operations (ED, BC 186).

To address this problem, it proposes the use of operating profit as a starting point for the OCF calculation using the indirect method, as it will be made in this process since this variable includes less income and expenses whose cash effects can be classified as ICF or FCF (ED, BC 188a). Another factor that led to the choice of this variable is related to the difference between the operating profit and the OCF, which consists of a measure of operating increases considered useful for users of financial statements since it helps them to understand how the operating profit was converted into cash flows (ED, BC 188b).

Similarly, a comparability problem was also identified concerning the classification of some components of the SCF, depending, for instance, on the entity's economic sector of activity (ED, BC 189). Thus, one of the concerns of the IASB's ED was to restrict the entities' choices in matters related to the classification of their cash flows, to increase the comparability of the SCF (ED, BC12).

Thus, as for the classification of interest and dividends paid it is specified that the entities should classify them as FCF (ED, BC191, BC196b). Regarding the interest paid, it is argued that this component represents the entities' cost of obtaining external financing, being also consistent with its recognition as an expense, within the financing category in the statement of profit or loss (ED, BC 196b). Concerning the dividends paid, the argument is that this type of flow stems from a source of financing and, as such, it is not considered that classification as OCF allows a more reliable representation (ED, BC 191, BC192a). On the other hand, entities should classify interest and dividends received as ICF, to improve the consistency with the changes foreseen for the statement of profit or loss, since interest and dividends, when recognised as income, are expected to be classified in the statement of profit or loss within the investing category (ED, BC 196a).

There is, however, an exception for entities from the financial sector, whose dividends received and interest are classified into a single category, leaving it up to the entities to rank them (ED, BC 200, BC 201). Notwithstanding, it is expected that this classification should be consistent with those for income and expenses within the statement of profit or loss (ED, BC202). Dividends paid, in turn, should be classified as FCF for all entities (ED, BC 191).

Figure 4 summarises the proposed amendments within the IASB's ED for the SCF concerning the above-mentioned matters.

Figure 4. Changes proposed by the IASB's ED for SCF

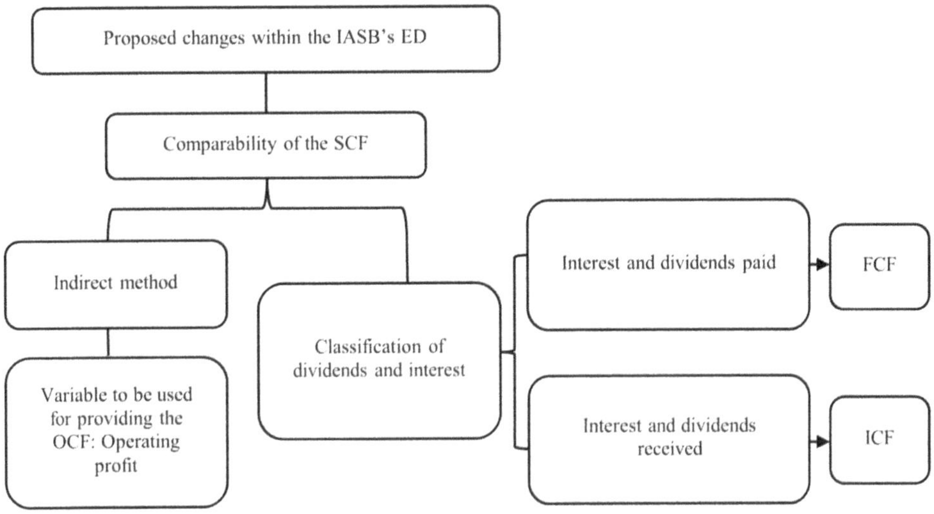

Finally, and as previously mentioned, one of the objectives of the IASB's ED was to align the classifications used between the statement of profit or loss and the SCF, increasing not only the comparability but also the global understandability of the financial information reported by the entities (ED, BC194). Thus, the IASB also proposes the classification of associates and joint ventures between integral and non-integral for SCF preparation purposes. However, cash flows from the net acquisition of associates and joint ventures should be classified as ICF in the SCF (ED, BC185, BC 206).

Figure 5 provides a non-exhaustive example of the SCF aligned with those considerations.

Based on Figure 5, the main changes can be highlighted as follows:

i. the definition of the net operating profit for the OCF calculation using the indirect method;
ii. the specification of the classification of interest and dividends; and
iii. separation of the cash flow classification of associates and joint ventures integral and non-integral in the ICF category.

In summary, the proposed amendments are expected to benefit the information provided for analysis purposes and, consequently, for the decision-making process (ED, BC 239). Thus, an improvement in the quality of the financial statements is expected, since the IASB's ED responds overall to the criticism regarding their structure and content (ED, BC250).

Figure 5. The structured model for the SCF proposed in the ED
Source: **Adapted from IFRS Foundation (2020)**

SCF (using the indirect method)	
Operating Profit	(+/-)
Adjustments for (accrual basis income and expenses):	
Depreciation / amortisations / provisions / fair value changes / defaults, etc. (...)	X
Income taxes paid	(x)
(...)	
Cash flows from operating activities	(+/-)
Acquisition/disposal of **integral** associates and joint ventures	(+/-)
Acquisition/disposal of **non-integral** associates and joint ventures	(+/-)
Dividends received from **integral** associates and joint ventures	x
Dividends received from **non-integral** associates and joint ventures	x
Dividends received from investments in equity instruments other than associates and joint ventures	x
Interest received	x
(...)	
Cash flows from investing activities	(X)
Dividends paid	(x)
Interest paid	(x)
(...)	
Cash flows from financing activities	(X)
Net increase in cash and cash equivalents	(+/-)

A consistent variable as starting point for providing the OCF using the indirect method

New requirements for the classification of cash flows from associates and joint ventures between integral and non-integral within the ICF

Guidance for the classification of interest and dividends in their categories

As mentioned earlier, the IASB asked stakeholders for feedback on the proposed changes by September 2020. After receiving their comments, it was possible to verify that, overall, the proposals received positive assessments, indicating that the changes proposed might have a beneficial impact on the relevance of financial statements from the stakeholders' perspective (IFRS Foundation, 2020a). In this sense, the comments received also highlighted the importance of completing the project as soon as possible (EFRAG, 2022).

It worts to stress that some IAS and IFRS would likely be amended or replaced at the end of this project, i.e., when final changes under discussion are implemented by the IASB, which includes, in addition to IAS 1 and IAS 7 previously mentioned, the following ones (ED, BC1 and BC 2):

- IAS 8 - Accounting Policies, Changes in Accounting Estimates and Errors;
- IAS 33 – Earnings Per Share;
- IAS 34 - Interim Financial Reporting.

- IFRS 7 - Financial Instruments: Disclosures; and
- IFRS 12 - Disclosure of Interests in Other Entities.

Finally, the deadline for implementing the ED proposals has not been disclosed yet, as meetings for analysis and deliberations, based on the comments received, are still taking place by 2023 (IFRS Foundation, 2022). Overall, it can be said that the IASB's ED content was generally well received by stakeholders, although some stakeholders' suggestions for expanding on certain topics, such as the NGM. The statement of profit or loss and the SCF proposals generally received positive feedback, although some criticism stemmed from inconsistencies between the proposed categories. Furthermore, based on the analysis developed by the IASB in its pilot study, it was confirmed that the entities were capable of responding to the proposed changes without excessive constraints (IFRS Foundation, 2021a,b,c,d).

The next section provides the empirical analysis of the study carried out in this chapter.

Empirical Analysis

This section is dedicated to the presentation of the exploratory research developed for this chapter. It is divided into two subsections. The first concerns the methodology used for the development of the empirical study. The second one is dedicated to the presentation, analysis and discussion of the findings.

Material and Methods

The exploratory study presented in this section is eminently quantitative. Its quantitative nature is verified by the analysis of the data gathered from the sources of information used for this purpose. As a method of investigation, archival research was carried out, using content analysis as a research technique. The statistical analysis uses univariate descriptive statistics.

The data source is comprised of the annual consolidated reports of entities included in the European regulated markets that use the IAS and IFRS for preparing their financial reporting. More specifically, the entities included in the Euronext indices were selected, namely: Euronext Paris (CAC-40), Euronext Lisbon (PSI-20), Euronext Amsterdam (AEX), Euronext Brussels (BEL-20), Euronext Dublin (ISEQ-20) and Euronext Oslo (OBX). To ensure data comparability, entities from the financial and insurance sector were excluded since they integrate institutional sectors that may be subject to local and European-specific regulation and supervision.

A total of 121 entities from those Euronext indexes were selected. Data comprises the period between 2018 and 2021. Therefore, 484 consolidated annual reports were collected for those four years.

The entities' reference country was based on the indices in which the sample entities are listed.

Table 1 summarizes the classification attributed to the entities' countries.

Table 1. Entities' classification by country

Euronext Index	Country	Number of entities	% of entities
CAC-40	France	35	28.9%
PSI-20	Portugal	17	14.1%
AEX	The Netherlands	20	16.5%
BEL-20	Belgium	14	11.6%
ISEQ-20	Ireland	14	11.6%
OBX	Norway	21	17.4%
Total	-	**121**	**100%**

Table 2 summarizes the classification attributed to the entities' economic activity sectors according to the Industry Classification Benchamark.

Table 2. Entities' classification by sector

Industry Classification Benchmark	Sector	Number of entities	% of entities
10 and 15	Telecommunications and technologies	21	17.4%
20	Health care	9	7.4%
40 and 45	Consumer discretionary and staples	37	30.6%
50 and 55	Industrials and basic material	39	32.2%
60 and 65	Energy and utilities	15	12.4%
Total	-	**121**	**100%**

The identification of entities included in those indices was based on the Euronext website. The annual consolidated reports were gathered, in turn, from the official website of each entity included in this sample research. Entities were classified by country and economic activity sector for analysis purposes.

For the objective underlying the **comparability**, different dummies (or dichotomic variables) were created for the variables underlying the proposed analysis, to which the value "1" was attributed to those cases whether the information was accordingly and "0" otherwise. Those variables were defined according to the requirements from the IASB's ED and used as a reference for the interest paid, interest received, dividends paid, dividends received and the variable used as starting point for providing OCF. Furthermore, for assessing the method used by entities to disclose the OCF, a specific variable was also created for this purpose. Therefore, such variables were computed as follows:

- The interest and dividends paid assumed the value "1" whether they were classified as FCF and "0" otherwise;
- The interest and dividends received assumed the value "1" whether they were classified as ICF and "0" otherwise;

- The method used to disclose the OCF assumed the value "1" whether the direct method was used and "0" otherwise;
- The variable used for providing the OCF through the indirect method assumed the value "1" whether the operating profit was used and "0" otherwise;

For the objective underlying the **understandability**, it was proposed different dummies (or dichotomic variables) based on the identification of items related to the disclosure of financial information on the NGM related to cash flows (for instance, the free cash flow). Thus, it was first identified whether the entities reported NGM related to cash flows. Therefore, it was assumed the value "1" whether any NGM on this topic was found and "0" otherwise. Subsequently, considering the requirements from the IASB's ED, variables associated with the disclosure matters were defined. Therefore, for each entity under assessment, the following variables were proposed, which they were duly codified again as "1" whether the information was disclosed and "0" otherwise, as follows:

- the identification and justification of the relevance of the NGM concerning proposed cash flows;
- additional references on the NGM used, in particular, the information it seeks to supplement;
- the disclosure of the proposed NGM formula;
- the possibility of reconciliation of the NGM with the information present in the financial statements (GAAP information).

Following the methodological lines underlying the proposed study, the next subsection is dedicated to the presentation and analysis of the findings.

Analysis of Results

To meet the two objectives proposed in this chapter, the findings will be first presented and assessed and, then, the results will be discussed having the literature on this topic as a reference.

The Comparability of the Information on Cash Flows

Based on the first objective proposed for this study, related to comparability, it was intended to assess the choices made by entities as regards the presentation of items within SCF. Through the descriptive analysis, it was sought to identify the accounting choices of interest and dividends, as well as the method adopted by the sample entities for presenting the OCF as well as the variables used for providing it using the indirect method, whenever applicable.

In this sense, Table 3 summarizes the accounting choices adopted by the entities of this research sample for the period under assessment.

Table 3. Frequencies: choices identified in the SCF

	Number		%	
	0	1	0	1
Interest received	292	176	62	38
Interest paid	273	211	56	44
Dividends received	200	200	50	50
Dividends paid	0	460	0	100
OCF disclosure method	407	77	84	16
The variable used for providing the OCF	460	24	95	5

Table 3 shows that most of the interest received and paid was classified as OCF (62% and 56%, respectively). In turn, dividends received were classified equally as ICF (50%) and OCF (50%). Dividends paid, on the other hand, were exclusively classified as FCF. In terms of the OCF disclosure method, 84% of the observations indicated that the indirect method was being used. However, in only 5% of the cases, the OCF was calculated based on the operating profit as proposed by the IASB's ED. Despite not being significant in the overall analysis, it is worthwhile to also mention that missing data were recorded for some cases.

Table 4 provides the entities' accounting choices by country.

According to Table 4, all entities from Portugal classified interest received and paid as ICF and FCF, respectively, while most entities from the remaining countries classified these items as OCF. For Portugal, there is one exceptional case in which the interest paid was classified as OCF in 2018 but changed this option for the remaining years. Regarding dividends received most entities from Portugal, The Netherlands and Ireland classified them as ICF while the remaining cases were classified as OCF. As far as the OCF disclosure method is concerned, all entities from France and Norway preferred the indirect method, compared to those from Portugal, which preferred the direct method. For the remaining entities, there is also a preference for the indirect method.

Table 4. Frequencies: choices identified in the SCF by country

	France				**Portugal**				**The Netherlands**			
	Number		**%**		**Number**		**%**		**Number**		**%**	
	0	**1**	**0**	**1**	**0**	**1**	**0**	**1**	**0**	**1**	**0**	**1**
Interest received	100	36	74	26	0	68	0	100	51	28	65	35
Interest paid	92	48	66	34	1	67	1	99	51	28	65	35
Dividends received	92	44	68	32	4	52	7	93	27	36	43	57
OCF disclosure method	140	0	100	0	7	61	10	90	72	7	91	9
The variable used for providing the OCF	136	4	97	3	7	0	100	0	64	8	89	11
	Belgium				Ireland				Norway			
	Number		%		Number		%		Number		%	
	0	1	0	1	0	1	0	1	0	1	0	1
Interest received	45	12	79	21	32	12	73	27	64	20	76	24
Interest paid	37	20	65	35	48	8	86	14	44	40	52	48
Dividends received	29	12	71	29	8	24	25	75	40	32	56	44
OCF disclosure method	56	1	98	2	48	8	86	14	84	0	100	0
The variable used for providing the OCF	52	4	93	7	44	4	92	8	80	4	95	5

Table 5 provides, in turn, the entities' accounting choices by sector.

Table 5. Frequencies: Choices identified in the SCF by sector

	Telecommunications and technologies				Health care				Consumer discretionary and staples			
	Number		%		Number		%		Number		%	
	0	1	0	1	0	1	0	1	0	1	0	1
Interest received	64	20	76	24	28	8	78	22	80	52	61	39
Interest paid	64	20	76	24	28	8	78	22	69	79	47	53
Dividends received	44	20	69	31	20	4	83	17	52	76	41	59
OCF disclosure method	68	16	81	19	32	4	89	11	130	18	88	12
The variable used for providing the OCF	68	0	100	0	29	4	88	12	122	8	94	6

	Industrials and basic material				Energy and utilities			
	Number		%		Number		%	
	0	1	0	1	0	1	0	1
Interest received	96	60	62	38	24	36	40	60
Interest paid	92	64	59	41	20	40	33	67
Dividends received	64	68	48	52	20	32	38	62
OCF disclosure method	132	24	85	15	45	15	75	25
The variable used for providing the OCF	124	8	94	6	41	4	91	9

According to Table 5, the entities from the energy and utilities sector mostly follow the current proposal of the IASB's ED to classify interest and dividends received as ICF, whereas other sectors prefer to classify the items as OCF. Furthermore, the majority of entities in all sectors (higher than 75%) choose the indirect method for disclosing the OCF. In addition, no entity in the telecommunications and technologies sectors used the operating profit as a starting point for the OCF.

The findings from the objective related to the understandability of the information on cash flows are presented in the next subsubsection.

The Understandability of the Information on Cash Flows

Based on the second objective proposed for this study, regarding the understandability, several variables were proposed for the analysis of disclosures associated with the NGM related to cash flows. For this purpose, those variables included the identification of the NGM proposed and its relevance, the existence of additional explanation concerning the information that this measure is intended to complement, the presentation of its formula and, finally, the possibility of reconciliation between the NGM with the GAAP information presented by the entities.

Then, Table 6 initially presents the data collected concerning the use by the entities of any NGM related to the identified cash flows, and the free cash flow in particular, as it is the predominant indicator used in this context.

Table 6. Frequencies: disclosures on NGM (overall) and free cash flow (in particular)

	Number		%	
	0	**1**	**0**	**1**
Disclosures on NGM (overall)	179	305	37	63
Disclosure on free cash flow (in particular)	69	236	22	78

Table 6 shows that there are references to NGM related to cash flows in 305 out of 484 cases (63%), of which 236 (78%) are concerned, specifically, the free cash flow. Following, the four items associated with the further explanations on the NGM for those 305 cases mentioned were assessed, with data identified in Table 7.

Table 7. Frequencies: disclosures on NGM related to cash flows

	Number		%	
	0	**1**	**0**	**1**
Relevance of the NGM disclosed	196	109	64	36
Information aimed to complement	281	24	92	8
Presentation of the formula used	28	277	9	91
Reconciliation process	28	277	9	91

Table 7 shows that about one-third of the observations (36%) contained information on the explanation of the relevance of the NGM. In addition to this, only 8% of the observations justified its use with the information that aimed to complement. On the other hand, in more than 90% of the cases, the formula and its reconciliation with the GAAP information were provided to the entities. Consequently, in all cases where the formula is presented, it has also become possible to reconcile the values associated with the NGM related to the cash flows.

Following, Table 8 provides the same information with a breakdown by country.

Table 8. Frequencies: disclosures on NGM by country

	France				Portugal				The Netherlands			
	Number		%		Number		%		%		Number	
	0	1	0	1	0	1	0	1	0	1	0	1
Relevance of the NGM disclosed	94	34	73	27	32	0	100	0	23	39	37	63
Information aimed to complement	124	4	97	3	32	0	100	0	58	4	94	6
Presentation of the formula used	4	124	3	97	12	20	37	63	4	58	6	94
Reconciliation process	4	124	3	97	12	20	37	63	4	58	6	94
	Belgium				Ireland				Norway			
	Number		%		Number		%		Number		%	
	0	1	0	1	0	1	0	1	0	1	0	1
Relevance of the NGM disclosed	21	8	72	28	16	16	50	50	10	12	45	55
Information aimed to complement	25	4	86	14	28	4	88	12	14	8	64	36
Presentation of the formula used	8	21	28	72	0	32	0	100	0	22	0	100
Reconciliation process	8	21	28	72	0	32	0	100	0	22	0	100

By country, it is noteworthy that there was no case in which the NGM relating to cash flows, disclosed by these entities from Portugal, was complemented with additional explanations. However, the information on the relevance of the NGM was mostly disclosed (more than 50%) by entities from the Netherlands, as well as from Norway and Ireland. All entities from Ireland and Norway provided the formula and the possibility of reconciliation between the NGM and their GAAP information. On the other hand, entities from Portugal and Belgium present a lower level of disclosures on those matters. Finally, Table 9 provides similar data by sector.

Table 9. Frequencies: disclosures on NGM by sector

	Telecommunications and technologies				Health care				Consumer discretionary and staples			
	Number		%		Number		%		Number		%	
	0	1	0	1	0	1	0	1	0	1	0	1
Relevance of the NGM disclosed	20	36	36	64	8	12	40	60	66	33	67	33
Information aimed to complement	44	12	79	21	16	4	80	20	95	4	96	4
Presentation of the formula used	12	44	21	79	0	20	0	100	4	95	4	96
Reconciliation process	12	44	21	79	0	20	0	100	4	95	4	96
	Industrials and basic material				Energy and utilities							
	Number		%		Number		%					
	0	1	0	1	0	1	0	1				
Relevance of the NGM disclosed	75	24	76	24	26	4	87	13				
Information aimed to complement	95	4	96	4	30	0	100	0				
Presentation of the formula used	11	88	11	89	0	30	0	100				
Reconciliation process	11	88	11	89	0	30	0	100				

According to Table 9, entities from telecommunications and technologies and health care sectors usually provided references to justify the relevance of NGM disclosed (more than 60%). No entities from the energy and utilities sectors have disclosed any indication regarding the information the NGM aimed to complement. Entities from health care and energy and utilities sectors, however, provided the NGM formula and the possibility of reconciling it with GAAP data.

The following subsection is dedicated to discussing the findings.

Discussion of Results

This subsection discusses the findings considering the literature on this topic. For this purpose, it is divided into two subsubsections according to the two objectives proposed for the comparability and understandability of the information on cash flows, respectively.

The Comparability of the Information on Cash Flows

In the context of the objective related to the comparability of the information on cash flows, proposed by this study, it was mostly identified a classification for the interest (paid or received) as OCF and the dividends paid as FCF, being, in this last case, aligned with the IASB's ED. The dividends received, in turn, are classified either as OCF or as ICF and in the latter case, the same alignment is found for dividends paid.

Therefore, and despite a global non-alignment with the IASB's ED, it is observed that, except for the dividends received, the accounting choices of the entities assessed do not present significant comparability issues as regards the matters on the SCF presentation, which is corroborated by the literature on this topic (for example, Costa et al., 2019; Maciel, et al., 2019; Morais & Martins, 2016; Silvestre & Malaquias, 2015; Scherer, et al., 2012).

The classification identified for interest (paid or received), although not aligned with the IASB's ED proposal, finds support in several studies on the subject (for instance, Costa et al., 2019, Gordon et al., 2017; Hosser et al., 2016; Kiaupaite-Grušniene & Alver, 2019; Kretzmann et al., 2015; Łazarowicz, 2019; Mafra 2016; Morais & Martins, 2016; Scherer, et al., 2012; Silva et al., 2018; Silvestre & Malaquias, 2015). As far as dividends paid are concerned, the findings can also be supported by the existing literature (for instance, Costa et al., 2019; Gordon et al., 2017; Hosser et al., 2016; Kiaupaite-Grušniene & Alver, 2019; Kretzmann et al., 2015; Łazarowicz, 2019; Mafra, 2016; Morais & Martins, 2016; Scherer, et al., 2012; Silva et al., 2018; Silvestre & Malaquias, 2015).

Regarding the method used to disclose the OCF, the findings indicated that the indirect method remains the most used, according to previous research on this topic (Clacher et al., 2013; Hosser et al., 2016; Kiaupaite-Grušniene & Alver, 2019; Łazarowicz, 2019; Nobes, 2011; Silva et al., 2018; Scherer et al., 2012). Regarding the starting point for disclosing the OCF by the indirect method, the operating profit was not used, as identified in the study by Łazarowicz (2019) and Silva (2018). Although this profit or loss measure will potentially change upon implementation of the ED, since the statement of profit or loss will also need to be revised in an aligned manner, these findings indicate a likely impact on the current presentation of SCF.

Despite being out of the scope of this explanatory research, it should be mentioned that literature has been searching for the explanatory factors of higher levels of SCF comparability, within the accounting choices theories. Among those factors, the entities' location and sector were found as relevant matters

(Costa et al., 2019; Maciel et al., 2019; Mafra, 2016; Nascimento & Zanolla, 2020; Kretzmann et al. 2015; Silva, 2018). The first is explained by their entities' alignment with local standards, in a way that allows them to increase the comparability of the information provided to different stakeholders at a national level (Andrade et al., 2017; Costa et al. 2019; Maciel et al., 2019; Silva et al., 2018). As regards the sector, a possible explanation relates to the entities' intention to improve their comparison with others sharing similar activities, to also improve the information provided to their stakeholders (Nascimento & Zanolla, 2020; Kretzmann, et al., 2015). Therefore, the findings corroborate these previous indications, since there is consistency in the presentation of the SCF according to those factors.

The next subsubsection provides the discussion of results for the objective related to the understandability of the information on cash flows.

The Understandability of the Information on Cash Flows

In the context of the objective related to the understandability of the information on cash flows, also proposed by this study, it was found that most entities disclose the NGM related to cash flows (63%), using for this purpose the free cash flow, in particular (78% of the NGM found). Few entities (less than half) provide additional explanations along with their proposed NGM. On the other hand, most entities (91%) present the formula and, simultaneously, disclose information that enables stakeholders to reconcile the values underlying the NGM to the GAAP.

Besides being widely used and disclosed, as highlighted by Brown (2020), the findings from this research on the NGM indicate that some of the suggestions proposed in the IASB's ED regarding the related disclosures are already implemented by some entities, particularly on the underlying formula and the possibility of reconciliation of information, conversely to those by Black (2016) and Marques (2010) studies. On the other hand, the implementation of IASB's ED will potentially increase the disclosure of more qualitative information, including explanations about the framework of the NGM disclosed, such as their relevance and the information it aims to complement, as highlighted by a few research found on this topic (for instance, Black, 2016; Cardeira, 2012; Hosser et al., 2016; Marques, 2010; Souza, 2020).

Again, despite being out of this research scope, it is worthwhile to mention that the literature has been also assessing the relationship between disclosure levels and possible explanatory factors, including location (Cardeira, 2012; Isidro & Marques, 2008) and sector (Baik et al., 2008; Cardeira, 2012; Isidro & Marques, 2008; Murcia & Santos, 2009). Isidro & Marques (2008), for instance, argue that the local social environment can increase NGM disclosure transparency in the sense that entities comply with stakeholders' expectations regarding higher performance in the market where they operate. Moreover, those authors found that sectors with less competition tend to exclude information that may be essential to understanding certain disclosed information. In contrast, sectors with more competition usually reconcile GAAP and non-GAAP data. Cardeira (2012), in turn, states that entities belonging to more competitive sectors should disclose more information to meet stakeholders' expectations. Based on the findings of this study, it can then be concluded that NGM disclosures are consistent with the entities' location and sector assumptions in the literature.

The next section provides the conclusions from the study carried out in this chapter, as well as its limitations and future avenues.

CONCLUSION

The empirical analysis performed in this chapter aimed to focus on the analysis of two qualitative characteristics of financial information (comparability and understandability), within the specific context of the information related to the cash flows. Data from European listed companies were assessed for this purpose and the suggestions underlying the IASB's ED current proposals were used as reference.

Regarding comparability, this research assessed the accounting choices of those entities for the presentation of different items in the SCF, given that IAS 7 currently provides distinct options. As a result, this chapter revealed that the dividend paid is the single item that is presently classified according to the IASB's ED. For the remaining items, distinct classifications than those proposed by the IASB's ED can be found. Therefore, changes can be likely expected as regards SCF for some countries and sectors.

In what concerns understandability, the analysis carried out assessed the disclosures (transparency) on the NGM related to the cash flow information. The findings showed that the entities often disclose NGM related to cash flows, especially the free cash flow, also presenting its formula and the possibility of reconciliation, as suggested by IASB's ED. Notwithstanding, the information on the relevance of such indicators as well as further explanations, as suggested in the IASB's ED, are not provided. It is therefore expected that its implementation will provide more qualitative information on the NGM provided by those entities.

To sum up, the chapter provides evidence on the likely future impacts of the ED proposed by the IASB, at the time of its implementation, mainly in matters related to the comparability and understandability of the information related to cash flows by the European entities listed.

Underlying those findings, however, some limitations should be considered. The limitation relates to the subjectivity of the analyses performed as well as, concerning the objective of comparability in particular, the difficulty of, despite being in a few cases tough, obtaining explicit information on the choices for classifying interest and dividends in the SCF.

Future investigations should be analysed by unlisted entities or include listed entities from other countries, to identify potential differences and compare the findings with those obtained in the present study. Country, sector and other explanatory factors for the accounting choices and the compliance level of disclosures related to the NGM can be also further explored by future research. Finally, it is suggested that those matters, i.e., the two objectives proposed in this study, should be explored in a post-implementation analysis of the IASB's ED.

The study presents contributions to academics and business due to its transversal approach to the analysis of the information on cash flows. Regarding the objective related to the comparability, its findings contribute to the discussion on the applicability of the IASB's ED, identifying the future implications that may arise for the entities in terms of presentation matters within the SCF. In what concerns understandability, this study provides the current disclosure items related to SCF on the NGM provided by entities and which ones need to be strengthened for the potential fulfilment of the IASB's ED.

REFERENCES

Albuquerque, F., Cariano, A., & Marques, L. (2017). Os gastos e rendimentos financeiros reportados pelas entidades cotadas em Portugal (The Financial Expenses and Incomes Reported by the Listed Entities in Portugal). *Revista Suma de Negocios*, *9*(19), 45–55. doi:10.14349umneg/2018.V9.N19.A6

Andrade, M. E. M., & da Silva, D. M. (2017). Demonstração dos Fluxos de Caixa pelo Método Direto ou Indireto? *Revista Mineira de Contabilidade, 18*(1), 5-14. https://revista.crcmg.org.br/rmc/article/view/638

Arena, C., Catuogno, S., & Moscariello, N. (2021). The unusual debate on non-GAAP reporting in the current standard practice. The lens of corporate governance. *The Journal of Management and Governance, 25*(3), 655–684. doi:10.100710997-020-09515-z

Baik, B., Billings, B., & Morton, R. (2008). Reliability and transparency of non-GAAP disclosures by real estate investment trusts (REITs). *The Accounting Review, 83*(2), 271–301. doi:10.2308/accr.2008.83.2.271

Black, E. L. (2016). O Relato Ético das Mensurações de Desempenho Não Consideradas no GAAP. *Revista Contabilidade & Finanças-USP, 27*(70), 7–11. doi:10.1590/1808-057x201690090

Brown, N. (2020). Going Public: The benefits and pitfalls of non-GAAP metrics. *Revista de Educação E Pesquisa Em Contabilidade, 14*(2), 145-157. doi:10.17524/repec.v14i2.2670

Cardeira, J. M. R. (2012). *Manipulação de resultados e a divulgação de resultados non GAAP* [Master thesis, ISCTE]. Repositorio.iscte-Iul.pt. https://repositorio.iscte-iul.pt/handle/10071/6122

Chen, H. C., Lee, Y. J., Lo, S. Y., & Yu, Y. (2021). Qualitative characteristics of non-GAAP disclosures and non-GAAP earnings quality. *Journal of Accounting and Economics, 72*(1), 101–125. doi:10.1016/j.jacceco.2021.101402

Clacher, I., Duboisée de Ricquebourg, a., & Hodgson, a. (. (2013). The value relevance of direct cash flows under IFRS. *Abacus, 49*(3), 367–395. doi:10.1111/abac.12010

Coelho, L. V. (2016). Nível de comparabilidade das práticas contábeis dos estoques de entidades brasileiras do setor de varejo listadas na bm&fbovespa [Master thesis, Repositório Institucional USCF]. https://repositorio.uSCF.br/handle/123456789/166675

Costa, P. D. S., Pinto, A. F., Nunes, F. M., & Lemes, S. (2019). Comparability of accounting choices in the statement of cash flow: Evidence from Brazil. *Contaduría y Administración, 64*(3), 1–20. doi:10.22201/fca.24488410e.2018.1445

Daga, K., Kruger, S. D., & Mazzioni, S. (2015). Demonstração dos fluxos de caixa: Controle gerencial ou obediência normativa? *Revista de Contabilidade da UFBA, 9*(1), 93–112. doi:10.9771/rcufba.v9i1.9977

Dias, C., Neves, I. R. B. D., Oliveira, J. R. S., & Martinez, A. L. (2004). *Ruídos na comunicação entre a contabilidade e os seus usuários.* Congresso USP. https://congressousp.fipecafi.org/anais/artigos42004/160.pFS

EFRAG. (2022). *Summary report and recommendations. Targeted outreach events on primary financial statements: From September to December 2022.* EFrag. https://efrag.org/news/project-626/Primary-Financial-Statements---Summary-Report-and-Recommendations---Targeted-Outreach-Roundtables

Gope, A. (2017). Accounting for Derivative Financial Instruments: An Analysis of Disclosure Determinants. *Amity Journal of Management Research, 2*(1), 10-19. https://amity.edu/UserFiles/admaa/e85baPaper%202.pFS

Gope, A., & Mitra, G. (2015). IFRS for Derivative Financial Instruments: Disclosure Level and Uniformity. *Journal of Advanced Research in Accounting & Finance Management*, *1*(2), 11–16. https://www.researchgate.net/profile/Arjun-Gope/publication/340633562_IFRS_for_Derivative_Financial_Instruments_Disclosure_Level_and_Uniformity/links/5e95f7754585150839db42da/IFRS-for-Derivative-Financial-Instruments-Disclosure-Level-and-Uniformity.pdf

Gordon, E. A., Henry, E., Jorgensen, B. N., & Linthicum, C. L. (2017). Flexibility in cash-flow classification under IFRS: Determinants and consequences. *Review of Accounting Studies*, *22*(2), 839–872. doi:10.100711142-017-9387-1

Guimarães, E. F., & Rover, S. (2018). Comparabilidade da mensuração das propriedades para investimento das companhias abertas listadas na b3: Uma análise sob a ótica dos índices T e H. *Revista Catarinense da Ciência Contábil*, *17*(52), 23–40. doi:10.16930/2237-7662/rccc.v17n52.2555

Hosser, C., Quintana, A. C., & da Cruz, A. P. C. (2016). Demonstração dos fluxos de caixa: Juros e dividendos. *Revista UNEMAT de Contabilidade*, *5*(10), 1–17. doi:10.30681/ruc.v5i10.852

IFRS Foundation. (2003). IAS 7: *Statement of Cash Flows*. IFRS. https://www.ifrs.org/issued-standards/list-of-standards/ias-7-statement-of-cash-flows/

IFRS Foundation. (2016). *Primary Financial Statements: Comment letter analysis – feedback received from the Agenda Consultation process*. IFRS. https://www.ifrs.org/content/dam/ifrs/meetings/2016/april/iasb/primary-financial-statements/ap21-comment-letter-analysis.pFS

IFRS Foundation. (2018). *Conceptual Framework for Financial Reporting*. IFRS. https://www.ifrs.org/issued-standards/list-of-standards/conceptual-framework/

IFRS Foundation. (2019). *General Presentation and Disclosures*. IFRS. https://cdn.ifrs.org/-/media/project/primary-financial-statements/exposure-draft/ed-general-presentation-disclosures.pFS

IFRS Foundation. (2020). Exposure Draft: Illustrative Examples. IFRS. https://www.ifrs.org/content/dam/ifrs/project/primary-financial-statements/exposure-draft/ed-illustrative-examples-general-presentation-disclosures.pdf

IFRS Foundation. (2020a). *Feedback summary: Subtotals and categories—general model*. IFRS. https://www.ifrs.org/content/dam/ifrs/meetings/2020/december/iasb/ap21b-pfs.pFS

IFRS Foundation. (2021). *Principles of aggregation and disaggregation and roles of the primary financial statements and the notes*. IFRS. https://www.ifrs.org/content/dam/ifrs/meetings/2021/april/iasb/ap21a-primary-financial-statements.pFS

IFRS Foundation. (2021a). *Primary Financial Statements: Plan for redeliberations*. IFRS. https://www.ifrs.org/content/dam/ifrs/meetings/2021/january/iasb/ap21-primary-financial-statements.pFS

IFRS Foundation. (2021b). *Primary Financial Statements: Scope of management performance measures.* IFRS. https://www.ifrs.org/content/dam/ifrs/meetings/2021/june/iasb/ap21a-scope-of-management-performance-measures.pFS

IFRS Foundation. (2021c). *Primary Financial Statements: Statement of cash flows.* IFRS. https://www.ifrs.org/content/dam/ifrs/meetings/2021/january/iasb/ap21b-primary-financial-statements.pFS

IFRS Foundation. (2021d). *Primary Financial Statements: Paper topic- Associates and Joint Ventures.* IFRS. https://www.ifrs.org/content/dam/ifrs/meetings/2021/september/iasb/ap21f-pfs-associates-and-jvs.pFS

IFRS Foundation. (2022). *Global Preparers Forum: Primary Financial Statements.* IFRS. https://www.ifrs.org/content/dam/ifrs/meetings/2022/november/gpf/ap4-pfs-gpf-nov-2022.pFS

Isidro, H., & Marques, A. (2008). Industry competition and non-GAAP disclosures. *Accounting and Business Research, 51*(2), 156–184. doi:10.1080/00014788.2020.1798209

Jacinto, J. M. (2019). *Compliance do reporte de informações Non-GAAP e a presença do comitê de auditoria.* [Master thesis, Universidade Federal Da Paraíba] Repositório UFPB. https://repositorio.ufpb.br/jspui/handle/123456789/17298

Kiaupaite-Grušniene, V., & Alver, L. (2019). Comparability of cash flow statements: Evidence from Baltic Countries. *Accounting and Management Information Systems, 18*(3), 307–329. doi:10.24818/jamis.2019.03001

Kretzmann, C., Teuteberg, T., & Zülch, H. (2015, Maio-21). *Comparability of Reported Cash Flows Under IFRS: Evidence from Germany.* [Conference session]. International Conference Corporate and Institutional Innovations in Finance and Governance, Paris. http://www.virtusinterpress.org/IMG/pFS/10-22495_cocv12i4csp11.pFS

Łazarowicz, E. (2019). The comparability of IFRS statements of cash flows in Poland. The influence of national regulations. *Zeszyty Teoretyczne Rachunkowości, 157*(101), 149–166. doi:10.5604/01.3001.0013.0760

Macedo, M. A. D. S., Machado, M. R., Murcia, F. D. R., & Machado, M. A. V. (2011). Análise da relevância do Ebitda versus fluxo de caixa operacional no mercado brasileiro de capitais. *ASAA-Advances in Scientific and Applied Accounting, 5*(1), 99-130. https://asaa.anpcont.org.br/index.php/asaa/article/view/72

Maciel, F. F. D. S., Salotti, B. M., & Imoniana, J. O. (2019). Incentivos para opções contábeis na demonstração dos fluxos de caixa. *Revista Contabilidade & Finanças, 31*(2), 244–261. doi:10.1590/1808-057x201908670

Mafra, R. M. (2016). *Escolha contábil na classificação dos juros pagos na Demonstração dos Fluxos de Caixa de empresas listadas na BM&FBovespano período de 2010 a 2015.* [Master thesis, Universidade Federal de Santa Catarina] Repositório USCF. https://repositorio.uSCF.br/handle/123456789/172496

Magro, N. (2014). *A comparabilidade das demonstrações financeiras na Europa.* [Master thesis, ISCTE Business School]. Repositóro ISCTE. https://repositorio.iscte-iul.pt/handle/10071/8695

Marques, A. (2010). Disclosure strategies among s&p 500 firms: Evidence on the disclosure of non-GAAP financial measures and financial statements in earnings Press releases. *The British Accounting Review*, *42*(2), 119–131. doi:10.1016/j.bar.2010.02.004

Morais, V. O., & Martins, V. F. (2016). Opções Contábeis na Evidenciação da Demonstração dos Fluxos de Caixa de Empresas do Setor de Energia Elétrica da BM&FBOVESPA. *Revista de Auditoria, Governança e* Contabilidade, *4*(13), 162-172. https://revistas.fucamp.edu.br/index.php/ragc/article/view/796

Murcia, F., & Santos, A. (2009). Fatores determinantes do nível de disclosure voluntário das companhias abertas no Brasil. *Revista de Educação e Pesquisa em Contabilidade*, *3*(2), 72–95. doi:10.17524/repec.v3i2.68

Nascimento, D. F., & Zanolla, E. (2020). Accounting Choices in the Cash Flow Statement: Analysis in Latin American Companies. *Journal of Accounting. Management and Governance*, *23*(3), 424–441. doi:10.51341/1984-3925_2020v23n3a8

Neto, A. M. D. N. (2020). *Informações GAAP e Non-GAAP: um estudo sobre o value relevance do EBITDA e fluxo de caixa operacional.* [Trabalho final de curso, Universidade Federal Da Paraíba] Repositório UFPB. https://repositorio.ufpb.br/jspui/handle/123456789/17401

Nobes, C. (2011). IFRS practices and the persistence of accounting system classification. *A Journal of Accounting. Abacus*, *47*(3), 267–283. doi:10.1111/j.1467-6281.2011.00341.x

Oliveira, H. M. S., Lopes, C. M. F. P., & da Silva, C. A. (2008). A transparência da informação por parte dos emitentes. *Revista Universo Contábil*, *4*(2), 93–104. doi:10.4270/ruc.20084

Oliveira, S. R. S. (2017). *A demonstração de fluxos de caixa como instrumento estratégico de gestão.* [Tese de doutoramento, Instituto Politécnico de Coimbra]. Repositório comum. https://comum.rcaap.pt/handle/10400.26/21157

Regulation (EC) No. 1606/2002 of the European Parliament and of the Council of 19 July 2002 on the application of international accounting standards. https://op.europa.eu/pt/publication-detail/-/publication/063990c7-2ce2-4e5c-b0cc-5eba713d7d08/language-en

Rodrigues, D. (2019). *Comparação do nível de divulgação de elementos da demonstração da posição financeira das entidades do PSI-20.* [Master thesis, ISCAL]. Repositório Científico IPL. https://repositorio.ipl.pt/handle/10400.21/12878

Santos, E. M. D., Lima, J. D. D., & Bonfim, M. P. (2021). Demonstrações Financeiras Primárias: Impactos das Mudanças Propostas pelo IASB. *Pensar contábil, 1*(2), 1-15. http://atena.org.br/revista/ojs-2.2.3-06/index.php/pensarcontabil/article/viewFile/3613/2738

Scherer, L. M., Teodoro, J. D., Anjos, R. P., & Kos, S. R. (2012). Demonstração dos fluxos de caixa: Análise de diferenças de procedimentos de divulgação entre empresas listadas nas bolsas de valores de São Paulo, Frankfurt, Milão e Londres. *Revista Contabilidade e Controladoria*, *4*(2), 37–51. doi:10.5380/rcc.v4i2.29025

Silva, D. M. D., Martins, V. A., & Lima, F. G. (2018). Opções Contábeis na Evidenciação da Demonstração dos Fluxos de Caixa. *Revista de Auditoria e Governança de Contabilidade*, *4*(13), 162–172. doi:10.5007/2175-8069.2018v15n36p143

Silva, K. R. D. (2020). *Fluxo de caixa e suas contribuições na geração de informações gerenciaSPL: um estudo de caso na Guararapes Confecções S/A*. [Master thesis, Universidade Federal do Rio Grande do Norte]. Repositório UFRN. https://repositorio.ufrn.br/handle/123456789/41253

Silvestre, L. N., & Malaquias, R. F. (2015). Classificação dos juros e dividendos na Demonstração dos Fluxos de Caixa das empresas brasileiras. *Revista ambiente contábil, 7*(2), 119-134. https://ojs.ccsa.ufrn.br/index.php/contabil/article/view/547

Souza, F. J. V. D. (2020). *Compreensibilidade da informação contábil por usuários tomadores de decisão.* [Tese de doutoramento, Universidade Federal da Paraíba Centro de Ciências Sociais Aplicadas] Repositório Institucional UFPB. https://repositorio.ufpb.br/jspui/handle/123456789/18314

Taplin, R. H. (2011). The Measurement of Comparability in Accounting Research. *A Journal of Accounting*. *Abacus*, *47*(3), 383–409. doi:10.1111/j.1467-6281.2011.00345.x

Chapter 5
An Integrative View of Corporate Transparency in Family Businesses

María-Pilar Martín-Zamora
Lusófona University, Portugal

Joao Miguel Borralho
https://orcid.org/0000-0003-2860-0692
Lusofona University, Portugal

Remedios Hernández-Linares
https://orcid.org/0000-0001-7836-4670
Universidad de Extremadura, Spain

ABSTRACT

Transparency is a key factor in ensuring family firms' commercial success and establishing and nurturing trust among stakeholders, including managers and teams. However, transparency appears to depend on business contexts and, more specifically, on family members' involvement in these companies, which helps explain researchers' growing interest in corporate transparency in family firms. This chapter examines the most relevant literature on this topic to provide an integrative overview of studies of transparency practices in family businesses and identify the main research gaps that comprise paths for future investigations. To this end, a non-systematic compilation and review was conducted of 50 related articles published in journals included in the Academic Journal Guide 2021. Content analysis revealed that the majority are based on empirical research focusing on the quality of information disclosed via earnings management. The most significant findings are discussed in this chapter, including research questions to be answered in further studies of this topic.

DOI: 10.4018/978-1-6684-7293-4.ch005

INTRODUCTION

Corporate transparency has been defined as 'the availability of firm-specific information to those outside publicly traded firms' (Bushman et al., 2004, p. 207). Another possible definition is 'the widespread availability of relevant information on the performance, financial position, investment opportunities, governance, value . . ., and risks of [the] listed entity' (Fülöp, 2014, p. 228). A more recent definition is 'the visibility of the company's internal situation relative to external investors. . . . [I]ts focus is the external investors' grasp of the nature of the company' (Wu et al., 2022, p. 2567). These quotations provide just three examples of the plethora of definitions available.

Most authors have emphasised corporate transparency's importance in terms of supporting corporate governance structures. This transparency ensures that companies can provide shareholders with reliable information about the firm's worth and activities and motivates managers to maximise company values rather than pursue personal objectives (Bushman et al., 2004; Vaccaro & Madsen, 2009). However, corporate transparency appears to depend on business contexts and, more specifically, on family versus non-family businesses (Borralho et al., 2020b, 2022).

This variability is unsurprising as the literature reveals a strong consensus among scholars about family firms' singular environments (e.g. Gómez-Mejía et al., 2007; Habbershon & Williams, 1999; Habbershon et al., 2003). For example, owners and managers' interests are closely aligned in family businesses (Wang, 2006), which combines with these firms' long-term orientation to create incentives for developing more powerful governance structures (Liu et al., 2016). In addition, the relationships between companies and their stakeholders are closer in family than non-family businesses (Block & Wagner, 2014). These and other distinctive features have inspired researchers to focus on family firms' transparency (e.g. Borralho et al., 2020a, 2020b, 2022; Chen et al., 2014; Paiva et al., 2019; Zhong et al., 2022).

The present study sought to integrate the knowledge generated thus far by researchers' increasing interest in the convergence of corporate transparency and family business (e.g. Borralho et al., 2022; Corten et al., 2021; Umans & Corten, 2022; Zhong et al., 2022) for two reasons. First, scholars widely acknowledge the problems created by multiple interpretations of what constitutes transparency (Biondi & Lapsley, 2014; Heald, 2006). Second, the literature on family firms' transparency practices is spread across quite diverse journals covering multiple fields (e.g. management, business, finance and accounting).

Thus, the current study's main objectives were to review the main contributions of publications on family businesses' corporate transparency and to offer an integrative view of the relevant literature's state of the art. The goal was to generate a fuller understanding of this subject and challenge scholars to conduct research on the 'black holes' still left in the available knowledge. That is, the overall objective was to go beyond a simple systematic literature review and integrate different interpretations and ways of analysing corporate transparency in family business contexts in order to identify future lines of research based on the gaps identified and thus stimulate further studies.

This chapter contributes to the literature in at least two ways. The first contribution consists of identifying and amalgamating relevant papers that have shaped the current state of the art of research on family businesses' corporate transparency. The results provide a holistic guide that should be useful to both practitioners and academics. The second contribution is that, building on the review of prior literature, the findings provide a better understanding of both the gaps in and limitations of the current knowledge. Potential avenues for future research are presented that could offer meaningful ways to consolidate this field of study further.

The remainder of the chapter is structured as follows. The above introduction identified the research gaps and presented the main goals. The next section explores the corporate transparency concept and explains why transparency scholars need to pay attention to family business contexts. Section three describes the literature review conducted and the studies covered. Section four summarises prior research on the convergence between corporate transparency and family business, and section five presents suggestions for future research. The concluding section discusses this study's contributions and limitations.

FRAMEWORK

Corporate Transparency

The vast majority of scholars take the concept of corporate transparency for granted, assuming that this idea is common knowledge and thus that no further description or more detailed explanation is required (Wehmeier & Raaz, 2012). In reality, the literature offers many diverse definitions of corporate transparency (see Table 1 for specific examples), most of which emphasise the intentional, voluntary and free disclosure of business information (i.e. the volume of detail disclosed) (e.g. Fülöp, 2014; Seyoum, 2009). However, transparency not only relies on the volume of information provided (Albu & Flyverbom, 2019) but also on the quality of the details reported. This point is emphasised by Bushman and Smith (2003), among other authors, when discussing company reports' reliability. Corporate transparency depends on information disclosure and, more directly, the provided details' quality, quantity, transmission and degree of observability (Albu & Flyverbom, 2019).

Table 1. Corporate transparency definitions

Author(s) (year, page)	Definition
Bushman & Smith (2003, p. 66)	'the widespread availability of sufficient, relevant, and reliable information about the periodic performance, financial position, investment opportunities, governance, value, and risk of firms'
Bushman et al. (2004, p. 207)	'the availability of firm-specific information to those outside publicly traded firms'
Ali et al. (2007, p. 240)	'[the] disclos[ure of] more information about their [the company's] corporate governance practices in their proxy statements'
Seyoum (2009, p. 30)	'the degree to which companies regularly reveal substantial information about their financial condition and accounting practices to outsiders and the government in a reliable manner'
Vaccaro & Madsen (2009, p. 115)	'the widespread availability of relevant and reliable information about such aspects as short and long-term performance, financial position, investment opportunities, governance, value and risk'
Kim et al. (2012, p. 790)	'[the] financial transparency . . . associated with ethics and reputation as factors affecting corporate financial reporting'
Fülöp (2014, p. 228)	'the widespread availability of relevant information on the performance, financial position, investment opportunities, governance, value . . ., and risks of [the] listed entity'
Bozzolan et al. (2015, p. 363)	'[the] transparency . . . expected to be a tool of accountability because it enables stakeholders to confront companies and collectively organise against them if necessary'
Baraibar-Díez et al. (2017, p. 484)	'[the] availability of company specific information to those who are outside listed companies'
Heinberg et al. (2021, p. 47)	'a firm trait that determines whether the information provided is objective and accessible to its stakeholders'
Wu et al. (2022, p. 2567)	'the visibility of the company's internal situation relative to external investors, and its focus . . . [on] the external investors' grasp of the nature of the company'
Yuan et al. (2022, p. 3)	'nonfinancial information disclosure [that] helps reduce information asymmetry and investors' uncertainty . . . [and] related information [that] plays a complementary role for financial information, [by] contributing to higher transparency'

High-profile corporate scandals (e.g. Enron in 2001, WorldCom in 2002, Lehman Brothers in 2008, Madoff Investment Securities in 2009, Banco Espírito Santo in 2014 and Wirecard in 2020) have made transparency an increasingly prominent area of research (Etzioni, 2010; Mohammadi & Nezhad, 2015; Schnackenberg & Tomlinson, 2016) whose findings permeate many contemporary sociopolitical discourses (Albu & Flyverbom, 2019). This trend is unsurprising given that corporate transparency is a key factor in companies' ability to generate trust among stakeholders (Bidabad et al., 2017; Hultman & Axelsson, 2007; Plumlee et al., 2015; Schnackenberg & Tomlinson, 2016; Williams, 2005) and a source of other important benefits for organisations. For example, this transparency has a positive impact on liquidity (Goldstein et al., 2007), decreases information asymmetry (Chang et al., 2007; Chiyachantana et al., 2013), boosts firms' value (Gu & Hackbarth, 2013; Li et al., 2018; Liu et al., 2022) and improves employee engagement (Men & Hung-Baesecke, 2015).

The literature reports that corporate transparency depends on company contexts and, more specifically, businesses' family or non-family nature (e.g. Ali et al., 2007; Chen et al., 2008; Palma et al., 2022). Family firms can be defined as those 'in which the family, . . . [more] broadly defined, either has significant ownership or management control' (Lee, 2006, p. 104). Family members' involvement in family businesses appears to affect these organisations' corporate transparency, as explained in greater detail in the next subsection.

Corporate Transparency and Family Businesses

Family firms are usually managed by the founding families and their descendants (Anderson & Reeb, 2003; Martins & André, 2013; Villalonga et al., 2015). This feature generates significant differences between family and non-family businesses' agency problems (Ben-Amar & André, 2006; Cheng, 2014; Li & Zuo, 2020; Schulze et al., 2001; Villalonga et al., 2015). For instance, majority shareholders in family businesses are less often exposed to severe Type I agency problems as compared to shareholders in non-family firms (Ang et al., 2000; Basheer et al., 2021; Li & Zuo, 2020). The family's greater proximity to their business can also result in closer supervision of managers and thus prevent their engagement in opportunistic behaviours (Ali et al., 2007; Corte et al., 2021). However, these companies face a higher risk of expropriation by controlling shareholders who may become entrenched and seek to extract private benefits (Claessens et al., 2002; Li & Zuo, 2020; Morck et al., 1988; Purkayastha et al., 2022; Shleifer & Vishny, 1997; Villalonga & Amit, 2006).

Given the above findings, researchers have concluded that discrepancies in agency issues produce different corporate transparency patterns in family versus non-family firms (Ali et al., 2007; Chaudhary et al., 2021; Chen et al., 2008, 2014; Wan-Hussin, 2009). The present study thus focused on family business contexts because of not only their economic importance (Pieper et al., 2021; Prencipe et al., 2014; Sharma et al., 2012) but also, more importantly, their uniqueness (Carney et al., 2015; Cunha et al., 2021; Gómez-Mejía et al., 2007; Habbershon & Williams, 1999; Habbershon et al., 2003; Sirmon & Hitt, 2003). The current research examined how the family business literature has dealt with corporate transparency policies and practices.

METHODOLOGY

A non-systematic literature review was conducted to explore how scholars have addressed family business transparency. This type of review does not require systematic procedures to select (Gaspar et al., 2019), analyse and summarise the existing knowledge, but clear criteria were adopted to identify pertinent publications, that is, a search of the Web of Science and Google Scholar ending with 13 April 2023. More specifically, the search identified and selected the most relevant articles published on the research topic so far. Books, book chapters and grey literature were excluded because only publications in peer-reviewed journals were considered validated knowledge (Podsakoff et al., 2005).

The high quality of the studies reviewed was ensured – as is commonly done in family business research (e.g. Hernández-Linares & López-Fernández, 2018) – by limiting the search and selection processes to articles published in English-language peer-reviewed journals. These criteria were imposed for two reasons. First, these journals follow blind review procedures, which is a standard quality control mechanism used to guide the creation and validation of new knowledge (Akram et al., 2022). These publications are considered by scholars to be the only validated knowledge and are expected to have the largest impact on academic discourse (Podsakoff et al., 2005). Second, English-language peer-reviewed journals tend to be more accessible to international readers (Xiao et al., 2022).

In addition, the review only included articles published in academic journals listed in the *Academic Journal Guide* as a way to guarantee quality publications as other scholars have done before in reviews (e.g. Balzano, 2022). The *Academic Journal Guide* is compiled by the Chartered Association of Business Schools and is a widely accepted journal list in the business and management fields (Wu et al., 2018).

More specifically, the *Academic Journal Guide 2021* was used,[1] which was the most up-to-date version at the time the present research was conducted.

The search process resulted in a list of 50 articles, which were included in the literature review. The earliest publication was Fan and Wong's (2002) article. This chapter thus covers the most relevant literature on family firms' corporate transparency from 2002 to 2023, although 2023 had not ended when the study was completed.

DISCUSSION OF RESULTS

The results reveal that the literature on family businesses' corporate transparency can be grouped into two categories: the (1) quantity and (2) quality of information disclosed (Albu & Flyverbom, 2019). Content analysis also identified a third set of papers focused on strategic issues that may affect family firms' corporate transparency. Each category is discussed in greater detail below.

Quantity of Information Disclosed

Disclosure is the principal means by which companies can become transparent (Solomon, 2007). Firms may divulge information via mandatory annual reports, but businesses can also provide additional information voluntarily. The first group of articles identified in the present review focuses on whether family firms disclose more or less information than non-family firms do (see Table 2). These studies have produced contradictory findings.

Table 2. Main research on quantity of information disclosed

Author(s) (year)	Study type	Short sample description	Main findings/conclusions
Fan & Wong (2002)	E/Qt	977 East Asian firms from 1991 to 1995	Firms with concentrated ownership have low earnings informativeness as they avoid disclosing proprietary information about their rent-seeking activities.
Chen et al. (2008)	E/Qt	Standard & Poor's 1500 index from 1996 to 2000	FBs are less likely to provide management forecasts than non-FBs, whether good or bad trends are forecasted. FBs are less likely than non-FBs to use conference calls as a voluntary disclosure channel. FBs are also less inclined to issue long-run forecast and short-run good news forecasts, but these firms are more likely to issue warnings of bad news about earnings.
Chau & Gray (2010)	E/Qt	273 listed firms in Hong Kong in 2002	Voluntary disclosure is relatively low at moderate to low levels of family shareholding (i.e. 25% or less). More family shareholding is associated with a stronger entrenchment effect and higher voluntary disclosure.
Vural (2018)	E/Qt	314 Swedish publicly listed firms from 2001 to 2010, of which 163 are FBs	FBs are less forthcoming regarding overall disclosure than non-FBs are, especially information about corporate governance matters.
Louie et al. (2019)	E/Qt	120 Australian firms of which 60 are FBs and 60 are non-FBs, randomly chosen from 2001 to 2006	FBs disclose information voluntarily to signal to the market their growth potential and abide by government regulations to improve their reputation.
Zaini et al. (2019)	E/Ql&Qt	Malaysian listed companies for the 2009–2013 period	FBs tend to disclose information voluntarily about external factors and global conditions. Most FBs also provide financial warnings in their releases.
Gjergji et al. (2021)	E/Qt	132 Italian listed SMEs	ESG disclosure for SMEs tends to provoke an increase in capital costs, yet this pattern is reversed for FBs.
Boubaker et al. (2022)	E/Qt	French listed firms during the 2007–2013 period	FBs in which the founding family does not have full control can use voluntary disclosure as a tool for reducing tax avoidance activities. Family control below 40% has a significant negative effect on voluntary disclosures of tax avoidance practices.
Palma et al. (2022)	E/Qt	360 companies from 17 European countries, of which 180 are FBs and 180 are non-FBs	FBs attach greater importance to sustainability reporting than non-FBs do. Corporate websites attribute this emphasis to sustainability issues when the FBs' CEO is a family member and family ownership levels are lower.
Rahman & Zheng (2022)	E/Qt	Chinese listed companies for the 2010–2020 period	Family ownership influences the positive relationship between corporate social responsibility and earnings management. Compared with non-FBs, FBs tend to disclose less ESG performance but engage in fewer accrual-based earnings management behaviours.
Ma (2023)	E/Qt	Chinese listed firms from 2009 to 2016	FBs disclose significantly more information about their ESG activities than non-FBs do. The positive relationship between FBs and more transparent ESG disclosure exists mainly in FBs with relatively high state ownership, which helps mitigate government expropriation risks.

Note: CEO = chief executive office; E = empirical; ESG = environmental, social and governance disclosure; FB = family business; Ql = qualitative; Qt = quantitative; SMEs = small and medium-sized enterprises.

On the one hand, family businesses' management is usually consigned to the founding family and its members (Anderson & Reeb, 2003; Martins & André, 2013; Villalonga et al., 2015), so they are in a better position than other stakeholders to access information about the firm. Scholars have thus argued that family firms have fewer incentives to disclose information voluntarily (Chau & Gray, 2010). In this vein, some studies have confirmed that family businesses disclose less overall information than non-family firms do (Chen et al., 2008; Zaini et al., 2019), especially about corporate governance matters (Vural, 2018) and environmental, social and governance (ESG) performance (Rahman & Zheng, 2022).

However, family businesses' environmental disclosure is positively associated with their capital costs (Gjergji et al., 2021). This group of articles also provides empirically robust evidence that family firms are more likely to provide warnings of bad news about earnings due to the family owners' greater concerns about litigation and reputation damage, but these companies are less likely to report earnings forecasts. The latter could be explained by both lower information asymmetry between owners and managers and family owners' desire to avoid the potential cost of providing timely information (Chen et al., 2008).

On the other hand, the researchers in this category state that family firms can be more inclined to engage in activities that conform to stakeholder disclosure standards because of the owners' concerns about social capital and reputation (Liu et al., 2016). Various studies have found that family businesses provide more information than non-family firms do to signal to the market their potential for growth and to comply with government regulations in order to improve their reputation (Louie et al., 2019; Ma, 2023). The results thus corroborate that family businesses use corporate social responsibility (CSR) disclosure to legitimise their behaviour (Ma, 2023).

All the publications included in this first category (see Table 2 above) indicate that family firms show heterogeneous behaviours regarding the quantity of information disclosed, which may be due to these companies' different levels of family ownership. More specifically, Chau and Gray's (2010) empirical research provided evidence that, when the family's shareholding falls below 25%, the degree of voluntary disclosure is relatively low, while higher percentages are associated with more voluntary disclosure.

Quality of Information Disclosed

The present review identified a second group of articles that assess corporate transparency based on the quality of information disclosed. The disclosed details' quality can be defined as the degree to which investors can easily read and understand the reported details (Hopkins, 1996). Earnings management affects firms' value when information asymmetry exists between managers and investors who are focused on serving private interests (Chaney & Lewis, 1995), so the quality of disclosed information has often been studied via earnings management quality (see Table 3).

Table 3. Main research on family firms' earnings disclosure quality

Author(s) (year)	Study type	Short sample description	Main findings/conclusions
Ali et al. (2007)	E/Qt	S&P 500 firms	FBs report better quality earnings. They are more likely to issue warnings for significantly bad news, but FBs make fewer disclosures about their corporate governance practices.
Prencipe et al. (2008)	E/Qt	44 Italian listed companies with research and development activities	FBs are less affected by income-smoothing motivations, while they are similar to other companies in being inclined to manage earnings to alleviate debt covenant concerns.
Cascino et al. (2010)	E/Qt	778 nonfinancial listed Italian firms for the 1998–2004 period, of which 507 are FBs and 271 non-FBs	FBs have a higher accruals quality compared to non-FBs. The family's presence rather than its ownership concentration has beneficial effects on accounting information quality.
Stockmans et al. (2010)	E/Qt	132 Flemish FBs	SEW can play a role as a motive for upward earnings management when firms perform poorly. First-generation and founder-led private FBs appear to have greater incentives to engage in upward earnings management in order to preserve their SEW.
Setia-Atmaja et al. (2011)	E/Qt	Australian listed firms from 2000 to 2004	A higher proportion of independent directors on FB boards reduce earnings management. FB managers are also less aggressive in managing earnings via discretionary long-term accruals than non-FBs are.
Pazzaglia et al. (2013)	E/Qt	All nonfinancial firms listed on the Milan Stock Exchange from 1995 to 2008	Firms acquired by families through market transactions display lower earnings quality due to the new owners' lower firm identification compared to companies still owned by founding families. Acquired FBs' earnings quality improves with a nonfamily CEO, while non-acquired FBs benefit from having a family CEO.
Stockmans et al. (2013)	E/Qt	79 Belgian FBs	In private FBs, the potential presence of agency conflicts moderates the relationship between board characteristics and earnings management.
Achleitner et al. (2014)	E/Qt	402 German listed companies, of which 402 are FBs and 436 non-FBs	FBs use earnings management activities strategically, avoiding those that inhibit the firm's long-term value (i.e. real earnings management) and engaging in activities that help family owners retain transgenerational control (i.e. accrual-based earnings management).
Martin et al. (2016)	E/Qt	S&P 500 firms in the United States	Earnings management's potential reputational consequences lead FBs to engage in these practices less often than non-FBs do, and founder FBs are less likely than non-founder FBs to use earnings management.
Paiva et al. (2016)	LR	Not applicable	This literature review focuses on earnings management in FBs, using agency theory as its main theoretical framework. The authors call for further research on earnings management in different types of FBs, more qualitative and experimental research and theoretical frameworks better able to capture FBs' peculiarities.
Rodríguez-Ariza et al. (2016)	E/Qt	1,169 listed companies for the 2006–2010 period from 20 countries	FBs have more incentives for controlling and monitoring managerial decisions, avoiding information asymmetries and thus minimising earnings management and the potential loss of reputation. A negative link exists between family control and earnings management.

Continued on following page

Table 3. Continued

Author(s) (year)	Study type	Short sample description	Main findings/conclusions
Vieira (2016)	E/Qt	All Portuguese nonfinancial listed companies on the Euronext Lisbon from 1999 to 2011	No significant differences appear between public FBs and non-FBs' incentives to manage earnings, suggesting that theoretical adjustments are needed to explain the interactions between the entrenchment effect and the goal alignment hypothesis, FBs' long-term orientation and their desire to pass the business on to future generations.
Duréndez & Madrid-Guijarro (2018)	E/Qt	252 Spanish family small and medium-sized enterprises	To promote financial reporting quality, FBs should increase family involvement in terms of company culture and business experience but limit family members' power inside the company.
Ferramosca & Allegrini (2018)	E/Qt	793 Italian firms	An inverted U-shaped relationship exists between discretionary accruals and family involvement in FBs' management and control.
Paiva et al. (2019)	E/Qt	1,043 United Kingdom listed firms	FBs have higher levels of earnings management as compared to non-FBs except for when FBs are monitored by a significant number of analysts.
Borralho et al. (2020a)	E/Qt	263 audited Spanish companies	FBs are less prone to earnings management practices than non-FBs are. The association between FBs' status and earnings management is moderated by the generation in charge.
Borralho et al. (2020b)	E/Qt	650 large Spanish firms	FBs' earnings quality is higher than that of non-FBs. This tendency is reinforced by a different president and CEO, the proportion of female board of director members and the use of non-Big 4 audit firms.
Corten et al. (2021)	E/Qt	218 managers of 37 private FBs	Private FBs' earnings management can be increased by differences in SEW goals among members of top management teams. Earnings management is mainly regarded as a mechanism to cover poor team performance due to these conflicting goals.
Borralho et al. (2022)	E/Qt	114 listed companies, of which 77 are from France and 37 from Spain	All ESG disclosure dimensions are not equally important in terms of reducing earnings management. The association between ESG disclosure and earnings management is affected by companies' family or non-family status.
Brahem et al. (2022)	E/Qt	French listed firms from 2005 to 2016	Firms committed to CSR activities are more likely to provide high earnings quality. The positive association between CSR performance and earnings quality is stronger in FBs.
Chen et al. (2022)	E/Qt	Nonfinancial FBs listed on the Taiwan and Taipei Stock Exchanges between 2005 and 2014	FBs' disclosure quality is, at least partly, determined by their level of control-ownership divergence. Greater control-ownership divergence causes FBs to improve their credit ratings via better disclosure quality achieved by hiring a Big-4 auditor.
Umans and Corten (2022)	E/Qt	331 Belgian private FBs	FBs seeking to transfer ownership to non-family members engage in more earnings management than FBs planning to transfer ownership to family members.
Zhong et al. (2022)	E/Qt	Chinese A-share listed FBs for the 2008–2017 period	FBs dominated by founders are unlikely to engage in earnings management activities. This link is enhanced by industry growth and weakened by industry competition.

Note: CEO = chief executive office; CSR = corporate social responsibility; E = empirical; ESG = environmental, social and governance disclosure; FB = family business; LR = literature review; Qt = quantitative; SEW = socioemotional wealth; S&P = Standard and Poor's.

The articles in this group include studies that have focused on family and non-family firms, which mostly report that family businesses present higher earnings quality than non-family firms do (Borralho et al., 2020a, 2020b; Cascino et al., 2010; Martín et al., 2016; Rodríguez-Ariza et al., 2016). Achleitner et al. (2014) qualify their findings by observing that, as family members can be more concerned about their firm's transgenerational sustainability, the level of real earnings management in family businesses is lower than in non-family firms due to these practices' negative implications for future value. The cited authors add that family businesses have more negative accruals than non-family firms because lower reported earnings can, for instance, reduce pressure from shareholders to pay higher dividends. In addition, this strategy helps the family retain more value for future investments and their business survive in the long run.

Contrary to most researchers in this category, Vieira (2016) reports no significant differences exist between public family and non-family firms regarding incentives to manage earnings. Paiva et al. (2019) further found that family firms have higher levels of earnings management than non-family businesses do, unless the former are tracked by multiple analysts. The literature on corporate transparency in family and non-family firms also reveals that the relationship between ESG disclosure and earnings management is stronger in family businesses (Borralho et al., 2022).

However, not all family firms appear to display the same earnings quality. Studies that have concentrated on family firms exclusively have verified that these organisations are more concerned about preserving or increasing socioemotional wealth (SEW) (Corten et al., 2021; Stockmans et al., 2010) or being more socially responsible (Brahem et al., 2022), which can promote earnings quality. Similarly, earnings management has potential reputational consequences that make founder-owned firms less likely than other types of family firms to use this strategy (Martín et al., 2016). The latter finding confirms that family businesses dominated by the founders are unlikely to engage in earnings management activities (Zhong et al., 2022).

In addition, Chen et al. (2022) report that the quality of information disclosed is, at least partly, determined by the level of divergence between family firm ownership and control. Duréndez and Madrid-Guijarro (2018), in turn, used the Family Influence on Power, Experience, and Culture scale (Astrachan et al., 2002) to examine family firm heterogeneity via the family's influence on earnings management practices. Their study found that, to strengthen financial reporting quality, family firms need to promote family members' involvement in terms of company culture and work experience, as well as limiting their power inside the organisation.

KEY FACTORS THAT PROMOTE FAMILY BUSINESS CORPORATE TRANSPARENCY

The present literature review also found a set of papers that highlighted three key strategy-related variables that can improve family businesses' corporate transparency (Craig & Moores, 2005; Dello Sbarba & Marelli 2010, 2018; Kang et al., 2015): using risk management techniques, holding family managers accountable and utilising the balanced scorecard (BSC). The latter is a performance measurement and management methodology that translates firms' mission and strategies into objectives and initiatives in four dimensions: finance, customers, internal business and opportunities to learn and growth (Kang et al., 2015, p. 126).

Family managers are bound to their company by kinship, trust, strong firm identification and deep emotional investment in the business (Dello Sbarba & Marelli, 2018). This natural alignment among family managers may lead some firms to dispense with management tools that encourage greater transparency (Liu et al., 2016). However, management and control instruments, such as strategic planning, are critical for family businesses that are more concerned about preserving their image and good reputation (Deephouse & Jaskiewicz, 2013) because they need to inspire trust in their stakeholders (Craig & Moores, 2005).

In this context, the BSC is a strategic tool for aligning varied interests at all organisational levels around the firm's mission, vision, objectives and performance measures, allowing managers to report results more easily (Craig & Moores, 2005, 2010). Including financial and non-financial objectives helps reconcile family and business interests, which may promote more open and shared decisions. This strategy has a positive effect on corporate transparency, as shown by the studies summarised in Table 4 (Kang et al., 2015).

Table 4. Main research on risk management, accountability and BSC in family firms

Author(s) (year)	Study type	Short sample description	Main findings/conclusions
Craig & Moores (2005)	E/Ql	1 Australian retail industry FB	The BSC can help businesses develop and facilitate communication among FB staff members.
Craig & Moores (2010)	E/Ql	1 third-generation Australian FB	The BSC ensures that employees understand new developments in the mission, strategies, objectives, measures and goals. This tool facilitates communication within and outside companies, and changes can be more easily scrutinised by multiple stakeholders.
Kang et al. (2015)	E/Ql	2 family-owned hotels	CSR has a positive impact on FB performance and encourages firms to use the BSC to facilitate meaningful, transparent communication across diverse stakeholder groups.
Dello Sbarba & Marelli (2018)	E/Ql	1 Italian FB operating in different industries	Financial management practices can provide accountability mechanisms for family managers and influence FBs' ability to survive, grow and succeed.
Note: BSC = balanced scorecard; CSR = corporate social responsibility; E = empirical; FB = family business; Ql = qualitative.			

FUTURE LINES OF RESEARCH

This chapter presents a first attempt to review comprehensively and integrate the results reported in the literature on corporate transparency in family businesses. To confirm this review's findings are empirically robust, researchers need to conduct more systematic reviews of this literature. In addition, six research questions (RQ) should be addressed to expand the knowledge about corporate transparency's antecedents and outcomes in family firm contexts.

Corporate Transparency Antecedents

Most articles covered by the above review have focused on analysing the differences between family and non-family businesses (e.g. Fang & Wong, 2002; Martín et al., 2016; Rodríguez-Ariza et al., 2016). These studies evidently assume that family firms are homogeneous organisations (Chua et al., 2012), so multiple differences remain unexplored or underresearched within the category of family businesses. Further investigations are needed to explore these variations to improve the knowledge about heterogeneity in family firms (Nordqvist et al., 2014).

More specifically, the present literature review revealed that first-generation family businesses have more incentives to engage in upward earnings management because of family members' dedication to preserving SEW (Stockmans et al., 2010). The association between family business status and earnings management is also stronger among family firms run by the second or later generations (Borralho et al., 2020a).

Researchers may get especially interesting results by exploring whether family businesses' generation has a moderating role in the relationship between the status of family business and quality of information disclosed. The owners and/or managers' generation may further have a direct effect on these organisations' corporate transparency in terms of not only the quality of disclosures but also the quantity. Therefore, the first question proposed is as follows:

RQ 1. *How does family firms' generation affect their corporate transparency policies and practices?*

Family businesses often stress non-financial objectives, and these organisations' behaviour may not always be financially rational (Cabrera-Suárez et al., 2014). This pattern is why agency theory's explanatory power is restricted (Prencipe et al., 2008). For this reason, SEW theory, the only related approach developed specifically for the family business field (Berrone et al., 2012), has been used as a theoretical framework by various articles included in the present review (e.g. Borralho et al., 2020a; Corten et al., 2021; Stockmans et al., 2010).

Family firms' focus on maintaining SEW is one of the main differences between family and non-family businesses (Berrone et al., 2012), so scholars must include SEW as a variable in empirical research. The concept of SEW can be broken down into the five dimensions proposed by Berrone et al. (2012): family control and influence, identification with the business, dynastic succession, emotional attachment and social ties. Further research is thus needed to answer the following question:

RQ 2. *How does family firms' interest in maintaining SEW affect their corporate transparency?*

This literature review also revealed that the composition and diversity of family businesses' board of directors may contribute to these firms' heterogeneity in terms of transparency. Various studies reviewed provide empirically robust evidence that a higher proportion of independent (Setia-Atmaja et al., 2011; Stockmans et al., 2013) or women board members improves the quality of family businesses' financial information (Borralho et al., 2020b).

In line with the above findings, scholars could explore how board diversity affects the quantity of information disclosed (Orazalin & Baydauletov, 2020). The current results also indicate that special attention needs to be paid to chief executive officer (CEO) gender's effect on family firms' transparency as they tend to offer more supportive settings for leaders (Englisch et al., 2015; Montemerlo et al., 2013). Thus, the following RQ should be addressed:

RQ 3. *How does CEO gender in family firms influence their corporate transparency?*

This literature review verified that researchers have paid insufficient attention to one of family businesses' greatest challenges: succession (Cabrera-Suárez et al., 2001; Corrales-Villega et al., 2019). The type of succession (i.e. planned versus unexpected and intra-family versus external) may influence these firms' corporate transparency. Therefore, the following question still needs to be answered:

RQ 4. *How do succession processes affect family firms' quantity and quality of information disclosures?*

Corporate Transparency Outputs

A major difference between family and non-family businesses is that the former pursue not only financial and non-financial goals to satisfy their stakeholders but also family-oriented goals (Chrisman et al., 2012; Kotlar & De Massis, 2013). The latter include, among others, securing family members' jobs and lifestyles and maintaining family culture, cohesion and well-being (Block & Wagner, 2014; Gómez-Mejía et al., 2007; Revilla et al., 2016). A deeper understanding is needed of corporate transparency's consequences for family firms, which means that another important task is for scholars to find answers to the following question:

RQ 5. *How do family firms' information disclosure quality and quantity affect family members' cohesion and well-being?*

In addition, researchers could explore any positive associations between corporate transparency and reputation in the general literature (Bravo, 2015; Fombrun & Rindova, 2000; Landgraf & Riahi-Belkaoui, 2003; Rawlins, 2009) that can be extended to family business contexts. This topic is especially important because family firms are widely thought to be more concerned about preserving their image and corporate reputation than non-family firms are (Deephouse & Jaskiewicz, 2013). In particular, the relationship between corporate transparency and corporate reputation needs to be explored in non-listed family businesses as transparency in these firms remains underresearched (Pazzaglia et al., 2013; Umans & Corten, 2022). Further studies should be conducted to answer the following question:

RQ 6. *How does family firms' transparency affect their corporate reputation?*

Finally, most of the articles summarised in Tables 2 to 4 above are quantitative. This review's results thus reinforce Paiva et al.'s (2016) call for additional research on family firms' information disclosure to broaden this field's methodological spectrum with diverse types of qualitative and experimental studies.

CONCLUSION

The above findings contribute to both the accounting and family business literature. The review conducted provides an overview of the state of the art regarding the knowledge generated by the most significant publications on family business corporate transparency. The results constitute a significant contribution as the literature on this topic (i.e. family firms' corporate transparency) has expanded in an extremely fragmented way (i.e. publications in a broad range of journals), which increases the present overview's value. In addition, this non-systematic compilation and review of the relevant literature constitutes a more comprehensive survey of previous research's gaps and short comings, thereby exposing multiple potential lines of research.

However, this study is not without limitations. For example, the review focused on articles published in peer-reviewed journal articles – which is common in the field of family business (e.g. Andreini et al., 2020; Hernández-Linares & López-Fernández, 2018; Kubíček & Machek, 2020; Pindado & Requejo,

2015). Various books have been published by important authors, with contents that have had a significant impact on this area of study (Hernández-Linares et al., 2018), so other types of publications (e.g. books, proceedings and grey literature in general) would have enriched the present results.

In addition, the articles reviewed were published in English, which is also a common practice in this field (e.g. Campopiano et al., 2022; Hernández-Linares & Arias-Abelaira, 2022; Hernández-Linares et al., 2017, 2018; Su & Daspit, 2021). Nonetheless, the literature on family business has grown in other languages such as Spanish (see, for example, López-Fernández et al., 2017), so important papers may have been omitted. Finally, the current literature review was non-systematic, which means further research should be conducted based on other types of reviews (e.g. systematic literature reviews) to consolidate the findings on this topic.

In summary, the increasing number of publications on the convergence between corporate transparency and family business indicates, according to Chen et al. (2008, p. 500), that 'family firms' unique ownership structure has important implications for their voluntary disclosure practices'. This literature's dispersed nature makes a coherent synthesis of these publications imperative. The present review was the first step in that direction, but much remains to be done by researchers willing to take up this challenge.

REFERENCES

Achleitner, A. K., Günther, N., Kaserer, C., & Siciliano, G. (2014). Real earnings management and accrual-based earnings management in family firms. *European Accounting Review*, *23*(3), 431–461. doi:10.1080/09638180.2014.895620

Akram, M. U., Ghosh, K., & Sharma, D. (2022). A systematic review of innovation in family firms and future research agenda. *International Journal of Emerging Markets*, *17*(7), 1759–1792. doi:10.1108/IJOEM-06-2021-0936

Albu, O. B., & Flyverbom, M. (2019). Organizational transparency: Conceptualizations, conditions, and consequences. *Business & Society*, *58*(2), 268–297. doi:10.1177/0007650316659851

Ali, A., Chen, T., & Radhakrishnan, S. (2007). Corporate disclosure by family firms. *Journal of Accounting and Economics*, *44*(1–2), 238–286. doi:10.1016/j.jacceco.2007.01.006

Anderson, R. C., & Reeb, D. M. (2003). Founding family ownership and firm performance: Evidence from the S&P 500. *The Journal of Finance*, *58*(3), 1301–1328. doi:10.1111/1540-6261.00567

Andreini, D., Bettinelli, C., Pedeliento, G., & Apa, R. (2020). How do consumers see firms' family nature? A review of the literature. *Family Business Review*, *33*(1), 18–37. doi:10.1177/0894486519890229

Ang, J. S., Coles, R. A., & Lin, J. W. (2000). Agency costs and ownership structure. *The Journal of Finance*, *55*(1), 81–106. doi:10.1111/0022-1082.00201

Astrachan, J. H., Klein, S. B., & Smyrnios, K. X. (2002). The F-PEC scale of family influence: A proposal for solving the family business definition problem. *Family Business Review*, *15*(1), 45–58. doi:10.1111/j.1741-6248.2002.00045.x

Attig, N., Boubakri, N., Ghoul, S., & Guedhami, O. (2015). The global financial crisis, family control, and dividend policy. *Financial Management*, *45*(2), 291–313. doi:10.1111/fima.12115

Bae, S. C., Chang, K., & Yi, H. C. (2018). Corporate social responsibility, credit rating, and private debt contracting: New evidence from the syndicated loan market. *Review of Quantitative Finance and Accounting*, *50*(1), 261–299. doi:10.100711156-017-0630-4

Balzano, M. (2022). Serendipity in management studies: A literature review and future research directions. *Management Decision*, *60*(13), 130–152. doi:10.1108/MD-02-2022-0245

Baraibar-Díez, E., Odrizola, M. D., & Fernández-Sánchez, J. L. (2017). A survey of transparency: An intrinsic aspect of business strategy. *Business Strategy and the Environment*, *26*(4), 480–489. doi:10.1002/bse.1931

Basheer, M. F., Gupta, S., Raoof, R., & Waemustafa, W. (2021). Revisiting the agency conflicts in family owned pyramidal business structures: A case of an emerging market. *Cogent Economics & Finance*, *9*(1), 1–18. doi:10.1080/23322039.2021.1926617

Ben-Amar, W., & André, P. (2006). Separation of ownership from control and acquiring firm performance: The case of family ownership in Canada. *Journal of Business Finance & Accounting*, *33*(3-4), 517–543. doi:10.1111/j.1468-5957.2006.00613.x

Berrone, P., Cruz, C., & Gómez-Mejía, L. R. (2012). Socioemotional wealth in family firms: Theoretical dimensions, assessment approaches, and agenda for future research. *Family Business Review*, *25*(3), 258–279. doi:10.1177/0894486511435355

Bidabad, B., Amirostovar, A., & Sherafati, M. (2017). Financial transparency, corporate governance and information disclosure of the entrepreneur's corporation in Rastin banking. *International Journal of Law and Management*, *59*(5), 636–651. doi:10.1108/IJLMA-01-2016-0003

Biondi, L., & Lapsley, I. (2014). Accounting, transparency and governance: The heritage assets problem. *Qualitative Research in Accounting & Management*, *11*(2), 146–164. doi:10.1108/QRAM-04-2014-0035

Block, J., & Wagner, M. (2014). The effect of family ownership on different dimensions of corporate social responsibility: Evidence from large US firms. *Business Strategy and the Environment*, *23*(7), 475–492. doi:10.1002/bse.1798

Borralho, J., Gallardo-Vázquez, D., & Hernández-Linares, R. (2020a). Earnings management in private family versus non-family firms. The moderate effect on family business generation. Spanish Journal of Finance and Accounting / Revista Española de Financiación y Contabilidad, *49*(2), 210–233. doi:10.1080/02102412.2019.1616480

Borralho, J., Gallardo-Vázquez, D., Hernández-Linares, R., & Paiva, I. (2020b). The effect of corporate governance factors on the quality of financial reporting in family and non-family firms. *Revista de Contabilidad/Spanish Accounting Review*, *23*(2), 167–179. doi:10.6018/rcsar.358451

Borralho, J. M., Hernández-Linares, R., Vázquez, D. G., & Paiva, I. (2022). Environmental, social and governance disclosure's impacts on earnings management: Family versus non-family firms. *Journal of Cleaner Production*, *379*, 134603. doi:10.1016/j.jclepro.2022.134603

Boubaker, S., Derouiche, I., & Nguyen, H. (2022). Voluntary disclosure, tax avoidance and family firms. *The Journal of Management and Governance*, *26*(1), 129–158. doi:10.100710997-021-09601-w

Bozzolan, S., Fabrizi, M., Mallin, C. A., & Michelon, G. (2015). Corporate social responsibility and earnings quality: International evidence. *The International Journal of Accounting*, *50*(4), 361–396. doi:10.1016/j.intacc.2015.10.003

Brahem, E., Depoers, F., & Lakhal, F. (2022). Corporate social responsibility and earnings quality in family firms. *Journal of Applied Accounting Research*, *23*(5), 1114–1134. doi:10.1108/JAAR-05-2021-0139

Bravo, F. (2015). Forward-looking disclosure and corporate reputation as mechanisms to reduce stock return volatility. *Revista de Contabilidad/Spanish Accounting Review*, *19*(1), 122–131. doi:10.1016/j.rcsar.2015.03.001

Bushman, R., Piotroski, J., & Smith, A. J. (2004). What determines corporate transparency? *Journal of Accounting Research*, *42*(2), 207–252. doi:10.1111/j.1475-679X.2004.00136.x

BushmanR. M.SmithA. J. (2003). Transparency, financial accounting information, and corporate governance. *Economic Policy Review*, *32*(1-3), 237-333. Available at SSRN: https://ssrn.com/abstract=795547

Cabrera-Suárez, K., De Saa-Pérez, P., & Garcia-Almeida, D. (2001). The succession process from a resource-and knowledge-based view of the family firm. *Family Business Review*, *14*(1), 37–48. doi:10.1111/j.1741-6248.2001.00037.x

Cabrera-Suárez, M. K., Déniz-Déniz, M. C., & Martín-Santana, J. D. (2014). The setting of non-financial goals in the family firm: The influence of family climate and identification. *Journal of Family Business Strategy*, *5*(3), 289–299. doi:10.1016/j.jfbs.2014.05.003

Campopiano, G., Gabaldón, P., & Giménez-Jiménez, D. (2022). Women directors and corporate social performance: An integrative review of the literature and a future research agenda. *Journal of Business Ethics*. Advance online publication. doi:10.100710551-021-04999-7

Carney, M., van Essen, M., Gedajlovic, E. R., & Heugens, P. P. (2015). What do we know about private family firms? A meta-analytical review. *Entrepreneurship Theory and Practice*, *39*(3), 513–544. doi:10.1111/etap.12054

Cascino, S., Pugliese, A., Mussolino, D., & Sasone, C. (2010). The influence of family ownership on the quality of accounting information. *Family Business Review*, *23*(3), 246–265. doi:10.1177/0894486510374302

Chaney, P. K., & Lewis, C. M. (1995). Earnings management and firm valuation under asymmetric information. *Journal of Corporate Finance*, *1*(3-4), 319–345. doi:10.1016/0929-1199(94)00008-I

Chang, J., Cho, Y. J., & Shin, H. H. (2007). The change in corporate transparency of Korean firms after the Asian financial crisis: An analysis using analysts' forecast data. *Corporate Governance*, *15*(6), 1144–1167. doi:10.1111/j.1467-8683.2007.00637.x

Chau, G., & Gray, S. J. (2010). Family ownership, board independence and voluntary disclosure: Evidence from Hong Kong. *Journal of International Accounting, Auditing & Taxation*, *19*(2), 93–109. doi:10.1016/j.intaccaudtax.2010.07.002

Chaudhary, S., Dhir, A., Ferraris, A., & Bertoldi, B. (2021). Trust and reputation in family businesses: A systematic literature review of past achievements and future promises. *Journal of Business Research*, *137*(7-8), 143–161. doi:10.1016/j.jbusres.2021.07.052

Chen, J., Chen, N. Y., He, L., & Patel, C. (2022). The effect of ownership structure on disclosure quality and credit ratings in family firms: The moderating role of auditor choice. *Family Business Review*, *35*(2), 140–158. doi:10.1177/08944865211057854

Chen, S., Chen, X., & Cheng, Q. (2008). Do family firms provide more or less voluntary disclosure? *Journal of Accounting Research*, *46*(3), 499–536. doi:10.1111/j.1475-679X.2008.00288.x

Chen, T. Y., Dasgupta, S., & Yu, Y. (2014). Transparency and financing choices of family firms. *Journal of Financial and Quantitative Analysis*, *49*(2), 381–408. doi:10.1017/S0022109014000313

Cheng, Q. (2014). Family firm research. A review. *China Journal of Accounting Research*, *7*(3), 146–163. doi:10.1016/j.cjar.2014.03.002

Chiyachantana, C. N., Nuengwang, N., Taechapiroontong, N., & Thanarung, P. (2013). The effect of information disclosure on information asymmetry. *Investment Management and Financial Innovations*, *10*(1), 225–234. doi:10.1017/S0022109014000313

Chrisman, J. J., Chua, J. H., Pearson, A. W., & Barnett, T. (2012). Family involvement, family influence, and family-centered non-economic goals in small firms. *Entrepreneurship Theory and Practice*, *36*(2), 267–293. doi:10.1111/j.1540-6520.2010.00407.x

Chua, J. H., Chrisman, J. J., Steier, L. P., & Rau, S. B. (2012). Sources of heterogeneity in family firms: An introduction. *Entrepreneurship Theory and Practice*, *36*(6), 1103–1113. doi:10.1111/j.1540-6520.2012.00540.x

Claessens, S., Djankov, S., Fan, J. P. H., & Lang, L. H. P. (2002). Disentangling the incentive and entrenchment effects of large shareholdings. *The Journal of Finance*, *57*(6), 2741–2771. doi:10.1111/1540-6261.00511

Corrales-Villegas, S. A., Ochoa-Jiménez, S., & Jacobo-Hernández, C. A. (2019). Leadership in the family business in relation to the desirable attributes for the successor: Evidence from Mexico. *European Journal of Family Business*, *8*(2), 117–128. doi:10.24310/ejfbejfb.v8i2.5193

Corten, M., Vandekerkhof, P., & Steijvers, T. (2021). The effect of socioemotional wealth diversity within the top management team on earnings management in private family firms: The moderating role of the board of directors. *MDE. Managerial and Decision Economics*, *42*(7), 1886–1896. doi:10.1002/mde.3352

Craig, J., & Moores, K. (2005). Balanced scorecards to drive the strategic planning of family firms. *Family Business Review*, *18*(2), 105–122. doi:10.1111/j.1741-6248.2005.00035.x

Craig, J., & Moores, K. (2010). Strategically aligning family and business systems using the Balanced Scorecard. *Journal of Family Business Strategy*, *1*(2), 78–87. doi:10.1016/j.jfbs.2010.04.003

Cunha, M. P., Soares Leitão, M. J., Clegg, S., Hernández-Linares, R., Moasa, H., Randerson, K., & Rego, A. (2021). Cognition, emotion and action: Persistent sources of parent–offspring paradoxes in the family business. *Journal of Family Business Management*, *12*(4), 729–749. doi:10.1108/JFBM-11-2020-0104

Deephouse, D., & Jaskiewicz, P. (2013). Do family firms have better reputations than non-family firms? An integration of socioemotional wealth and social identity theories. *Journal of Management Studies*, *50*(3), 337–360. doi:10.1111/joms.12015

Dello Sbarba, A., & Marelli, A. (2018). Family-controlled businesses and management control: The framing of "shareholder-oriented" practices. *Journal of Management Control*, *28*(4), 417–456. doi:10.100700187-018-0255-3

Duréndez, A., & Madrid-Guijarro, A. (2018). The impact of family influence on financial reporting quality in small and medium family firms. *Journal of Family Business Strategy*, *9*(3), 205–218. doi:10.1016/j.jfbs.2018.08.002

Englisch, P., Hall, C., Burgess, I., Macoto, H., Astrachan, J., & Pieper, T. M. (2015). Women in leadership: Family business advantage. *Special report based on a global survey of the World's largest family businesses.* EY. https://familybusiness.ey-vx.com/pdfs/ey-women-in-leadership-the-family-business-advantage.pdf

Etzioni, A. (2010). Is transparency the best disinfectant? *Journal of Political Philosophy*, *18*(4), 389–404. doi:10.1111/j.1467-9760.2010.00366.x

Fan, P. H. J., & Wong, T. J. (2002). Corporate ownership structure and the informativeness of accounting earnings in East Asia. *Journal of Accounting and Economics*, *33*(3), 401–425. doi:10.1016/S0165-4101(02)00047-2

Ferramosca, S., & Allegrini, M. (2018). The complex role of family involvement in earnings management. *Journal of Family Business Strategy*, *9*(2), 128–141. doi:10.1016/j.jfbs.2018.01.001

Fombrun, C., & Rindova, V. (2000). The road to transparency: Reputation management at Royal Dutch/Shell. In M. Schultz, M. J. Hatch, & M. H. Larsen (Eds.), *The expressive organization: Linking identity, reputation and the corporate brand* (pp. 77–97). Oxford University Press.

Fülöp, M. T. (2014). Why do we need effective corporate governance? *International Advances in Economic Research*, *20*(2), 227–228. doi:10.100711294-013-9430-3

Gaspar, R., Rohde, P., & Giger, J. C. (2019). Unconventional settings and uses of human enhancement technologies: A non-systematic review of public and experts' views on self-enhancement and DIY biology/biohacking risks. *Human Behavior and Emerging Technologies*, *1*(4), 295–305. doi:10.1002/hbe2.175

Gjergji, R., Vena, L., Sciascia, S., & Cortesi, A. (2021). The effects of environmental, social and governance disclosure on the cost of capital in small and medium enterprises: The role of family business status. *Business Strategy and the Environment*, *30*(1), 683–693. doi:10.1002/bse.2647

Goldstein, M. A., Hotchkiss, E. S., & Sirri, E. R. (2007). Transparency and liquidity: A controlled experiment on corporate bonds. *Review of Financial Studies*, *20*(2), 235–273. doi:10.1093/rfs/hhl020

Gómez-Mejía, L. R., Haynes, K. T., Núnez-Nickel, M., Jacobson, K. J., & Moyano-Fuentes, J. (2007). Socioemotional wealth and business risks in family-controlled firms: Evidence from Spanish olive oil mills. *Administrative Science Quarterly*, *52*(1), 106–137. doi:10.2189/asqu.52.1.106

González, M., Guzmán, A., Pombo, C., & Trujillo, M. A. (2014). Family involvement and dividend policy in closely held firms. *Family Business Review*, *27*(4), 365–385. doi:10.1177/0894486514538448

Gu, L., & Hackbarth, D. (2013). Governance and equity prices: Does transparency matter? *Review of Finance*, *17*(6), 1989–2033. doi:10.1093/rof/rfs047

Habbershon, T. G., & Williams, M. L. (1999). A resource-based framework for assessing the strategic advantages of family firms. *Family Business Review*, *12*(1), 1–25. doi:10.1111/j.1741-6248.1999.00001.x

Habbershon, T. G., Williams, M. L., & MacMillan, I. C. (2003). A unified systems perspective of family firm performance. *Journal of Business Venturing*, *18*(4), 451–465. doi:10.1016/S0883-9026(03)00053-3

Heald, D. (2006). Transparency as an instrumental value. In C. Hood & D. Heald (Eds.), *Transparency: The Key to Better Governance?* (pp. 59–74). Oxford University Press. doi:10.5871/bacad/9780197263839.003.0004

Heinberg, M., Liu, Y., Huang, X., & Eisingerich, A. B. (2021). A bad job of doing good: Does corporate transparency on a country and company level moderate corporate social responsibility effectiveness? *Journal of International Marketing*, *29*(2), 45–61. doi:10.1177/1069031X20981870

Hernández-Linares, R., & Arias-Abelaira, T. (2022). Adapt or perish! A systematic review of the literature on strategic renewal and the family firm. *European Journal of Family Business*, *12*(2), 137–155. doi:10.24310/ejfbejfb.v12i2.14718

Hernández-Linares, R., & López-Fernández, M. C. (2018). Entrepreneurial orientation and the family firm: Mapping the field and tracing a path for future research. *Family Business Review*, *31*(3), 318–351. doi:10.1177/0894486518781940

Hernández-Linares, R., Sarkar, S., & Cobo, M. J. (2018). Inspecting the Achilles heel: A quantitative analysis of 50 years of family business definitions. *Scientometrics*, *115*(2), 929–951. doi:10.100711192-018-2702-1

Hernández-Linares, R., Sarkar, S., & López-Fernández, M. C. (2017). How has the family firm literature addressed its heterogeneity through classification systems? An integrated analysis. *European Journal of Family Business*, *7*(1-2), 1–13. doi:10.1016/j.ejfb.2017.06.003

Hopkins, P. (1996). The effect of financial statement classification of hybrid financial instruments on financial analysts' stock price judgements. *Journal of Accounting Research*, *34*(3), 33–50. doi:10.2307/2491424

Hultman, J., & Axelsson, B. (2007). Towards a typology of transparency for marketing management research. *Industrial Marketing Management*, *36*(5), 627–635. doi:10.1016/j.indmarman.2006.04.001

Kang, J.-S., Chiang, C.-F., Huangthanapan, K., & Downing, S. (2015). Corporate social responsibility and sustainability balanced scorecard: The case study of family-owned hotels. *International Journal of Hospitality Management*, *48*, 124–134. doi:10.1016/j.ijhm.2015.05.001

Kim, Y., Park, M., & Wier, B. (2012). Is earnings quality associated with corporate social responsibility? *The Accounting Review*, *87*(3), 761–796. doi:10.2308/accr-10209

Kotlar, J., & De Massis, A. (2013). Goal setting in family firms: Goal diversity, social interactions, and collective commitment to family-centered goals. *Entrepreneurship Theory and Practice*, *37*(6), 1263–1288. doi:10.1111/etap.12065

Kubíček, A., & Machek, O. (2020). Intrafamily conflicts in Family businesses: A systematic review of the literature and agenda for future research. *Family Business Review*, *33*(2), 194–227. doi:10.1177/0894486519899573

Landgraf, E., & Riahi-Belkaoui, A. (2003). Corporate disclosure quality and corporate reputation. *Review of Accounting and Finance*, *2*(1), 86–95. doi:10.1108/eb027003

Lee, J. (2006). Family firm performance: Further evidence. *Family Business Review*, *19*(2), 103–114. doi:10.1111/j.1741-6248.2006.00060.x

Li, S., & Zuo, X. (2020). Agency Costs in Family Business: A Review. *Journal of Service Science and Management*, *13*(2), 377–387. doi:10.4236/jssm.2020.132025

Li, Y., Gong, M., Zhang, X. Y., & Koh, L. (2018). The impact of environmental, social, and governance disclosure on firm value: The role of CEO power. *The British Accounting Review*, *50*(1), 60–75. doi:10.1016/j.bar.2017.09.007

Liu, C., Li, Q., & Lin, Y. E. (2022). (in press). Corporate transparency and firm value: Does market competition play an external governance role? *Journal of Contemporary Accounting & Economics*. Advance online publication. doi:10.1016/j.jcae.2022.100334

Liu, Y., Valenti, A., & Chen, Y. (2016). Corporate governance and information transparency in Taiwan's public firms. The moderating effect of family ownership. *Journal of Management & Organization*, *22*(5), 662–679. doi:10.1017/jmo.2015.56

López-Fernández, M. C., Serrano-Bedia, A. M., Pérez-Pérez, M., Hernández-Linares, R., & Palma-Ruiz, M. (2017). A review of the academic literature on family business in Spanish. In F. W. Kellermanns & F. Hoy (Eds.), *The Routledge Companion to Family Business* (pp. 522–548). Routledge.

Louie, J., Ahmed, K., & Ji, X. D. (2019). Voluntary disclosures practices of family firms in Australia. *Accounting Research Journal*, *32*(2), 273–294. doi:10.1108/ARJ-04-2016-0042

Ma, L. (2023). Corporate social responsibility reporting in family firms: Evidence from China. *Journal of Behavioral and Experimental Finance*, *37*, 100730. doi:10.1016/j.jbef.2022.100730

Martin, G., Campbell, J., & Gómez-Mejía, L. R. (2016). Family control, socioemotional wealth and earnings management in publicly traded firms. *Journal of Business Ethics*, *133*(3), 435–469. doi:10.100710551-014-2403-5

Martins, J. J., & André, M. A. (2013). Governance bodies of family business. *European Journal of Family Business*, *3*(1), 47–58. doi:10.24310/ejfbejfb.v3i1.4040

Men, L. R., & Hung-Baesecke, C. J. F. (2015). Engaging employees in China: The impact of communication channels, organizational transparency, and authenticity. *Corporate Communications*, *20*(4), 448–467. doi:10.1108/CCIJ-11-2014-0079

Mohammadi, S., & Nezhad, B. M. (2015). The role of disclosure and transparency in financial reporting. *International Journal of Accounting and Economics Studies*, *3*(1), 60–62. doi:10.14419/ijaes.v3i1.4549

Montemerlo, D., Minichilli, A., & Corbetta, G. (2013). The determinants of women's involvement in top management teams: Opportunities or obstacles for family-controlled firms? In K. X. Smyrnios, P. Z. Poutziouris, & S. Goel (Eds.), *Handbook of Research in Family Business* (pp. 301–322). Edward Elgar. doi:10.4337/9781781009383.00025

Morck, R., Schleifer, A., & Vishny, R. W. (1988). Management ownership and market valuation: An empirical analysis. *Journal of Financial Economics*, *20*(1-2), 293–315. doi:10.1016/0304-405X(88)90048-7

Nordqvist, M., Sharma, P., & Chirico, F. (2014). Family firm heterogeneity and governance: A configuration approach. *Journal of Small Business Management*, *52*(2), 192–209. doi:10.1111/jsbm.12096

Orazalin, N., & Baydauletov, M. (2020). Corporate social responsibility strategy and corporate environmental and social performance: The moderating role of board gender diversity. *Corporate Social Responsibility and Environmental Management*, *27*(4), 1664–1676. doi:10.1002/csr.1915

Paiva, I., Lourenço, I., & Branco, M. (2016). Earnings management in family firms: Current state of knowledge and opportunities for future research. *Review of Accounting and Finance*, *15*(1), 85–100. doi:10.1108/RAF-06-2014-0065

Paiva, I., Lourenço, I., & Curto, J. (2019). Earnings management in family versus non-family firms: The influence of analyst coverage. *Spanish Journal of Finance and Accounting/Revista Española de Financiación y Contabilidad*, *48*(2), 113–133. doi:10.1080/02102412.2018.1463764

Palma, M., Costa, I., & Castelo, M. (2022). Web-based sustainability reporting by family companies: The role of the richest European families. *Accounting Forum*, *46*(4), 344–368. doi:10.1080/01559982.2021.1979331

Pazzaglia, F., Mengoli, S., & Sapienza, E. (2013). Earnings quality in acquired and non-acquired family firms: A socioemotional wealth perspective. *Family Business Review*, *4*(26), 374–386. doi:10.1177/0894486513486343

Pieper, T. M., Kellermanns, F. W., & Astrachan, J. H. (2021). *Family businesses' contribution to the US economy*. Washington, DC: Family Enterprise USA.

Pindado, J., & Requejo, I. (2015). Family business performance from a governance perspective: A review of empirical research. *International Journal of Management Reviews*, *17*(3), 279–311. doi:10.1111/ijmr.12040

Plumlee, M., Brown, D., Hayes, R. M., & Marshall, R. S. (2015). Voluntary environmental disclosure quality and firm value: Further evidence. *Journal of Accounting and Public Policy*, *34*(4), 336–361. doi:10.1016/j.jaccpubpol.2015.04.004

Podsakoff, P. M., Mackenzie, S. B., Bachrach, D. G., & Podsakoff, N. P. (2005). The influence of management journals in the 1980s and 1990s. *Strategic Management Journal*, *26*(5), 473–488. doi:10.1002mj.454

Prencipe, A., Bar-Yosef, S., & Dekker, H. (2014). Accounting research in family firms: Theoretical and empirical challenges. *European Accounting Review*, *23*(3), 361–385. doi:10.1080/09638180.2014.895621

Prencipe, A., Markarian, G., & Pozza, L. (2008). Earnings management in family firms: Evidence from R&D cost capitalization in Italy. *Family Business Review*, *21*(1), 71–88. doi:10.1111/j.1741-6248.2007.00112.x

Purkayastha, S., Veliyath, R., & George, R. (2022). Type I and type II agency conflicts in family firms: An empirical investigation. *Journal of Business Research*, *153*(3), 285–299. doi:10.1016/j.jbusres.2022.07.054

Rahman, M. J., & Zheng, X. (2022). Whether family ownership affects the relationship between CSR and EM: Evidence from Chinese listed firms. *Journal of Family Business Management*. doi:10.1108/JFBM-03-2022-0030

Rawlins, B. (2009). Give the emperor a mirror: Toward developing a stakeholder measurement of organizational transparency. *Journal of Public Relations Research*, *21*(1), 71–99. doi:10.1080/10627260802153421

Revilla, A. J., Pérez-Luño, A., & Nieto, M. J. (2016). Does family involvement in management reduce the risk of business failure? The moderating role of entrepreneurial orientation. *Family Business Review*, *29*(4), 365–379. doi:10.1177/0894486516671075

Rodríguez-Ariza, L., Martínez-Ferrero, J., & Bermejo-Sánchez, M. (2016). Consequences of earnings management for corporate reputation: Evidence from family firms. *Accounting Research Journal*, *29*(4), 457–474. doi:10.1108/ARJ-02-2015-0017

Sarumpaet, S., Nelwan, M. L., & Dewi, D. N. (2017). The value relevance of environmental performance: Evidence from Indonesia. *Social Responsibility Journal*, *13*(4), 817–827. doi:10.1108/SRJ-01-2017-0003

Schnackenberg, A. K., & Tomlinson, E. C. (2016). Organizational transparency: A new perspective on managing trust in organization-stakeholder relationships. *Journal of Management*, *42*(7), 1784–1810. doi:10.1177/0149206314525202

Schulze, W. S., Lubatkin, M. H., Dino, R. N., & Buchholtz, A. K. (2001). Agency relationships in family firms: Theory and evidence. *Organization Science*, *12*(2), 99–116. doi:10.1287/orsc.12.2.99.10114

Setia-Atmaja, L., Haman, J., & Tanewski, G. (2011). The role of board independence in mitigating agency problem II in Australian family firms. *The British Accounting Review*, *43*(3), 230–246. doi:10.1016/j.bar.2011.06.006

Seyoum, B. (2009). An empirical analysis of the impact of corporate transparency on foreign direct investment. *Multinational Business Review*, *17*(3), 29–48. doi:10.1108/1525383X200900016

Sharma, P., Chrisman, J. J., & Gersick, K. E. (2012). 25 years of family business review: Reflections on the past and perspectives for the future. *Family Business Review*, *25*(1), 5–15. doi:10.1177/0894486512437626

Shleifer, A., & Vishny, R. (1997). A survey of corporate governance. *The Journal of Finance*, *52*(2), 737–783. doi:10.1111/j.1540-6261.1997.tb04820.x

Sirmon, D. G., & Hitt, M. A. (2003). Managing resources: Linking unique resources, management, and wealth creation in family firms. *Entrepreneurship Theory and Practice*, *27*(4), 339–358. doi:10.1111/1540-8520.t01-1-00013

Solomon, J. (2007). *Corporate governance and accountability*. John Wiley & Sons, Ltd.

Stockmans, A., Lybaert, N., & Voordeckers, W. (2010). Socioemotional wealth and earnings management in private family firms. *Family Business Review*, *23*(3), 280–294. doi:10.1177/0894486510374457

Stockmans, A., Lybaert, N., & Voordeckers, W. (2013). The conditional nature of board characteristics in constraining earnings management in private family firms. *Journal of Family Business Strategy*, *2*(4), 84–92. doi:10.1016/j.jfbs.2013.01.001

Su, E., & Daspit, J. (2021). Knowledge management in family firms: A systematic review, integrated insights and future research opportunities. *Journal of Knowledge Management*, *26*(2), 291–325. doi:10.1108/JKM-08-2020-0658

Umans, I., & Corten, M. (2022). Ownership succession intentions affecting earnings management in private family firms. *Small Business Economics*, 1–16. doi:10.100711187-022-00696-5

Vaccaro, A., & Madsen, P. (2009). Corporate dynamic transparency: The new ICT-driven ethics. *Ethics and Information Technology*, *11*(2), 113–122. doi:10.100710676-009-9190-1

Vieira, E. (2016). Earnings management in public family firms. *Australian Accounting Review*, *77*(26), 190–207. doi:10.1111/auar.12096

Villalonga, B., & Amit, R. (2006). How do family ownership, control and management affect firm value? *Journal of Financial Economics*, *80*(2), 385–417. doi:10.1016/j.jfineco.2004.12.005

Villalonga, B., Amit, R., Trujillo, M. A., & Guzmán, A. (2015). Governance of family firms. *Annual Review of Financial Economics*, *7*(1), 635–654. doi:10.1146/annurev-financial-110613-034357

Vural, D. (2018). Disclosure practices by family firms: Evidence from Swedish publicly listed firms. *Accounting in Europe*, *15*(3), 347–373. doi:10.1080/17449480.2018.1479531

Wan-Hussin, W. N. (2009). The impact of family-firm structure and board composition on corporate transparency: Evidence based on segment disclosures in Malaysia. *The International Journal of Accounting*, *44*(4), 313–333. doi:10.1016/j.intacc.2009.09.003

Wang, D. (2006). Founding family ownership and earnings quality. *Journal of Accounting Research*, *44*(3), 619–656. doi:10.1111/j.1475-679X.2006.00213.x

Wehmeier, S., & Raaz, O. (2012). Transparency matters: The concept of organizational transparency in the academic discourse. *Public Relations Inquiry*, *1*(3), 337–366. doi:10.1177/2046147X12448580

Williams, C. C. (2005). Trust diffusion: The effect of interpersonal trust on structure, function, and organizational transparency. *Business & Society*, *44*(3), 357–368. doi:10.1177/0007650305275299

Wu, D., Li, J., Lu, X., & Li, J. (2018). Journal editorship index for assessing the scholarly impact of academic institutions: An empirical analysis in the field of economics. *Journal of Informetrics*, *12*(2), 448–460. doi:10.1016/j.joi.2018.03.008

Wu, X., Tong, X., & Wang, Y. (2022). Managerial ability and idiosyncratic volatility. *International Journal of Finance & Economics*, *27*(2), 2566–2581. doi:10.1002/ijfe.2287

Xiao, Q., Cooke, F. L., & Chen, L. (2022). Nurses' well-being and implications for human resource management: A systematic literature review. *International Journal of Management Reviews*, *24*(4), 599–624. doi:10.1111/ijmr.12295

Yuan, X., Li, Z., Xu, J., & Shang, L. (2022). ESG disclosure and corporate financial irregularities – Evidence from Chinese listed firms. *Journal of Cleaner Production*, *332*, 129992. Advance online publication. doi:10.1016/j.jclepro.2021.129992

Zaini, S. M., Sharma, U., Samking, G., & Davey, H. (2019). Impact of ownership structure on the level of voluntary disclosure: A study of listed family-controlled companies in Malaysia. *Accounting Forum*, *44*(1), 1–34. doi:10.1080/01559982.2019.1605874

Zhong, X., Ren, L., & Wu, X. (2022). Founder domination, industry environment, and family firms' earnings management. *Baltic Journal of Management*, *17*(5), 565–585. doi:10.1108/BJM-09-2021-0360

KEY TERMS AND DEFINITIONS

Corporate transparency: Business practices that promote open access to all information about organisations' reality to all interested stakeholders

Family firm/business: Companies in which ownership and/or management is in the hands of a family and which are dedicated to continuity, that is, that family descendants will continue to run the business in the future

Financial disclosure: Communication to all stakeholder of relevant information about organisations' shareholder equity, financial position and results of operations

Non-financial disclosure: Communication to all stakeholders of significant details related to companies' corporate social responsibility activities and their impact on society at large

Socioemotional wealth (SEW): Family businesses' characteristic intangible assets that make these firms unique, including affective values taken on by family members in their capacity as company owners and/or managers that allow the company to gain non-financial benefits

Type I agency conflict: Agency theory's understanding of contractual relations between principals and agents that identifies conflict as occurring between company owners and their managers

Type II agency conflict: Agency theory's conceptualisation of contractual relations between principals and agents that defines conflict as existing between companies' majority and minority shareholders

ENDNOTE

1 Available at https://charteredabs.org/academic-journal-guide-2021 (last accessed: 10 April 2023).

Chapter 6
Normative Guidelines and Financial Disclosure:
Relationship Between OCPC07 and Readability of Notes

Thiago Rios Sena
https://orcid.org/0000-0003-0261-7381
Universidade Federal de Pernambuco, Brazil

Jorge Luiz de Santana Junior
Universidade de São Paulo, Brazil

Sheizi Calheira de Freitas
Universidade Federal da Bahia, Brazil

ABSTRACT

Accounting communication has attracted substantial attention in the last decade since several regulators issued guidelines that aim to increase financial reporting quality. In this chapter, the authors aim to study the association between the issuance of the technical guidance 07 (OCPC 07) by the Brazilian Accounting Standard Committee (CPC) and the readability of notes to the financial statements of Brazilian public firms. The authors use a multiple linear regression of panel data, controlling by industry and year fixed effect. The results suggest that there is no significant change in the average readability of financial notes after the issuance of OCPC 07. The authors contribute with additional disclosure to accounting literature by collecting empirical evidence on the relationship between the publication of normative guidance and accounting evidence. Moreover, these results may contribute to regulatory decisions made by regulatory agencies, which are certainly among the main stakeholders in the impacts caused by the issuance of norms and guiding the preparation and disclosure of economic-financial information.

DOI: 10.4018/978-1-6684-7293-4.ch006

INTRODUCTION

The International Financial Reporting Standards (IFRS) provided managers with greater discretion in accounting choices, both in bookkeeping and in disclosure. In addition, after IFRS adoption, Brazilian standards began to require the disclosure of additional information in notes to financial statements, which increased the information content of financial reporting (Antunes et al., 2012).

Cunha (2008) states that narrative information is as much used for decision-making as numerical information, and the former have occupied a higher percentage in the size of the statements. Lo et al. (2017) document that the textual narrative represents an average of 80% of an annual report, highlighting the relevance of clarity of notes for understanding and interpreting the quantitative information contained in financial reporting.

In the last decade, several regulatory bodies around the world began to pay more attention to the accounting disclosure process with the aim of making narrative statements more useful in the decision-making process of external users, especially with regard to the clarity of information. Some examples of international organizations that issued documents related to this matter are the Securities and Exchange Commission (SEC), the European Financial Reporting Advisory Group (EFRAG), the International Accounting Standards Board (IASB).

In view of this worldwide movement aimed at improving the disclosure of qualitative information, in 2014, the Brazilian Accounting Standard Committee (CPC) issued Technical Guidance 07 (OCPC 07) – Disclosure of General Purpose Financial Reporting. Since Brazilian standards are in line with IFRS, OCPC 07 follows guidelines similar to EFRAG. This document was intended to guide developers in the preparation and dissemination of higher quality notes to the financial statements (Cruz Junior, 2018).

In this sense, one of the characteristics that is expected to be improved is the readability of financial reports. Readability refers to the inherent ability of the text to be read quickly and easily, therefore it is a property of the complexity of the narrative (Smith & Taffler, 1992). Distorted and confusing writing impedes the fluid understanding of messages by the reader, especially if unfamiliar or unnecessary polysyllabic words are used, in addition to long sentences (Courtis, 2004).

Recent studies have sought to verify characteristics of narrative statements before and after the issuance of OCPC 07 (Silva, 2017; Gomes et al., 2018; Cruz Junior, 2018; Telles, 2020). However, the results are conflicting, since they vary depending on the strategies to measure readability or statistically analyses used. Thus, this chapter contributes with additional information to the accounting literature by exploring the following research question: Did Brazilian public firms change the readability of notes to the financial statements after the issuance of OCPC 07?

To answer this research question, it is used a sample of Brazilian public firms listed on B3 in the period from 2010 to 2018. The methodology is classified as a descriptive and quantitative approach, through a document examination. Data were analyzed using multiple linear regression with panel data controlled by sector and year fixed effect.

Thus, this chapter aims to verify the association between the issuance of OCPC 07 and changes in the level of readability of the notes to the financial statements of Brazilian public firms. This chapter differs from the previous studies in the following aspects: i) sample with longer period post-IFRS and observations; ii) the inclusion of financial firms, commonly excluded from the analysis; iii) use of fixed effects and control variables; iv) analysis of legibility variance by sector.

Rodrigues (2012) states that researchers, policy makers, regulators and investors are paying attention to the elements of disclosure and corporate governance. Therefore, in addition to the academic contribution, by reporting results from a different perspective, this study contributes to the issue of standards aimed at disclosure for different types of financial reporting users: managers, investors, market analysts, creditors, regulators, among others. Since external users use financial statements to assess the performance and future perspectives of firms for decision-making, the ease of reading narrative reports can interfere with users' perception and, consequently, with resource allocation.

Furthermore, it is expected that the results presented by this chapter will help in the accounting regulation process by providing information about readability, since accounting disclosure has become one of the main topics discussed by regulatory bodies internationally.

THEORETICAL FRAMEWORK

Readability Concepts and Characteristics

Distorted and confusing writing impedes the fluid understanding of messages by the reader, especially if unfamiliar or unnecessary polysyllabic words are used, in addition to long sentences (Courtis, 2004). Readability is one of the characteristics of text clarity, fundamental for fast and easy communication through the use of short sentences and easy-to-understand words (Borges, 2020). Readability refers to the inherent ability of the text to be read quickly and easily, therefore it is a property of the complexity of the narrative (Smith & Taffler, 1992).

Within the scope of accounting literature, Peleias (2017) defines readability as the quality of writing, linked to the quality of accounting information, whose objective is to facilitate the reading and understanding of financial statements, resulting in easier and faster communication of accounting information to your users.

To measure readability, tools called readability indexes are used, which are usually based on a mathematical model weighing different combinations of variables. In recent decades there has been an increase in the number and sophistication of readability measures, and these indices have similar basic characteristics: they are based on sentence length and word length as primary determinants of the reading level of a given document (Baker & Care, 1992).

This chapter uses the Flesch index adapted to Portuguese (Martins et al., 1996) as the main metric for measuring the readability of narrative statements. The option for this index is based on the extensive use of the Flesch index (1979) for analysis of accounting narratives, which is the only index adapted and validated for texts in Portuguese. Telles (2018) states that other techniques such as Dale-Chall and Gunning FOG do not yet have a correspondent for texts in Portuguese, meaning that their direct application may present distorted results.

The indices mentioned above were developed for the analysis of texts in English and have constant values for that language in their respective formulas. Based on the fact that the Portuguese language usually has words with a greater number of syllables, Martins et al (1996) adapted the Flesch index by adding 42 points to its original formula. The calculation of this index is exposed on Equation 1:

$$\text{Flesch Adapted} = 248{,}835 - (\text{MWPS} + \text{MSPW}) \quad (1)$$

Where MWPS is the mean words per sentence and MSPW is the mean syllables per word. This index has a scale ranging from 0 to 100 points, being interpreted as the higher the score, the easier the understanding of the text.

Moreno and Casasola (2015) highlight three important characteristics for using the Flesch index adapted for the Spanish language in their work and that can be equally reproduced for the Flesch index adapted for the Portuguese language: i) it provides comparability with analyzes on the evolution of readability; ii) the Flesch index is one of the most used in accounting studies in general; and iii) it is one of the few formulas adapted and tested in documents in Portuguese.

Financial Disclosure and the Readability of Financial Statements

According to IFRS, financial disclosures are intended to provide useful information for current and future users of an entity's information. The usefulness of information is understood as the ability to influence the user's economic decision-making, making it possible to evaluate past actions and make inferences about the future evolution of the entity's assets (Espíndula & Costa, 2008). If financial statements' users are not able to read and understand the content of the reports, it will not be possible to obtain a common understanding on the underlying economic events among insiders and outsiders (Hasan, 2018) and accounting information has its usefulness reduced in the decision-making process.

Lanzana (2004) points out disclosure as one of the most important ways for management to communicate with shareholders and other users. Financial reports also serve other stakeholders of the company, such as customers, suppliers, employees and society in general (Miranda et al., 2018). Moreover, a higher level of disclosure can bring benefits to the company itself by reducing information asymmetry. Gomes et al. (2018) list the following benefits of disclosure: increasing credibility, facilitating access to capital, decreasing the cost of capital and increasing firm value. It is also possible to emphasize that good communication provides a climate of trust between insiders and outsiders (Silva & Fernandes, 2009).

Dias Filho (2000) points out that there are at least three fundamental points regarding disclosure: the information content, the receptor of this information and the format of presenting it. When preparing the statements, the accounting professional must observe that each user, in addition to different and particular needs in relation to financial reporting, also has different levels of understanding of the information. Nevertheless, Hendriksen and Van Breda (1999) state that accounting users have limited capacity for attention and understanding, suggesting that investors, analysts and other professionals in the securities market may not pay attention to all available information (Lee, 2012). Therefore, a concise, clear, objective and accessible language must be adopted to achieve the objective of communicating the message (Peleias, 2017).

Silva and Fernandes (2009) point out that financial information is also communicated through narrative texts and that these are becoming increasingly important in external financial reports. The authors argue that the numerical presentation alone may not be sufficient for the adequate judgment of users of information about the entity's performance. However, financial statements have become excessively extensive by showing too much and irrelevant information. One of the aspects that caused an increase in the extent of qualitative information disclosed was the introduction of IFRS (Antunes et al., 2012). With the change in focus from rule-based accounting to principle-based accounting, financial statement preparers began to use subjective criteria for disclosing information (Li, 2008).

Among financial statements, notes to the financial statements are important sources of qualitative information, as they generate more comprehensive disclosures about relevant financial information and facts (Hendriksen & Van Breda, 2012). Gelbcke et al (2018) also point out that notes can be adopted in the description of accounting practices, additional explanation about operations and accounts, as well as their compositions and details. Lee (2012) identified consistent evidence, when evaluating companies registered with the SEC between 2001 and 2007, that longer and textually complex quarterly reports impair the market's ability to timely assimilate earnings-related information.

Qualitative statements with more complex and extensive reading increase the cost of transactions and information processing and, therefore, have a lower financial reporting quality, bringing inefficiencies in the establishment of contracts (Li, 2008). The difficulty in reading the statements increases the search for additional information and affects the sensitivity of investors' valuation judgments to information contained in external sources. Asay et al. (2017) conducted an experiment in which they showed to a group of investors financial reports with different levels of readability containing news about a firm's performance. When reports are less readable, investors are less comfortable evaluating the firm and, as a result, rely more on external information.

International Attention Toward Understandability and OCPC 07

Despite the growing guidelines on accounting disclosure, it is not possible to determine a single standard capable of subsidizing the decision-making process for all firms due to the specificities of each context. However, several regulatory bodies around the world have sought to prepare documents to assist in the construction of financial statements, especially the notes to the financial statements (Silva, 2017).

In the United States, in 1998, "A Plain English Handbook: How to create clear SEC disclosure documents" was issued by the SEC, with the aim of making disclosures clearer and more informative. Its content addressed various techniques and procedures for writing documents based on the "Plain Language", prepared by a group formed by employees of different US agencies with the aim of promoting the use of simple language for government documents. Therefore, the SEC sought, through this manual, to ensure that complex information is written in a clearer and more orderly way for the best quality of information and, in turn, greater understanding for decision making (Silva, 2017).

In terms of readability of financial reports, the SEC advises that some writing constructions be avoided in reports, such as: passive voice, weak or hidden verbs, superfluous words, legal and financial jargon, abstract words, unnecessary details, lengthy sentences, in addition to visual characteristics such as complex design and layout. The reduced use or absence of these constructions for better understanding of written texts has been confirmed in several contexts, including research in the military, health, law and business areas (Bonsall et al, 2017).

In Europe, in 2012, the European Financial Reporting Advisory Group (EFRAG) also showed concern with improving the quality of qualitative information disclosed by firms. This group discussed the difficulties and situations that compromise the relevance of the notes to financial statements and, through the document "Towards a Disclosure Framework for the Notes", suggested a disclosure structure, in addition to actions to improve the quality of information. Among various suggestions, the recommendation stands out that regulatory bodies start to address requirements on the form and criteria of disclosure, not just rules on their content (Silva, 2017).

Faced with this worldwide movement aimed at improving the disclosure of qualitative information, in 2014, the CPC issued Technical Guidance 07 – Disclosure of General Purpose Financial Reporting. Since Brazilian standards are in line with IFRS, OCPC 07 follows guidelines similar to EFRAG. OCPC 07 points out that the large volume of information in notes to the financial statements causes an increase in transaction costs, impairing decision-making by financial market agents and questions regarding the relevance of the statements. Among the main reasons for issuing this guidance, the CPC (2014) highlights: the large volume of information; reproduction of unnecessary information; presentation of reports apparently based on models with irrelevant features; and increased transaction costs. Despite the criticisms of the practices adopted until then and the new guidelines, the document reinforces the professional's judgment as an inherent element in the elaboration of the statements on a case-by-case basis.

Also in Brazil, the Guidance Committee for Disclosure of Information to the Market (CODIM) issued two Guidance Pronouncements (PO) for Best Practices for Preparation and Disclosure. In 2012, PO 13 was issued, which deals with the Annual Report, highlighting that "disclosure must be necessary and sufficient to facilitate the decision of investors and other interested parties, without confusing them with excessive information".

In 2016, OP 19 was released with the objective of providing guidance in the preparation of notes to the financial statements, after finding a greater volume of unnecessary text in the notes. The presence of repetitive text without prior reflection and judgment on the relevance of this content to the financial reporting. Despite criticisms regarding the length of the notes to the financial statements, CODIM points out that the quality of information should be prioritized and that the reduction of quantity of text does not imply omitting or partially disclosing information that is relevant.

Demonstrating concern with the disclosure of accounting information, in 2016 the IASB presented a work agenda for the period from 2017 to 2021 with one of the focuses for communication to the user, seeking mechanisms to improve the quality of disclosure. After consultation with investors, the IASB decided to focus on projects that result in better presentation, disclosure and communication in financial reports, rather than changes in recognition and measurement requirements. These actions emerged as a result of "Disclosure in Financial Reporting", a public discussion forum promoted by the IASB in 2013.

More recently, in 2023, IASB has concluded the Targeted Standards-level Review of Disclosures Project to help the development of Accounting Standards that would enable firms to provide more useful information to investors. It is based on improving its approach to developing and drafting disclosure requirements. The guidance approach involves: engaging to understand user needs, developing disclosure requirements, digital reporting implications, supporting specific disclosure objectives.

Among the possible proxies to measure the disclosure level of firms, someone can highlight readability measures. Despite criticism, readability measures are still widely used and recommended for this type of study for the following reasons: being an objective test, ease of use, and power of comparison between different texts (Toit, 2017).

Brazilian Studies About Regulations and Readability of Notes

Some Brazilian research aimed to identify the consequences of regulatory acts on the financial statements of publicly traded firms in Brazil. The process of harmonizing financial reporting standards led Brazil to adopt the IFRS as mandatory for public firms, promoting some changes in the preparation of financial statements and, consequently, in their extension. In view of this, Miranda et al. (2018) studied the degree of complexity of financial reports in different periods of the IFRS adoption process in Brazil, finding that readability increased in the post-IFRS period. Borges (2020) tests the relationship between the readability of financial standards and the readability of the notes to the financial statements when they refer to the same subject and the results show that standards with a higher degree of readability result in more readable notes.

Other studies address the consequences on accounting reports after the issuance of OCPC 07. Since the guidance of the CPC suggests practices to make the text less extensive, some studies have investigated whether there was a reduction in the size of the notes to the financial statements (Silva, 2017; Gomes, Ferreira, Martins, 2018; Cruz Junior, 2018). In addition, recent research has verified the impact on the readability of financial statements (Silva, 2017; Gomes et al., 2018; Cruz Junior, 2018; Telles, 2018).

Table 1 summarizes the main results of the aforementioned surveys:

Table 1. Brazilian studies about regulations and readability of notes to the financial statements

Authors (Ano)	Sample	Method	Results
Silva (2017)	Public firms of the food industry listed on BM&Fbovespa from 2010 to 2016.	Ordinary Least Squares Regression	Results show significant changes that could be attributed to OCPC 07 in the readability of the documents analyzed and in relation to disclosure, there is no change.
Miranda et al. (2018)	Public firms of Novo Mercado listed on BM&Fbovespa from 2005 to 2016.	Spearman	Most of the companies that submitted reports in the years 2005 (pre-adoption) and 2016 (post-adoption) decreased the complexity of their reports, suggesting that readability increased in the post-IFRS adoption period.
Gomes et al. (2018)	Public firms of Novo Mercado listed on BM&Fbovespa from 2013 to 2014.	Ordinary Least Squares Regression	Results indicate that the notes to financial statements became smaller, but they did not become easier to read.
Cruz Junior (2018)	Public firms of Novo Mercado listed on BM&Fbovespa from 2010 to 2017.	Mean	The notes to the financial statements exhibit a moderate degree of readability and there has also been an improvement, since the issuance of OCPC 07, in their degree of readability and length.
Telles (2018)	Check how readability impacts the understandability of the notes to the financial statements	Quali-quantitative	There are no differences in comprehension between texts with different levels of readability. Additionally, OCPC 07 did not impact the level of readability for the years studied.
Borges (2020)	Public firms of the IbrX 50 index listed on BM&Fbovespa from 2010 to 2017.	Ordinary Least Squares Regression (Random effects)	Accounting pronouncements with a higher degree of readability result in more readable notes to the financial statements

Results are mixed when comparing studies that analyzed the readability of notes before and after OCPC07. Silva (2017) and Cruz Junior (2018) find an improvement in readability after the issuance of OCPC 07, while Gomes et al. (2018) and Telles (2018) find no impact of OCPC 07 on the readability of financial reporting. Such divergences may be explained by differences in the sample of studies or methods used to analyze the data. This fact reinforces the need for additional studies to contribute to this discussion, using a sample with a greater number of observations and an extended period of time, as well as multiple linear regression of panel data with fixed effect of industry and year. Therefore, this chapter seeks to fill this gap.

METHODOLOGY

This chapter is classified by a descriptive approach of document analysis, using quantitative methods for data analysis through multivariate regression of panel data with fixed effects to verify the relationship between the issuance of the OCPC 07 and readability of the notes to the financial statements.

It is analyzed notes released between 2010 and 2018. The initial period is characterized by different disclosure requirements through the mandatory adoption of IFRS and review of accounting standards by the CPC (Borges & Rech, 2018). The final period was chosen in order to balance the number of statements issued before and after OCPC 07, that is, four years before and after 2014.

Population comprises all firms listed on Brazilian Stock Exchange (B3), which represents 310 firms with active registration at B3 and the Brazilian Securities and Exchange Commission (CVM). After applying the necessary filters to carry out the statistical procedures, 190 firms were excluded for not presenting all data. Thus, the final sample comprises 120 firms x 9 years, otherwise, 1,080 firm-years observations.

The notes to the financial statements were obtained directly from the website of the CVM in PDF format. Elements that cannot be measured for readability was excluded, such as headers, footnotes, single-line paragraphs, titles, tables, charts, graphics and others, as proposed by Li (2008).

To calculate the readability index, this study used the Pylinguistics program (Castilhos, 2016), a free open-source software for natural language analysis in English and Portuguese. Then, electronic spreadsheets were used to organize the data extracted from the various sources mentioned above and then proceed with the econometric calculations through the Stata software.

The main variables (readability of the notes and issuance of OCPC 07) are established as follows:

1. The Flesch index adapted to Portuguese (Martins et al., 1996) is the measure for the readability of notes. This index is used because of the extensive use of the Flesch index (1979) for analysis of accounting narratives, which is the only index adapted and validated for texts in Portuguese. Based on the fact that the Portuguese language usually has words with a greater number of syllables, Martins et al (1996) adapted the Flesch index by adding 42 points to its original formula;
2. OCPC 07 was issued in 2014 by the CPC based on the arguments the identified presence of unnecessary text in financial reporting, therefore this variable is measured using a dummy equal to 1 for firm-year observations after 2014, and zero otherwise (Silva, 2017; Gomes, Ferreira & Martins, 2018)

To isolate external interferences on the coefficient of the main variable (OCPC 07), control variables was added that are related to readability according to recent studies, which includes: profitability, corporate governance, auditing, listing age, indebtedness, and company size. Table 2 reports summarized characteristics of all variables used in this study.

Table 2. Summary of the variables

Variables	Acronyms	Formulas	References
Readability	Read	Adapted Flesh Index (Martins et al., 1996)	Telles (2018)
OCPC 07	OCPC	Dummy equal to 1 for year periods after OCPC 07 (2014) and zero otherwise.	Silva (2017); Gomes et al. (2018).
Return on Assets	ROA	Ratio of earnings over total assets	Li (2008); Lo et al. (2017).
Corporate Governance	CG	Dummy equal to 1 whether firm is part of the Novo Mercado (certification of high-quality governance practices) and zero otherwise	Silva (2017); Borges and Rech (2018).
Audit quality	BigFour	Dummy equal to 1 whether the firm is audited by one of the big four audit firms and zero otherwise	Silva (2017); Borges and Rech (2018).
Listing age	Age	Difference between the current year and the year of listing on the Brazilian stock exchange.	Li (2008); Silva (2017); Lo et al. (2017); Hasan (2018); Borges and Rech (2018).
Market-to-Book	MtB	Ratio of the firm market value over book value assets	Li (2008); Lo et al. (2017); Hasan (2018).
Firm size	Size	Natural logarithm of total assets	Li (2008); Lo et al. (2017); Hasan (2018); Borges and Rech (2018); Hasan (2018).

A multiple linear regression of panel data with fixed effect of industry and year is used to analyze the relationship between readability of notes to the financial statements and the issuance of the OCPC07. The structure of this model is established in Equation 2.

$$Read_{it} = \beta_0 + \beta_1 OCPC_{it} + \beta_2 ROA_{it} + \beta_3 CG_{it} + \beta_4 BigFour_{it} + \beta_5 Age_{it} + \beta_6 MtB_{it} + + \beta_7 Size_{it} + \sum \beta_k OCPC * Industry_k + \text{Æ}_k + \text{É}_y + \varepsilon_{it} \quad (2)$$

Where i and t index the firm and the year, Read is the degree of readability; OCPC is a dummy variable for the OCPC 07; ROA is the return on assets; CG is the proxy for the corporate governance; BigFour is the proxy for audit quality; AGE is the listing age; MtB is the market-to-book ratio; Size is the firm size; OCPC*Industry is the interaction term of OCPC 07 and the industries; φ is the industry fixed effect; ω is the year fixed effect; and ε is the error term.

RESULTS ANALYSIS

Descriptive Analysis

Initially, the descriptive analysis of the variables used in this study are presented. Table 3 reports mean values, standard deviation, minimum and maximum values for each of all variables.

Table 3. Descriptive statistics

Variables	Mean	Standard Deviation	Minimum	Maximum
Read	16.653	4.581	0.877	39.455
ROA	0.126	0.129	-1.601	0.466
Age	16.462	8.742	1	32
MtB	1.383	0.946	0.350	12.298
Size	21.995	1.750	16.546	27.525

Note: Dummy variables are ommitted.

In this sample, the dependent variable "Read", measured by the Flesch index adapted to Portuguese (Martins et al, 1996), exhibit an average value that is classified as "very difficult". These results are similar to studies in other countries (Li, 2008; Lo et al., 2017), as well as studies in Brazil (Silva, 2017; Borges, 2020). When analyzing the minimum and maximum values, it is evident that all notes are classified as "difficult" or "very difficult" to be read.

Despite the readability metrics indicating that the financial statements present a "very difficult" level of readability, the language used in business usually includes words considered complex (three or more syllables), but which are presumably easy for external users to understand (Loughran & Mcdonald, 2014). Some examples of these words are: 'corporação', 'companhia', 'operações', 'administração', 'relatório', 'demonstração', 'desempenho', 'liquidez', 'rentabilidade', etc.

Table 3 does not show the dummy variables. However, this sample is characterized by the following characteristics: firms certified in the Novo Mercado represent 44% of the observations; Big Four audit firms are responsible for assuring 77% of the financial statements. In addition, 56% of the notes were released after 2014 (issue of OCPC 07), reflecting a balance in the sample between the number of notes released before and after OCPC 07. About the characteristics related to the industry, the following proportions are presented: Financial, 19%; Communications, 1,7%; Consumer Cyclicals, 26,4%; Consumer Non-Cyclicals, 7,4%; Industrial Goods, 10,7%; Basic Materials, 9,9%; Oil and Gas, 2,5%; Health, 5%; Information Technology, 0,8%; Utilities, 16,5%.

Still regarding the description of the sample, Table 4 presents the association between the variables through Pearson's correlation.

Table 4. Correlation Matrix

Variables	Read	OCPC	ROA	CG	Big Four	AGE	MtB	Size
Read	1,000							
OCPC	0,004	1,000						
ROA	0,063	-0,179	1,000					
CG	0,119	0,025	0,068	1,000				
BigFour	0,214	-0,082	0,251	0,249	1,000			
Age	-0,074	0,256	-0,116	-0,618	-0,226	1,000		
MtB	0,092	-0,062	-0,108	0,091	0,034	-0,061	1,000	
Size	0,215	0,042	0,177	0,043	0,420	0,089	-0,113	1,000

Table 4 indicates that the correlation between the OCPC 07 and the readability of the notes to the financial statements is not statistically significant. Thus, the issuance of OCPC 07 possibly did not change the readability of the notes. On the other hand, control variables are weakly correlated but with coefficient is statistically significant. This suggests that control variables may influence the readability of notes. Moreover, listing age is the only negatively correlated with the readability index, that is, the longer the company is listed on the stock exchange, the greater the difficulty in reading notes.

Test of Means and Multivariate Analysis

After descriptive analysis, the test of means is used to compare the mean of the readability index of the group of firm-year observations before and after the issuance of OCPC 07. The results are reported in Table 5.

Table 5. Test for difference of means on readability before and after OCPC 07

Group	Observations	Mean	Standard Error	Standard Deviation	Confidence Interval (95%)	
Before	484	16.63565	0.2138853	4.705476	16.21539	17.05591
After	605	16.66762	0.1822982	4.483942	16.30961	17.02564
All	1,089	16.65341	0.1388370	4.581621	4.58162	16.92583
Difference		-0.03197	0.2795309		-0.58045	-0.58045
Ho: Difference = 0						
Ha: Difference < 0 Pr(T < t) = 0.4545			Ha: Difference != 0 Pr(|T| > |t|) = 0.9090		Ha: Difference > 0 Pr(T > t) = 0.5455	

According to test, it is not possible to reject the null hypothesis that there is no difference in the level of readability between the period before and after the issuance of OCPC 07. That is, the notes to the financial statements remains with similar reading difficulty regardless of the guidelines issued in the OCPC 07. Telles (2018) documents similar results, finding no improvement in the characteristics of textual quality and readability in the pre and post OCPC 07 periods.

Since the mean difference tests are characterized by limited statistical power and do not allow testing specific hypotheses, it is necessary to use additional tests in order to control for the effect of other characteristics on the dependent variable. Thus, Equation 2 is estimated using a multiple linear regression model.

To ensure the necessary hypotheses for the analysis using Ordinary Least Squares (OLS), violation tests is performed to verify statistical assumptions of homoscedasticity (Wald test), serial-autocorrelation (Wooldridge test), cross-sectional independence (Pesaran test), and multicollinearity (VIF test). Tests indicates the presence of heteroscedasticity and serial-autocorrelation, then robust estimator proposed by Huber-White is used. Furthermore, it is assumed that residuals are normally distributed based on the Central Limit Theorem.

The results obtained from Equation 2 are reported in Table 6 and Table 7, segregating the analysis into two parts: i) OCPC and control variables; ii) OCPC and Industries. It should be noted that this is the execution of the same regression, being divided into two tables for explanatory purposes only.

Table 6. Results of the multivariate analysis of the relationship between OCPC 07 and Readability

Variables	Coefficients	Standard Errors (Robust)	t	P > I t I	
Intercept	3.0588	2.2521	1.36	0.17	
OCPC	1.0627	1.0810	0.98	0.32	
ROA	0.9885	1.0418	0.95	0.34	
CG	0.4826	0.3717	1.30	0.19	
BigFour	1.0512	0.3744	2.81	0.00	*
Age	-0.0482	0.0237	-2.03	0.04	*
MtB	0.6358	0.1350	4.71	0.00	*
Size	0.4686	0.1003	4.67	0.00	*
Comunications	3.3627	1.1033	3.05	0.00	*
Consumer Cyclicals	0.9539	0.8273	1.15	0.24	
Consumer Non-Cyclicals	1.7445	1.0041	1.74	0.08	
Industrial Goods	1.3004	0.8781	1.48	0.14	
Basic Materials	3.5415	0.9644	3.67	0.00	*
Oil and Gas	1.7378	0.9911	1.75	0.08	
Health	1.7424	1.0692	1.63	0.10	
Information Technology	-1.1371	1.0271	-1.11	0.27	
Utilities	1.3808	0.8973	1.54	0.12	
OCPC * Comunications	-2.5474	1.4209	-1.79	0.07	
OCPC * Consumer Cyclicals	0.5272	1.0606	0.50	0.62	
OCPC * Consumer Non-Cyclicals	-1.2164	1.3488	-0.90	0.37	
OCPC * Industrial Goods	-0.0382	1.0980	-0.03	0.97	
OCPC * Basic Materials	0.4548	1.1529	0.39	0.69	
OCPC * Oil and Gas	-2.4589	1.2908	-1.90	0.06	
OCPC * Health	-1.2327	1.4358	-0.86	0.39	
OCPC * Information Technology	4.0281	1.2397	3.25	0.00	*
OCPC * Utilities	-0.7862	1.0957	-0.72	0.47	

Note: * Significant correlation at the level of 5%

The sign of the coefficients reported in Table 6 indicate that the relationships in the multivariate analysis reinforce the results of the Pearson correlations reported in Table 4. The association between OCPC 07 issuance and the readability of the notes to the financial statements is consistent with the test of means, confirming that the issuance of OCPC 07 did not influence the readability of notes. This result differs from Silva (2017) and Cruz Junior (2018). It is important to highlight that the choice of statistical procedures adopted may result in different coefficients and their respective significance.

OCPC 07 guides the preparation and presentation of notes to the financial statements, seeking to increase the quality and transparency of the information. As a consequence, it is expected that the decision-making of the users of these reports (such as investors, creditors and other stakeholders) will be more assertive for a better allocation of resources.

However, this guidance does not mention the term "readability". Based on the Rational Choice Theory (Scott, 2000), it is possible that the financial statement preparers only complied with the explicit guidelines in the text of OCPC 07, avoiding additional efforts to promote changes that are perceived as not advantageous to them. Thus, it is plausible that the authors made changes to other textual elements that did not cause significant changes in the level of readability.

OCPC 07 presents the basic requirements to the notes for preparation and disclosure of accounting information. Firms are expected to improve the understandability of their statements, once it is one of the requirements, but it is very difficult to measure it (Telles, 2018). It should be noted that the readability factors analyzed in this research are not based on ontological or semantic aspects, therefore it is not possible to make inferences about the understandability of the text.

Additionally, the association between readability level and the issuance of the OCPC 07 is tested in each industry separately. Thus, the coefficient related to the interaction of each industry variable and OCPC variable is estimated. Financial industry is omitted since all dummy variables of the same categorical variable cannot be inserted to avoid perfect multicollinearity. Thus, the interpretation of the coefficients in Table 6 are comparisons between the different industries in reference to financial industry. Financial industry is this reference because it has specific requirements from the regulatory agent (Central Bank) and because it presents vocabulary, expressions and information needs inherent to financial activity that can cause greater difficulty in reading.

With the insertion of the interaction between the OCPC and industry variables, the coefficients of industry reflect the association between a particular industry and the change in the level of readability in relation to the financial industry before the issue of OCPC 07. On the other hand, coefficients of interaction of each industry variable and OCPC report the marginal effect of this relationship after the issuance of OCPC 07.

The analysis of the coefficients for the period prior to the issuance of OCPC 07 indicates that companies other than the financial industry have, on average, notes to the financial statements that are less difficult to read, except for companies in the Information Technology industry. This result indicates that the notes of companies in the financial industry are more difficult to read, which can be explained by the terms and jargon used in this area. In addition, the specific regulations of the Central Bank may require a greater level of detail of information, leading to the writing of longer sentences to explain the facts more completely.

When it comes to the coefficients of the interactions, that is, the change after OCPC 07, the relations are in opposite directions in general, but are not statistically significant, except for companies in the Information Technology industry. The lack of statistical significance in these coefficients reinforces the idea that the issuance of OCPC 07 is not associated with changes in the level of readability of the notes of listed companies in Brazil.

In general, even if some estimators of industry are statistically significant, the difference in the reported readability level would not cause a change in the classification of reading difficulty, since the industry difference would cause an average increase of 3 to 4 points in the Flesch index, in a scale ranging from 0 to 100.

CONCLUSION

This chapter aimed to verify the association between the issuance of OCPC 07 and changes in the level of readability of the notes to the financial statements of Brazilian public firms. The sample comprises 1,080 observations from 120 firms listed on B3 in the period from 2010 to 2018. The analysis was performed using the difference of means test and multiple linear regression.

It is documented unprecedented contributions within this theme by using a sample with a longer period post-IRFS and observations, analyzing different industries (including financial firms) and controlling other factors that may influence the level of readability of financial statements.

The results of the study point to the non-existence of a relationship between the OCPC 07 issued by the CPC and the readability of the notes to the financial statements of the firms listed on B3. The tests of means and multivariate analysis show similar results: there is no association between the studied variables. Thus, it cannot state that the issuance of OCPC 07 caused a change in the readability of notes in the analyzed sample.

By not finding the expected result for the investigated relationship, it is possible to raise questions about the effectiveness of non-mandatory guidelines. Based on the Rational Choice Theory, which states that people analyze the costs and benefits to make choices (Scott, 2000), it can be expected that the preparers of the financial statements do not make changes that are perceived as not advantageous for them.

It is worth mentioning that it is not possible to make inferences about the comprehensibility of accounting information users from the results found in this study, since the readability measures used are not based on semantic or ontological aspects. This factor constitutes one of the main limitations of this chapter. In addition, the reported results cannot be extrapolated to other scenarios, such as private firms, different time periods or different economic environments.

Due to the growing discussion on accounting disclosure by regulatory bodies around the world, it is expected that this chapter adds to the current literature on guidance regulations, helping in the process of accounting regulation by providing information related to this topic. Moreover, this chapter does not exhaust the discussion on this topic, and in view of not having found a relationship between the issuance of OCPC 07 and the ease of reading the notes to the financial statements, it is suggested that studies be carried out to identify whether there were changes in other disclosure characteristics in the notes due to the issuance of OCPC 07.

REFERENCES

Antunes, M. T. P., Grecco, M. C. P., Formigoni, H., & Neto, O. R. D. M. (2012). A adoção no Brasil das normas internacionais de contabilidade IFRS: O processo e seus impactos na qualidade da informação contábil. *Revista de Economia e Relações Internacionais*, *10*(20), 5–19.

Asay, H. S., Elliott, W. B., & Rennekamp, K. (2017). Disclosure readability and the sensitivity of investors' valuation judgments to outside information. *The Accounting Review*, *92*(4), 1–25. doi:10.2308/accr-51570

Baker, H. E., & Kare, D. D. (1992). Relationship between annual report readability and corporate financial performance. *Management Research News*, *15*(1), 1–4. doi:10.1108/eb028188

Bonsall, S. B. IV, Leone, A. J., Miller, B. P., & Rennekamp, K. (2017). A plain English measure of financial reporting readability. *Journal of Accounting and Economics*, *63*(2-3), 329–357. doi:10.1016/j.jacceco.2017.03.002

Borges, G. F. (2020). *Análise da Legibilidade dos BR_GAAP X Legibilidade das Notas Explicativas de Empresas Brasileiras Abertas*. [Doctoral dissertation, Universidade de São Paulo, São Paulo, SP].

Castilhos, S. Pereira. (2016). *Pylinguistics: an open source library for readability assessment of texts written in Portuguese*. [Graduate school dissertation, Universidade Federal do Rio Grande do Sul, Porto Alegre, RS].

Comitê de Pronunciamentos Contábeis. (2019). CPC 00 R2: *Estrutura Conceitual para Relatório Financeiro*. CPC. http://www.cpc.org.br/Arquivos/Documentos/573_CPC00(R2).pdf

Courtis, J. K. (2004). Colour as visual rhetoric in financial reporting. *Accounting Forum*, *28*(2), 265–281. doi:10.1016/j.accfor.2004.07.003

Cruz, H., Junior. (2018). *Legibilidade de notas explicativas em empresas de capital aberto no Brasil*. [Undergraduate thesis, Universidade Federal de Uberlândia, Uberlândia, MG].

Cunha, R. K. C. (2008). *Análise da facilidade de leitura das demonstrações contábeis das empresas brasileiras*: *uma investigação do gerenciamento de impressões nas narrativas contábeis*. [Master's thesis, Universidade de Brasília, Brasília, DF].

Dias Filho, J. M., & Machado, L. H. B. (2004). *Abordagens da pesquisa em contabilidade. Teoria avançada da contabilidade*. Atlas.

Espíndula, R. P., & Costa, P. S. (2008). Análise da influência da publicação e da legibilidade dos atos ou fatos relevantes no preço da ação das empresas brasileiras de capital aberto no período de 2002 a 2006. Horizonte Científico, Uberlândia, 2(1).

Flesch, R. F. (1979). *How to write plain English: A book for lawyers and consumers*. Harpercollins.

Gelbcke, E. R. (2018). Manual de contabilidade societária: aplicável a todas as sociedades de acordo com as normas internacionais e do CPC.

Hasan, M. M. (2020). Readability of narrative disclosures in 10-K reports: Does managerial ability matter? *European Accounting Review*, *29*(1), 147–168. doi:10.1080/09638180.2018.1528169

Hendriksen, E. S., & Van Breda, M. F. (1999). *Teoria da contabilidade* (A. Z. Sanvicente, Trans.). Atlas.

Hendriksen, E. S., & Van Breda, M. F. (2012). *Teoria da contabilidade* (10th ed.). Atlas.

Lanzana, A. P. (2004). *Relação entre disclosure e governança corporativa das empresas brasileiras*. [Master's thesis, Universidade de São Paulo, São Paulo, SP].

Lee, Y.-J. (2012). The effect of quarterly report readability on information efficiency of stock prices. *Contemporary Accounting Research*, *29*(4), 1137–1170. doi:10.1111/j.1911-3846.2011.01152.x

Li, F. (2008). Annual report readability, current earnings, and earnings persistence. *Journal of Accounting and Economics*, *45*(2-3), 221–247. doi:10.1016/j.jacceco.2008.02.003

Lo, K., Ramos, F., & Rogo, R. (2017). Earnings management and annual report readability. *Journal of Accounting and Economics*, *63*(1), 1–25. doi:10.1016/j.jacceco.2016.09.002

Martins, T. B., Ghiraldelo, C. M., Nunes, M. D. G. V., & de Oliveira, O. N. Junior. (1996). *Readability formulas applied to textbooks in brazilian portuguese*. Icmsc-Usp.

Miranda, I. A., Reina, D., & Lemes, S. (2018). Grau de legibilidade dos relatórios financeiros em empresas do novo mercado. In *USP International Conference in Accounting* (Vol. 18).

Moreno, A., & Casasola, A. (2016). A readability evolution of narratives in annual reports: A longitudinal study of two Spanish companies. *Journal of Business and Technical Communication*, *30*(2), 202–235. doi:10.1177/1050651915620233

Peleias, F. D. 'A. (2017). *Mecanismos linguísticos (des)favoráveis para a readability das demonstrações financeiras: uma análise das empresas listadas no mercado de capitais brasileiro*. [Master's dissertation, Fundação Escola de Comércio Álvares Penteado, São Paulo, SP].

Rodrigues, F. F. (2012). *Fatores determinantes da evolução das informações divulgadas no relatório da administração das empresas brasileiras de capital aberto*. [Doctoral dissertation, Programa Multi-institucional e Inter-regional de Pós-Graduação em Ciências Contábeis. Brasília, DF].

Scott, J. (2000). Rational choice theory. *Understanding contemporary society: Theories of the present*, *129*, 671-85.

Silva, C. A. T., & Fernandes, J. L. T. (2009). Legibilidade dos fatos relevantes no Brasil. *Revista de Administração Contemporânea - RAC Electronica*, *3*(1), 142-159.

Silva, R. B. (2017). *Implicações da OCPC 07 no disclosure e na forma das notas explicativas das demonstrações contábeis*. [Master's dissertation, Universidade Federal do Ceará, Fortaleza, CE].

Smith, M., & Taffler, R. (1992). Readability and understandability: Different measures of the textual complexity of accounting narrative. *Accounting, Auditing & Accountability Journal*, *5*(4), 0-0.

Telles, S. V. (2018). *Readability and understandability of notes to the financial statements*. [Doctoral dissertation, Universidade de São Paulo, São Paulo, SP].

Toit, E. (2017). *The readability of integrated reports*. Meditari Accountancy Research.

KEY TERMS AND DEFINITIONS

CPC: Brazilian Accounting Standard Committee.
Flesch index: A measure of readability.
IFRS: International Financial Reporting Standards.
Notes: Narrative Report that includes additional information supporting Financial Statements.
OCPC: Technical Guidance issued by Brazilian Accounting Standard Committee.
OCPC 07: Technical Guidance about Disclosure of General Purpose Financial Reporting.
Readability: Inherent ability of text to be read quickly and easily.
Understandability: Reader's ability to understand a text.

Chapter 7
The Secret of the Best:
The Practice of Risk Management in Brazilian Educational Institutions

Rômulo Brito Oliveira
Universidade Federal de Pernambuco, Brazil

Fernando Gentil de Souza
Universidade Federal de Pernambuco, Brazil

Darlene Silva S. Santana
Instituto Federal de Educação Ciência e Tecnologia da Bahia, Brazil

ABSTRACT

The theme of governance has occupied the spaces of debate and practice in public administration. The evaluation of good examples of institutional management, in the current scenario, is always linked to the implementation of governance principles and their guidelines. In this sense, this chapter aims to indicate an initial step to increase risk management in Brazilian educational institutions. To this end, the authors present the historical path of the concept of governance until its adoption by public management in Brazil, seeking to understand the current political-economic-social; then, in order to show that good practices lead to good results, the authors list some Brazilian educational institutions that present a high Government Management Index, pointing out some of their actions that contributed to the excellence status. Finally, in the last chapter, the authors describe the initial stages of implementation of risk management, using the Swot Matrix as a useful tool for the systematic knowledge of the institution, which enables decision making more consistent with the reality of the context.

DOI: 10.4018/978-1-6684-7293-4.ch007

INTRODUCTION

The topic of governance dates back to ancient times. The term governance can be broadly defined as a complex decision-making process that anticipates and transcends government (Rodhes, 1996). But it is from the administration of private organizations by third-party agents that its concept was delineated in the sense of presenting regulatory principles to secure the interests of investors and owners. Since then, the term has expanded in meaning and achieved trustworthy status, gaining the title of Corporate Governance and becoming present in the various actions of private and governmental institutions around the world. According to Bhatta (2003), corporate governance in the public sector refers to the management of public institutions through private sector corporate governance principles, adapted to the reality of state agencies.

In this historical path, the global crisis of the 1980s demanded a reformulation of the State's role in the economy in order to increase its credibility and efficiency. To this end, a new global discussion began, whose agenda indicated the expansion of the principles of Corporate Governance to the public sphere, that is, the systematic construction of a regulation of the roles and responsibilities of the organizations' managers in order to minimize the impacts of conflicts of interest. This means that governance mechanisms should be instituted in the public administration in an attempt to ensure that the objectives of the owner/principal, citizens, are achieved and preserved.

Thus, in recent decades we have seen significant contributions from multilateral and private institutions such as the World Bank, the Organization for Economic Cooperation and Development (OECD), the International Monetary Fund (IMF), the International Federation of Accountants (IFAC), and the Brazilian Institute of Corporate Governance (IBGC). It is important to recognize these contributions with emphasis on the insertion of corporate governance practices, favoring the consolidation of basic governance principles in public administration shared worldwide. This systematization of good governance practices continues to be on the agenda of organizations such as the World Bank, the IMF, and the OECD (TCU, 2004) with a view to making public service more efficient, ethical, and committed to the real interests of society.

Public Governance in Brazil has a milestone in the 1988 Federal Constitution and, since then, a series of legal documents have been reformulating the organization of state agencies in order to improve governance practices in public service, such as the Fiscal Responsibility Law; the National Program of Public Management; the Access to Information Law; among others. Besides these legal instruments, other independent institutions, such as the IBGC and the Tribunal de Contas da União - TCU, contribute to the acquis on the subject, with periodical publications such as the Code of Best Corporate Governance Practices (IBGC) and the Basic Governance Reference (TCU) that serve as models and samples of good practices that can be incorporated in public instances.

More recently, with the recommendation expressed in the 2014 judgment of the TCU, the topic occupied definitive space in the government agenda, inserting the theme in Brazilian legislation with the publication of the joint Normative Instruction MP/CGU of 2016, which determines that "the agencies and entities of the federal executive branch shall adopt measures for the systematization of practices related to risk management, internal controls, and governance" (Art. 1º of IN 01/2016) and of Decree 9,203/2017, which "provides for the governance policy of the direct federal public administration, autarchic and fundamental" (Art. 1º of Decree 9,203 of November 22, 2017). Among the guidelines described for the materiality of what was put, the documents present risk management as a fundamental process, without which the practice of governance is not effective, since the mapping of possible events that may compromise institutional activities ensures quick and preventive decision-making to nullify or mitigate errors and problems, thus promoting more satisfactory results as to what is desired.

In this sense, it is important the careful study of the available tools for an adequate risk management, starting from the context of application, as well as institutional maturity regarding the applicability of governance practices in the specific body. Thus, in order to collaborate with this study, this research aims to present the SWOT technique to support risk management in the governance process in Brazilian federal educational institutions.

The SWOT matrix, according to Appio, Scharmach & Sampaio (2009), is a tool that, by identifying the positive and negative institutional aspects and correlating them, allows a holistic, complete and real knowledge of the performance context and of the institution itself, collaborating in decision making to improve the company's performance.

Furthermore, in addition to describing the SWOT Matrix as an important tool for the practice of risk management, we extend the discussion to analyze how risk management is applied in the contextual reality of Brazilian federal education institutions, verifying the way in which it has been adopted by each management and its impacts on institutional results. Thus, this work is characterized methodologically as qualitative in nature with documentary and bibliographic survey procedures.

According to Richardson (2008), qualitative research consists in understanding a given phenomenon by means of a subjective and grounded analysis. Thus, this research consists of a subjective analysis by presenting the authors' considerations on the subject when discussing the SWOT tool as effective in the preliminary implementation of a risk management policy. The documentary procedure supported the survey and the selection of Brazilian educational institutions that obtained the best averages of the Integrated Governance and Management Index (iGG) of the Federal Court of Audit - TCU in 2021. From the result, it was sought to investigate the governance and risk management measures disclosed on the official websites of the respective institutions to understand the secret of success. Finally, based on the bibliographic survey for theoretical foundation and aiming to contribute to the dissemination of good governance practices, the last theoretical chapter simulates the use of the SWOT Matrix as a first step to implement a risk policy in Brazilian federal educational institutions.

To organize the discussions, this article is structured into four sections: the first consists of this introduction, in which we contextualize the topic to be discussed and the objectives. In the second section, we present the concept of risk management within the practice of governance, as well as describe the risk management practices in some Brazilian institutions. The third section details the first steps for an educational institution to implement a risk management policy through a study based on the SWOT analysis. Finally, the last section is the conclusion, in which we present the limitations, difficulties, and suggestions for future studies.

RISK MANAGEMENT: THE PILLAR OF GOVERNANCE

Risk management is one of the processes that make up good corporate governance, and appears in several best practice models as a pillar of corporate governance. Risk is the possibility that results will differ from expectations, which may involve serious losses or new opportunities (Damodaran, 2003). ISO 31000 defines risk as the effect of uncertainty on objectives. And risk management involves coordinated activities aimed at directing and controlling an organization in relation to risks. Article 2 of Decree 9.203/2017 conceptualizes risk management as "a process of permanent nature, established, directed and monitored by senior management, which contemplates the activities of identifying, evaluating and managing potential events that may affect the organization" (BRASIL, 2017) and, in its Article 3 item VI, states, as a guideline of public governance, "to implement internal controls *based on risk management*, which will privilege *strategic prevention actions* before sanctioning processes" (BRASIL, 2017 - our emphasis). Based on this proposition, risk management is a concrete action in the search for improvement of institutional work and fundamental to the practice of governance, since it guides structuring protocols to reduce possible losses, as well as increases the power of positive results, increases the effectiveness of activities and, consequently, increases the reliability index before society.

As for Normative Instruction 01/2016, in addition to conceptualizing the terms for the purpose of collective understanding, it highlights risk management as "the process of identifying, assessing, managing and controlling potential events or situations to provide reasonable certainty regarding the achievement of the organization's objectives," which means that it is a fundamental step to ensure the organization's efficiency in meeting its goals and its role in society. Without risk management, companies are unaware of the true extent of the operational risks they face, leaving them vulnerable to unpleasant surprises (Westerman & Hunter, 2008). In this sense, it is worth stating that it is from the mapping and assessment of risks that decisions must be taken, since it is up to management to prepare strategic planning, procedural standardization, financial investments, among other measures, consistent with the circumstances that may interfere directly and/or indirectly in institutional results.

Thus, the lack of risk measurement can cause losses to the institution, both financial and operational (since the lack of protocols to mitigate risks can lead to waste or allocation of resources and human energy in nonessential activities, compromising the competent execution of activities) and prestige, since once the activities are not executed with efficiency and transparency, society's confidence can be affected by the agency's poor functional management and apparent inability to fulfill its mission and purpose for which it was created. For Gromoff & Stavenko (2012), the effectiveness of risk management depends on flexibility, adaptability, and speed of response, factors that are directly related to the ability of an organization to quickly deal with adverse situations. It is in light of these considerations that it behooves us to conduct a survey of how educational institutions have appropriated the risk management policy to improve their activities and, consequently, raise their approval rating before regulatory agencies and society.

Due to the constant updates in public administration, the institutions need better prepared managers, because the exercise of activities in the public sector has particular characteristics, aiming to produce positive results for the population. In this context, the central concern of risk management is to look out for the public interest; the risks must always be managed in the public interest. This makes the most important aspect of risk management to decide how to balance potential gains and losses. Estimating risks and evaluating technically valid and socially acceptable alternatives is a complex task for policy makers who must be prepared to make decisions: "A government's ability to manage risk depends on the skills of its officials" (2000, PCO4).

Public servants cannot avoid making risky decisions. Therefore, everyone must have the skills and abilities to deal with these risks. Stephen Hill (2006, p. 30) highlights three ways to help staff identify and manage potential risks, facilitate decision making and direct the management of risks, identify and control the management of these risks, and know the best ways to manage them.

In the first of these learning alternatives, case studies are a useful tool for equipping staff with knowledge from a wide variety of past experiences. In the second approach, it is important to allow public service managers to actively participate in managerial experiments based on trial and error also known as "adaptive management". In the third case, it is advisable to help managers see how their mental models affect their understanding of risks - perhaps through scenario development, interdisciplinary efforts, or public dialogues.

In many cases, the risk management process requires that public managers ponder, evaluate, and maintain a balance between the conflict of interests until the best acceptable measure is determined, but these actions in most instances involve political choices, leaving technical decisions in the background. For this reason, the objective of risk management in public administration is ultimately that of the public interest, always improving the quality of the services provided by the Administration and the effectiveness of public policies. One of the challenges of public service is to continuously improve its activities in the face of increasingly complex and changing situations. The government's ability to plan, formulate, implement, and execute policies is continuously evaluated by those involved in the governance process and by the beneficiaries of public policies. Therefore, all leaders have responsibilities, a shared source of accountability, and the need for internal and external controls to monitor operational actions and events.

A Brief Overview of Risk Management in Federal Educational Institutions

In 2017, the TCU made the iGG available, which considers the governance and management capacity of federal public organizations and also of other entities under the jurisdiction of the TCU, based on the level of implementation of good leadership, strategy, and *accountability practices*, including risk management, as well as good governance, IT management, people management, and procurement practices. With the formalization of this index, the gathering of information on public institutions became annual and was inserted as an integral part of their accountability process. According to the (TCU, 2017), the action is part of a process that seeks to better understand the governance situation in the public sector, in addition to encouraging the implementation of policies, plans and actions aimed at good management practices provided in the TCU's Basic Governance Reference.

The TCU clarifies that the main purpose of the iGG is to help users identify aspects of governance and management with the greatest risks and opportunities for improvement, in their area of jurisdiction, influence or study. The users of the information can be multiple, among them the parliamentarians, the advisors, whether they are linked to public policies, the boards or collegiate superiors of public organizations, the senior management of these organizations and their assistants, the control bodies or higher governing bodies responsible for regulating and monitoring segments of the public administration, the academia (colleges, universities, research centers, etc.), the media, etc. The TCU also warns that the use of the iGG (or its sub-indicators) in the form of a ranking is not appropriate in most situations, since public organizations are often not directly comparable, if not with those of the same segment and conditions. Noting this information, this study sought to evaluate institutions in the same segment. Thus, comparisons between organizations using the iGG must be made with extreme care so that the conclusions to be drawn are valid and truly useful for the purpose of the research.

As this metric is based on responses from the organizations themselves, a margin of error must be taken into account, however this cannot be known. Therefore, it is impossible to say that a fabric with iGG 0.80 is better than a fabric with iGG 0.70, as in fact they could be tied or even 0.70 class better if the statistical error were ±0.10. Furthermore, iGG is measured against the minimum set of internal controls that the TCU believes facilitate the control of risks common to public organizations. It is for this reason that an organization with an iGG of 0.50, but little exposure, is likely to do better than another organization with an iGG of 0.70, but a lot of exposure. For example, organizations in the banking system face many risks and must implement tighter controls according to national and international rules, while small public foundations may face few risks, so there is no need to have such a high iGG as a target. It must be remembered that the implementation of internal controls is very costly for the state and should only be done if the risks justify its implementation (Law 200/1967, art. 14).

In the iGG survey conducted in 2021, 378 public organizations participated with valid responses . The data were collected in the period October 2022 from the ranking made available on the TCU portal. When analyzing the federal educational institutions linked to the Ministério da Educação - MEC, we captured to investigate the good practices those that occupied the ranking of the top three places, which are:

Table 1. TCU's iGG 2021 ranking of the Brazilian educational institutions linked to the MEC

Institution	Average iGG
Universidade Federal do Rio Grande do Norte (UFRN)	0.96
Universidade Federal de Itajubá (UNIFEI)	0.93
Universidade Federal de Mato Grosso do Sul (UFMS)	0.91

Source: portal.tcu.gov.br

UFRN created the Secretariat of Institutional Governance (SGI), in 2019, as one of the actions to strengthen university administration. The sector built a Governance Action Plan based on the survey and guidelines made by the TCU in 2018, aiming to develop, implement and monitor policies, based on the Basic Governance Benchmark that has plans and actions guided by good practices. In addition, from Resolution nº 016/2017 - CONSAD, it instituted the Risk Management Policy and created the Governance, Risks and Controls Committee with the goal of mapping and evaluating institutional risks, as well as advising management in decision-making. Among the results, UFRN developed the "Risk Management Dashboard" that graphically shows all events related to risks in a sectored way, which provides a broad view of institutional strengths and weaknesses, and contributes to a more strategic planning focused on results.

UNIFEI, in turn, has the Governance, Risk and Control Management Committee (CGRC) which is one of the advisory bodies to the Central Administration, whose goal is to implement and supervise the Risk Management Policy. The risk matrix of each body, as the Directorate of Information Technology - DTI, Pro-Rectory of Teaching and Extension - PROEX, Pro-Rectory of Administration - PRAD, among other bodies that make up the CGRC allows to evaluate the key risks that may compromise the achievement of the objectives of UNIFEI, provided in the Institutional Development Plan (PDI), thus providing reasonable assurance that the mission and vision of the University are fulfilled. In parallel to the risk matrices, the Committee's bodies performed the respective analyses of their strengths, weaknesses, opportunities and threats, known as SWOT Analysis that they perform in parallel to the risk matrices, composing the risk management process.

The UFMS, finally, exposes in its portal that the risk management became a permanent policy of the University, from the guidelines of the Integrity Management Policy, Risks and Internal Controls of the UFMS, approved by Resolution No. 134-COUN/UFMS, of October 15, 2021, which encourages, on an ongoing basis, the adoption of mechanisms for identification, mapping, monitoring and evaluation of risks and existing processes; the training of employees to improve management practices; the implementation and updating of models, with the purpose of identifying the degree of vulnerability in the institution and proposing measures for its mitigation. Besides this policy, UFMS has the Committee of Integrity, Risks and Internal Control Management (CGIRCI) that seeks to promote, together with the Institutional Governance Committee, a management instrument of actions, goals, and monitoring, which originated the Process and Risk Management Plan - 2022/2024. It is worth noting that a risk management structure, duly guided by processes, meets the main purpose of transparency to the Public Administration, thus, the plan presented by the institution is a complete instrument to meet the current needs of good governance and perfected to contribute to achieving the objectives of the institutional mission.

Some renowned institutions have also achieved outstanding iGG, such as the Universidade Federal de Pernambuco (UFPE), the Universidade Federal da Bahia (UFBA) among others. The TCU has been avoiding encouraging organizations to use simple goals to increase iGG. In fact, the incentive the TCU has been giving is for organizations to assess their true risk (for example, with the help of the iGG) and implement only the necessary controls. Therefore, each organization should set its own targets for each iGG sub-meter (according to its risk) and pursue only its own targets. The fact is that, to achieve the objectives of good governance, actions are required to establish the principles, guidelines, responsibilities and competencies for the implementation of integrity management, risks and internal controls with the purpose of fostering institutional credibility, ensuring security in the achievement of the mission, continuity and sustainability of the services provided to society.

Thus, we detail in the following chapter some guidelines to proceed with the implementation of a risk management policy in educational institutions in order to contribute to the studies in the area and, consequently, with the improvement of public administration.

FIRST STEPS TOWARDS A RISK MANAGEMENT POLICY

Firstly, it is necessary to state that organizations need to be concerned with the potential risks that may reach their objectives. According to Salles Júnior, de Souza, and de Souza (2010), the word risk is directly related to uncertainty, uncertain events in the future, which can be positive or negative.

First of all, it is necessary to analyze the context of the organization to understand its needs and expectations; this should be done based on criteria defined by the institution itself. Damodaran (2009) states that to manage risks, it is initially necessary to understand the risks to which an organization is exposed. For example, internal criteria can be organizational structure, governance, flows and processes, information systems, and others; while external criteria can be cultural, political, legal, economic, technological, or regional scenarios. Thus, based on this survey, it is possible to have a holistic view of the institution and, consequently, identify the risks that may compromise the achievement of its objectives.

To identify risks, some tools are used, which differ in their complexity and applicability. In this work, we will use the SWOT Matrix because it is the most appropriate for an initial stage of implementation of institutional risk management.

In a case study of exploratory nature, published in 2018 in the Journal Strategy & Development and entitled "SWOT Analysis: Case Study in a Higher Education Institution", the authors conclude that the impact of SWOT analysis on the company's strategy is like a kind of rudder, which guides to the best path to be followed, however, it takes skill to understand what actually needs to be done to achieve positive results. In another study, entitled "Institutional Diagnosis of the Universidade Federal da Paraíba from SWOT Analysis", the authors conducted an institutional diagnosis of the Universidade Federal da Paraíba

(UFPB) using SWOT analysis as a strategic management tool and concluded that SWOT analysis was a useful tool for the institutional diagnosis of the UFPB, allowing the identification of relevant aspects for the management of the university; in addition to the conclusion, the authors recommend the continued use of this tool to improve the management of the institution and ensure its long-term sustainability.

The SWOT analysis was created by Kenneth Andrews and Roland Cristensen, professors at Harvard Business School, and studies the competitiveness of an organization from the perspective of four variables: Strengths, Weaknesses, Opportunities and Threats Rodrigues, Eiras, Nunes, and Cardoso (2005). SWOT analysis is a tool used to evaluate the competitive position of an organization and identify its strengths, weaknesses, opportunities and threats. In other words, it is a necessary assessment model that measures what an organization can and cannot do and its potential risk areas. What makes SWOT particularly powerful is that it provides reflection and can help the organization discover valid opportunities to be exploited. And by understanding weaknesses, management can create strategic actions to eliminate threats and/or prepare to overcome them.

In this vein Chiavenato & Sapiro (2009, p. 181) explain how to use the SWOT matrix. After the survey of the factors based on the strategic intent of the organization (taking into account the mission, vision, values and organizational objectives), one must cross the opportunities and external threats with the strengths and weaknesses of the institution.

Table 2. Visual arrangement of the SWOT analysis

Swot analysis			
		Assists	**Disturbs**
Internal Factors	Organization	Strength	Weaknesses
External Factors	Environment	Opportunities	Threats

Source: adapted of SILVA (2009)

The primary function of SWOT analysis is to enable the choice of an appropriate strategy to achieve certain objectives from a critical evaluation of the internal and external environments (Serra, Torres & Torres, 2004).

Regarding the internal environments, according to Chiavenato & Sapiro (2003), the criteria to be evaluated are: financial resources, market leadership and image, competitive conditioning that generates barriers to the entry of new competitors, technologies, cost advantages, advertising, capabilities, and product innovations.

According to Rezende (2008), organizational strengths or strengths are internal and controllable variables that provide the organization with advantages over its environment. They are characteristics or qualities of the organization that can positively influence its performance, thus strengths should be widely exploited by the organization. To list some possibilities of strengths in federal public educational institutions, we can mention: its differential in quality teaching, being a reference in promoting the citizen's education; tradition, which ensures high credibility with its public by offering teaching, research, and extension with socially referenced quality; experience in teaching, research, and extension; fostering of cultural, social, technological, and entrepreneurship/innovation projects through public notices; servers with higher qualifications than required for the position; teams committed to performing their activities;

workplace suitable for the development of activities; processes in a virtual way and better communication of servers; managers act strongly so that the activities are developed in order to meet the institution's objectives; faculty dominates the expertise in their respective academic areas.

Weaknesses are considered deficiencies that inhibit the organization's ability to perform and must be overcome to avoid bankruptcy (Matos, Matos, & Almeida, 2007). Regarding weaknesses, federal public educational institutions have a strong and polarized political process, sometimes causing changes in management and project profiles. The lack of process standardization can also be a weakness, which ends up demanding more time and use of more resources to complete certain tasks, decreasing individual and collective productivity levels and increasing the risk of errors and rework. In addition, other conditions can be defined as weaknesses, such as: the organizational structure of the unit is fragile and does not contemplate strategic servers and functions for governance; deficiency in the levels of training of the internal community (including employees) in matters related to governance; low level of maturity for the development of governance policies, risks and internal controls in the institution; failure in communication between administration and the units; absence of goals and performance indicators defined for each sector in accordance with the strategic objectives; absence of a technical tool for the implementation of organizational climate survey; lack of specific internal training for the development of the sectors; absence of a system for project management.

Regarding external factors, according to Sobral & Peci (2008), the external environment consists of the socio-geographical context where organizations exist and operate, being formed by the elements that are not within their boundaries. It can be understood as a collection of factors that, despite being outside the institution, influence it directly and/or indirectly. The external factors are organized into two groups: opportunities and threats.

Opportunities are the external and non-controllable variables that can create favorable conditions for the organization, provided it is able or interested in using them (Rezende, 2008). In the context of the public service of educational institutions, it is possible to seek the implementation of actions to promote the use of technology to improve their own activities. These measures are evident when institutions start to make partnerships with the public and private sectors in order to, besides promoting the quality of education, attract new audiences and opportunities, showing their importance in society and opening options for the implementation of new courses, contributing even more to the social development of the country. Among other opportunities linked to the external environment, we can cite: the university's adherence to Transforma.gov and the implementation of digital government; the emergence of new digital services offered by the Federal Government for service and management activities; post-pandemic economic heating; alignment with municipal, state and federal governments; government incentives for modernization of management and governance; growing incentives from the Federal Government, with offers of online training for teams; exchange of experiences with other universities; promote the training of faculty for their development through postgraduate programs, raising the quality of teaching, research and extension actions offered.

According to Oliveira (2010), threats are external conditions that have influence over the institution and may bring certain difficulties. In relation to this aspect, federal educational institutions suffer recurrent cuts and contingencies that affect budgets, leading to economic conditions that compromise the power of investment. The constant changes in legislation and regulation are also threats to the administrative and operational activities, since, if the institutions do not promote updates and training to their employees, they may suffer with notifications from the control bodies and also with the payment of fines and interest due to errors and delays in the delivery of information. Other possible threats can be: the non-replacement of the work force, due to retirement, requisition, etc.; extinction of positions in the career of Technical and Administrative Servants in Education; constant changes in government systems regarding procedures; uncertainties related to the pandemic; demand for speed X legal insecurity; increase of the administrative burden resulting from legislation; insecurity in the official sites and systems (cyber attacks); change of government/management, intrinsic characteristic to the public administration, discontinuing projects.

To better elucidate this discussion, we illustrate below a SWOT matrix with the factors listed from possible occurrences in Brazilian educational institutions.

Table 3. SWOT analysis with a survey of possible internal and external factors linked to the Brazilian educational institutions

Swot analysis			
		Assists	**Disturbs**
Internal FactorsExternal Factors	OrganizationEnvironment	**StrengthQuality teaching, being a reference in promoting the formation of the citizenExperience in teaching, research and extension**	**WeaknessesStrong and polarized political process sometimes the projects suffer with the change of management profileThe unit's organizational structure is weak and does not include employees and strategic functions for governance**
		What are the organization's assets and skills?Tradition, which ensures high credibility with its public, offering teaching, research and extension with socially referenced qualityPromotion of cultural, social, technological, and entrepreneurial/innovation projects through public notices	Any competence deficits in the organization?Lack of process standardization, generating increased time and use of more resources to complete certain tasksDeficiency in the levels of training of the internal community (including employees), in matters related to governance
		Servers with qualifications higher than those required for the position	Low level of maturity for the development of governance policies, risks and internal controls in the institution
		Teams committed to performing their activities	Faulty communication between management and the units
		Workplace adequate for the development of activities	Non-existence of performance goals and indicators defined for each sector in accordance with the strategic objectives of the University
		Virtual processes and better server communication	Non-existence of a technical tool to implement the organizational climate survey
		The managers act strongly so that the activities are developed to meet the institution's objectives	Lack of specific internal training for the development of the sectors
		Faculty master the expertise in their respective academic areas	Non-existence of a system for project management
		Opportunities	**Threats**
		What external factors benefit the organization?	What are the organization's risks?
		Implementation of actions to encourage the use of technology to improve their own activities	Recurrent cuts and contingencies that affect the budgets of federal educational institutions
		Partnerships with the public and private sector publicize the quality of education, attract new audiences	Constant changes in legislation and regulation
		The university joins Transforma.gov and implements digital government.	Non-replenishment of the work force, due to retirement, requisition, etc.
		Emergence of new digital services offered by the Federal Government for attendance and management of activities	Extinction of Positions in the career of Technical and Administrative Servants in Education
		Post-pandemic economy heating up	Keep track of as many changes in government systems regarding procedures
		Alignment with municipal, state and federal governments	Uncertainties related to the pandemic;
		Government incentive for management modernization and governance	Demanding speed vs. legal insecurity
		Growing incentives from the Federal Government, with online training offers for the teams	Increased administrative burden from legislation;
		Exchange of experiences with other universities	insecurity on official sites and systems (Cyber attacks)
		promote the qualification of the teaching staff for its development through post-graduate programs, raising the quality of the teaching, research and extension offered	Change of government/management, an intrinsic characteristic of public administration, discontinuing projects

Source: author's elaboration

With the visual arrangement of the survey carried out according to the SWOT matrix guidelines, it is possible for everyone linked to the institution to become aware of the set of factors that directly and indirectly affect the activities developed, favoring a collective participation in institutional conservation and improvement.

In order to obtain a more complete and objective result, it is recommended that the construction of the SWOT matrix be done from different groups of action and interest within the organization. The individualized application by internal sectors can contribute to a real and legitimate picture. Promoting workshops to bring teams together is also a great opportunity to encourage engagement and integration of those involved.

For Pereira (2010, p. 114), the SWOT analysis aims to "gather all items considered as Strengths and relate them to Weaknesses, Opportunities and Threats". After the data survey, a correlation of the strengths with the opportunities is applied, seeking to take advantage of some strength of the organization that can be transformed into an opportunity. In the same way it is done with the threats and weaknesses, that is: look for some strong point that helps to minimize the impact of some threat or weakness. Thus, the organization must have a perception of how it is and, based on a collective collaboration, seek the best strategies to optimize results.

In order to promote the correlation of the points raised in each of the four variables, one can adopt the procedure of obtaining answers from questions. To correlate the organization's weaknesses with the external environment, we can start by relating the opportunities with the weaknesses. Thus it is possible to ask: What should we do with our weaknesses to take better advantage of our opportunities? As answers, it is possible to infer: 1) Promote an internal regulation that guarantees the continuity of projects mainly focusing on fostering the use of technology in the improvement of the activities themselves; 2) Improve the standardization of processes using external benchmarking actions, seeking partnerships with the public and private sector.

In the relationship between threats and weaknesses, we try to answer the following question: What should we do to strengthen our weaknesses and prevent the threats from damaging us even more? Possible answers: 1) Demonstrate with data the ongoing projects and the planning for the coming years regardless of the change in management profile, seeking a sense of continuity and possible alternatives to eventual cuts and contingencies; 2) Standardize the processes according to the current legislation being aware of their changes and the readjustment of processes.

In the analysis of the strengths with the external environment, it is possible to correlate the opportunities with the strengths by answering the following question: How can our strengths be used to take advantage of our opportunities? Among the answers, one can obtain: 1) Use the tradition, high credibility and quality teaching to reach the opportunities of partnerships with the public and private sector to attract new publics; 2) In the search for the implementation of actions to promote the use of technology to improve its own activities, one can use the strength of its own quality teaching referenced in the technological area, such as IT and Robotics courses.

Finally, in the same way as above, we can correlate the threats with the organization's strengths, answering the question: How can our strengths be used to prevent threats from hindering our strategies? Possible answers: 1) Demonstrate, with positive data, to higher education institutions, the importance of the organization and its quality teaching to avoid recurrent cuts and contingencies; 2) Promote courses and qualification for employees on changes in legislation and regulation of academic and administrative activities.

Next we present figure 3, which shows a simulation of the correlation of the four variables. It is worth pointing out that this action plan depends on the organization's strategy and available resources.

Table 4. Correlation of internal and external factors of the SWOT analysis

Swot analysis		
Swot analysis correlation	**External Analysis Opportunities O**	**External Analysis Threats T**
Internal Analysis Weaknesses W	What should we do with our weaknesses to take better advantage of our opportunities?	What should we do to strengthen our weaknesses and prevent the threats from harming us further?
	Promote an internal regulation that guarantees the continuity of the projects, mainly focusing on the promotion of the use of technology in the improvement of its own activities	Demonstrate with data the ongoing projects and the planning for the coming years, regardless of the change in management profile, seeking a sense of continuity and avoiding recurrent cuts and contingencies
	Improve process standardization using external benchmarking actions, seeking partnerships with the public and private sectors	Standardize the processes according to the legislation in force, being aware of its changes and the readjustment of the processes
Internal Analysis Strengths S	How can our strengths be employed to take advantage of our opportunities?	How can our strengths be used to prevent threats from hindering our strategies?
	Use tradition, high credibility, and quality teaching to reach out to public and private sector partnership opportunities to attract new audiences	Demonstrate with positive data to higher bodies the importance of the organization and its quality teaching to avoid recurring cuts and contingencies
	In the search for Implementation of actions to promote the use of technology in the improvement of its own activities, one can use the strength of its own quality education referenced in the technological area as IT and Robotics courses	Promote courses and qualifications to prepare employees for changes in legislation and regulation of academic and administrative activities

Source: author's elaboration

For Pereira (2010, p. 116) in relation to the analysis of the environment (internal and external), says that the most important thing is the decision made after the analysis, and states that "recognizing and applying the SWOT matrix is the most important thing, because it allows the organization to have a general and deep view of its situation". Thus, from the SWOT matrix, we get an accurate and real survey of the comprehensive conditions that involve the internal and external environment variables of the institution. And, by making the correlation, we can explore how the variables contribute to a greater self-knowledge of the organization, favoring the obtaining of valuable insights to define which strategies should be put into practice. By following these steps, the institution can promote its initiation into risk management.

The practical implementation of the SWOT Matrix is an activity that must be carried out in a detailed and organized manner. Considering this information, for a good execution of the application of the tool, process management is necessary to ensure that the action reaches its objectives. Process management can be defined as the organization and structuring of all the steps and tasks that contribute to the achievement of the organization's strategic objectives in order to ensure their correct execution. Enabling the institution to act effectively, achieving maximum production with minimum effort. Seeking to optimize and do more with less is a central responsibility of managers, from the highest decision-making level to the simplest level of execution (Davenport, 1994).

According to Melo (2000), the corporate environment must be adequate for the management by processes to produce the expected results, having to have its global structure interconnected with other management tools such as: strategic planning, organizational structure, total quality, logistics, managerial reports, participation systems and the server promises. As a suggestion, we present a flowchart of the main steps for the implementation of the SWOT matrix. It is worth noting that the deeper the analysis, the more complete the diagnosis will be.

1. Gather the entire strategic team in a workshop, demonstrating the benefits of using the SWOT technique, explaining in detail what the Strengths and Weaknesses are, demonstrating examples and possible results. Space is recommended for the exposure of ideas with the goal of raising information and discussing about events and factors in each sector. Through this meeting, data and aspects that will be part of the analysis are collected and shared.
2. Establish a deadline for each unit to do the internal analysis, raising the Strengths and Weaknesses, and the external analysis, describing the Opportunities and Threats.
3. After the analysis of each unit, the team responsible for the implementation should conduct a review, clarifying possible misunderstandings or seek to produce more information.
4. Close the matrix by describing in each section the negative aspects (threats and weaknesses) and in the other the positive factors (strengths and opportunities). These should be recorded in a visible place, physical or virtual, being ideal a matrix of easy and quick visualization and understanding.
5. Each unit should make the correlation between the elements (Strengths, Opportunities, Weaknesses and Threats). It is necessary to allow time for this discussion. For this you can answer some questions as presented.
6. Perform an action plan with the objective of promoting actions to achieve the correlated factors, using the strengths to take advantage of the opportunities, minimize the weaknesses, and avoid the threats. At this stage, the organization already has a good analysis of where it stands, because the SWOT matrix provides an overview of the entire organization.

Table 5. Flowchart of SWOT analysis implementation in an organization

How to implement SWOT Matrix Analysis in an organization?	
Main steps to implement and use the SWOT matrix.	**Flowchart**
1. Gather the entire strategic team, promoting a workshop, demonstrating the benefits of using the SWOT technique, explaining in detail what the Strengths and Weaknesses are, demonstrating examples and possible results. Space is recommended for the exposure of ideas with the goal of raising information and discussing about events and factors in each sector. Through this meeting, data and aspects that will be part of the analysis are collected and shared.	Workshop with strategic team
2. Establish a deadline for each unit to do an internal analysis of its Strengths and Weaknesses, and an external analysis describing opportunities and Threats.	Internal and External Analysis of each sector
3. After the analysis of each unit, the team responsible for the implementation should conduct a review, clarifying possible misunderstandings or seek to produce more information.	Review of the data by the responsible team
4. Close the matrix by describing in each section the negative aspects (threats and weaknesses) and in the other the positive factors (strengths and opportunities). These should be recorded in a place that should be visible, physically or virtually, ideally in a matrix that is easy and quick to visualize and understand.	Closing and elaboration of the SWOT matrix
5. Each unit should make the correlation between the elements (Strengths, Opportunities, Weaknesses and Threats). It is necessary to allow time for this discussion. For this you can answer some questions as presented.	SWOT Analysis Correlation
6. Perform an action plan with the objective of promoting actions to achieve the correlated factors, taking advantage of the strengths to take advantage of the opportunities, minimize the weaknesses and avoid the threats. At this stage the organization already has a good analysis of how it is, because the SWOT matrix provides an overview of the entire organization.	Promote an action plan

Source: author's elaboration

In light of the above, we realize the importance of using techniques to aid organizational performance. With training, low cost, and willingness, an environment for risk analysis, matrix development, and benchmarking can be quickly established. Little by little, as in private organizations, these strategic departments will improve their work, optimize resources, reduce risks, and help ensure effective communication and compliance with laws and regulations, avoiding damage to the entity's reputation and its painful consequences. From this perspective Almatrooshi, Singh & Farouk (2016), highlight that organizational performance refers to its ability to effectively implement strategies to achieve institutional goals and objectives, achieving real results.

CONCLUSION

This paper presented SWOT analysis as an option for initiating a risk management policy in educational institutions. The use of this technique helps management to become aware of the factors that help and hinder the achievement of the institution's objectives, enabling greater engagement and participation of the strategic team in risk management. In this sense, considering risk management as an initiative that results in the improvement and quality of management, we present a contribution to the literature on the benefits that SWOT analysis can provide in the work context.

Governance and risk management in the public service is a relatively new topic, and for it to be well applied it is necessary to understand the bases and guidelines that permeate the scope of this subject. In this vein, there is a strong need for the training of public servants with the objective of promoting the appropriate competence in the survey and analysis of the risks raised.

After all, what is the secret of the best institutions? We realize that good results are not by chance. The actions implemented by the institutions that are at the top of the average IGG are good governance practices based on technical and contextual knowledge that, consequently, lead to positive results. Factors such as leadership, strategy, and *accountability* are maintained by a cohesive team that, by achieving specific objectives, help achieve the overall goal, contributing to the fulfillment of the institution's mission, vision, and values.

In this research, the possible limitations described in the SWOT Matrix are simulated data that may not accurately reflect the reality of each institution. However, we indicate a path to initiate the practice of risk management with the intention of showing that it should not be restricted only to data tabulation and information gathering, but should expand to the applicability of knowledge and possible maintenance of management quality in public administration.

SWOT analysis is a management tool widely used in various contexts, whether in business, government or academia. By performing a SWOT analysis in an appropriate and contextualized manner, it is possible to obtain a clearer and more accurate view of the organization's current situation. However, it is important to emphasize that the SWOT analysis is not just a simple listing of factors, but should be contextualized so that it becomes clear that its use aims to contribute to a good diagnosis, and that the methodologies for goal setting and strategy formulation should also be followed. This is the only way to identify opportunities for improvement and risks to be controlled. With this, it is also possible to establish realistic and effective objectives, and outline strategies to achieve them, ensuring greater control of the risks involved. In summary, SWOT analysis is a fundamental tool for risk management, but its use must be carried out in a careful and methodological manner, to ensure a complete and accurate diagnosis of the organization's situation, allowing the establishment of clear and effective objectives and the development of strategies to achieve them.

Finally, it should be noted that Governance is a constant process. Thus, it is up to the institutions to promote strategic planning with direction of actions in the search for excellence in their activities, and may take advantage of techniques such as SWOT analysis, to achieve better collaboration between servers, promoting efficient communication between departments and teams. In addition, it can guide the course of the institution in the search for service satisfaction before the public. Moreover the institution can use the strengths and opportunities to improve the quality of management, making processes and procedures faster and more efficient, allowing the identification and elimination of unnecessary or repetitive steps, providing better results. In addition to greater agility to respond quickly to weaknesses and threats, reducing time and resources, which can lead to a reduction in costs. This process, finally, may be the first major step towards the materialization of institutional knowledge and consequent change in behavior in face of institutional reality, as analyzed in this study.

REFERENCES

Adm Working Group On Risk Management. (2000). Risk Management for Canada and Canadians: Report of the ADM Working Group on Risk Management. Ottawa: Privy Council Office (PCO), Government of Canada.

Almatrooshi, B., Singh, S. K., & Farouk, S. (2016). Determinants of organizational performance: A proposed framework. *International Journal of Productivity and Performance Management*, *65*(6), 844–859. doi:10.1108/IJPPM-02-2016-0038

Appio, J., Scharmach, Alr, Silva, Akld, Carvalho, Lcd, & Sampaio, Cac. (2009). SWOT analysis as a competitive differential: An exploratory study in Cooperativa Muza Brasil. *Revista Interdisciplinar Científica Aplicada*, *3*(3), 1–18.

Bhatta, G. (2003). Post-NPM issues. In Public Sector Governance, Wellington: State Services Commission. Working Paper no. 17.

Brazil Court of Auditors of the Union. (2014). Referencial Básico de governança aplicável aos órgãos e entidades da administração pública. Brasília: Secretariat of Planning, Governance and Management.

Cavalcanti, L. M. R., & Guerra, M. G. G. V. (2019). Institutional diagnosis of the Federal University of Paraíba from SWOT Analysis. *Electronic Journal of Social Development*, (33), 120–137. doi:10.22347/2175-2753v11i33.2270

Chiavenato, I., & Sapiro, A. (2009). *Planejamento estratégico* (2nd ed.). Elsevier.

Damodaran, A. (2003). *Investment philosophies: Successful investment philosophies and the greatest investors who made them work*. Wiley and Sons.

Damodaran, A. (2009). *Strategic risk management: reference for enterprise risk taking*. Bookman.

Davenport, T. H. (1994). *Reengenharia de processos*. Campus.

de Oliveira, D. (2010). *Planejamento estratégico: conceitos, metodologias e prática* (28th ed.). Atlas.

Gromoff, A., & Stavenko, J. (2012). An attempt at a systems approach to operational risk management. *Far East Journal of Psychology and Business*, *8*(3), 38–49.

Hill, S. (2003). A basis for developing learning strategies for risk management in public service (LMBL de Vasconcelos, Trad.). Brasília: National School of Public Administration - Enap.

Hill, S. (2006). Guide on risk management in the public service (LMBL de Vasconcelos, Trad.). Brasília: National School of Public Administration. (Cadernos Enap, 30).

Jr, S. Cac, S, Am, V. J., & Rabechini, R. (2010). Gerenciamento de riscos em projetos (2a ed.). Rio de Janeiro: Editora FGV.

Melo, M. S. (2000). A Gestão da Qualidade Total e as perspectivas dessa tendência nos serviços públicos [Dissertação de mestrado, Universidade Federal da Paraíba, João Pessoa, PB, Brazil].

Pereira, M. F. (2010). *Planejamento estratégico: teorias, modelos e processos. São Paulo: Atlas. Matos, J. G. R., Matos, R. M. B., & Almeida, J. R. DE. (2007). Análise do Ambiente Corporativo: do caos organizado ao planejamento*. E-papers.

Ramos, V. (2019). A proposal for using risk management for Academic Planning at a Public University. *Journal of Management and Projects*. https://doi.org/ . doi:10.5585/gep.v10i1.14777

Rezende, D. A. (2008). *Planejamento estratégico para organizações: públicas e privadas*. Brasport.

Richardson, R. J. (2008). *Social research: methods and techniques* (3rd ed.). Atlas.

Sdi Unifei. (n.d.). *Risk Management and Controls*. Sdi Unifei. https://sdi.unifei.edu.br/governanca-riscos-e-controles-internos/gestao/

UFNS. (n.d.). Risk Management Policy. Ufms. https://www.ufms.br/comite-de-gestao-de-integridade-riscos-e-controle-interno/gestao-de-riscos/

Rodhes, R. (1996). The new governance: Governing without government. *Political Studies*, *44*(4), 652–667. doi:10.1111/j.1467-9248.1996.tb01747.x

Rodrigues, J. N., Eiras, R., Nunes, C., & Cardoso, J. F. (2005). 50 gurus for the 21st century. Lisbon: Centro Atlântico.PT.

Santos, R., Ribeiro, H. C. M., & Moreira, A. A. A. P. (2018). Swot analysis: A case study in a higher education institution. *Strategy & Development Journal*, *2*(3), 18–34.

Serra, F., Torres, A., & Torres, M. (2004). *Administração estratégica: conceito, roteiros práticos e casos*. Reichmann & Affonso Editores.

Silva, B. (2015). *Proposta de modelo de gestão de riscos para uma ifes visando a realização de auditoria baseada em riscos* [Master's thesis, Universidade Federal do Rio Grande do Norte, Natal]

Sobral, F., & Peci, A. (2008). *Administração: teoria e prática no contexto brasileiro*. Pearson Prentice Hall.

Tcu. (n.d.). *Levantamento de governança*. TCU. https://portal.tcu.gov.br/governanca/governancapublica/organizacional/levantamento-de-governanca/levantamento-de-governanca.htm

Ufrn achieves 1st place in governance and management. (2022, August 11). UFRN. https://ufrn.br/imprensa/noticias/52219/ufrn-alcanca-1o-lugar-em-governanca-e-gestao

Westerman, G., & Hunter, R. (2008). *O risco de TI: convert ameaças aos negócios em vantagem competitiva*. M. Books do Brasil.

KEY TERMS AND DEFINITIONS

External benchmarking: When the comparison of practices and performance is carried out between different organizations, within or outside the same operating segment.

Cyber-attacks: This is a set of actions directed against information systems.

Governance: A complex decision-making process that anticipates and transcends government.

Integrated Governance and Management Index (iGG): This considers the governance and management capacity of federal public organizations and also of other entities under the TCU's jurisdiction.

Fiscal Responsibility Law: This establishes a set of public finance norms aimed at responsible fiscal management.

Access to Information Law: This regulates the constitutional right of citizens to access public information.

National Program of Public Management: This is a program that aims to contribute to improving the quality of public services provided to citizens.

Chapter 8
An Assessment of the Stakeholders' Participation and View in IPSASB Due Processes

Paula Gomes dos Santos
https://orcid.org/0000-0003-2192-8855
Instituto Politécnico de Lisboa, Portugal

Fábio Albuquerque
https://orcid.org/0000-0001-8877-9634
Instituto Politécnico de Lisboa, Portugal

Maria Eugênia Paiva da Penha
Universidade Federal de Pernambuco, Brazil

ABSTRACT

Despite being an international reference, the majority of countries did not fully adopt international public sector accounting standards (IPSAS). Given the importance of due processes to the IPSAS Board (IPSASB) legitimation, this chapter uses the comment letters sent by different stakeholders within its due processes to assess their level of participation and agreement with the IPSASB position concerning their distinctive characteristics. For this purpose, seven ongoing projects in August 2021 are used as a source of information, and contingency tables and the chi-square test as statistical analysis techniques. The findings show, as matters of constraint to the IPSASB legitimacy, a low level of responses overall, as well as a lower level of agreement by government entities and national standards setters. The study provides inputs to the understanding of the limited implementation of IPSAS, proposing as a future avenue the inclusion of some elements that can be particularly useful to explain stakeholders' engagement and interests in IPSASB public consultation processes.

DOI: 10.4018/978-1-6684-7293-4.ch008

INTRODUCTION

The international public sector accounting standards (IPSAS) are global standards for public sector accounting issued by the International Public Sector Accounting Standards Board (IPSASB), designed in convergence with the International Accounting Standards Board (IASB) standards, which aim at the comparability of financial information among countries (Schmidthuber et al., 2020). IPSAS has been seen as a benchmark for high-quality public sector accounting standards, which has led some international institutions, such as the International Monetary Fund (IMF), the World Bank (WB), and the Organization for Economic Cooperation and Development (OECD), to encourage countries to adopt standards consistent with IPSAS, especially in emerging countries (Association of Chartered Certified Accountants (ACCA), 2017; Toudas et al., 2013).

It is observed a trend in countries of moving towards accrual-based accounting standards (OECD/International Federation of Accountants (IFAC), 2017; Cavanagh et al., 2016), which is due, namely, to the development of accrual-based international standards for government fiscal and financial reporting including Government Finance Statistics Manual (GFSM) and IPSAS (Cavanagh et al., 2016).

Despite this trend, since IPSAS adoption is not mandatory (IPSASB, 2020; Oulasvirta & Bailey, 2016), the majority of the jurisdictions apply national standards, and only a reduced number of countries have fully adopted IPSAS (Chartered Institute of Public Finance and Accountancy (CIPFA)/IFAC, 2021; OECD/IFAC, 2017).

The scientific interest in the development of IPSAS and the harmonization of public sector accounting standards has been growing (Schmidthuber et al., 2020). The studies about IPSAS implementation sets out that it is a challenge, takes time, and is costly (Schmidthuber et al., 2020). Also, IPSAS has been criticized, namely for not being adequate for public sector accounting (Polzer et al., 2022; European Commission, 2013).

Given the limited number of countries that fully adopted IPSAS, it is important to study the IPSASB due processes through public consultations, which are relevant to the IPSASB's efforts to maintain and strengthen its legitimacy (Pittrof, 2021; Baskerville & Grossi, 2019). They address the broad public to participate in and influence the process of standard development by commenting on the published exposure drafts during the due process (Schmidthuber et al., 2020). Therefore, it is relevant to know what the involvement of the stakeholders in the due processes is, and how they position themselves regarding the IPSASB arguments (Kidwell & Lowensohn, 2019).

Research on the IPSASB due processes is still scarce and is mainly focused on the study of the affiliation and country of origin of respondents to public consultation processes, as well as on the level of agreement with the IPSASB position (Kidwell & Lowensohn, 2019; De Wolf & Christiaens, 2019; Manes Rossi & Aversano, 2015; Bisogno et al., 2015; Mitu & Tiron-Tudor, 2013). Also, most studies assess the comment letters (CL) submitted by stakeholders for a single project.

Due to the literature gap on the IPSASB due processes, namely in what concerns the influence of stakeholders' characteristics on the views on IPSASB's position, this chapter uses, as a source of information, the answers provided by different groups of stakeholders who responded to the different questions posed in the public consultation related to seven ongoing projects undertaken by the IPSASB at the time the data were collected (July and August 2021). Then, it aims to assess the level of stakeholders' participation and agreement with the IPSASB position, assessing the differences concerning their distinctive characteristics, namely the groups of interest (types of stakeholders), localisation (based on the country-level of alignment with the IPSASB's legitimacy), and the public sector accounting framework (accounting and reporting standards) used.

As a result of the proposed approach, this chapter intends to offer further insights that may explain stakeholders' responses during public consultations, which include their engagement and interests in these processes. Those inputs can be particularly useful to understand the limited implementation of IPSAS, adding to the literature on public sector accounting harmonization.

The structure of this proposed chapter is as follows. The next section reviews the relevant literature. Section three provides the objectives and the proposed methodology. The analysis for this chapter is presented and the main findings are discussed in section four. Finally, the last sections provide the future research directions and the conclusion from this research.

LITERATURE REVIEW

In many countries, the setting of accounting standards for the public sector has been the responsibility of the Minister of Finances (MoF). By introducing accrual accounting, some of them externalized the standard-setting by having independent advisory boards of the governments (e.g. France, and the United Kingdom), by having independent national standards setters (e.g. New Zealand, Australia, Canada, and South Africa); by adopting standards developed by an international standard setter (e.g. Chile); or by consulting the supreme audit institutions before enacting new accounting standards in the public sector (e.g. Austria) (Cavanagh et al., 2016).

In the context of OECD countries, about 50% have the MoF as the standard-setting authority, while only 24% have the standard setting as a duty of independent national standard-setting boards (Australia, Canada, France, Israel, Mexico, New Zealand, and the United States) (OECD/IFAC, 2017).

IPSAS intends to enable comparability (IPSASB, 2020), which may help countries to improve, for instance, their borrowing conditions (ACCA, 2017). However, given the importance of accountability in the IPSASB Framework, which usually operates within the borders of countries and for national users, there is less pressure for international comparability in the public sector (Baskerville & Grossi, 2019).

By not being mandatory (IPSASB, 2020; Oulasvirta & Bailey, 2016), governments may implement IPSAS through its unaltered adoption, its partial adoption (only adopting some standards), by adapting certain standards, or may not implement IPSAS at all (Polzer et al., 2022).

According to OECD/IFAC (2017), only 3% of OECD countries have fully applied IPSAS, and the majority (57%) apply national standards.

The CIPFA and the IFAC assessed the current frameworks used by federal and central governments around the world and concluded that 69 out of 166 countries use other national standards (42%), of which 40 adopted IPSAS with no modifications (24%). It also identifies countries that apply national standards with reference to IPSAS (23%), IPSAS modified for the local context (10%), and national standards based on the International Financial Reporting Standards (IFRS) (2%) (CIPFA/IFAC, 2021).

Governments and national standard setters use IPSAS as guidelines for their national accounting standards, which can comply to a higher or lower degree with IPSAS (Caruana, 2019). Due to the several IPSAS adaptations to the national accounting rules, every national transition to IPSAS is different, with some IPSAS being ignored, which translates into a low level of consistency and comparability among countries (Schmidthuber et al., 2020; PwC, 2019; EY, 2016).

Polzer et al. (2022) assessed the IPSAS implementation in Austria, Estonia, Iceland, France, Poland, Spain, Sweden, Switzerland, and the United Kingdom, concluding that none of them has implemented the IPSAS directly, having adopted national rules or standards influenced by IPSAS. Several reasons may explain this evidence, based on the criticisms around the IPSAS implementation. Polzer et al. (2022) summarized them as follows: i) they are inadequate for public sector accounting; ii) being principle-based, they allow too many disclosures and valuation options; iii) they disregard certain accounting issues, such as social benefits, pension provisions, and heritage assets; iv) there are contradictions and conflicts between IPSAS and established national accounting standards; v) countries have limited incentives or pressures to adopt IPSAS; and, finally, vi) IPSAS adoption may not be economically feasible.

European Union (EU) supported some of these critics when proposing the establishment of European Public Sector Accounting Standards (EPSAS). The European Commission noted that, despite being a reference, IPSAS could not be easily implemented in the EU Member States as it stood, proposing the implementation of EPSAS to "reduce the complexity of methods and compilation processes used to transform these data onto a quasi-harmonised basis and minimise risk as regards the reliability of the data notified by the Member States and published by Eurostat" (European Commission, 2013, p. 9). The proposal, according to Kidwell and Lowensohn (2019), decreased the likelihood that EU Member States would fully adopt IPSAS.

Given that governments and international organizations are not obliged to apply IPSAS, due processes through public consultations are relevant for the IPSASB legitimation (Pittrof, 2021; Baskerville & Grossi, 2019). According to Richardson and Eberlein (2011), this legitimacy can be based on the participation of the various stakeholders (input legitimacy), may result from the process (throughput legitimacy), or be based on the quality of the standards issued (output legitimacy). The first form is of particular importance to IPSASB, namely through public consultation processes that allow the collection of the stakeholders' opinions (De Wolf & Christiaens, 2019; Richardson & Eberlein, 2011).

The IPSASB due processes are similar to those of other international standards setters, allowing stakeholders to provide input through public consultations. The Board starts new projects, namely with an Exposure Draft (ED) or a Discussion Paper (DP), which are placed in public consultation (free of charge). Stakeholders may contribute through CL, which can lead to changes in those documents that, whenever significant, may be placed in a new public consultation process (IPSASB, 2016).

As far as the literature on the IPSASB's due processes is concerned, few studies have assessed the representativity of respondents and their level of agreement with the IPSASB's position based on their interest groups and geographical location, primarily focusing on legitimation issues. Few studies also assess the level of participation by the public sector accounting framework used. However, none was found that assessed different patterns for the respondents' agreement level with IPSAS's position based on that distinctive characteristic.

Regarding the stakeholders' affiliations or groups, the literature has been distinctly classifying them for assessment purposes, as their responses may influence the standard-setting proposals, for instance:

i. Manes Rossi and Aversano (2015) grouped the respondents into the following three categories: Professional Organizations; Public Organizations; and Standard Setters.
ii. Bisogno et al. (2015) classified the respondents into six interest groups, as follows: International Organizations; Governmental Organizations; Professional Organizations; Counties; Academics; and Audit/Consulting firms.

iii. De Wolf and Christiaens (2019) identified the following nine groups: Standard-Setting Boards; Governmental Organizations; Intergovernmental Organizations; Individuals; Professional Associations; Firms; Universities; Others; and Unknown. In the study by De Wolf et al. (2021), the respondents were classified as follows: Academics; Auditors; Public Sector Entities; Interest Groups; International Organisations; Professional Associations; Professional Organisations; and Standard Setters.
iv. Kidwell and Lowensohn (2019), finally, identified 14 distinct stakeholders groups, proposing a more detailed division of different categories, as follows: professional associations; standard setters; Treasury/Ministry of Finance; Court of Accounts/National or State Auditors; Standards Advisory Group; External Accounting Firms; Academics; Government; Practitioners; International agency; Local Government; Central Banks; Regulators; User Groups; Analysts; and Other.

Despite the different entities' classifications found in literature, there is a set of common classifications that can be divided into additional groups, as follows: i. standard setters; ii. public entities, such as government entities and other public sector entities; iii professionals, such as consultants, preparers, and professional associations; iv. academics, which sometimes include those residual categories not included in the previous groups (others). Concerning their participation in the IPSASB due processes, entities classified as governmental entities, professional associations, and standard setters are the ones that most respond, while academics have a low level of representation (Bisogno et al., 2022; De Wolf & Christiaens, 2019; Kidwell & Lowensohn, 2019; De Wolf et al., 2021; Manes Rossi & Aversano, 2015; Bisogno et al., 2015). According to De Wolf and Christiaens (2019), the lower level of representation by academics may compromise, not only the IPSASB's input legitimacy but also the throughput legitimacy, due to the relevance of the contributions of those stakeholders. Kidwell and Lowensohn (2019) note the existence of a reduced level of individual engagement (unlike what happens in the GASB due process), which may result from their belief that individuals have opportunities to influence these processes more at the national level than internationally.

Regarding the geographic area, the literature has been classifying the regions by continents, as follows: Africa, Asia, Europe, and Oceania, with America being divided into Central and South America and North America, and, finally, a seventh group comprised of the international organizations (De Wolf et al., 2021; De Wolf & Christiaens, 2019; Kidwell & Lowensohn, 2019). As for the localisation of respondents, most of the answers come from Europe, North America, Oceania, and Africa; there is also relevant participation from international organizations (Bisogno et al., 2022; De Wolf et al., 2021; Kidwell & Lowensohn, 2019; Bisogno et al., 2015).

Finally, regarding the public sector accounting framework used by respondents, it was also possible to find out that countries in which IPSAS have been fully implemented or are planning to implement them have a higher level of participation in these processes (De Wolf & Christiaens, 2019). Also, there is a positive relation between a higher implementation level of IPSAS and the stakeholders' participation in the IPSASB's due process by De Wolf and Christiaens (2022).

In what concerns the alignment between stakeholders' opinions and the IPSASB's position, in general, research has found a higher level of agreement, as the examples provided below indicate:

- Kidwell and Lowensohn (2019) studied the public comments in the IPSAS setting through the period of 2010 to 2017 and found a higher level of agreement;

- Also, concerning the Consultation Paper (CP) on Public Sector Combinations (Mitu & Tiron-Tudor, 2013) and the CP on Reporting Service Performance Information (Manes Rossi & Aversano, 2015), there was a general agreement with the position of IPSASB;
- As for the CP on Financial Reporting for Heritage in the Public Sector, the majority of respondents agreed with the IPSASB, although they expressed some concerns about the accounting perspective proposed for this specific type of asset (De Wolf et al., 2021);
- Regarding the ED 63 Social Benefits, respondents disagreed with the IPSASB position, raising questions on the IPSASB conceptual framework, as well as the alignment with other frameworks with different users and objectives, such as the National Accounts or the Government Financial Statistics (Brown et al., 2018);
- Finally, concerning the EDs '70 Revenue with Performance Obligations', 71 'Revenue without Performance Obligations', and 72 'Transfer Expenses', Bisogno et al. (2022) found a high percentage of responses that, despite agreeing with the IPSASB position, make several comments providing additional explanations and suggestions.

Considering the analysis of the differences in agreement levels based on the respondents' distinctive characteristics, there are different patterns found in the literature as follows.

In this sense, the research found indicates that neither De Wolf et al. (2021) nor Manes Rossi and Aversano (2015) found any evidence of different agreement levels based on the respondents' geographic location.

As for the interest groups, Manes Rossi and Aversano (2015) concluded that there were no significant differences in the responses. Conversely, according to De Wolf et al. (2021), the differences found between governmental entities and professional associations suggested that the interest group influenced the responses.

The next section presents the chapter's objective and methodology.

OBJECTIVES AND METHODOLOGY

This chapter aims at studying the IPSASB due processes concerning the stakeholders' participation and their level of agreement with the IPSASB position. Differences in those matters from their distinctive characteristics are also assessed, which includes the interest groups (based on the stakeholders' affiliations or groups), localisation (based on the country-level of alignment with the IPSASB's legitimacy), as well as the public sector accounting framework (based on the accounting and reporting standards used).

This study is based on the archival research method, with content analysis as a research technique for classifying the stakeholders' answers to each question posed by IPSASB in its public consultations. Notwithstanding, it is worthwhile to stress that the objective is limited to the assessment of the stakeholders' agreement levels with the different questions proposed and, therefore, the use of that technique was limited to this purpose.

The answers were collected during July and August 2021, from the IPSASB projects, in the CP and ED phases, whose consultation ended during the period between the last quarter of 2019 and the period of data gathering, which include the seven ongoing projects presented in Table 1.

Table 1. The ongoing projects assessed

	CL	Number of questions	Total observations	Valid observations
ED 75 Leases	50	3	150	148
ED 74 IPSAS 5: Borrowing Costs	18	1	18	16
ED 72 Transfer Expenses	66	10	660	563
ED 71 Revenue without Performance Obligations	68	7	476	383
ED 70 Revenue with Performance Obligations	75	5	375	304
ED 69 Public Sector Specific Financial Instruments, Amendments to IPSAS 41: Financial Instruments	19	1	19	18
CP Measurement	30	15	450	363
Total	326		2,148	1,795

Since a given CL comprises a diverse set of questions, it was not considered the following set of answers: i) those that did not identify the question to which they were concerned, only providing general comments; ii) non-answers to a given question. Also, some CL contains distinctive responses from more than one entity, so they were considered individually in this context. Therefore, the reference sample comprises 326 CL and 1,795 valid observations out of 2,148 total observations collected, including a total of 104 stakeholders and 44 different countries, representing all continents.

The answers were classified into dichotomic variables according to the stakeholders' agreement ("1") or not ("0") with the proposed question (adapting the methodology followed by Kidwell & Lowensohn, 2019). Therefore, the answers that fully or partially agree (although making some caveats) were considered as agreeing ("1"), while the others were included in the opposite situation ("0").

As the chapter's objective is to assess the different perspectives between the subgroups according to their distinctive characteristics, they were classified by interest groups, geographic location, and accounting framework, as follows.

Regarding the **interest group**, the various respondents were classified into four groups as follows: national standard setters; government entities and other public sector entities (public entities group); consultants, preparers, and professional associations (professionals' group); and academics (based on De Wolf et al., 2021; De Wolf & Christiaens, 2019; Kidwell & Lowensohn, 2019; Manes Rossi & Aversano, 2015; Bisogno et al., 2015).

In what concerns **geographic location**, it was considered two different classifications. Based on the respondent's country, the first relates to the continent and, based on the literature, seven groups were identified, namely: Africa, Asia, Europe, Central and South America, North America, Oceania, and International. The latter includes respondents from international organisations and those who represent two or more countries of more than one of the previous groups (De Wolf et al., 2021; De Wolf & Christiaens, 2019; Kidwell & Lowensohn, 2019). Given the European Commission's position of implementing EPSAS (and not IPSAS), evidencing a minor alignment with the IPSASB's legitimacy, the second one is related to the European Union (EU) classification, considering the respondents from, or not from, any of the EU Member States or the European Commission. International organisations and those who represent more than one country were classified as 'International'.

Concerning the **accounting framework**, five groups were initially distinguished, namely those located in countries that used national standards based on IFRS (NS IFRS-based), national standards based on IPSAS (NS IPSAS-based), other national standards (other NS), IPSAS modified for the local context (IPSAS modified), or IPSAS with no modifications (IPSAS not modified) (following the classification from IFAC). Respondents from international organisations and those who represent two or more countries with different frameworks were classified in a sixth group, named 'non-applicable'. The information on the accounting framework relates to the year 2020 and was obtained from the global impact map, available on the website of the IFAC.

The chapter uses contingency tables and the non-parametric chi-square test as statistical analysis techniques. As this test requires two non-related answers as samples and dichotomic variables, all of them were performed by comprising all possible combinations of two groups at a time.

RESULTS AND DISCUSSION

This section presents and discusses the results obtained from the answers to the questions for the projects identified in the preceding section.

Table 2 presents the geographic distribution of respondents by continent and international organisations with a breakdown by their accounting framework.

As shown in Table 2, most responses came from Europe (19%), followed by North America (17%), Africa (16%), and Oceania (13%). International organizations (15%) have also relevant participation. The results corroborate the literature about the high engagement of the stakeholders of those localisations with the IPSASB due process (Bisogno et al., 2015 and 2022; De Wolf et al., 2021; Kidwell & Lowensohn, 2019).

Regarding the accounting framework, 28% of the responses are from countries that have other national standards (not related to IPSAS or IFRS), and 17% have IPSAS modified for the local context. Only 10% have adopted IPSAS with no modifications, which does not follow the conclusions by De Wolf and Christiaens (2019) about a higher level of participation of these countries in such processes.

European responses are mainly from countries that have national standards based on IFRS (38%), other national standards (25%), and IPSAS modified for the local context (22%), while the respondents from North America have mainly other national standards (72%). The respondents from countries who have adopted IPSAS with no modifications are exclusively from Africa, Asia, and North America, having more expressive rates in Asia (with 34% of the respondents), and in Africa (with 29% of the responses from these countries). These results show the possible influence of international institutions (such as IMF, MB, or OECD) on the adoption of IPSAS, particularly in emerging countries (ACCA, 2017; Toudas et al., 2013).

Table 2. Respondents by geographic distribution and accounting framework

	Other NS		NS IFRS -based		NS IPSAS-based		IPSAS modified		IPSAS not modified		NA		Total	
	No.	%	No.	%	No.	%	No.	%	No.	%	No.	%	No.	%
Africa	18	35%	0	0%	4	8%	9	17%	15	29%	6	12%	52	16%
Asia	15	47%	0	0%	6	19%	0	0%	11	34%	0	0%	32	10%
Europe	16	25%	24	38%	0	0%	14	22%	0	0%	9	14%	63	19%
North America	41	72%	0	0%	8	14%	0	0%	8	14%	0	0%	57	17%
Oceania	0	0%	17	40%	0	0%	21	49%	0	0%	5	12%	43	13%
Central and South America	1	3%	0	0%	18	58%	12	39%	0	0%	0	0%	31	10%
International	0	0%	0	0%	0	0%	0	0%	0	0%	48	100%	48	15%
Total	91	28%	41	13%	36	11%	56	17%	34	10%	68	21%	326	100%

Table 3 presents the geographic distribution of respondents considering countries from EU, non-EU and international organisations, with a breakdown by their accounting framework.

Table 3. Respondents from EU versus others by accounting framework

		Other NS	NS IFRS -based	NS IPSAS-based	IPSAS modified	IPSAS not modified	NA	Total
EU countries	No.	16			6		9	31
	%	52%	0%	0%	19%	0%	29%	10%
Non-EU countries	No.	75	41	36	50	34	11	247
	%	30%	17%	15%	20%	14%	4%	76%
International organisations	No.						48	48
	%	0%	0%	0%	0%	0%	100%	15%
Total	No.	91	41	36	56	34	68	326
	%	28%	13%	11%	17%	10%	21%	100%

In what concerns respondents from the EU, Table 3 identifies that 52% of the respondents are from countries that have implemented other national standards, having no responses from countries with IPSAS with no modifications (as seen before). Most of the CL comes from non-EU respondents (76%). The reduced level of EU countries' participation may result from the EU's option to implement EPSAS.

Following, Table 4 presents the distribution of respondents by project, with a breakdown by their interest group.

As seen in Table 1, not all of the EDs have the same level of participation. Therefore, Table 4 evidence that the EDs about specific public sector matters (ED 70, ED 71, and ED 72) have higher rates of CL (23%, 21%, and 20%, respectively). Not surprisingly, those projects also had more participation from public entities and national standard setters. According to Bisogno et al. (2022), these high levels of participation may be due to being part of the same project and published together and also because they deal with public sector-specific issues.

Table 4. Respondents by project and interest group

	Standard setters		Public entities		Professionals		Academics		Total	
	No.	%	No.	%	No.	%	No.	%	No.	%
ED 75	8	13%	10	9%	30	21%	2	20%	50	15%
ED 74	7	11%	4	4%	5	4%	2	20%	18	6%
ED 72	12	19%	27	24%	26	18%	1	10%	66	20%
ED 71	12	19%	28	25%	27	19%	1	10%	68	21%
ED 70	12	19%	34	31%	28	20%	1	10%	75	23%
ED 69	6	9%	2	2%	10	7%	1	10%	19	6%
CP	7	11%	6	5%	15	11%	2	20%	30	9%
Total	64	20%	111	34%	141	43%	10	3%	326	100%

Regarding the interest group, respondents are mainly professionals (43%), public entities (34%), and standard setters (20%), having academics only 3% of responses. These results corroborate the literature on what concerns greater participation in IPSASB due processes for the first three interest groups, conversely to which was found for the last (Bisogno et al., 2022; De Wolf & Christiaens, 2019; Kidwell & Lowensohn, 2019; De Wolf et al., 2021; Manes Rossi & Aversano, 2015; Bisogno et al., 2015).

In what concerns the level of agreement with the IPSASB proposals, the analysis considers the different sets of questions proposed in each project, which motivates a total of 1,795 observations based on 326 CL collected.

Table 5 shows the level of agreement with the IPSASB position by each project.

Table 5. Level of agreement with the IPSASB position by project

	Agreement		Non-agreement		Total	
	No.	%	No.	%	No.	%
ED 69	16	89%	2	11%	18	100%
ED 70	222	73%	82	27%	304	100%
ED 71	231	60%	152	40%	383	100%
ED 72	405	72%	158	28%	563	100%
ED 74	15	94%	1	6%	16	100%
ED 75	129	87%	19	13%	148	100%
CP	274	75%	89	25%	363	100%
Total	1,292	72%	503	28%	1,795	100%

The figures in Table 5 show that the overall agreement is 72%, although this level may differ amongst the projects under assessment. The ED 70 'Revenue with Performance Obligations' (73%), ED 72 'Transfer Expenses' (72%), and ED 71 'Revenue without Performance Obligations' (60%) have the lowest levels of agreement. Concerning those three ED, it is also important to mention that respondents expressed concerns about their complexity, cost implementation, and the lack of 'mirroring' in some transactions, which hinders the consolidation process, being those criticisms of IPSAS aligned with the literature (Polzer et al., 2022; European Commission, 2013). Also, some respondents have questioned the possible alignment with other frameworks (Brown et al., 2018). Regarding these EDs, Bisogno et al. (2022) also found that respondents asked for clarification on some matters and raised several doubts.

As seen in the literature, the feedback expressed in the CL is generally aligned with the IPSASB position (De Wolf et al., 2021; Kidwell & Lowensohn, 2019; Bisogno et al., 2015; Mitu & Tiron-Tudor, 2013; Manes Rossi & Aversano, 2015). Nevertheless, whenever the matter is specific to the public sector, respondents seem to express concerns about some positions and, therefore, a lower level of agreement can be observed (as seen by Bisogno et al., 2022; De Wolf et al., 2021; Brown et al., 2018).

Table 6 presents the level of agreement between responses and the IPSASB position by geographic distribution.

Table 6. Level of agreement with the IPSASB position by geographic region

	Agreement		Non-agreement		Total	
	No.	%	No.	%	No.	%
Africa	259	89%	33	11%	292	16%
Asia	116	83%	24	17%	140	8%
Europe	276	71%	112	29%	388	22%
North America	194	68%	91	32%	285	16%
Oceania	163	62%	98	38%	261	15%
Central and South America	125	67%	62	33%	187	10%
International	159	66%	83	34%	242	13%
Total	1,292	72%	503	28%	1,795	100%

From Table 6, it can be observed that respondents from Africa (89%), and Asia (83%) are the ones that most agree with IPSASB, being the ones from Oceania (62%) with a lower level of agreement. It is worthwhile to remember that the former are the ones that most apply IPSAS with no modifications, oppositely to the latter.

The chi-square test revealed statistically significant differences between the answers from Africa and all the other regions at a significance level of 1%, except for Asia where it was only at a 10%-level. Also, there are statistically significant differences between the answers from Asia and all the other regions at a significance level of 1% (except for Africa, as mentioned before). There are also statistically significant differences (at a 5%-level) between answers from Europe and Oceania. Contrary to the literature (De Wolf et al., 2021; Manes Rossi & Aversano, 2015), these results evidence differences in their responses by geographic localisation.

Table 7 presents the level of agreement between responses and the IPSASB position by accounting framework.

Table 7. Level of agreement with the IPSASB position by accounting framework

	Agreement		Non-agreement		Total	
	No.	%	No.	%	No.	%
Other NS	370	74%	127	26%	497	28%
NS IFRS-based	182	71%	73	29%	255	14%
NS IPSAS-based	130	73%	49	27%	179	10%
IPSAS modified	216	65%	115	35%	331	18%
IPSAS not modified	130	81%	30	19%	160	9%
NA	264	71%	109	29%	373	21%
Total	1,292	72%	503	28%	1,795	100%

The figures in Table 7 identify that respondents who have adopted IPSAS with no modifications are the ones who most agree with the position of the IPSASB (81%). On the contrary, the ones who have modified IPSAS for the local context show the lowest rate of agreement (65%).

The chi-square test pointed out statistically significant differences between those who have IPSAS modified for the local context and the ones who have other national standards, and national standards based on IPSAS (at 1%-level, and 10%-level, respectively).

It was found statistically significant differences between respondents who have IPSAS with no modifications and the ones with IPSAS modified for the local context (at a 1%-level), and between the first ones and who have national standards based on IFRS (at a 5%-level). At a significance level of 10%, there are also statistically significant differences between respondents who have IPSAS with no modifications, and the ones with national standards based on IPSAS, and with other national standards. Finally, there are statistically significant differences between respondents who have IPSAS modified for the local context and those who have other national standards (at a 1%-level), and between the first ones and who have national standards based on IPSAS (at a 10%-level).

The level of agreement between responses and the IPSASB position by EU countries, non-EU countries, and international organisations is shown in Table 8.

Table 8. Level of agreement with the IPSASB position by EU countries, non-EU countries, and international organisations

	Agreement		Non-agreement		Total	
	No.	%	No.	%	No.	%
EU countries	132	69%	58	31%	190	11%
Non-EU countries	1,001	73%	362	27%	1,363	76%
International organisations	159	66%	83	34%	242	13%
Total	1,292	72%	503	28%	1,795	100%

Table 8 shows that, regardless of being or not from the EU, the respondents largely agree with the IPSASB positions. The chi-square test did not reveal any statistically significant differences.

Table 9 presents the responses by interest groups and their level of agreement with IPSASB.

Table 9. Level of agreement with the IPSASB position by interest groups

	Agreement		Non-agreement		Total	
	No.	**%**	**No.**	**%**	**No.**	**%**
Standard setters	263	73%	95	27%	358	20%
Public entities	407	69%	187	31%	594	33%
Professionals	595	75%	198	25%	793	44%
Academics	27	54%	23	46%	50	3%
Total	1,292	72%	503	28%	1,795	100%

Based on the figures in Table 9, professionals are the ones who most agree with the IASB positions, with an agreement rate of 75%, with the lowest levels of agreement attributable to public entities and academics. A statistically significant difference can be found through the chi-square test between the answers from academics and other interest groups (standard setters, and professionals, at a 1%-level, and public entities, at a 5%-level). They are also differences at a significance level of 1% between public entities' answers and the ones from professionals. However, this is in contrast to the findings of Manes Rossi and Aversano (2015), who have not found significant differences in respondents' interest groups but aligned with those of De Wolf et al (2021). Specifically, responses from professionals and governmental entities were influenced by interest groups.

Table 10, in turn, presents the agreement level with the IPSASB position of the interest groups, according to the several projects studied.

Table 10. Level of agreement with the IPSASB position by interest groups and projects

	Standard setters				Public entities				Professionals				Academics			
	Agree		Opposite		Agree		Opposite		Agree		Opposite		Agree		Opposite	
	No.	%	No.	%	No.	%	No.	%	No.	%	No.	%	No.	%	No.	%
ED 75	20	83%	4	17%	24	80%	6	20%	82	93%	6	7%	3	50%	3	50%
ED 74	6	100%		0%	3	75%	1	25%	5	100%		0%	1	100%		0%
ED 72	83	77%	25	23%	152	70%	65	30%	163	71%	65	29%	7	70%	3	30%
ED 71	43	61%	27	39%	76	51%	74	49%	107	69%	49	31%	5	71%	2	29%
ED 70	41	76%	13	24%	92	76%	29	24%	85	69%	39	31%	4	80%	1	20%
ED 69	5	83%	1	17%	2	100%		0%	8	89%	1	11%	1	100%		0%
CP	65	72%	25	28%	58	83%	12	17%	145	79%	38	21%	6	30%	14	70%

Figures in Table 10 identify that the public entities are the ones who have the lowest level of agreement (51%), which is observed in ED 71, specific to the public sector, followed by standard setters in the same ED (61%). These results reinforce the concerns of these groups with the solutions proposed by IPSAS in matters that are specific to public sector accounting (in line with Polzer et al., 2022; De Wolf et al., 2021; Brown et al., 2018; European Commission, 2013).

The next section proposes future avenues for research on the topic proposed for this chapter.

FUTURE RESEARCH DIRECTION

Although many countries have been implementing accrual-based accounting standards (OECD/IFAC, 2017; Cavanagh et al., 2016), the majority opted for applying national standards, and only a few of them have fully adopted IPSAS (CIPFA/IFAC, 2021; OECD/IFAC, 2017). Although IPSAS are seen as a benchmark for public sector accounting standards, they are not mandatory and are often applied with several adaptations which may limit their objective of contributing to comparability.

As governments are not obliged to apply IPSAS, and given the several criticisms made to them, it is relevant to study the IPSASB due processes in what concerns the stakeholders' participation, and the level of agreement with the IPSASB position, understanding whether their viewpoint is related to distinctive characteristics. The analysis proposed in this chapter was driven by this objective, which can be useful to the understanding of the limited implementation of IPSAS. Also, these results can be used by IPSASB to try to collaborate with governmental entities, and national standard setters (namely, the MoF) to address their several concerns.

As future research, it is suggested to continue studying the IPSASB due processes to understand the factors that are limiting the IPSAS implementation, namely in what concerns specific public sector matters. In this sense, more robust statistical methods can be applied in future research, also including further distinctive characteristics, such as different levels of country development, cultural factors, as well as other contextual factors influenced by the political, legal, social, or economic environment of countries.

Finally, it is important to stress the limitations associated with this study, which mainly concern the subjectivity associated with the interpretation of the answers, which are not always sufficiently objective or properly structured. Also, it was only used two categories to classify the answers, agreement or not. These constraints can be mitigated with future research using different methods.

Following, the next section presents the main conclusions found.

CONCLUSION

As main conclusions, this research found that major respondents to the IPSASB due process are professionals, public entities, and standard setters, having a low rate of academic's participation, as seen in the literature (Bisogno et al., 2022; De Wolf & Christiaens, 2019; Kidwell & Lowensohn, 2019; De Wolf et al., 2021; Manes Rossi & Aversano, 2015; Bisogno et al., 2015). As highlighted by other authors, the low involvement by individuals may result from not believing in their capacity in influencing these processes (e.g., Kidwell & Lowensohn, 2019).

Regarding the respondents' geographic location, the majority are from Europe, North America, Africa, and Oceania (Bisogno et al., 2022; De Wolf et al., 2021; Kidwell & Lowensohn, 2019; Bisogno et al., 2015).

As for the accounting framework, most of the responses are from countries that have local standards not IPSAS-based, oppositely to countries that have adopted IPSAS with no modifications, which had a lower level of participation as a finding not aligned with the ones by De Wolf & Christiaens (2019).

In what concerns the alignment with the IPSASB positions, despite the overall agreement with them, the agreement level is not the same in all the projects assessed. The EDs about specific matters of the public sector, such as Revenue with Performance Obligations, Revenue without Performance Obligations, and Transfer Expenses had higher participation of the stakeholders, namely from the public/governmental entities, and from the national standard setters. Also, these are the ones with the lower rate of agreement with the position of the IPSASB. The fact that they had concerns may have motivated them to participate in the process of public discussion. The results pointed out that there are statistically significant differences between the stakeholders' positions according to their region, framework, and interest group.

While IPSAS is an international reference standard, it hasn't seen much implementation progress, since several countries chose not to adopt them directly and, when implementing them, adopted only some of those standards or adapted them domestically. The criticism stems from the inapplicability of several standards to the public sector, as well as the complexity and cost of implementing some. The low level of responses to the EDs, as well as the lower level of agreement by government entities and national standards setters in specific public sector matters, highlight this reality and may limit the legitimacy of IPSASB, which may be related to the efforts and the cost of IPSAS implementation, and the differences to other frameworks, such as Eurostat's.

Therefore, as in public sector accounting, international comparability is not of most relevance, accountability focuses on national users (Baskerville & Grossi, 2019), and in several countries, the standard setter is the duty of the MoF (Cavanagh et al., 2016; OECD/IFAC, 2017), the non-agreement position of the public entities and the standard setters regarding the specific matters, may give insights to the understanding of the low adoption of full IPSAS.

REFERENCES

ACCA. (2017). IPSAS implementation: Current status and challenges. *Professional insight report*. ACCA.

Baskerville, R., & Grossi, G. (2019). Glocalization of accounting standards: Observations on neo-institutionalism of IPSAS. *Public Money & Management*, *39*(2), 101–110. doi:10.1080/09540962.2019.1580894

Bisogno, M., Manes-Rossi, F., & Sicilia, M. (2022). Designing international public sector accounting standards: An analysis of constituents' participation through comment letters. *Financial Accountability & Management*, *38*(4), 661–685. doi:10.1111/faam.12343

Bisogno, M., Santis, S., & Tommasetti, A. (2015). Public-Sector Consolidated Financial Statements: An Analysis of the Comment Letters on IPSASB's Exposure Draft No. 49. *International Journal of Public Administration*, *38*(4), 311–324. doi:10.1080/01900692.2015.999605

Caruana, J. (2019). Shades of governmental financial reporting with a national accounting twist. *Accounting Forum*, *40*(3), 153–165. doi:10.1016/j.accfor.2016.06.002

Cavanagh, J., Flynn, S., & Moretti, D. (2016). *Implementing Accrual Accounting in the Public Sector. Technical Notes and Manuals*. International Monetary Fund - Fiscal Affairs Department.

CIPFA/IFAC. (2021). *International Public Sector Financial Accountability Index: 2020*. IFAC. https://www.ifac.org/what-we-do/global-impact-map/accountabi lity

De Wolf, A., & Christiaens, J. (2019). *Stakeholder Participation in the Development of International Public Sector Accounting Standards (IPSAS): A Multi-Issue and Multi-Period Analysis of the Due Process* [Paper presentation]. *International Conference on Public Organization (ICONPO)*, Khon Kaen Province, Thailand. 10.2139srn.3635566

De Wolf, A., & Christiaens, J. (2022): The hurdle model: Analysing the influence of country characteristics on participation in IPSASB's due process. *Public Money & Management*. https://doi.org/10.1 080/09540962.2022.2066817

De Wolf, A., Christiaens, J., & Aversano, N. (2021). Heritage assets in the due process of the International Public Sector Accounting Standards Board (IPSASB). *Public Money & Management, 41*(4), 325–335. doi:10.1080/09540962.2020.1727114

European Commission (EC). (2013). Towards implementing harmonised public sector accounting standards in Member States. Report from the Commission to the Council and the European Parliament. EC.

EY. (2016). *Approach for narrowing down of options within IPSAS*. EYGM.

IPSASB (2016). *Due Process and working procedures*. International Public Sector Accounting Standard Board.

IPSASB. (2020). *Handbook of international public sector accounting pronouncements* (Vol. I). IFAC.

Kidwell, L., & Lowensohn, S. (2019). Participation in the Process of Setting Public Sector Accounting Standards: The Case of IPSASB. *Accounting in Europe, 16*(2), 177–194. doi:10.1080/17449480.2019 .1632466

Manes Rossi, F, & Aversano, N. (2015). Advancing performance measurement: Italian local government vis-à-vis the IPSASB project. *International Journal of Productivity and Performance Management, 64*(1), 76- 93. htpps://doi.org. a0.1108/IJPPM-07-2013-0134

Mitu, I., & Tiron-Tudor, A. (2013). Public Sector Combinations: A New Challenge For IPSASB. [University of Oradea]. *Annals of Faculty of Economics, 1*(2), 540–549.

OECD/IFAC. (2017). *Accrual Practices and Reform Experiences in OECD Countries*. OECD Publishing. doi:10.1787/9789264270572-

Oulasvirta, L. O., & Bailey, S. J. (2016). Evolution of EU public sector financial accounting standardisation: Critical events that opened the window for attempted policy change. *Journal of European Integration, 38*(6), 653–669. doi:10.1080/07036337.2016.1177043

Pittroff, E. (2021). The legitimacy of global accounting rules: A note on the challenges from path-dependence theory. *The Journal of Management and Governance, 25*(2), 379–396. doi:10.100710997-020-09546-6

Polzer, T., Grossi, G., & Reichard, C. (2022). Implementation of the international public sector accounting standards in Europe. Variations on a global theme. *Accounting Forum*, *46*(1), 57–82. doi:10.1080/01559982.2021.1920277

PwC. (2019). *Accounting maturity update. 2019 preliminary results*. PricewaterhouseCoopers.

Richardson, A., & Eberlein, B. (2011). Legitimating Transnational Standard-Setting: The Case of the International Accounting Standards Board. *Journal of Business Ethics*, *98*(2), 217–245. doi:10.100710551-010-0543-9

Schmidthuber, L., Hilgers, D., & Hofmann, S. (2020). International Public Sector Accounting Standards (IPSASs): A systematic literature review and future research agenda. *Financial Accountability & Management*, *38*(1), 119–142. https://doi.org/https://doi.org/10.1111/faam.12265. doi:10.1111/faam.12265

Toudas, K., Poutos, E., & Balios, D. (2013). Concept, regulations and institutional issues of IPSAS: A critical review. *European Journal of Business and Social Sciences*, *2*(1), 43–54.

ADDITIONAL READING

Aversano, N., Nicolò, G., Sannino, G., & Polcini, P. (2022). *Accounting for Collective Services, Individual Services, and Emergency Relief: Reconsideration in Times of a Pandemic*. Public Sector Accounting, Financial Accountability and Viability in Times of Crisis.

Biondi, L., Grandis, F., & Mattei, G. (2021). Heritage assets in financial reporting: A critical analysis of the IPSASB's consultation paper. *Journal of Public Budgeting, Accounting & Financial Management*, *33*(5), 533–551. doi:10.1108/JPBAFM-09-2020-0158

De Wolf, A. (2021). Stakeholder participation in the IPSASB's due process. Ghent University.

De Wolf, A., & Christiaens, J. (2020). Het consultatieproces van de IPSASB: Een blik op de Europese participatie. *Accountancy & Bedrijfskunde*, *2020*(12), 115–126.

KEY TERMS AND DEFINITIONS

Accounting Framework: Financial reporting standards adopted by each country.

Accrual Basis: Accounting assumption under which transactions and other events are recognized whenever they occur, regardless of the timing of the related cash flow.

IPSAS modified for the local context: IPSAS adopted indirectly via national standards.

IPSAS with no modifications: IPSAS adopted directly.

National standards based on IFRS: National standards using IFRS as a reference.

National standards with reference to IPSAS: National standards using IPSAS as a reference.

Other national standards: National financial reporting standards other than those previously mentioned.

Chapter 9
Developing a Social Accounting System for European Social Enterprises Based on Public Accounting

Ilias Anastasios Gerakos
https://orcid.org/0009-0000-6662-7226
Panteion University of Political and Social Sciences, Greece

Manolis Tzouvelekas
https://orcid.org/0000-0002-1876-2551
Hellenic Mediterranean University, Greece

John Filos
https://orcid.org/0009-0000-6662-7226
Panteion University of Political and Social Sciences, Greece

ABSTRACT

The growing popularity of the social enterprises (SEs) discourse highlights the need for accounting-focused research. The SEs aim to create mainly social and environmental impact, rather than merely economic value for shareholders; hence, conventional accounting is often not suitable for SEs. Furthermore, the literature unfolds that social accounting is defined as a metric for measuring social and environmental impact. The authors argue that this one-sided accounting worldview is not sufficient, and they propose a well-known and operational accounting system that is based on the relationship between SEs and public organizations in the broader context of accounting, social finance, and public accounting. This chapter makes both theoretical and practical contributions by developing a common accounting language and practices between the public and social sectors in order to provide and distribute public and social value to society and organisations.

DOI: 10.4018/978-1-6684-7293-4.ch009

INTRODUCTION

The growing popularity of the Social Enterprises (SEs) discourse highlights the need for accounting-focused research. The SEs aim to create mainly social and environmental impact rather than merely economic value for shareholders; hence, conventional accounting measures are often not suitable for SEs (Fazzi, 2010; Andreaus & Costa, 2014; Mäkelä, 2021). Furthermore, the literature, unfolds that social accounting is defined as a metric for measuring social and environmental impact (Bebbington & Gray, 1993; Brown & Fraser, 2006; Yongvanich & Guthrie, 2006; Baba, Ishida & Aoki, 2015; Dey & Gibbon, 2017; Rinaldi, 2019).

The authors argue that this one-sided accounting worldview is not sufficient, and they propose a well-known and operational accounting system that is based on the relationship between SEs and public organizations in the broader context of accounting, social finance and public accounting. This study suggests adhering to the framework design and rationale of public accounting rather than conventional accounting without overlooking other operational or proposed models of social or non-conventional accounting. It should be considered that traditional accounting as Mook (2014) emphasizes developed for for-profit organisations, servicing other goals and underestimate the nonfinancial performance or as Retolaza et al. (2016) mention "conventional accounting is only concerned with reflecting value for shareholders" and not for stakeholders and society in general.

The features that the use of public accounting brings together are what prompted the authors to focus on this issue:

(1) the accrual basis, which refers to recording the financial status of transactions when they occur rather than when cash settlement occurs. Many governments have already adopted the accrual accounting as point of reference, and many more are in the process of doing so.

Many international organizations also are pushing for the implementation of the accrual accounting because of the attempts of economic crime to use social enterprises as mob business. Taking into account the data collected for 150 governments, (International Federation of Accountants, 2018) the break-down of how they report their finances, reveal that 37 governments (25%) proceeded with accrual reporting in the last published financial statements, 68 governments (45%) are moving to accrual reporting or already have some elements of accrual reporting in their financial statements and 45 governments (30%) still report on a cash basis,

(2) the organizational design of SEs, which is based on the classification of economic, operational, and administrative factors, that enables the recording of all SEs activities,
(3) the accrual principle is the foundation of the uniform accounting scheme,
(4) all SEs could receive access to a compact Enterprise Resource Planning (ERP) system that has been developed,
(5) using GFS (Government Finance Statistics), one can assess each SE's financial information and assist it in becoming profitable, which will provide prosperity to its partners and society at large,
(6) through COFOG (Classification of the Functions of Government) control is achieved in the spending areas and is developed based on the principles set by the COFOG International Standards issued by the United Nations,

(7) the administrative classification reflects the organizational and hierarchical structure of the obliged entities and determines the administrative positions that are legally responsible for the management of expenses, income, assets, and obligations of the entities and
(8) other classifications.

The plan of accounts, combined with the information system of each entity, allows the integration of other types of classifications, such as Classification by programme, which reflects sectoral programmes that consume resources and allows the measurement of their performance consumed resources, classification by source of financing, which reflects the main sources of financing of expenses, as well as the connection between them, geographic classification, which reflects the spatial distribution of financial reporting data and classification for costing purposes.

Concerning the financial statements, they consist of the statement of financial position, statement of financial performance, statement of changes in equity, statement of cash flows, and explanatory notes to the financial statements.

The legislation in this area specifies who is in control of finances. The protocols in place help to keep decision-making under control. They improve efficiency by changing the control tools and basing them on the new accounting plan.

The potential usage of Enterprise Resource Systems (ERP), which are the finest instrument for setting up SEs and can incorporate other business operations like administration, warehouse, etc.

Artificial Intelligence can be used to develop tools that support the operation of the business, and integrated reporting (see also Bashkar & Flower, 2021) such as software that will be integrated into the ERP system and will automate control, as long as one can support an ERP system that will be based on this structured and properly structured accounting system.

The International Public Sector Accounting Standards (IPSAS) are relatively simple to understand and do not cause problems in jurisprudence or law enforcement. This paper recommends that social accounting use IPSAS because (a) it is simpler than International Accounting Standards (IAS), (b) it has an international application, and (c) it can be implemented after training a group of executives without causing problems with bookkeeping (Gerakos, 2021).

The Social Economy and its enterprises aim to generate more than 10% in the EU GDP and globally because it has the sociability and purpose of supply, to fit the logic of the public sector and, as a result, of the public accounting system.

To provide adequate feedback to this research on the proposed accounting system, a quantitative analysis was conducted with a group of key informants, presidents from various Unions of social enterprises and other social economy and entrepreneurship entities from Greece.

Furthermore, the purpose of this research is to depict the design and development of a new digital multilingual platform that will incorporate the proposed sectoral public accounting system for SEs using agile software design and development principles and practices. This chapter makes both theoretical and practical contributions that are innovative. It is expected that by developing a common accounting language and practices between the public and social sectors in order to provide and distribute public and social value to society and organisations, rather than mixing their services by substituting public services through SEs, as critics accuse social economy enterprises of doing, the social and economic role and positive impact of SEs will be enhanced.

BACKGROUND

Social Economy and Social Enterprises

Third or social economy organisations are presented in this section to demonstrate how they differ significantly from traditional business in national and international contexts. Although they are private entities, they are distinct from businesses seeking to meet corporate or entrepreneurial financial objectives.

Third or social economy institutions, according to the United Nations Department of Social Affairs, are organisations that are self-governing, non-compulsory in nature, significantly limited in its distribution of surplus (profit) and are finally private entities not controlled by government (United Nations Department of Social Affairs, 2018).

Social enterprises are the type of third sector business entities that bear the following characteristics:

- A continuous activity producing goods and/or selling service
- A high degree of autonomy
- A significant level of economic risk
- A minimum amount of paid work
- An explicit aim to benefit the community
- An initiative launched by a group of citizens
- A decision-making power not based on capital ownership
- A participatory nature, which involves the persons affected by the activity
- Limited profit distribution (Defourny, 2001, pp. 16-18)

This definition provides a common line of analysis in the European Union because it is the result of a long and in-depth EMES Network research defining social enterprise reclassified along three lines: the social dimension, the entrepreneurial dimension, and the inclusive ownership-governance dimension (Defourny & Nyssens, 2014). In the United States, however, the concept of social enterprise is much broader and more focused on entrepreneurial initiatives established by nonprofit organisations for the purpose of revenue generation (Kerlin, as cited in Borzaga & Galera, 2014).

Defourny and Pestoff (2014) provide a comprehensive picture of the European nonprofit sector.

A Venn diagram (Mook et al., 2007), is shown in Figure 1 below. It illustrates the interaction of the three economic sectors—public, private, and third sector. The intersection of these three sectors is referred to as the "social economy" which demonstrates explicitly the function of social economy institutions, such as enterprises, as a buffer between the public and the private sectors while simultaneously upholding the Defourny (2001) definitional criteria.

Figure 1. The Social Economy in relation to the private and Public Sectors
(Source: Mook et al., 2007, p. 24, Fig. 2.1)

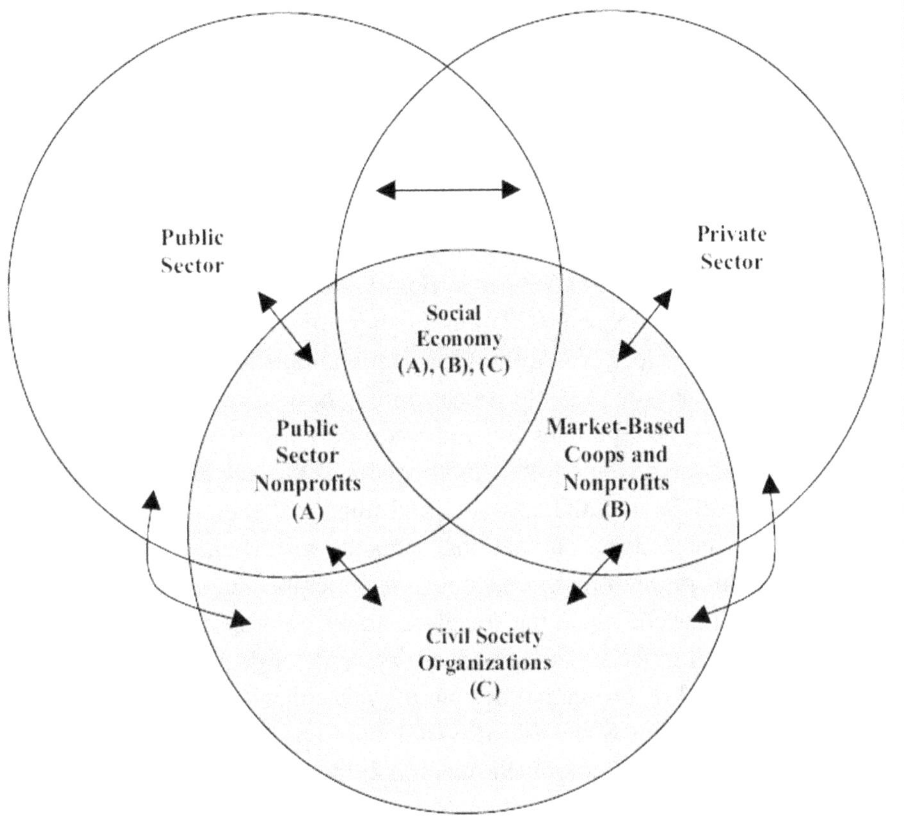

Recent evidence measures social economy activities along with proximity economy as an important factor in European business environment, given that "2.8 million social economy entities in Europe offer concrete and innovative solutions to key challenges" (European Commission, 2021, p.2). Social enterprises and third-sector enterprises are distinct entrepreneurial models in Europe and elsewhere, and as such, their organisational goals, policies, and business model necessitate separate economic and financial management and accounting.

MAIN FOCUS OF THE CHAPTER

Issues, Controversies, Problems

The main argument of this chapter is that traditional accounting, despite its long-standing contribution to business vendors and for-profit organisations, is insufficient for capturing the essence, dynamics, and multiplicity of the galaxy of stakeholders of social economy in general, and social enterprises in particular, in the context of the nonprofit sector.

To address this gap, various initiatives, models, and tools have been developed in so far in various national and international contexts, with social reporting, as well as to economic reporting, at their core.

Several initiatives in the field of social impact investment and social finance have been established and are in operation, according to Nicholls, Paton, Emerson (2015) including integrated ESG accounting, the Global Reporting Initiative (GRI), the Sustainable Accounting Standards Board (SASB), the Global Impact Investing Network's Impact Reporting and Investment Standards (IRIS) and the European Union's Standard for Social Impact.

In the field of sustainability reporting there are also other frameworks like Climate Disclosure Standards Board, the Global Reporting Initiative, the International Integrated Reporting Council, the Sustainability Accounting Standards Board, and the Task Force on Climate-Related Financial Disclosures parts of the Environment, Society and Governance or ESG reporting (Eccles & Mirchandani, 2022).

As Eccles and Mirchandani propose (2022) this plethora of models could be unified on a single model as it is proposed with the global solution of International Sustainability Standard Board (ISSB).

One of the most difficult issues in the field is determining how to capture, evaluate, and present the non-monetary aspects of social entrepreneurship and enterprises, such as the social and environmental impact, in addition to the measurable outcomes. Another issue is the lack of connectivity between micro and macro accounting, as well as how the activities and impact of social enterprises and third-sector entities inform overall national statistics and national accounts with validated data.

Finally, as depicted in this piece of research, "only a few member states have adapted their national accounting systems... satellite accounts on the social economy" (European Commission, 2021, p. 22). In the next nine sections equal models and systems are presented in order to inform the reader on the literature and practice on social reporting and accounting other than conventional accounting, namely Social Accounting, Social Reporting Standard (SRS), Global Reporting Initiative (GRI), IRIS+ impact accounting system, Polyhedral model, Integrated Accountability Model, Human Resources Accounting, Blended Value Accounting Social Cost-Benefit analysis.

Social Accounting

Apart from mainstream accounting, social accounting has been the epicenter of various authors. Lazkano and Beraza (2019) explain in their research "how social accounting can generate legitimacy for a social company and make companies more sustainable".

There is a distinction between social accounting as applied in the for-profit and nonprofit sectors. Gray, Dillard, & Spence, (as cited in Mook, 2014), mention that "for-profit sector social accounting is "a response by principally economic organizations to demonstrate that they are not purely economic" while social accounting for nonprofit organizations developed "to justify their pursuit of social and environmental goals in economic terms".

The use of the term "social accounting" in this chapter differs from the concept of the Social Accounting Matrix (SAM) as a component of the national accounts. Although it is an illustration of a satellite account, a concept that will be discussed in a following section, a SAM is "a matrix presentation which shows the links between the Supply and Use Tables (SUT) and the institutional sector accounts" and provides information on "the level and composition of employment" (ESA, 2010, p. 499).

Kay, the pioneering social audit network's founder in 2001, published the social accounting and audit guide (2011), a practical tool that aids in the development of the social accounting profession and the field of social accounting and audit, with the goal of assisting organisations:

to be able to prove the difference they have made in terms of outputs, outcomes and an overall impact; ... [t]o improve their services and operations, ...[t]o account for their work to all stakeholders as well as the wider public (Kay & McMullan, 2017, p.2).

Figure 2 depicts a comparison between financial accounts on the one hand and social, environmental, and economics on the other, as well as related processes in terms of reporting and auditing in accordance with social auditing practice (Kay, 2011).

Figure 2. Comparison of social, environmental and economic accounts with financial accounts
(Source: Kay, 2011, p. 59, Diagram)

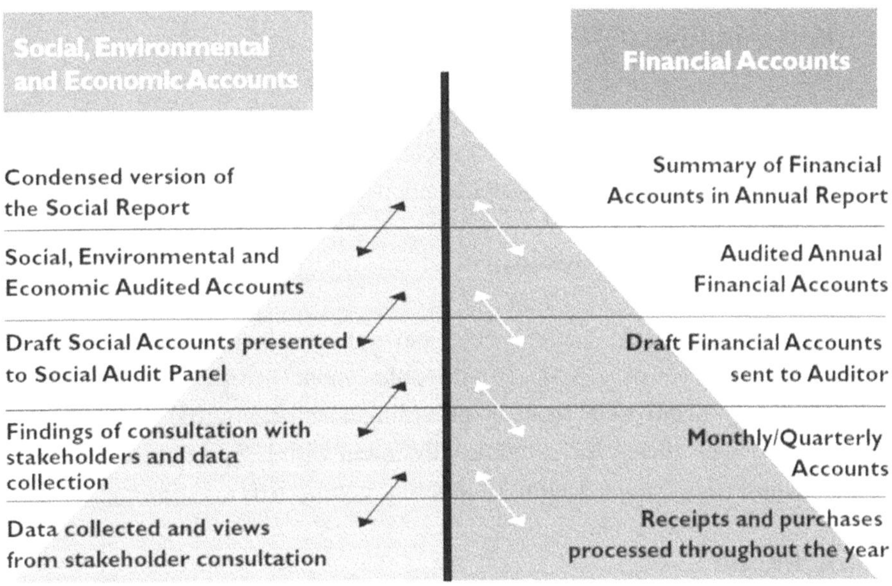

Kay and McMullan (2017) acknowledge that the complexity of the "social value" field makes it difficult for the vast majority of social enterprises to demonstrate systematically social accounts on their annual reporting of activities.

Furthermore, the authors pose four key challenges for organisations that want to report on their social, environmental, and economic fields of activities, namely: (a) what should be included in the reporting that really matters, (b) where should social impact assessment fit within an organisation, (c) how to ensure credibility in social impact reporting, and (d) how to deal with the financialisation of social impact assessment.

Apart from the Kay and McMullan social accounting model, other indicative models are presented in brief to help the reader better understand social accounting methodology and reporting.

The Social Reporting Standard (SRS) Model

The SRS model "covers all the other essential elements associated with the reporting process, from the organisational side right through to the financial", making it appropriate for both internal reports and transparent representation of organisational results to the public. It is divided into three sections.

"Part A" of the model introduces the model by stating the report's vision and scope. Model's "Part B" presents the social problem and offers an organisational solution, as well as resources and results from the reporting period. This section concludes with planning and forecasting as well as organisational structure. Finally, "Part C" defines the organisation as a whole, including the organisational framework, governance, and finance and accounting principles and practices. SRS is the most prominent reporting standard in Germany (von Ravensburg et al., 2018).

Global Reporting Initiative (GRI)

The Global Reporting Initiative model addresses three classes of interconnected sustainability reporting standards. The GRI universal standards, GRI sector standards, and GRI topic standards, with the first dealing with all organisations, the second with specific sectors, and the third with specific topics.

The IRIS+ Impact Accounting System

The IRIS+ impact accounting system is a widely accepted system in the field of impact investing, powered by the Global Impact Investing Network (GIIN), that enables impact investors to make informed decisions about their investing priorities and preferences by providing a well-designed, thoroughly interconnected set of targets, core metrics sets, thematic taxonomy, alignment with UN Sustainable Development Goals (SDGs), and other features that paint a picture of a public good (GIIN).

The Polyhedral Model

This model according to Retolaza, San-Jose and Ruiz-Roqueni "integrates stakeholder theory into an analytical-synthetic framework, from a phenomenological perspective and using fuzzy logic" (Retolaza et al., 2016, p. 39) and portrayed in Figure 3. Its main focus is the monetization of social value and its integration with economic and financial information.

Figure 3. The Polyhedral model
(Source: Retolaza et al., 2016, p. 40, Fig 6.1)

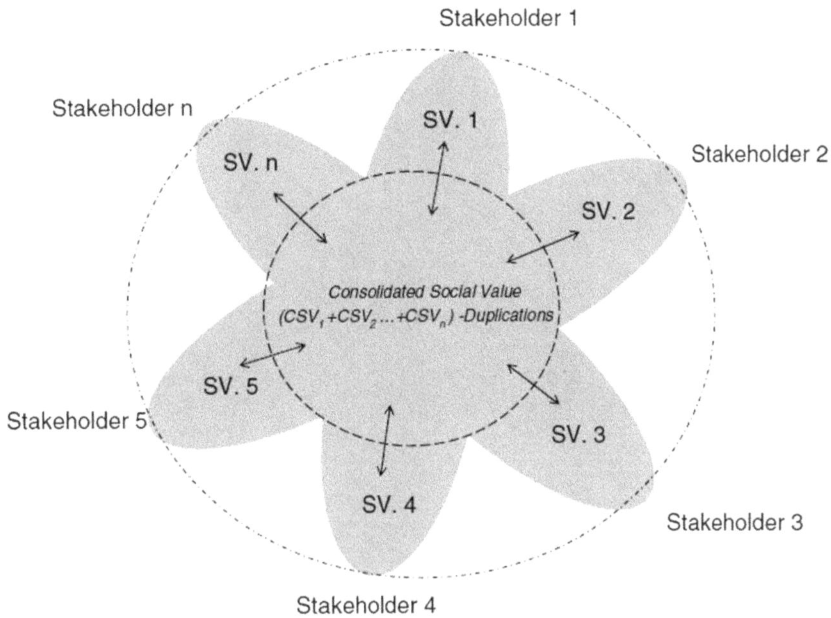

The Integrated Accountability Model

Apart from the development of new tools in the nonprofit sector other models integrate existing tools and approaches, like the integrated accountability model of Andreaus and Costa (2014). The authors delineate three interrelated accountability dimensions, namely economic and financial, mission-related and social related, comprising the Integrated Accountability model as schematically portrayed by Andreaus and Costa (2014) shown in Figure 4.

Figure 4. The Integrated Accountability Model (IAM)
(Source: Andreaus & Costa, 2014, p. 185, Fig. 1)

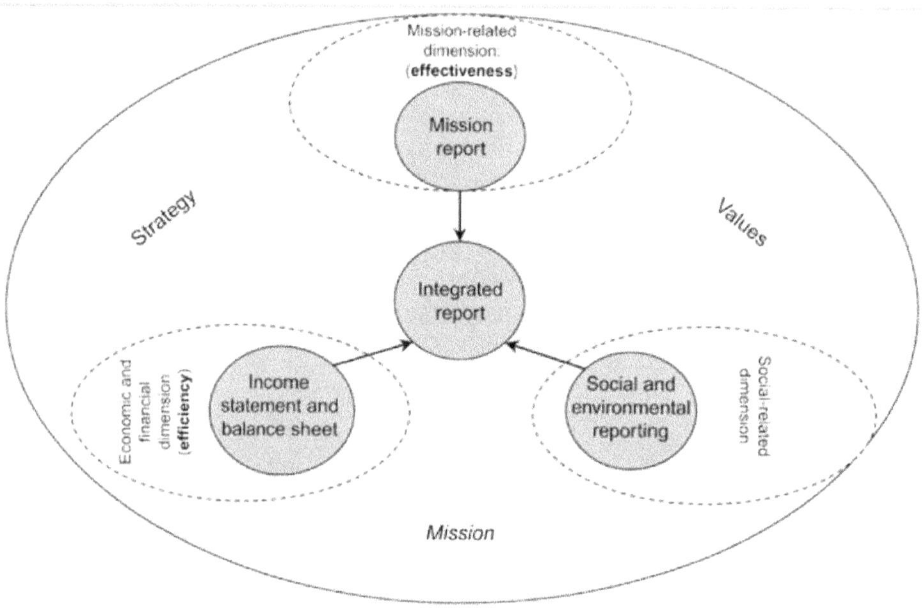

Each one of the three dimensions is summarized and portrayed through discrete statements and reports like Income Statement and Balance Report (economic-financial dimension, the efficiency side of the model), the Social and Environmental Reporting (social-related dimension) and the Mission Report (mission-related dimension, the effectiveness side of the model).

Human Resources Accounting

Human asset accounting theory emerged in the 1960s (Johnson and Kleiner, 1987) as a challenge to neoclassical economics-based Anglo-American Accounting (Mathews, 1995). According to Filios "Human resource accounting is the branch of accounting which is used extensively non-financial measures of human asset performance and social accounting has been advanced" (Filios, 1991, p. 133).

Following Flamholz possible methods of presenting investment in human assets in corporate financial reports include (a) the president's letter, (b) a statement of intangibles, (c) an unaudited pro forma supplementary financial statement, and (d) integration into conventional financial statements (Flamholz, 1999, p. 46).

Regardless the fact that Human assets accounting is not a typical accounting method it is a practical and efficient way to focus on staff as an asset rather than a cost to the organization, considering both human and capital costs, measuring employee effectiveness and resulting in improved performance (Johnson & Kleiner, 1987).

Blended Value Accounting

In his research project Nicholls, (2009), conducts an exploratory analysis of reporting practices in five case studies from the field of social entrepreneurship, and as a result, the theoretical model of Blended Value Accounting is presented. Emerson coined the term "Blended Value" (as cited in Nicholls, 2009), to describe the creation of both financial and social value in an organisation in a positive rather than a zero-sum game.

The social reporting tools that are considered in the model are the Annual Report of Audited Financial Accounts, the Social Return on Investment (SROI), the CIC34, the Enhanced Social Audit and Trustee's Report. The model is presented graphically in Figure 5.

Figure 5. The spectrum of Blended Value Accounting
(Source: Nicholls, 2009, p.765, Fig. 1)

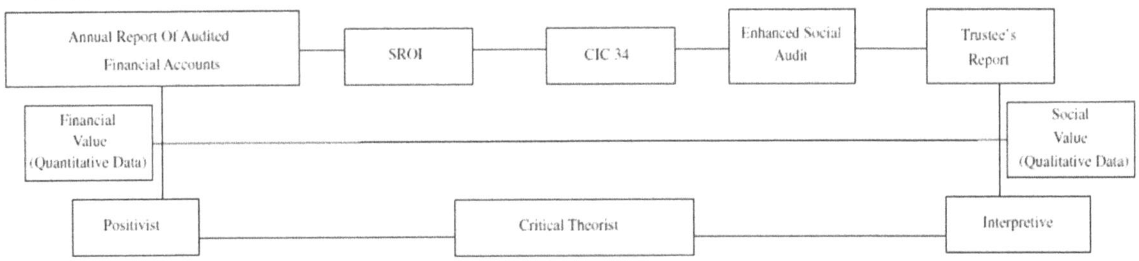

Nicholls (2009) explains that the rationalist/positivist, critical realist, and interpretative interpretation approaches are the three approaches within the framework of accounting sociology. "At the conceptual level, this may appear theoretically chaotic, but on the ground, it fits well with the innovation, boundary blurring, strategic instrumentalism, and bricolage typical of social entrepreneurship in general" the author adds (Nicholls, 2009, p. 756).

The Social Cost-Benefit Analysis

In addition to the models mentioned above, Thirlwall's work on developmental economics stated that social cost-benefit analysis demonstrated that:

A project will be profitable to society if the social benefits of the project exceed the social costs, or, to put it another way, if the net present value of the project to society is greater than zero (Thirlwall, 1983, p. 202).

The essence of social-cost-benefit analysis is summarized in the following equation:

$$NPV = \sum_{t-0}^{T} \left(\frac{Vt - Ct}{(1+r)t} \right) - K$$

Where: Vt is the annual flow of social benefit

C, is the social cost of variable inputs

r is the rate at which future benefits and costs are discounted

K is the fixed cost of the investment

By transferring a project to the level of total activity of a social enterprise, the social cost and social benefit of a social business could be calculated analogously. Thirlwall's important concept of shadow wages is beyond the scope of this study.

All of the above models provide valuable insights on how to calculate the social impact of social enterprises, but they, to our knowledge, lack the capacity to deploy accredited accounting system which is mingle the financial performance and reporting with the social performance and related social reporting.

The various approaches discussed in the preceding sections should be integrated or, preferably, adjusted in a unified and integrated accounting system measuring the social and environmental impact of the (social) business sector and producing accurate accounting and statistical reporting.

Relevant models and tools in the field of Environment, Society and Governance (ESG) with the proposed global solution of International Sustainability Standard Board (ISSB) are valuable along with integrated models such as Blended Value Accounting in Social Entrepreneurship and the Integrated Accountability Model for the present and future of social accounting.

Table 1 identifies and summarize the models, initiatives and systems of social accounting of this section.

Table 1. Models, Initiatives and Systems of Social Accounting

Model/ Initiative/ System	Author(s) /developers	Focus	Key characteristic
1. Social Accounting	Kay & McMullan, 2017	• micro, • what should be included in the reporting that really matters	• prove in terms of outputs, outcomes and an overall impact • improve services and operations, • account for work to all stakeholders and wider public
2. Social Reporting Standard (SRS)	Ashoka, Auridis, BonVenture, Phineo, Schwab Foundation	• micro	• organisational and financial reporting
3. Global Reporting Initiative (GRI)	CERES and Tellus Institute 1997	• Micro, • global, • financial and sustainability reporting	Deal with, •all organisations, •specific sectors, and •specific topics
4. IRIS+ impact accounting system	Global Impact Investing Network (GIIN)	• micro, • impact investing, • indicators	• Contribution to positive social and environmental impact • Evidence and impact data in investment design • Manage impact performance • Contribution to the Impact Investing growth
5. Polyhedral model	Retolaza et al., 2016	• micro, • monetization of social value	Action research, stakeholder theory, phenomenological perspective and fuzzy logic
6. Integrated Accountability Model	Andreaus & Costa, 2014	• micro, • three interrelated accountability dimensions, economic and financial, mission-related and social related	• three dimensions are summarized and portrayed through discrete statements and reports
7. Human Resources Accounting	Flamholz, 1999	• micro, • focus on staff as an asset rather than a cost to the organization	• not a typical accounting method, • a branch of accounting used extensively non-financial measures of human asset performance and social accounting
8. Blended Value Accounting	Nicholls, 2009	• micro, • Blended Value, to describe the creation of both financial and social value in an organisation	social reporting tools: • Annual Report of Audited Financial Accounts, • the Social Return on Investment (SROI), • the CIC34, • the Enhanced Social Audit and Trustee's Report
9. Social cost-benefit analysis	Thirlwall, 1983	• micro •macro • Social Cost, Social Benefit	• social benefits of the project exceed the social costs, or, the net present value of the project to society is greater than zero
10. Social Accounting Matrix (SAM)	Stone & Brown, 1962	• macro, • the level and composition of employment	• linking the Supply and Use Tables (SUT) and the institutional sector accounts

The next section presents the deployed quantitative research with Social Enterprises in Greece in order to examine their leading teams' opinion on a new proposed accounting model as it will be presented in the following sections. This proposes the ESA 2010 and IPSAS, a well-known and operational accounting system based on the relationship between SEs and public organizations in the broader context of accounting, social finance, and public accounting that closes the gap between the conventional accounting and the various social accounting models that do not consider the accounting science per se.

In comparison to conventional accounting, this study proposes a new conceptual and applicable model based on the framework design and rationale of public accounting.

Social Enterprises and Social Accounting - the Empirical Analysis

Mixed research was conducted with representatives of the Unions of Social Enterprises and the confederation collective representation of the Unions of Social Enterprises in Greece in order to gain a thorough understanding of the introduction and implementation of social accounting.

Social enterprise representatives are the most well-informed and competent in the field of social enterprise management, bearing extensive expertise in the social enterprise organisation system. They really need E.R.P. information systems as well as an accounting system that meets their needs according to the distinct characteristics of social enterprises. Given the authors' experience and knowledge of the SE environment gained through long discussions with SEs members and representatives since 2011 it has been demonstrated proved that accountants are not familiar with the social and non-monetary, non-financial characteristics of a social enterprise. Their primary responsibility is to the corresponding state agencies for tax and labor obligations.

Methodologically, the research was designed and conducted in December 2022, with the following preprocessing taking place in order to design the semi-structured interview. The questionnaire was first drafted, and two experts provided feedback on it. Then the authors formulated the final questionnaire and distribute it.

The questionnaire had 10 questions (with a "yes", "no", "do not know/do not answer" choices) and was distributed to participants via a google forms query. The majority of participants were presidents of the boards of directors of social enterprise unions from across the country. This decision was made due to the high level of involvement of these SEs members in management, communications, relationships with lawyers and accountants, government agencies and political personnel, primarily from the responsible Ministry of Labor. As a result, rather than conducting quantitative research with SE representatives across Greece, which would take more time and likely fewer responses to build a coherent and robust sample, a small but highly informative target group of key informants has been selected to provide accurate information for this research. Another important factor is that all of them have operational and strategic experience in the Greek social entrepreneurial environment, representing democratically hundreds of Social Enterprises.

In order to fine-tune the questions before they were distributed to the participants, a semi-structured interview was also conducted with three representatives of the Greek SE unions with scientific or technocratic jargon to be explained in order every participant would understand the questions unambiguously. The results obtained from this study are depicted in Figure 6.

Figure 6. Greek Confederation and Unions of Social Enterprises answers on Social Accounting and ERP operational use

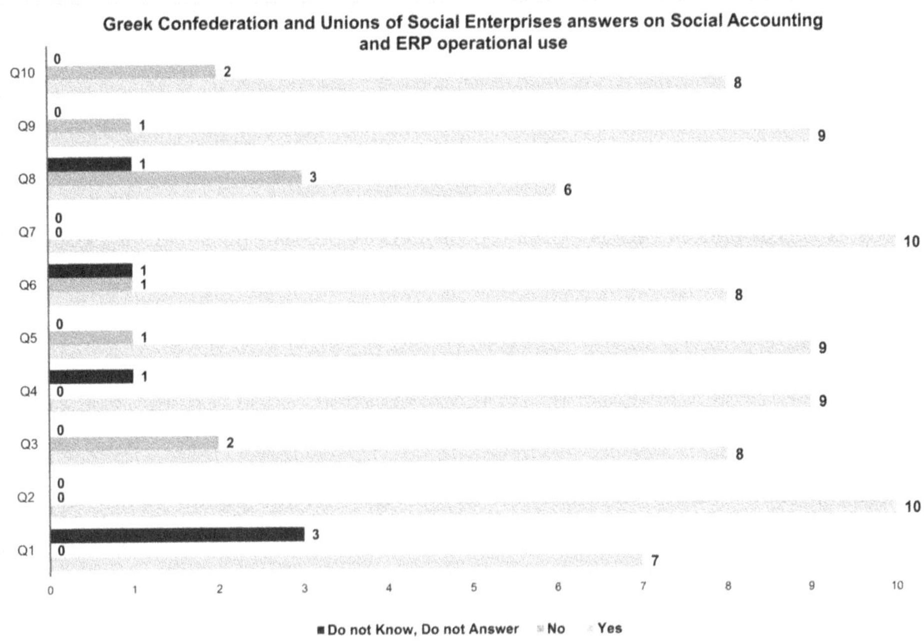

In Figure 6 the codified questions have been positively transcripted and portrayed as follows:

Q1. The proposed accounting system (ESA, 2010, IPSAS) is necessary for SEs.
Q2. An accounting system for social enterprises is necessary/useful.
Q3. The accounting system is supporting social enterprises in decision-making.
Q4. Social enterprises members are interested in a new system that keeps them updated also in legality and regularity.
Q5. Social enterprises members are interested in a common accounting system with other EU social enterprises for possible cooperation.
Q6. Social enterprises executive board and members interested in an ERP system that integrates with the Social enterprises accounting system and provides quick results.
Q7. Interested in an IT system also allowed for the provision of business plan
Q8. Accounting system, if designed exclusively for social enterprises, keep away adventurists.
Q9. Accounting and ERP systems useful for collaborating with other European and social enterprises.
Q10. National and European/international organisations would treat social enterprises and slanted social enterprises and social economy agents better in terms of funding and legal support.

The representatives of the SE Unions and Confederation voted overwhelmingly (87.5%) in favor of establishing an accounting system based on the European System of Accounts, or ESA, in 2010. The participants responded with an astounding 100% on the need for social enterprises to have their own discrete accounting system, as well as an 80% on an accounting system that supports decision making.

Participants are also 90% positive about a new system that will keep them on track with legal and regulatory issues.

When asked about the possibility of collaborating with other social enterprises in the European Union and sharing a common accounting system, participants responded positively on a 90% scale. On the question of whether an integrated Enterprise Resource System (ERP) with an accounting system development provides quick and reliable results, representatives from social enterprises unions answered with an 80% "yes" and only 10% negatively.

The positive responses for joined ERP and accounting systems for social enterprises on EU level collected an 80%. The respondents also considered by an 80% the national, European and international organisations more prone to provide funding and legal support by an 80%. The negative answers gathered low rates in all questions apart from a 30% on the question that a social accounting system would keep away the adventurists.

The Proposed Model for Social Accounting Based on Public Accounting (ESA)

The proposed accounting framework is mainly focused on IPSAS (International Public Sector Accounting Standards) and addresses the fundamental principles of initial recognition, subsequent measurement, and financial reporting item presentation.

Uniform adoption of an accrual accounting system for all Social Enterprises and Social Economy entities and a standard set of financial classification accounts used for budgeting and accounting are key features of the accounting framework.

The proposed system can include entities of Social Entrepreneurship as defined by the register of the Statistical Authority of each country or by the relevant registers kept in each country separately. To cover all aspects of social entrepreneurship comprehensively and consistently, and to present all necessary information on an accrual basis in order to provide data based on European System of Accounts (ESA) standards.

The accrual basis of reporting refers to recording the economic substance of transactions when they occur rather than when cash settlement occurs. Before proceeding with the detailed presentation of the proposed accounting model, a brief digression will be made to present two of the model's main parameters and core values, the European System of Accounts and the Social Economy Satellite Accounts. These two clearly differentiate the proposed model from the previously mentioned social accounting models, and especially from conventional accounting, by combining business finance and public fiscal accounting, as well as social reporting of social enterprises. Furthermore, the model is intended to connect a social enterprise's discrete accounting system with the rest of the social enterprises, aggregating from micro accounting to macro accounting, leading in this way to a more rational public funding and resource allocation.

European System of Accounts (ESA)

Regulation (EU) 549/2013 of the European Parliament and of the Council of 21 May 2013, which establishes the European Union (EU) system of national and regional accounts for the methodology and transmission of statistical data to Eurostat, the Commission's statistical office, is known as the European System of National and Regional Accounts.

The ESA 2010 lays out the methodology for compiling comparable accounts and tables for the needs of the EU, including common standards, definitions, nomenclatures, and accounting rules.

Among the arguments in favor of the accounting system are the following:

- Policymaking in the Union, as well as the monitoring of the EU countries' social enterprises and the Economic and Monetary Union (EMU), require comparable, up-to-date, and reliable information on the structure of the economy and the development of the economic situation of each EU country or region.
- The Commission can monitor the economies of EU member states and report to the Council on the progress made by social enterprises on a regular basis.
- EU citizens require financial accounts as a critical tool for analyzing social enterprises' financial situation.
- The Commission has the authority to use aggregated figures from national and regional accounts for EU administrative purposes, including fiscal calculations.

Entities subject to the application of Regulation (EU) 549/2013 must maintain an appropriate accounting system for: (a) monitoring revenues, profits, expenses, losses, other comprehensive income, assets, contingent assets, contingent liabilities, provisions, and other financial flows; and (b) Creating the necessary financial reports.

The management of obligated entities is responsible for ensuring the integrity of the accounting system. Accounting system reliability is ensured when:

(a) Accounting records are kept in an orderly, complete, and accurate manner in terms of accounting data identification, recording, and processing in accordance with prescribed policies.
(b) The procedures applied can be easily verified. Accounting system procedures are considered easily controllable if:
(b1) There is a two-way correlation between: events, transactions, and other operations, accounting records, and financial reports.
(b2) Persons with the requisite knowledge and experience can obtain an understanding of the structure and operation of the accounting system, the records maintained in which transactions, events, and other events are recorded, and the entity's financial position within a reasonable time.
(c) The transactions, events, and other operations are documented appropriately and adequately.

The accrual accounting system and allows for the monitoring of financial reporting data at the final level.

The proposed accounting system for social enterprises has several advantages, including the ability to transfer reporting statements from ERP based on ESA and IPSAS to SESA and form the social accounts. Furthermore, the identification of each social enterprise via administrative classification will be easily verifiable by the supervising public agency or organisation.

Through subsidies, tax policy, labor legislation etc, the state will be able to design effective policies in assisting social enterprises to their statutory mission. This is significant in society segments in need because vulnerable groups will find employment and personal well-being through the enjoyment of activity and social inclusion. Essentially, there will be a transition from Micro accounting to Macro accounting, which is accomplished by ESA and IPSAS, as well as a flexible and properly configured ERP system.

The Social Economy Satellite Accounts

National Accounts deal with aggregate sums that influence policy decisions in a variety of economic and social activity domains in the area of macro or national accounting. Regardless the fact of the multi origins of the data used to compile national accounts, "national accounts do not always meet the information needs of increasingly demanding users" (Ramos, 2019).

A satellite account is "a framework linked to the central (national or regional) accounts that permits attention to be focused on a specific field or feature of economic and social life in the context of national accounts", according to Eurostat (Eurostat, n.a.). Furthermore, ESA 2010 delineates a satellite account as the type of accounts that are used in cases of:

(a) showing more detail where necessary and leaving out superfluous detail; (b) enlarging the scope of the accounting framework by adding non-monetary information, e.g. on pollution and environmental assets; (c) changing some basic concepts, e.g. by enlarging the concept of capital formation by including expenditure on education (Eurostat, 2013).

ESA 2010 has established the structure to deal with satellite accounts by "connecting them to the national accounts facilitating the non-monetary statistics" as is clear from observation (Eurostat, 2013, p.9). To this end voluntary work can be included in the added value of social enterprises and or third sector organisations, an important issue that rarely has been calculated (Richmond et al., 2003).

Statistics Portugal and Statistics Poland have designed operate and maintain Social Economy Satellite Accounts, as special sector accounts for their countries (Ramos, 2019; Statistics Poland, 2021; Eurostat, 2013). Based on a thorough appraisal of the aforementioned accounts, an emphasis could be placed on the use of non-monetary data in satellite accounts, which, along with monetary data, provide key ratios (Eurostat, 2013). These key ratios are of major importance to social economy enterprises.

ESA also includes a framework of environmental accounts (Eurostat, 2013) satellite accounts that integrate and connect the environment and the economy and, as a result, measure environmental effect in addition to social impact both comprise the desideratum of social economy and social entrepreneurship.

The Sectoral Public Accounting For Social Enterprises

Financial statements and ERP reports will be presented by the ERP system as information. Because they are based on international standards supported by internationally recognized organisations that create them and are recognizable to all, financial statements and reports will be more streamlined and quantified than those used by the coordinating public agency, easier to capture, and can be analysed quickly and easily. According to ESA, the financial reports of Social Enterprises include the following:

- Budget – Annual Report
- Balance Sheet
- Statement of Fiscal Account
- Cash Flow Statement
- Profit and Loss Account
- Statement of Net Position
- Statement of Financial Position

The proposed ERP architecture shown in Figure 7, includes as inputs “Revenues” and “Expenditure” which operate as two parallel systems of the model’s Financial part, as well as “Social” and “Environmental” inputs. “Budget”, “Revenues”, “Social Procurement”, and “Other revenue streams” are included on the Revenues side, while the Expenses side includes “Budget”, “Expenditure Planning”, “Invoicing”, and “Other expense streams”.

The revenue and expense streams are integrated in the following process by processing revenues and expenses according to ESA and IPSAS through accounting recordings. Following that, we proceed to the next step, which is ESA reporting, as previously described, resulting in the above seven financial reports. In the same box (processing of Revenues and Expenditures) additional inputs feed the process, named under the codified names G, P1 and P2 respectively. The notion of G stands for the accounts in the chart of accounts which are classified into eight groups as following:

Group 1: Revenues,
Group 2: Expenditure,
Group 3: Property, Plant and Equipment, intangible assets and inventories,
Group 4: Financial assets,
Group 5: Financial liabilities,
Group 6: Provisions,
Group 7: Other financial flows,
Group 8: Equity accounts.

The notion of P1 stands for Government Finance Statistics or GFS as shown in Table 1. (For more elaboration, Eurostat 2013, p. 429, box. 20.1,).

Table 2. Government Finance Statistics (GFS) presentation according to ESA 2010 (Eurostat, 2013, p. 427)

	Government finance statistics (GFS) presentation
	Revenue Taxes Social Contributions Sales of goods and services Other current revenue Capital transfer revenue
less	Expenditure Intermediate consumption Compensation of employees Interest Subsidies Social Benefits Other current expenditure Capital transfer expenditure Investment expenditure
equals	Net lending/net borrowing
equals	Net financial transactions

As of the notion of P2 it is portraying the structure of the accounts of the economic classification of all groups , up to the fourth grade and the fifth grade from 90 to 99 is defined by the ESA. In order to adequately meet the information needs and the correct presentation of revenues, expenditure, tangible fixed assets, intangible fixed assets and inventories, financial assets, financial liabilities, provisions and other financial flows, in order to be consistent with those of the State Budget, the accounts are broken down into the fifth and sixth grades of economic classification. The fifth grade is expanded to two (2) digits (from 01 to 89), while the sixth grade is expanded to three (3) digits (from 001 to 899). The fifth grade of the chart of accounts indicates the accounting entry of transactions, while the sixth grade indicates the entry and monitoring of the execution of the Budget. The above analysis is shown in Table 2.

Table 3. Analysis of the structure of the financial classification of accounts according to ESA (source: Eurostat, 2013; Gerakos, in press, for the 6th Grade)

Analysis of the structure of the financial classification of accounts according to ESA								
Grade		1st		2nd	3rd	4th	5th	6th
Account		2		6	5	02	02	001
		2.6.5.02.02.001						
Grade	1st	2	=	Group of Accounts				2
Grade	2nd	6	=	Major Class of Accounts (GFS)				2. 6
Grade	3rd	5	=	Category according to ESA				2. 6 .5
Grade	4th	02	=	Analysis into further categories of previous grade				2. 6.5.02
Grade	5th	02	=	Accounting recording of transactions				2. 6.5.02.02
Grade	6th	001	=	Registration and monitoring of Budget execution				2.6.5.02.02.001

The ESA Reporting is the last process of the ERP system. Moving to the right side of Figure 7 the COFOG taxonomy (counting only for the expenditures side), the Social Economy Satellite Account and the National Account are the macro accounting part hence dealing with aggregates.

Figure 7. The proposed social accounting ERP model based on ESA and IPSAS

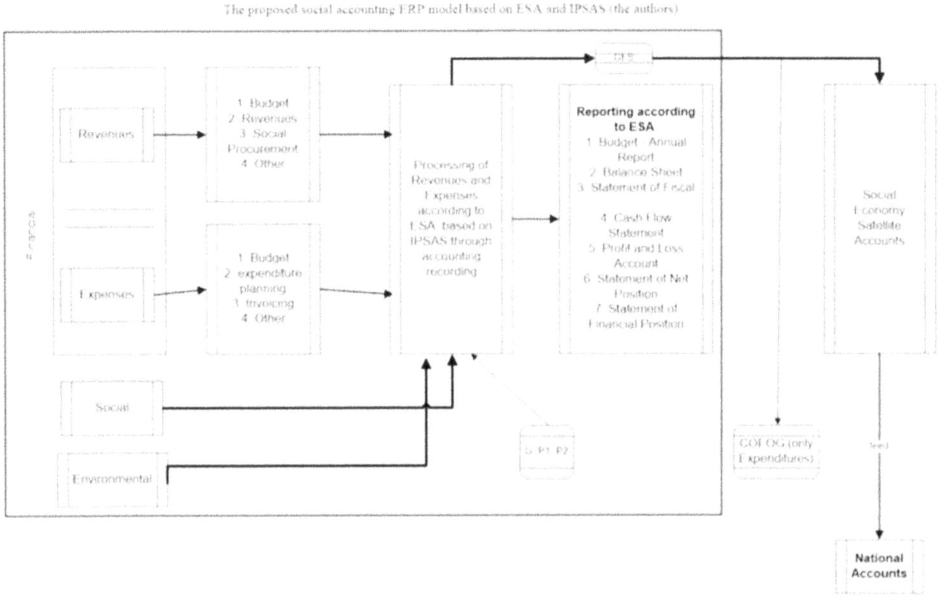

For functional classification purposes, the chart of accounts shall incorporate at least two levels of information. The Organisation for Economic Cooperation and Development, the United Nations, and the International Monetary Fund developed the Classification of Government Functions (COFOG), which is the primary model for classifying general government expenditure and includes the following codes:

01 General public services,
04 Economic Affairs,
05 Environmental Protection,
06 Housing and Community Amenities,
07 Health,
08 Recreation Culture and Religion,
09 Education,
10 Social Protection (Eurostat, 2013, p. 434).

The work and activities of social enterprises and nonprofit or third-sector entities can be classified in the above COFOG categories because they provide the required uniformity in common nomenclature, taxonomy, and methodology with the public sector.

The macro accounting parameter, Social Economy Satellite Accounts, is provided by the financial and non-financial (Social and Environmental) processing of Revenues and Expenses, and it is linked to National Accounts in sequence.

We share Kay and McMullan's (2017, p. 6) line of thought on "how to ensure credibility in reporting on social impact" and "how to handle the financialisation of social impact assessment" after presenting the social accounting model based on IPSAS and ESA, thus public accounting

Concerning the first challenge, the proposed model introduces a widely accepted and understandable model of public accounting into the discourse as well as in practice, with no controversies regarding its structuring and performance in terms of balancing and reporting. Accounting issues affect not only the social enterprise's accountants but also its management team and members, so IPSAS and ESA ensure credibility, openness, transparency, and a common language.

With regard to second challenge, the proposed model operates within a framework that includes monetized and non-monetized values but does not operate in terms of monetary return due to the intrinsic and external nature of social business. Money and financialisation are not required for social investors to invest in a social enterprise or a third sector organization and wait for (social) returns on investment.

A sectoral accounting plan based on group 1 (income) and group 2 (expenses) is required to serve the business activity of social enterprises.

The authors acknowledge that the submitted proposal is a good starting point and that it is feasible to implement. The accounting system proposal based on IPSAS and ESA is a supplemental structure known as a "sectoral accounting system" that will be further developed to improve the business operations of social enterprises. As a result, this discussion is being shared with the scientific community in order to aid in the development of a framework for accounting for social enterprises.

As a result, an actual implementation of the aforementioned system cannot be presented at this time. A significant amount of effort is being made in this direction. Greece has been granted a two-year extension with an implementation beginning on January 1, 2025 rather than January 1, 2023. A lengthy research process and strict timeline adherence are required.

Adoption of International Public Sector Accounting Standards (IPSAS) is a global trend that has received a lot of attention recently. States with higher comparative levels of development, larger public sectors, and greater participation in international organisations such as the United Nations have been found to be more likely to adopt IPSAS (Ben Amor & Damak Ayadi, 2019; Chow, & Aggestam Pontoppidan, 2019).

Implementing IPSAS could improve transparency and accountability. it is critical to consider the local context and cultural factors when developing standards (Dabbicco & Mattei, 2020; Chytis et al., 2020).

Despite the challenges, social enterprises, according to Apostolopoulos et al. (2019) have played an important role in promoting social cohesion and community empowerment, as well as sustainable development and environmental crisis management. This is how more integrated and sustainable economies can be built thereby contributing to the development of more resilient and just communities. To this end the proposed model builds on the view that:

Beyond traditional accounting tools suitable to provide an overview of the financial situation of the entity, a high attention has been progressively devoted to consider to what extent a public sector entity operates coherently with its own mission...

[A]t the same time, a large number of initiatives have emerged in the last decades promoting voluntary sustainability reporting in the public sector...

[S]cholars are paying growing attention to the flourishing different kinds of sustainability and environmental reporting, claiming the leading role of public sector organizations in a more sustainable future and the related relevance of sustainability accounting and accountability. (Katsikas et al., 2017, p. 2)

FUTURE RESEARCH DIRECTIONS

This research undertaking is still in its early stages. The sectoral public accounting model for social enterprises, based on ESA 2010 and linked with Social Economy Satellite Accounts, will be further developed and tested with the assistance of social firms in Greece and hopefully elsewhere in Europe through the deployment of the designed ERP system in Figure 7.

Following the development and implementation of the proposed system, trained and familiarized accountants with solid knowledge of public accounting and the discrete accounting singularity of the Social Economy must assist social enterprises.

The same holds true for public servants and public sector's personnel in economic services and agencies with jurisdiction over social economy organizations.

Given the importance of the Social Economy as one of the 14 industrial ecosystems in European Union, under the title of "Proximity, Social Economy and Civil Security", additional qualitative and quantitative research focused on transferring the social accounting notions and models to public sector with important contribution in local business and short value chains for mainly local production and consumption is required (European Commission, 2022).

As previously discussed, the Social Accounting Matrix (SAM) needs to be researched further in terms of social accounting given that it deals with employment and that gives us the idea of using it, with the use of a micro database (Eurostat, 2013) to calculate the contribution of volunteers and compare the results with the model of Richmond et al. (2003).

The polyhedral model, with its emphasis on monetizing social value/impact and its integration with economic and financial reporting, and the Integrated Accountability Model could be examined as pair models with the GRI model.

Another future challenge will be integrating social accounting in general, and the proposed sectoral accounting model for social enterprises in particular, into ESG practices and reporting in order develop a common field of understanding and bring corporations and traditional businesses closer to social enterprises in order to facilitate CSR actions and campaigns. In terms of materialising effective and long-term sustainability actions towards a resilient society, a greener and sustained environment, and an economy for the common good, social enterprises and social entrepreneurs are the best complements to traditional business.

CONCLUSION

Although social accounting has been tested in social enterprises (Gibbon and Affleck, 2008), this chapter's research provided the first theoretical and empirical analysis of the introduction of public accounting in social enterprises.

The authors propose the ESA 2010 and IPSAS, a well-known and operational accounting system based on the relationship between SEs and public organisations in the broader context of accounting, social finance, and public accounting, because it has been suggested in the literature and here that the mainstream accounting worldview is insufficient for the scope and impact of social economy enterprises.

In comparison to conventional accounting, this study proposes a new conceptual and applicable model based on the framework design and rationale of public accounting. Despite being in use for more than four decades, social accounting has yet to become a mainstream accounting system. The various approaches discussed in this chapter's preceding section should be integrated or, preferably, adjusted in a unified and integrated accounting system measuring the social and environmental impact of the (social) business sector and producing accurate accounting and statistical reporting. The same is true for other relevant models and tools in the field of Environment, Society and Governance (ESG) with the proposed global solution of International Sustainability Standard Board (ISSB).

Of course, integrated models such as Blended Value Accounting in Social Entrepreneurship (Nicholls, 2009) and the Integrated Accountability Model (Andreaus & Costa, 2014) are in use and are valuable tools for the present and future of social accounting. In any case we must take seriously what Gray (2001, p.14) concludes as one of many lessons in regard to social accounting, that is "Clarity of objectives, a systematic approach, quality evidence, completeness, integrity and independence are the sine qua non of good social accounts".

Our findings indicate that social enterprises in Greece are generally willing to adopt a discrete social accounting model based on public accounting logic structured on IPSAS and ESA via an ERP system that will provide accuracy, speed, and accountability.

Furthermore we propose the "sectoral accounting system for SEs" to facilitate the business activity of social enterprises, it is necessary to develop a sectoral accounting plan which will be based on income and expenses to serve the business activity of social enterprises and to expand the information of financial report.

Accountability, performance, and democracy all rely on the interdependence of micro and macro accounting. Bridging and connecting Social Accounting via Public Accounting with Satellite Accounts such as those in the Social Economy (Ramos, Statistics Poland, 2021) and National Accounts via ESA 2010 will be a valuable tool based on a common accounting language at the European level. The use of Social Cost-Benefit Analysis (Thirlwall, 1983) in the framework of the proposed social accounting analysis is also critical. This research project contributes to the debate about how to improve evidence-based policies in the European Union, specifically in the field of social economy and social enterprises, by developing an ERP system (micro accounting) that will collect comparable and quantifiable data on social economy, taking into account social and environmental contributions of social enterprises as well as their economic contribution.

By doing so, the EU and its member states will be able to design more effective and efficient policies in the field when it comes to financial support for this industrial sector.

ACKNOWLEDGMENT

This research received no specific grant from any funding agency in the public, commercial, or not-for-profit sectors.

REFERENCES

Andreaus, M., & Costa, E. (2014). Toward an integrated accountability model for nonprofit organizations. In Costa, E., Parker, D. L., and Andreaus, M. (Eds). Accountability and social accounting for social and nonprofit organizations (pp. 37–106). Howard House: Emerald.

Apostolopoulos, N., Newbery, R., & Gkartzios, M. (2019). Social enterprise and community resilience: Examining a Greek response to turbulent times. *Journal of Rural Studies*, *70*, 215–224.

Baba, H. Ishida, & Y., Aoki, T. (2015). Social Accounting for Nonprofit Organizations: Visualizing the Invisible Value of Social Impacts. Kansai University Review of Business and Commerce, 16, 1–22. Retrieved from: http://baba-hi72.up.seesaa.net/image/KandaiReview2015_baba_etal.pdf

Bashkar, K., & Flower, J. (2021). *Disruption in Financial Reporting A Post-pandemic View of the Future of Corporate Reporting*. Routledge.

Bebbington, J., & Gray, R. (2007). Corporate Accountability and the Physical Environment: Social Responsibility and Accounting Beyond Profit. *Business Strategy and the Environment*, *2*, 1–11. doi:10.1002/bse.3280020201

Ben Amor, D., & Damak Ayadi, S. (2019). The profile of IPSAS-adopters. *Journal of Accounting and Management Information Systems*, *18*(2), 262–282.

Borzaga, C., & Galera, E. (2014). New Trends in the Nonprofit sector in Europe: The emergence of social enterprises. In E. Costa, D. L. Parker, & M. Andreaus (Eds.), *The Accountability and Social Accounting for Social and Non-profit Organisations* (pp. 107–130). Emerald.

Borzaga, C., & Tortia, E. (2010). The economics of social enterprises. In L. Becchetti & C. Borzaga (Eds.), *The Economics of Social Responsibility, The world of social enterprises* (pp. 15–33). Routledge.

Brown, J., & Fraser, M. (2006). Approaches and Perspectives in Social and Environmental Accounting: An Overview of the Conceptual Landscape. *Business Strategy and the Environment*, *15*, 309–321. doi:10.1080/0969160X.2021.1872397

Chan, J., & Chan, E. (2010). Social Audits. In: Anheier, K.H., Toepler, S., List, R. (Eds). *International Encyclopedia of Civil Society, 1384-1388*. New York: Springer. https://doi.org/10.1007/978-0-387-93996-4

Chow, D., & Aggestam Pontoppidan, C. (2019). The United Nations' (UN) decision to adopt International Public Sector Accounting Standards (IPSAS). *Journal of Public Budgeting, Accounting &. Financial Management*, *31*(2), 285–306.

Chytis, E., Georgopoulos, I., Tasios, S., & Vrodou, I. (2020). Accounting Reform and IPSAS Adoption in Greece. *European Research Studies Journal*, *XXIII*(4), 165–184.

Dabbicco, G., & Mattei, G. (2020). The reconciliation of budgeting with financial reporting: A comparative study of Italy and the UK. *Public Money & Management*, *41*(2), 127–137.

Defourny, J. (2001). Introduction. From third sector to social enterprise. In C. Borzaga & J. Defourny (Eds.), *The Emergence of Social Enterprise* (pp. 1–28). Routledge.

Defourny, J., & Pestoff, V. (2014). Towards a European conceptualization of the third sector. In Costa, E., Parker, D. L., and Andreaus, M. (Eds). Accountability and social accounting for social and nonprofit organizations (pp. 37–106). Howard House: Emerald.

Dey, C., & Gibbon, J. (2017). Moving on from Scaling Up: Further Progress in Developing Social Impact Measurement in the Third Sector. *Social and Environmental Accountability Journal*, 37(1), 66-72. DOI: doi:10.1080/0969160X.2017.1285712

Eccles, G. R., & Mirchandani, B. (2022). We need universal ESG Accounting Standards. *Harvard Business Review*. Retrieved from https://hbr.org/2022/02/we-need-universal-esg-accounting-standards

European Commission. (2022). *Investment Support for Ecosystems Proximity and Social Economy*. Retrieved from https://ec.europa.eu/docsroom/documents/ 51115/attachments/2/translations/en/renditions/native

European Commission. (2021). *Investment Building an economy that works for people: an action plan for the social economy*. COM(2021)778 final. Retrieved from https://eur-lex.europa.eu/legal-content/EN/TXT/PDF/?uri=CELEX:52021DC0778

Eurostat, (2013). *European Systems of Account (ESA 2010)*. Retrieved from https://ec.europa.eu/eurostat/web/esa-2010

Eurostat, a. *Statistics explained*. Retrieved from https://ec.europa.eu/eurostat/statistics-explained/index.php?title=Glossary:Satellite_account

Facci, L. (2010). The provision of welfare and general-interest services. In L. Becchetti & C. Borzaga (Eds.), *The Economics of Social Responsibility, The world of social enterprises* (pp. 88–104). Routledge.

Flamholz, G. E. (1999). *Human Resource Accounting Advances in Concepts, Methods and Applications*. Springer.

Filios, R. (1991). Non-monetary accounting: A Necessary Development for Better managerial decisions. *Business Int. J. Value-Based Management*, *4*(2), 133–143.

Gerakos, I. (in press). *To plaisio gia to Neo Dimosio Logistiko (Proedriko Diatagma 54/2018)*. Athens. *Benos.*

Gerakos, I. (2021). *Dimosio Logistiko me vasi to PD 54/2018*. OTS.

Gibbon, J., & Affleck, A. (2008). Social enterprise resisting social accounting: Reflecting on lived experiences. *Social Enterprise Journal*, *4*(1), 41–56. doi:10.1108/17508610810877722

Gray, R. (2001). Thirty years of social accounting, reporting and auditing: What (if anything) have we learnt? *Business Ethics (Oxford, England)*, *10*(1), 9–15.

International Federation of Accountants. (2018). *International Public Sector Financial Accountability Index*. Retrieved from https://www.ifac.org/_flysystem/azure-private/IFAC-CIPFA-Public-Sector-Index-2018-Status.pdf

Johnson, B., & Kleiner, H. B. (1987). Human Asset Accounting: Where Are We Today? *International Journal of Manpower*, *8*(4), 3–4. doi:10.1108/eb045129

Katsikas, E., Rossi, M. F., & Orelli, L. R. (2017). *Towards Integrated Reporting Accounting Change in the Public Sector*. Springer.

Kay, A. (2011). *Prove, Improve, Account - The New Guide to Social Accounting and Audit*. Social Audit Network.

Kay, A., & McMullan, L. (2017). Contemporary Challenges Facing Social Enterprises and Community Organisations Seeking to Understand Their Social Value. *Social and Environmental Accountability Journal*, *37*(1), 1–5. doi:10.1080/0969160X.2017.1287583

Lazkano, L., & Beraza, A. (2019). Social Accounting for Sustainability: A Study in the Social Economy. *Sustainability*, *11*, 1–5. doi:10.3390u11246894

Mäkelä, H. (2021). Roles of Accounting for the Contested Terrain of Social Enterprises. *Social and Environmental Accountability Journal*, *41*(3), 150–171. doi:10.1080/0969160X.2021.1872397

Mäkelä, H., Gibbon, J., & Costa, E. (2017). Roles of Accounting for the Contested Terrain of Social Enterprises. *Social and Environmental Accountability Journal*, *37*(1), 1–5. doi:10.1080/0969160X.2017.1287583

Mook, L., Quarter, J., & Richmond, B. (2007). *What Counts: Social Accounting for Nonprofits and cooperatives*. Sigel Press.

Mook, L. (2014). An integrated social accounting model for nonprofit organizations. In Costa, E., Parker, D. L., and Andreaus, M. (Eds). Accountability and social accounting for social and nonprofit organizations (pp. 220–246). Howard House: Emerald.

Mook, L., & Quarter, J. (2010). Social Accounting for Social Economy Organisations. In: Anheier, K.H., Toepler, S., List, R. (Eds). International Encyclopedia of Civil Society, 1380-1384. New York: Springer. https://doi.org/ doi:10.1007/978-0-387-93996-4

Nicholls, A. (2009). "We do good thigs, don't we?": "Blended Value Accounting" in social entrepreneurship, *Social Accounting. Organizações & Sociedade*, *34*, 755–769. doi:10.1016/j.aos.2009.04.008

Nicholls, A., Paton, R., & Emerson, J. (2015). Social Impact Measurement. In A. Nicholls, R. Paton, & J. Emerson (Eds.), *Social Finance* (pp. 101–102). University Press Scholarship Online., doi:10.1093/acprof:oso/9780198703761.003.0016

Ramos, C. (2019). Social Economy Satellite Account (CSES) how to build a Satellite Account *(original article in Spanish), Economia Social Leituras and Debates*,6. Retrieved from https://knowledgehub.unsse.org/wp-content/uploads/2019/12/Ramos_2019_Social-Economy-Satellite-Account-in-Portugal.pdf

Regulation of the European Parliament and of the Council of 21 May 2013 on the European system of national and regional accounts in the European Union Text with EEA relevance. No 549/2013 (2013). https://eur-lex.europa.eu/legal-content/EN/ALL/?uri=celex:32013R0549

Retolaza, J. L., San-Jose, L., & Ruíz-Roqueñi, M. (2016). *Social Accounting for Sustainability Monetizing the Social Value*. Springer.

Richmond, J. B., Mook, L., & Quarter, J. (2003). Social Accounting for Nonprofits Two Models. *Nonprofit Management & Leadership*, *13*(4), 308–324.

Rinaldi, L. (2019). Accounting for Sustainability Governance: The Enabling Role of Social and Environmental Accountability Research. *Social and Environmental Accountability Journal*, *39*(1), 1–22. doi:10.1080/0969160X.2019.1578675

Statistics Poland. (2021). *Social Economy Satellite Account for Poland 2018*. Retrieved from https://stat.gov.pl/download/gfx/portalinformacyjny/en/defaultaktualnosci/3681/5/1/1/social_economy_satellite_account_for_poland_2018.pdf

Thirlwall, P. A. (1983). *Growth and Development with Special reference to developing economies* (3rd ed.). Macmillan.

United Nations, Department of Economic and Social Affairs. (2018). Satellite Account on Non-profit and Related Institutions and Volunteer Work. Studies in Methods, Handbook of national Accounting, Series F, No. 91, Rev. 1: New York

von Ravensburg, G. N., Krlev, G., & Mildenberge, G. (2018). *Social Enterprises and their Ecosystems in Europe. Country Report: Germany*. Luxemburg: European Union. https://ec.europa.eu/social/BlobServlet?docId=20563&langId=en

Yongvanich, K., & Guthrie, J. (2006). An Extended Performance Reporting Framework for Social and Environmental Accounting. *Business Strategy and the Environment*, *15*, 309–321. doi:10.1080/0969160X.2021.1872397

ADDITIONAL READING

Baldarelli, M. G., *Del Baldo, M., & Nesheva-Kios*seva, N. (2017). Sustainability Environmental A*c*-*counting and Reporting Theory and Practice. Springe*r.

Gal, G., Akişik, O., & Wooldridge, W. (2018). Sustainability and *Social Responsibility: Regulation and Reporting. Springer.*

*Jo*rdan, B. (2021). Social Value in Public Policy. Palgrave Macmillan.

Melville, *A. (2019). International Financial Reporting: A Practical Guide (7th ed.*). Pearson.

KEY TERMS AND DEFINITIONS

Accounting: is understood in its broadest notion, as "a complex", as a group of diverse elements, comprised not only of accounting and measurement tools but also of ideas, goals, reports, standards, laws and the human actors operating in this broad and fluid field of accounting (Miller and Power, 2013, cited in Mäkelä 2021).

Blended Value: all value is understood as being generated (by organizations and the application of capital) through the interaction over time of three primary value components: social, economic, and environmental, which together comprise organizational value creation and capital returns (Emerson, in Anheimer, et al., pp. 66-68).

Environmental Accounting: is the measurement and evaluation of natural resources and includes assigning an economic value to environmental goods and services, which are appreciated and recognized as important in society. (Mio, 2002, p. 31, cited in Baldarelli, Baldo and Kiosseva, 2017).

ESA 2010: the European System of Accounts (or "the ESA") is an internationally compatible accounting framework for a systematic and detailed description of a total economy (that is: a region, country or group of countries), its components and its relations with other total economies.

Human Resource Accounting: Human resource accounting is an attempt to identify, quantify, and report investments made in resources of an organization that are not presently accounted for under conventional accounting practice (Flamholz, 1999, p. 109).

Social Accounting: is a systematic analysis of the effects of an organization on its communities of interest or stakeholders, with stakeholder input as part of the data that is analyzed for the accounting statement. (Mook et al., 2007, p. 2, cited in Mook and Quarter, 2010).

Social Audit: is a systematic analysis of the effects of an organization on its communities of interest or stakeholders, with stakeholder input as part of the data that is analyzed for the accounting statement. (Chan and Chan, 2010).

Social Economy: covers entities sharing principles such as the primacy of people as well as social and/or environmental purpose over profit, the reinvestment of most profits to carry out activities in the interest of members or society at large and democratic and/or participatory governance (European Commission, 2022).

Chapter 10
External Auditors Discover Management Breach of Trust:
Evidence From Mexico

Flory Dieck-Assad
Tecnologico de Monterrey, Mexico

ABSTRACT

The importance of ethics in the accounting discipline has increased in recent years. A Mexican company reported a slower profit growth than expected, hiring external auditors to research the reasons behind this economic growth slowdown of a profitable company. This empirical research is the key for the success of any newly born firm (especially for small and medium sized firms), to establish the safeguards to avoid corruption and fraud, offering awareness to those eager to grow in the business environment. The firm needed an integral revision of the company's finances and operations to discover the role of the persons involved in the creation of the fake invoices and to enforce the needed safeguards to avoid recurrent breaches of trust. External auditors prove to be an important tool to provide a fresh perspective about the breach of trust in the accounting professional ethical code and its criminal implications.

INTRODUCTION

There was a breach of trust in a Mexican company. This chapter tells the story of this ethical violation and how it was resolved. Throughout the chapter, the reader will learn how to avoid future occurrences based on the professional code of ethics in accounting.

This chapter presents a real case where there was a breach of trust in a Mexican company, pinpointing the symptoms that triggered the suspicion of fraud and how it was found and corrected, and identifying important economic losses and the damage in the growth process of the company. The best tool that the company decided to use was an external audit. During a meeting where this Mexican company (CMInc) reviewed the possible breach of trust of its accountant (Loring & Sinclair, 2001), the Chief Financial Officer (CFO) decided to hire an external auditing company (AECG, Inc.), to do empirical research to find out the reasons behind the slowdown in the economic growth of this profitable company, suspecting of

DOI: 10.4018/978-1-6684-7293-4.ch010

a possible breach of trust. The CFO relied on their discretion and confidentiality. The main contribution of this chapter is to make this book multicultural, learning about the anguish of small private companies with a lack of accounting knowledge where the scarcity of resources suggests not investing in internal controls. After reading the chapter, small firms will understand the effectiveness of getting attached to an accounting ethical value code and the imposition of internal controls in the firm that does not need to be very expensive but could save the firm from financial problems and become more profitable in the long run. This chapter also emphasizes the role of an external auditing company to avoid retaliations, submitting the research to an external entity with the ability to enforce the law, and keeping the CFO and the owner of the company safe. This is how the search for the illegal behavior of one or more of CMInc´s employees started (Espino, 2014).

The structure of this chapter is as follows. The next section presents a background of what an Ethical Code is with reviews of relevant literature. The methodology is presented in the following section, specifying the objectives and the strategies to find the breach of trust in the company through an external auditing company. This section also includes an explanation of potential conflicts for unethical behavior. This chapter continues with the analysis of this real case beginning with the specification of the profile of the company, defining its structure and its challenges. This section also explains the way the external auditing company found the breach of trust. The hypothesis of the external auditing company in this real case asserts that there might have been a breach of compliance with the fundamental principles threatened by the following categories: self-interest, financial interests, inappropriate personal use of corporate assets, data being subject to review and justification by the same professional accountant responsible for making those decisions or preparing that data and the provision of statements with false or misleading information. These could be faults derived from the firms' lack of oversight. Based on the principle of professional behavior, this section also discusses if the professional accountant made a mistake or committed fraud and if it is proved that it was done, the question is if he acted alone or with a third party. The chapter follows with a discussion resulting from the external auditing report and the last section presents the conclusions with a specific recommendation for small and medium size entrepreneurs. At the end of the chapter, a reference section is presented as well as key terms and definitions used throughout the chapter.

BACKGROUND AND LITERATURE REVIEW

The chapter bases its analysis on the professional code published by The International Federation of Accountants (IFAC), which is a defense organization for good execution of the financial accounting and auditing professions (IFAC, 2006).

The sustainable development of a strong international economy is based on the establishment and adherence to high-quality professional standards. The key to a firm's failure could be focused on corruption and a lack of adherence to those professional standards. IFAC created the Ethics Standards Board for Accountants with the mission to develop and issue, under its authority, high-quality ethical standards and other pronouncements for professional accountants for use around the world. The result was the creation of The Code of Ethics for Professional Accountants establishing the ethical requirements for professional accountants.

The fundamental ethical principles of a professional accountant are Integrity, Objectivity, Professional Competence and Due Care, Confidentiality, and Professional Behavior (IFAC, 2006: Sections

110-150). In this case, the fundamental principles of Integrity, Professional Competence and Due Care, Confidentiality, and Professional Behavior were questioned. The professional accountant must devote his/her skills to the objective of offering his/her employer the reception of a competent professional service based on current developments in practice, legislation, and techniques.

To avoid any conflict of interest, an external auditing firm is hired as an independent third party that should work with those in charge of governance within the organization (CFO and the owner), as part of the auditing committee (Gantz, 2014). The hired auditing firm should determine the appropriate process to follow that is consistent with the identified violation of the fundamental principles and establish the consequences of each possible course of action.

On June 15, 2019, the accounting world heralded the coming into effect of the International Code of Ethics for Professional Accountants which had been revised and restructured (Yong, 2019). The objective was to propose clarity and usability of the Code, facilitating the Code´s adoption, effective implementation, and consistent application on a global basis. The hallmark of the Code remained unchanged: Integrity, Objectivity, Professional Competence and Due Care, Confidentiality, and Professional Behavior.

Integrity is defined by IFAC as the principle that imposes an obligation on all professional accountants to be straightforward and honest in professional and business relationships. Integrity also implies fair dealing and truthfulness (IFAC, 2006: Section 110) and is one of the principles that is researched in this chapter through an empirical case.

Objectivity is a principle that demands commitment from all professional accountants not to compromise their professional judgment because of bias, conflict of interest, or the undue influence of others (IFAC, 2006: Section 120). It is a fact that all professional accountants might be exposed to situations that may confuse their objectivity. It is impossible to describe all such situations; however, the professional accountant should develop a criterion to identify those situations, even though they might appear in a grey zone. Decisions are not always black or white; there appear to be a lot of grey situations that require the correct judgment of the professional accountant.

According to IFAC (IFAC, 2006: Section 130), Professional Competence and Due Care impose the following obligations on professional accountants: to maintain professional knowledge and skill at the level required to ensure that clients or employers receive competent professional service, and to act diligently under applicable technical and professional standards when providing professional services. Diligence encompasses the responsibility to act under the requirements of an assignment, carefully, thoroughly, and on a timely basis (IFAC, 2018). IFAC updated the fundamental ethical principles of a professional accountant in 2022, emphasizing quality management-related issues, including amendments to the Code that were issued as a result of the finalization of the International Auditing and Assurance Standards Board's (IAASB) suite of quality management standards (IFAC,2022).

The principle of Confidentiality imposes the obligation on professional accountants to refrain from using acquired confidential information because of professional and business relationships to their advantage or the advantage of third parties. The professional accountant should consider the need to maintain the confidentiality of information within the employing firm (IFAC, 2018).

According to IFAC, the principle of Professional Behavior imposes an obligation on professional accountants to comply with relevant laws and regulations and avoid any action that may bring discredit to the profession and impact the company's financials.

IFAC is concerned with professional accountants in public and private businesses. The following discussion of the IFAC Code is applied specifically to professional accountants in private businesses.

IFAC proposes that professional accountants in a private business may be solely or jointly responsible for the preparation and reporting of financial and other information, which both their employing organizations and third parties may rely on (IFAC, 2006: Section 300). They may also be responsible for providing effective financial management and competent advice on a variety of business-related matters.

According to the American Institute of CPAs (AICPA), a professional accountant in a private business holds a senior position within the firm with the possible opportunity to influence events, practices, and attitudes, and is expected to encourage an ethics-based culture in his employing organization that emphasizes the importance that senior management places on ethical behavior (AICPA, 2014).

IFAC provides an example (IFAC, 2006: Section 300) intended to illustrate how the conceptual framework of ethical values is to be applied and are not intended to be, nor should they be interpreted as, an exhaustive list of all circumstances experienced by a professional accountant in private business that may create threats to compliance with the principles. Consequently, it is not sufficient for a professional accountant in private business merely to comply with the examples; rather, the framework should be applied to the specific circumstances faced. This is the objective of this chapter.

Once the principles were reviewed it is important to learn more about threats and safeguards in a firm. Several threats could be obstacles to reaching the goals of a firm. IFAC (IFAC, 2006: Section 100) classifies the threats into five categories. The first concerns *self-interest threats*, which happen more frequently, and may occur when the professional accountant, or any of his/her family members, have a personal financial interest. The second involves *judgement threat*, which appears when a judgement is required from the professional accountant and should be made with objectivity and discernment. IFAC names the third threat as *advocacy threats*, which appear in any circumstance when the professional accountant promotes an opinion with a lack of objectivity; thus, his judgment might be compromised by certain circumstances or personal interests. The fourth threat is called *familiarity threat*, when the professional accountant has close relationships with specific persons becoming too sympathetic to the interests of others, and the last one is the *intimidation threat* when there are real threats that make the professional accountant fear consequences if he does not comply with the required decisions and lose objectivity in his decisions.

From the threats that IFAC lists, some fundamental ethical principles could be endangered by a broad range of circumstances that are discussed in this chapter. Specifically, *self-interest threats* may occur because of the financial or other interests of the professional accountant.

Safeguards were designed to eliminate or reduce such threats to an acceptable level. IFAC (IFAC, 2006: Section 100) presents two categories. The first ones are created by the profession itself, the legislation and/or the regulations, such as the university education, training, professional standards, established professional monitoring, and disciplinary procedures. It is suggested to hire an external reviewer empowered to examine and evaluate all reports, accountant statements, communications, or any information produced within the company with high scrutiny. The second one comes from the work environment itself, establishing paths to avoid unethical behavior. These must include, among others, an effective complaint system operated by the owner of the organization to empower colleagues to draw attention to unethical behavior. The nature of the safeguards to be applied will vary depending on the characteristics of every company, the size of the company, and the importance of the breach of trust that is being analyzed (Buffa, 2005).

Based on IFAC guidelines, the process to follow to analyze the symptom of providing higher efforts, more work but slow growth of profit throughout the years, is:

1. Identify relevant data related to the symptom.
2. Discover if fundamental principles related to the matter in question were violated.
3. Evaluate the effectiveness of internal procedures or safeguards.
4. Suggest alternative courses of action.

The following section explains the methodology of the company to face the symptom and identify the ethical violations.

METHODOLOGY

Once the symptom was identified, the company realized that it prevented the firm to grow and hinder the objective of the company to create new subsidiaries in other states of the country. A lack of financial health in the company made the company weak to afford its desired expansion in a dynamic market. Why is the company experiencing slow profit growth when the external economic indicators are characterized by a dynamic market? Thus, it was important to find out the reasons behind the symptom and this required the professional accountant to identify, evaluate, and address threats to compliance with the fundamental principles.

The hypothesis is that the slow growth of profit throughout the years (the symptom) was due to the breach of one or more of the principles described by IFAC. It is also assumed in the hypothesis that there could be a problem with, or within the company. The search for the reasons for the presented symptom of the company must be done by an external auditing consulting company and work with those in charge of governance within the organization, such as the CFO and the owner in this case.

The company needed to document the elements of possible fraud. As Kanade (2021) states, fraud is a serious business risk that needs to be identified and mitigated in time. If the assumed fraud is confirmed, the external auditing company should consider the CFO and owner's opinion to determine whether there is a requirement to report to the authorities. According to Mitz (2018), external audits of financial statements were the most commonly implemented anti-fraud controls with 80% of the organizations undergoing independent audits.

In 2021, Certified Fraud Examiners (CFEs) published a report based on data and facts that occurred throughout the world in 2021 (ACFE (Association of Certified Fraud Examiners), 2022). This global fraud survey was unique because it encompassed frauds that occurred during a global pandemic. This 12th edition of the report is a challenge to find new, innovative ways to detect fraud more quickly to limit losses. It was found that corruption was the most used scheme in every global region, causing on average a loss of $8,300 U.S. dollars per month and lasting 12 months before detection. (ACFE, 2022).

If, after exhausting all relevant possibilities, the ethical conflict remains unresolved, the external auditing company should determine if it is appropriate to enforce the law or to ask for the resignation of those who participated in the fraud from the employing organization. As Petrucelli (2013) explains in his book, subtle factors play a large role in identifying and ferreting out fraud in addition to the traditional knowledge of fraud schemes giving people and organizations the edge they need to be successful in prevention and deterrence. The decision should be taken in conjunction with the CFO and the owner of the company.

The company's professional accountant should not be involved with reports, returns, communications, or other information that may contain false or misleading statements. The CFO and the owner were concerned that the professional accountant may have not complied with the ethical principles and asked the external auditing company to research this issue to verify the ethical behavior of the professional accountant of this private firm. The management of the firm questioned the possible violation of the Professional Competence and Due Care principle but was unsure if there were other principles violated.

The hypothesis asserts that there might be a breach of compliance with the fundamental principles threatened by the following categories: self-interest, financial interests, inappropriate personal use of corporate assets, data being subject to review and justification by the same professional accountant responsible for making those decisions or preparing that data and the provision of statements with false or misleading information. These could be faults derived from the firms' lack of oversight.

Even though the recruitment procedures in the employing organization emphasized the importance of employing competent staff, temptations could arise that are derived from a lack of strong internal controls.

Even though the leadership of the firm stressed the importance of ethical behavior and the expectation that employees will act ethically, there could have been a lack of policies and procedures to implement and monitor the quality of employee performance (IFAC, 2018).

One of the safeguards that the company used to eliminate or reduce the self-interest threats was to implement an appropriate invoice emission system under the legislation and regulations (Murphy, 2022). However, this system was not working on time. It proved to be part of the company's weakness as shown in Figure 1. That is why, it was necessary in this case to add another work environment safeguard: hiring a legally empowered third party (external auditing company) to provide an independent review of these reports, returns, communications or information produced by the professional accountant.

Figure 1. Diagnosis of the company's weakness
Source: Own elaboration with the results from the empirical research

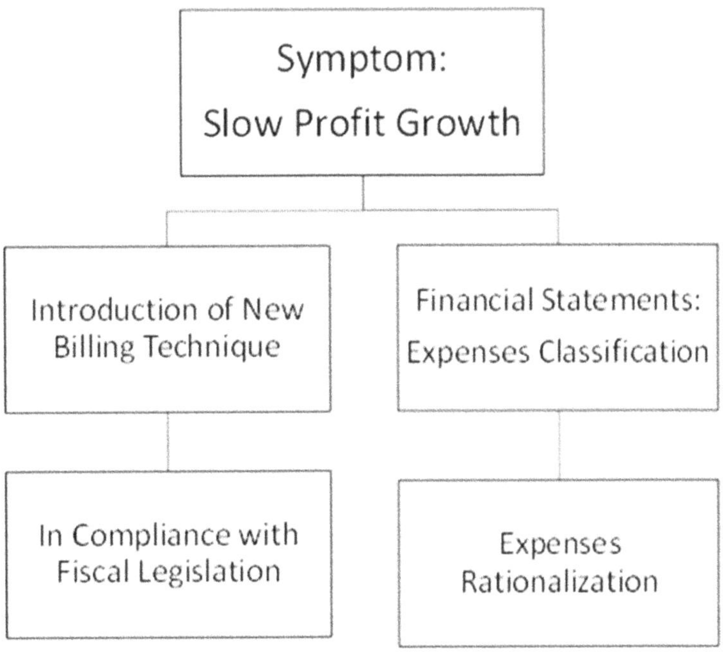

The company (CFO and owner) suspected that the emission of electronic receipts with the latest online techniques and according to the current legislation could be the problem. The technique of the emission of invoices was the main objective to be analyzed because if a firm shows less profit generation than expected, any accountant should have researched and analyzed the expenses to improve the business's profit generation (Antosz, 2022). It was important to identify the circumstances in which the firm's professional accountant failed to identify the reasons for this slow profit generation. Based on this analysis, there should be appropriate mitigating actions and define different safeguards if necessary (The Hartford Business Owners' Playbook, 2022). If there is suspicion of an existence of a significant threat to Professional Behavior and the professional accountant cannot implement appropriate safeguards, he should decline or discontinue the specific professional service involved, or when necessary, resign from the employing organization.

Based on the principle of Professional Behavior, in this case, the hypothesis to be tested is if the professional accountant made a mistake or committed fraud and if it is proved that it was done, the question is if he acted alone or with a third party.

To avoid confrontations, an external auditing firm was hired as an appropriate first safeguard for the company. It was important to simulate that everything continued operating normally and did not turn on high alerts to those involved in the possible threats to the company, especially if there is a possibility that the professional accountant might be violating a provision of this Code of Ethics.

In circumstances where the professional accountant in private business presents unethical behavior and it is not possible to reduce the threat to an acceptable level, the auditing firm may conclude that it is appropriate for the professional accountant to resign from the employing organization or face the law. The decision will be taken in conjunction with the CFO and the owner.

Once the ethical violation is discovered, it should be corrected immediately by designing and applying the needed safeguards. The circumstances encountered by the auditing firm must be corrected at once.

Potential Conflicts for Unethical Behavior

The empirical research began by hiring an external auditing firm to engage in financial statements audits and offered an independent analysis. According to IFAC (IFAC, 2006: Section 290.27), for financial statement audit clients, the external auditing firm is required to be independent of the financial statement audit client. Such independence requirements include prohibitions regarding certain relationships between members of the external auditing firm and directors, officers, and employees of the client in a position to exert direct and significant influence over the data to be analyzed (the financial statements, the financial position, financial performance, and cash flows).

The auditing firm must find financial information that could have impacted the financial statements of the firm about a broad range of transactions and events that have affected the profitability of the firm.

IFAC (IFAC, 2006: Section 310) emphasizes that the professional accountant has a professional obligation to comply with the fundamental principles. However, there may be times in which a conflict between their responsibilities to an employing organization and the professional obligations to comply with the fundamental principles may exist. Ordinarily, a professional accountant in private business should support the legitimate and ethical objectives established by the employer and the rules and procedures drawn up in support of those objectives. Nevertheless, where compliance with the fundamental principles is threatened, a professional accountant in private business who wanted to improve the company's results due to his ethical value code and also had the incentive to keep the jobs in a company that was meant to be successful might consider taking immediate action.

Thus, because of responsibilities to an employing organization, a professional accountant in private business may be under pressure to act or behave in ways that could directly or indirectly threaten compliance with the fundamental principles. Such pressure may be explicit or implicit and it is possible to come from a manager within the employing organization. He might feel pressure to act contrary to law or regulation, contrary to technical or professional standards, facilitating unethical or illegal earnings management strategies, lying intentionally with financial statements that mislead the outcome showing a company with slow profit growth and endangering its feasibility in the market. Thus, the financial statements misrepresented the facts which could lead to wrong decisions from the CFO and the owner.

The specific case presented in this chapter concerns topics about financial or management information, for example, forecasts and budgets, financial statements, management discussion and analysis. A professional accountant in private business should prepare or present such information fairly, honestly, and according to the relevant professional standards so that the information will be understood by any party involved.

IFAC states that the professional accountant should maintain information in a manner that clearly describes the true nature of business transactions, assets, or liabilities (IFAC, 2006: Section 320.3). The accountant also classifies and records information in a timely and proper manner and presents the data accurately and completely.

Threats to compliance with the fundamental principles, for example, self-interest or intimidation threats to objectivity or professional competence and due care, may be created where the professional accountant may be pressured (either externally or by the possibility of personal gain) to become associated with misleading information through personal actions or by the actions of others (IFAC, 2006: Section 320.4).

IFAC (IFAC, 2006: Section 320.6) also establishes that the significance of threats will depend on factors such as the source of the pressure and the degree to which the information is or may be misleading. In this case, the outcome of the threat is the stagnation of the expansion of the business in the Mexican market.

The significance of the threats should be evaluated and, if they are other than clearly insignificant, safeguards should be considered and applied as necessary to eliminate them or reduce them to an acceptable level. Such safeguards should be designed in agreement with the CFO and the owner. But if it is not possible to reduce the threats to an acceptable level, and the professional accountant was found guilty and aware that the issuance of misleading information was either significant or persistent, the auditing firm should consider informing the appropriate authorities in line with the guidance in Section 140 (IFAC, 2006) which states that the professional accountant in private business might be invited to look for legal advice or resign.

IFAC (IFAC, 2006: Section 330) states that the fundamental principle of professional competence and due care requires that the professional accountant in private business should only undertake significant tasks for which the professional accountant has, or can obtain, sufficient specific training or experience. A professional accountant in private business should not intentionally mislead an employer as to the level of expertise or experience possessed, nor should a professional accountant in private business fail to seek appropriate expert advice and assistance when required. That is why the external auditing company should review the selection process of the accountant of the firm, to verify that he complied with the required competencies and skills for the job.

Even though the hiring process was accurate, and the hired accountant had the required competencies, there could be complications in his performance, especially his financial interests as the main obstacle.

The personal financial interests of the hired accountant could in certain circumstances give rise to threats to compliance with the fundamental principles. For example, self-interest threats to objectivity or confidentiality may be created through the existence of the motive and opportunity to manipulate prices or sensitive information to gain financially. Examples of circumstances that may create self-interest threats are situations where the accountant holds a direct or indirect financial interest in the employing organization and the value of that financial interest could be directly affected by decisions made by the professional accountant.

To evaluate the significance of any threat and identify the appropriate safeguards to be applied to eliminate the threat or reduce it to an acceptable level, the external audit firm must examine the nature of the financial problem, and whether it was done para one or more persons in the firm. What constitutes a significant or valuable stake in an organization will vary from individual to individual, depending on personal circumstances.

If threats are other than clearly insignificant, safeguards should be considered and applied as necessary to eliminate or reduce them to an acceptable level. Such safeguards may include policies and procedures for certain key activities in the firm such as the electronic billing emission system, or the establishment of periodical internal and external auditing procedures.

The key thought is that a professional accountant should neither manipulate information nor use confidential information for personal gain. The next section presents the analysis of this empirical case.

ANALYSIS

This chapter presents the empirical case of CMInc, a small Mexican business which was seriously impacted by a breach of trust. This is its story.

CMInc Empirical Case

CMInc is a small company with approximately 40 employees, which manages the franchise of computer maintenance workshops. Some of their services include computer repair, replacement of parts in poor condition, and sale of spare parts for computer equipment.

CMInc started operations in August 2016. For approximately a year, it organized its legal, accounting, and financial operations to be prepared to open and operate its branches distributed in various states of Mexico. To do this, the company hired John as an administrative manager, in September 2016. John was a very organized and competent lawyer, but due to a lack of accounting skills, he only lasted in his position for two years and he left the company in June 2018. However, during that time he collaborated in the organization and successful opening of five CMInc branches in different states of Mexico (Querétaro, Mexico City, Durango, Chihuahua, and Sinaloa).

Since the company had plans to continue growing and increasing its branches, it needed to hire a replacement for John, with both an accounting and administrative profile. CMInc hired a headhunter to help them find the person they needed. CMInc titled the new job position "*Administrative Coordinator*" because the objective was to find a person who would follow up on all administrative issues and report directly to Sonia Ramos, the CFO and the CEO (the owner). The main function of the Administrative

Coordinator would be to monitor and follow up on the administrative and accounting operation of the company effectively and efficiently.

The job description of the activities that were required for that *Administrative Coordinator* position was:

- Must have the qualifications of a Certified Public Accountant with knowledge of administration and management processes.
- Follow up on branch real state lease contracts.
- Monitor and follow up on franchise contracts with CMInc.
- Provide support in the administration of branch development.
- Carry out recruitment, training, and payroll administration.
- Coordinate the management of suppliers (computers, tools, and supplies).
- Coordinate the management of service providers (advertising, marketing, maintenance, among others).
- Carry out the administrative control of financial and banking operations, such as:
    - Bank accounts of each service center (branch)
    - Accounts opening
    - Incomes
    - Expenses:
        - Bank account for local expenses
        - Scheduled expenses
        - Non-scheduled expenses
    - Coordination of accounting records and billing (invoices)
    - Weekly review of operational indicators of each service center

The headhunter worked on the search and proposed several candidates for the position that CMInc requested, and, in June 2018, the company finally found the ideal candidate and hired Charlie, a Certified Public Accountant (C.P.A.). His academic experience also included an MBA (Master of Business Administration). Charlie had an extensive 14-year experience in all the activities that CMInc required such as administrative control, accounting and management of expenses and banking operations, and a passionate character about the cyber industry, information technology, and computer and server repairs. This hiring seemed to be the perfect acquisition for the company.

Sonia Ramos (CFO) and the CEO (owner) of CMInc, welcomed the new *Administrative Coordinator*, C.P.A. Charlie, and explained the details of the company's operation and its growth objectives in the short and medium term. Because the company was small with branch offices just starting up, it did not have a sophisticated ERP (Enterprise Resource Planning) system in place. CMInc used a simple system for reporting operations and financial statements using worksheets and spreadsheets (Excel).

Monthly, each CMInc branch sent the accounting results of its operations to the corporate office so that the *Administrative Coordinator* could review them and send the consolidated statements to John, the General Tax Accountant (external accounting tax consultant), to prepare the final financial statements and the taxes to be paid. This process took about three to four months to be ready and updated so that the owner of the company could review the financial statements and make operational and corporate growth decisions. Therefore, one of the most important operational details that CMInc wanted to implement was a faster updating of the consolidated financial statements to reflect the profit of each branch more efficiently to be able to make financial decisions on time.

As mentioned earlier, while CMInc's CFO, Sonia Ramos, and the owner worked with John, the General Tax Accountant, to optimize the update of the financial statements, Charlie noticed the delay in reporting the monthly financial statements on time and took advantage of the situation. Charlie used his talent and experience in handling numbers within the monthly Income Statement to report fictitious expenses in Advertising, Marketing, Maintenance, Conservation (Upkeep), and Preservation for each branch to earn additional money for himself. Furthermore, to make these fictitious expenses legal and credible, several legal entities with an RFC (Federal Taxpayer Registry) legally registered with the SHCP (Ministry of Finance and Public Credit) in Mexico, billed and officially collected these fictitious expenses from CMInc.

Since CMInc was a company in the growth and consolidation of its branches, it effectively incurred considerable operating expenses related to Advertising and Maintenance. C.P.A. Charlie found it easier to report the fictitious expenses due to the high volume of transactions and billed these expenses to the false legal entities that he created.

For about one year, Charlie took advantage of CMInc's operational weakness to allocate fictitious Advertising and Maintenance expenses for each branch, starting with small amounts. While noting that neither the CFO nor the owner noticed these transactions because they reviewed them three months after they were issued and authorized, he gradually increased these false operating expenses, accumulating almost 100,000 Mexican pesos (more than $4,500 U.S.A dollars) per month paid to the name of the fictitious entities he had created.

However, the CFO and the owner continued to work closely with John, the General Tax Accountant, to shorten the delivery time of the monthly reports per branch to only one month, to prepare the monthly-consolidated financial statements faster. In this process, they also asked Charlie for faster delivery of the monthly spreadsheet reports.

The Breach of Trust Discovery

Finally, in August 2019, John, the General Tax Accountant, achieved the objective of shortening the delivery time of the consolidated financial statements to one month by sending the ones from July 2019 to Sonia Ramos, the CFO who reviewed them to verify the proper origin and destination of each of the company's accounts before taking the final files to the owner.

While reviewing the monthly Income Statements, Sonia Ramos noticed that certain branches experienced net losses rather than at least a small profit. Furthermore, in other branches, although the Net Income was positive, it did not represent the regular sales and expenses of the branch, and it seemed to provide a very low profit based on the operations of the branch. When Sonia Ramos arrived at the section of Operating Expenses of each branch, she noticed oddly high expenses with some of the Maintenance and Advertising accounts. She identified many inconsistencies in the classification of expenses and had several doubts, so Sonia Ramos decided to prepare a detailed analysis with her questions. Immediately, she sent an email to John, the General Tax Accountant, with a copy to C.P.A. Charlie (the Administrative Coordinator) to see if they could help her clarify the inconsistencies. Exhibit 1 shows the email sent by the CFO.

EXHIBIT 1

Email sent by Sonia Ramos, the CFO, to John, the General Tax Accountant

Good afternoon, John. Hope you are well.

I reviewed the financial statements for July 2019, but I have several doubts. Would the entire team clear them out before submitting the final files to the owner? My doubts are about some concepts within the Income Statements. I will specify them by branch as follows (I am cc'ing Charlie, The Administrative Coordinator so that he could be aware of my doubts and can support us in clearing them out.):

1. In the Income Statement of the Central Headquarters:
    a. The Expense of 955 Mexican Pesos (MXN) for promotion and advertising is misclassified in Headquarters. Charlie, please check what exactly is this expense for and to which branch it belongs, because I do not think it is correct to place it in promotion and advertising here.
2. In the Income Statement of Branch A:
    a. John: "*Glitchy Services*" has an expense of MXN 25,650 and it seems to be for the maintenance of the computer servers. Will you please verify that it is correctly classified? Charlie tells me that we probably need to reclassify it into several branches and not only in Branch A.
    b. MXN 2,000 worth of car fuel were spent on visits to this branch. Is it being applied well? Please check with the branch manager to learn if car fuel is being used correctly, or what it is being used for.
3. In the Income Statement of Branch B:
    a. Charlie: please review what the maintenance and machine preservation expenses are for in Branch B, which amount to MXN 21,300.
4. In the Income Statement of Branch C:
    a. John and Charlie: would you please check if the telephone charges are properly classified? There is no invoice supporting this expense.
5. In the Income Statements of Branches D and E:
    a. John and Charlie: I see very large amounts in the invoices billed from *"Esfuma Services"* as part of promotion and advertising. Would you please check if these numbers are correct since they are large amounts and I do not quite understand where they come from?
6. In the Income Statement of Branch F:
    a. John and Charlie: Would you explain to me what the "inactive maintenance and machine preservation" item means because it shows a charge of MXN 1,600 and MXN 16,800, respectively? I consider them to be very high amounts of charges. I do not know if they were misclassified expenses.

I am sending you the Excel file where I was working so that you can visualize my doubts, I highlighted them in yellow. In case you have more doubts, I also included the same comments from this email in each cell.

I look forward to your prompt response.

Please contact me if you have any additional questions or comments.

Sincerely,
Sonia Ramos
Chief Financial Officer CMInc.
Tel. +52 81 7474 3535 | Cel +52 81 9865 1212
Source: Original e-mail sent by the CFO in July 2019.

When she finished writing and sending the email, Sonia's mind was flooded with doubts, since she was not sure who could be responsible for this breach of trust and lack of ethics at CMInc. Could only one person be responsible, or could there be an act of collusion and complicity between several people?

DISCUSSION

Sonia Ramos as CFO of the firm was highly concerned about the ethical future of the company. She was not completely sure who was responsible and required the objective and transparent support of an external entity that was not "contaminated" with the internal operations of the corporation.

Sonia Ramos didn't want to involve John, the General Tax Accountant, in the process to avoid confrontation within the firm and decided to hire an external auditing company (AECG, Inc.).

Sonia Ramos shared her concerns with AECG, Inc., the external auditing company that was hired (Garcia, 2019). She required their valuable support and consultancy to have a fresh vision of the procedure to follow in the company: a diagnosis of who is the culprit and the best way to resolve this breach of trust and provide ethical safeguards based on the Code of Professional Ethics.

After locating the main threat in the process of electronic invoice emission (Onken, 2022), the external auditing company proposed corresponding safeguards to fill out a profile of every supplier of the firm with fiscal data and create a file of suppliers for the company. Each time that a new supplier arises, there should be a process to verify the credibility of this supplier as a trustworthy partner in the business.

The external auditing company also designed a descriptive catalog of needed expenses for each operation and its location in the financial statement.

The external auditing company recommended following random internal and external auditing to maintain control of the health of the financial statements.

The company decided to establish a code of conduct in practice for the firm, establishing specific rules. For example, a code of conduct when dealing with suppliers is to choose them properly according to the firm's wider mission, specifically to avoid fake billing.

The external auditing company also recommended remedial disciplinary action, such as requiring additional continuing education of its personnel. The diffusion of this Code among the firm could be the beginning because it provides a framework to assist the personnel to identify, evaluate and respond to threats to reach compliance with the fundamental principles.

AECG, Inc. advisers, as an external auditing company, dealt with issues related to the breach of trust of an accountant in a private company and the theft of money through the creation of false invoices originating from an ordinary person and attributed to the operating expenses of the company. Immediately, AECG, Inc. advisers proposed three possible scenarios:

Scenario 1: C.P.A. Charlie is guilty of collusion with John, the General Tax Accountant.

Scenario 2: C.P.A. Charlie is guilty of collusion with someone outside the company so that he can help him with the fictitious billing.
Scenario 3: C.P.A. Charlie is the only culprit because he has high experience in information technologies to falsify all the documents.

AECG, Inc. designed a research strategy to discover the origin of the breach of trust. They stated that the external auditing gave good results simulating that everything was fine to let the guilty person continue with the fraudulent activity (Quain, 2018). The hiring of external auditing was successful in helping the company discover that scenario 2 was correct. C.P.A. Charlie was guilty, and he was acting in collusion with someone outside the company.

AECG, Inc. advisers filed a report to the police and, as an external auditor, began the initial legal prosecution to protect the firm from any hate reactions from the perpetrators. The intervention of the external auditing company was a great success to avoid retaliations.

CONCLUSION

The main result of the external auditing process in the research of this Mexican company was to identify the impact of professional ethics for accountants who work in the private sector. They recommended enforcing the reflection and use of the Code of Professional Ethics for Public Accounting in the firm. They made the following discoveries:

- Identified the fundamental ethical principles applicable to this case (IFAC, 2006, 2018, and 2022).
- Located and analyzed the threats and proposed corresponding safeguards.
- Specified the ethical implications of the actions carried out by accountants in the private sector and the scope of their consequences in the future of the company.

The slow growth of the company for several years was not due to the operations of the company but to fraudulent activities from the people in charge of accounting. As the scope of their consequences in the future of the company shows the importance of identifying threats to the financial health of any company, designing the safeguards required to avoid a breach of trust, and the key role of external auditing companies to receive help in the process.

REFERENCES

ACFE. (2022). *Occupational Fraud 2022: A report to the Nations.* ACFE. https://legacy.acfe.com/report-to-the-nations/2022/

AICPA. (2014). *Professional Responsibilities.* AICPA. https://us.aicpa.org/interestareas/personalfinancialplanning/resources/practicecenter/professionalresponsibilities

Antosz, D. (2022). The best free invoicing software in 2022. *Zapier.* https://zapier.com/blog/best-free-invoice-software/

Buffa, D. W. (2005). *Breach of Trust*. Allen & Unwin.

Espino, G. (2014) Fundamentos de Auditoria. Grupo Patria Editorial (Hachette Livre Group).

Gantz, F. (2014). External Auditing. *Science Direct.* https://www.sciencedirect.com/topics/computer-science/external-auditing

Garcia, M. (2019). Roles & Responsibilities of External Audit Firms. *Small Business.* https://smallbusiness.chron.com/roles-responsibilities-external-audit-firms-73924.html

IFAC. (2006). *Code of Ethics for Professional Accountants.* IFAC. https://www.ifac.org/system/files/publications/files/ifac-code-of-ethics-for.pdf

IFAC. (2018). . *Final Pronouncement: International Code of Ethics for Professional Accountants (including International Independence Standards).* International Ethics Standards Board for Accountants. https://www.ifac.org/system/files/publications/files/Final-Pronouncement-The-Restructured-Code_0.pdf

IFAC. (2022). *2022 Handbook of the International Code of Ethics for Professional Accountants.* IFAC. https://www.ethicsboard.org/publications/2022-handbook-international-code-ethics-professional-accountants

Kanade, V. (2021). What Is Fraud Detection? Definition, Types, Applications, and Best Practices. *Spiceworks.* https://www.spiceworks.com/it-security/vulnerability-management/articles/what-is-fraud-detection/

Loring, J., & Sinclair, P. (2001). *Breach of the Trust Accounting Rules.* Discipline Case Digest Index. https://lawsociety.mb.ca/wp-content/uploads/2020/01/case_digest_01_05.pdf

Mitz, S. (2018). Fraud in Organizations. Fraud in Organizations. *Ethics Sage.* https://www.ethicssage.com/2018/04/fraud-in-organizations-fraud-can-be-defined-as-a-deliberate-misrepresentation-to-gain-an-advantage-over-another-party-fraud.html

Murphy, R. (2022). Best Invoicing Software for Small Business. *Nerd Wallet.* https://www.nerdwallet.com/article/small-business/best-invoicing-software-for-small-businesses

Onken, G. (2022). *Mexico is planning a major e-invoicing update to version 4 of CFDI 4.0 on 1st January 2022.* Product Manager software applications/services electronic business data exchange. https://blog.seeburger.com/mexico-is-planning-a-major-e-invoicing-update-to-version-4-of-cfdi-4-0-on-1st-january-2022/

Petrucelli, J. (2013). *Detecting Fraud in Organizations: Techniques, Tools, and Resources.* John Wiley & Sons, Inc., doi:10.1002/9781118555972

Quain, S. (2018). Importance of an External Audit. https://smallbusiness.chron.com/importance-external-audit-17630.html

The Hartford Business Owners' Playbook. (2022). Growing Safeguards. *Reduce Risk and Safeguard Your Growing Business.* The Hartford. https://www.thehartford.com/business-insurance/strategy/growing/safeguards

Yong, J. (2019). *Case Studies on Compliance with the IESBA Code of Ethics*. IFAC. https://www.ifac.org/knowledge-gateway/supporting-international-standards/discussion/case-studies-compliance-iesba-code-ethics

ADDITIONAL READING

American Bar Association. (2016). Model rules of professional conduct. ABA. https://www.americanbar.org/groups/professional_responsibility/publications /model_rules_of_professional_conduct/

Beck, M. (2021). *The Way of Integrity, Finding the Path to your true self.* Oprah's Book Club.

Carter, S. (1996) Integrity. *FTC Safeguards Rule: What Your Business Needs to Know.* Harpercollins, U.S.A. Federal Trade Commission. https://www.ftc.gov/business-guidance/resources/ftc-safeguards-rule-what-your-business-ne

Gaita, R. (2004). Breach of Trust, truth, morality, and politics. Quarterly Essay, (16). Australian Catholic University, Australia.

Hadfield, J. (2022). Internal Audit vs. External Audit. *Menzies*. https://www.menzies.co.uk/helping-you/audit-compliance/what-is-an-audit/internal-audit-vs-external-audit/

Henry & Home. (2022). IT safeguards, are you protecting your business? HHCPA. https://www.hhcpa.com/blogs/audit-accounting/it-safeguards-protecting-business/

Hong Kong Institute of Certified Public Accountants. (2018). Code of Ethics for Professional Accountants. HKICPA. https://www.hkicpa.org.hk/-/media/HKICPA-Website/Members-Handbook/volumeI/COErevised.pdf

Rae, S. Wong, K. (2012). Beyond Integrity: A Judeo-Christian Approach to Business Ethics. Zondervan.

Velasquez, M., Andre, C., Shanks, T., & Meyer, M. (2010). *What is Ethics?* Markkula Center for Applied Ethics at Santa Clara University.

KEY TERMS AND DEFINITIONS

Breach of Trust: A treason to the firm's professional ethical code. It could be envisioned as a failure to act with responsibility when a firm has given the employee its valuable records to keep them safe and successful for its economic and financial achievement. The most visible effect of a breach of trust is the financial and economic loss in the commercial achievement of a company which could endanger future investments and the firm's future survival.

Confidentiality: Avoid dissemination of information from the company with any other individual, company or organization. It is the strict need not to divulge information about the company with no one.

Ethics: The principles of ethics are part of a moral philosophy that encompasses the process of identifying and defending concepts to let every person establish a pattern to evaluate and recognize right from wrong.

External Auditor: An independent accountant who certifies a firm's financial statements and the accuracy and complete disclosure of a firm's accounting records. There are several reasons to hire an external auditor: if it is a requirement of investors and/or banks, for marketing purposes, or to establish safeguards in the company to eliminate corruption or fraud.

Integrity: Encompasses the principles to enhance the quality of being honest, establishing a moral and acceptable pattern of behavior, being eager to defend and refusing to be negatively influenced. Professionals must be strong enough to keep moral values from any bad influence in life.

Invoice System: The framework required by every country to submit valid invoices following a country's Secretary of Finance requirements. There could be breaches in the process.

Objectivity: The decision-making of a professional should be done without any favoritism towards one side or another. It is the principle that guides every professional to see and evaluate straightforward any situation avoiding a bias towards someone or something.

Professional Behavior: The respectful and courteous conduct, honoring the ethical codes of a company and values of human life. Even though a company lacks an ethical code, there is an inside ethical human code towards respect, tolerance, patience, teamwork, showing compassion for others, being supportive to everyone and team building within the company. But also, it must encompass the responsibility of developing personal skills to favor the success of the company, delivering excellent services to peers and clients, having an innovative spirit to find correct solutions to any problems, wisely using the resources towards the targets of the company, providing direction to others when it is required, etc.

Professional Competence and Due Care: There are principles that every firm expects every professional to execute, implementing his professional knowledge and skills to move the company towards its targets. This professional competence requires the awareness of current developments in the market, in any company's field practices, legislation changes, innovative techniques, etc. "Due Care" is a level of responsibility of the executive to be in tune with the changing business environment, moving according to the rules to successfully reach the goals of a company.

Professional Ethical Code: An enhanced conceptual framework that offers extensive revisions as a 'safeguard' throughout a firm's accounting activity that is better aligned to threats. This code offers the possibility to identify a breach of the fundamental principles, especially in the preparation and presentation of accounting reports and information. The base of this ethical code is objectivity, integrity, confidentiality, professional behavior, and professional competence and due care.

Safeguard: An action that might restrain activities to protect the firm against corruption, fraud, or other criminal threats. It is designed for protection before an economic injury in the company could lead it to bankruptcy.

The International Federation of Accountants (IFAC): A defense organization for good execution of the financial accounting and auditing professions. Every professional accountant must read the principles for outstanding execution of the profession. This organization summarizes these principles as follows: Integrity, Objectivity, Professional Competence and Due Care, Confidentiality, and Professional Behavior.

Chapter 11
The Impact of Auditor Rotation on Key Audit Matters (KAM):
Evidence From the Listed Portuguese Companies

Maria Albertina Barreiro Rodrigues
https://orcid.org/0000-0002-7858-5358
Universidade Europeia, Portugal

Carla Martinho
https://orcid.org/0000-0001-7675-7390
Lisbon Accounting and Business School, Instituto Politécnico de Lisboa, Portugal

Gabriel Correia Alves
Lisbon Accounting and Business School, Instituto Politécnico de Lisboa, Portugal

Miguel Ângelo Ribeiro Ladislau Ferreira
Lisbon Accounting and Business School, Instituto Politécnico de Lisboa, Portugal

ABSTRACT

One of the measures that emerged within the scope of the European audit reform was the report of key audit matters (KAM) with the objective of providing greater transparency in the auditor's reports. In 2015 the International Auditing and Assurance Standards Board (IAASB) approved the international standard on auditing (ISA) 701- Communicating KAM in the independent auditor's report. This chapter aims to analyse the evolution of the KAM report, in companies listed on Euronext Lisbon, from 2016 to 2019, and the impact of auditor rotation on that report. For this purpose, a mixed methodology was used with the KAM categorization followed by descriptive statistics. Through the research developed about the evolution of the report, it has been concluded that there was a decrease in the number of KAM reported during the period and that the majority of KAM reported each year are reported again in the following year. Regarding the impact that the audit firm change may have on KAM report, it was not possible to make a direct relationship between the audit firm change and KAM report.

DOI: 10.4018/978-1-6684-7293-4.ch011

INTRODUCTION

The increasing globalization of the economy, the quick growth of companies and their increasing complexity, combined with the need for users of financial statements to validate the economic and financial reality of companies, gave rise to the audit function (Rocha & Eugénio, 2019). According to Antle (1982), the purpose of auditing is to issue an independent opinion that provide reasonable assurance to the users, that financial report truly and appropriately reflects the economic and financial situation of the entity. For the audit to be provided with the highest quality and usefulness, the auditor should be objective, honest, and present a sceptical attitude. For this purpose, the independence in relation to the audited entity must be preserved and shown. The auditor's independence is related to its ability to carry out the audit process and express his opinion without the influence of factors that may compromise his work (IAASB, 2009).

However, the audit went through a difficult period at the beginning of the 21st century with the financial crisis, financial scandals, and bankruptcy of several companies, which frightened the audit sector, questioning the independence of the auditors and the transparency of their reports. Sequentially, regulatory bodies began a process of reforming the regulation of the audit sector (Cordos & Fulop, 2015). In this sense, with the aim of restoring confidence about the work carried out by auditing firms, some measures were implemented both in the European Union (EU) and in the United States of America (USA) to ensure compliance with all ethical principles such as Independence (Mayoral & Segura, 2008).

One of the measures implemented to face the problems of independence and transparency that the audit sector was experiencing, was the Sarbanes-Oxley Act (SOX), enacted in 2002 by the US President, that promoted a profound reform in the procedures for preparing financial reports and in the transparency aspects in the information disclosed by organizations.

In this way, the European Audit Reform process, among other measures, led to changes in the auditor's report. Following the evolution of the audit sector, a measure was imposed to address the need for greater transparency in the information provided by auditors to users of financial statements. This measure was the creation, in 2015, by the International Auditing and Assurance Standards Board (IAASB) of the International Standard on Auditing (ISA) 701 that has introduced the Key Audit Matters (KAM) in the auditor's report. The purpose was to provide greater transparency on the audit work performed, reporting more information on the matters that the auditor considered to be the more significant and that may allow the financial statements users to have a greater understanding of these same matters (IAASB, 2015).

Accordingly, it is possible to understand the need for evolution in the audit sector, with the introduction of KAM in the auditor's report being one of the most significant measures to allow greater transparency of the information provided by auditors to users of financial statements.

In view of what has been presented, this chapter aims to analyze the evolution of the reporting of KAM in the reports of companies, and to assess whether such matters change because of the auditor rotation. Considering that the inclusion of KAM in the audit report, is only mandatory for public interest entities, the focus will be on the companies listed in Portugal. This study aims to analyse the evolution from 2016, the beginning of the adoption of ISA 701, to 2019, of the reporting of KAM in listed companies on Euronext Lisbon, and the impact of auditor rotation on KAM reporting.

As stated, data for this study was taken from the financial reports between 2016 and 2019 of companies listed on Euronext Lisbon. Then, a mixed methodology was used, resulting in a complementary between qualitative and quantitative research. In a first phase of a qualitative nature, the financial reports of the companies were read, with the objective of organizing the KAM reported by categories. In a second phase, a quantitative methodology was used, which began with the organization of a database, in excel, recording the company's activity, the type and number of KAM reported per year and the audit firm responsible for the legal certification of accounts. The analysis continued via descriptive statistics, to establish some relationships between the variables.

As it is still a recent and yet not very explored topic, it is expected that the research will be relevant both in scientific terms and in professional practice. In scientific terms, the study will be relevant since it seeks to relate the rotation of auditors with the maintenance, or not, of the same relevant matters reported in the audit reports. At a practical level, the proposed study may be important to alert auditors if the nature of the KAM reported, the associated risks and the responses to these risks tend or not to remain constant, regardless of the evolution and development of audited companies, which may indicate that the KAM reported in the respective audit reports are out of date in view of the current situation of the company.

The structure of this proposed chapter is as follows. The next section reviews relevant literature. The following section presents the objectives and the proposed methodology. The last section presents the conclusions, the identified limitations, and suggestions for future studies.

LITERATURE REVIEW

Concept and Applicable Standards

With the financial crisis, which occurred in 2008, largely caused by the financial scandals of several companies around the world, associated with several auditing companies, the reputation of the auditor was seriously weakened (Pereira, 2019). The doubts raised in relation to auditors and their work, increased the interest of users of financial statements, the stakeholders', in the audit work performed (Cooper & Grose, 2010). The stakeholders' considered that the information provided by the auditor was not sufficient, since the auditor should not only express an opinion regarding the information disclosed by the companies, but rather present a more detailed and comprehensive information about the audited company, with the aim of being an added value for the stakeholders' decision making (Pereira, 2019).

It is possible to identify differences between the final product of the auditor's work and what users of the financial statements would expect the auditor to do. According to Gray et al. (2011), the disclosure of other important elements in the audit report and its discussion with the management body, could reduce the existing difference in expectations. With the inclusion of these new elements in the structure and content of the final audit report, its value could increase significantly and correspond to what is desired by users of financial statements (Simnett & Huggins, 2014).

With the aim of improving communication between auditors and stakeholders', and allow greater transparency, there was a need to include a new section in audit reports that allows highlighting certain aspects of the financial information of the audited company (Cordos & Fülöp, 2015). Thus, according to Simnett and Huggins (2014), to improve the quality of the auditor's work and of the audit report and with the aim of regaining market confidence, bodies such as the International Auditing and Assurance Standards Board (IAASB), the Public Company Accounting Oversight Board (PCAOB) and the European Union (EU) presented and developed studies and projects that intend to allow the standardization and harmonization of the audit work.

In this way, the European Audit Reform process began, which, among other measures, led to changes in the auditor's report. Thus, in 2015, the IAASB published the International Standard on Auditing (ISA)

701, which aims to communicate KAM in the auditor's report. The introduction of this new item in the audit report for Public Interest Entities (PIE) comes within the scope of paragraph 2 of article 10 of EU Regulation n.º 537/2014, of the European Parliament and of the Council of 16 April (UE, 2014), and of article 45 of the Statute of the Portuguese Institute of Statutory Auditors (OROC, 2017).

Within the scope of the 2nd paragraph of ISA 701, the objective of communicating the most relevant matters of the audit is to increase the value of the auditor's report, providing greater transparency about the audit carried out. The communication of these KAM provides a valuable information for users of financial statements, helping them to make their decisions. With this information, stakeholders' may make the analysis of the work carried out by the auditor in the most significant areas of the entity, which increases their knowledge of the audited entity (IAASB, 2016).

According to the 4th paragraph of the ISA under review, it is important to understand that the inclusion of this point in the audit report does not intend to replace (IAASB, 2016):

- **Disclosures:** Matters that the management body must disclose in the financial statements in accordance with the applicable accounting framework and necessary for a proper presentation.
- **Reserves or Emphases:** Matters that must be considered as such in the reports.
- **Uncertainty about going concern:** Events or conditions that may create significant doubt on the entity's ability to maintain its activities.
- **Opinions:** A separate opinion on matters.

Regarding determining the KAM to be communicated in the auditor's report, according to paragraph 9 of ISA 701 (IAASB, 2016) the auditor must determine the matters that require special attention in the performance of the audit work, considering the following points:

- Relevant higher risk areas, or significant risks identified in accordance with ISA 315.
- Significant audit judgments, which involve significant management judgments, including accounting estimates that were identified as having a large estimation uncertainty.
- The effect on the audit of significant events or transactions that occurred during the period.

According to PWC (2015) the KAM to be included in the auditor's report are determined as shown in Figure 1.

Figure 1. Determination of KAM
Source: Adapted from PWC (2015, p.4)

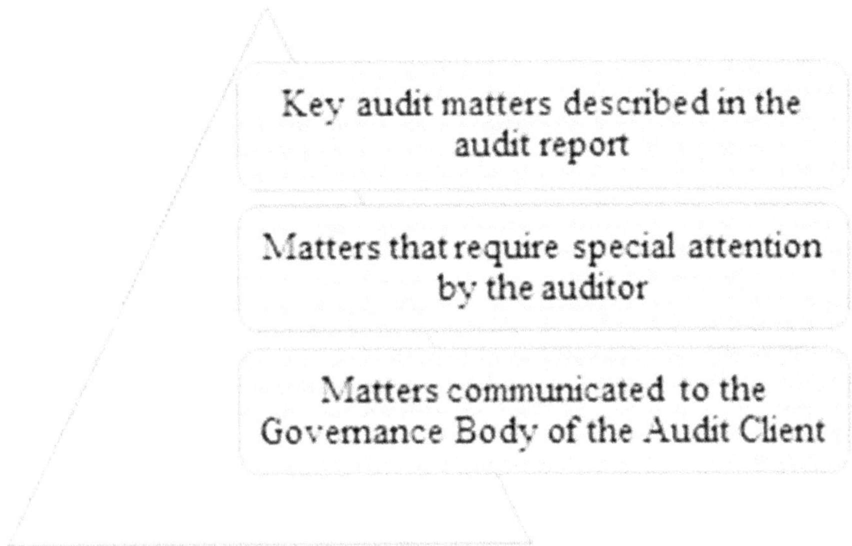

At the base of the pyramid, it is possible to verify the inclusion of all the matters that are communicated to the governance body, that is, the total population of matters. However, it is not expected that the majority will be considered as relevant audit matter. Subsequently, at the second level, the matters that require special attention on the part of the auditor are selected, in accordance with what was referred to above and that fall within what is defined in paragraph 9 of ISA 701. Finally, at the top of the pyramid, it is up to the auditor to identify the matters that are relevant and that must be described in the final audit report. The definition of KAM to be included in the audit report is a matter of professional judgment by the auditor, and the number of matters to be included can be directly affected by the complexity or size of the entity, or even by the business sector in which the entity is inserted (Figueiredo, 2015). For the author, the KAM described in the report should only be those of greatest importance.

Regarding the communication of KAM, the auditor should describe these matters using an appropriate subheading in the section created for this purpose called "Material Audit Matters" (IAASB, 2016). In this chapter, the term KAM is used to represent the material audit matters mentioned in ISA 701.

In accordance with paragraph 13 of ISA 701, auditors in the description of each of the KAM reported, must mention the reason why the respective matter was considered relevant to the audit and how it has been treated. The description of a certain material audit matter is intended, in a succinct and explicit way, to demonstrate to users of the financial statements why the matter was classified as having greater importance in the audit, identifying the significant risks associated with that matter (IAASB, 2016). The material audit matter must not only mention the nature and associated risks, but must also mention the auditor's approach, and be carried out as defined in paragraph A46 of ISA 701:

- Summary of audit procedures performed.

- Results of the procedures performed.
- Main observations regarding the matter.
- Aspects of the auditor's response or approach that were most relevant to the matter or more specific to the assessment of the risk of material misstatement.

Table 1 shows an example of the communication of a key audit matter of one of the companies analyzed in this study, where it is possible to verify the communication of the nature of the relevant audit matter, the significant risks associated with it and the audit team's response to the identified risks.

Table 1. Communication of KAM

Description of the most significant risks of material misstatement	Summary of our response to the most significant risks of material misstatement
As of June 30, 2019, the book value of the team amounts to 74,990 thousand euros, representing about 20% of the asset value. The football players passes are initially measured at acquisition cost, which includes the amounts paid to the original clubs and sports agents, and are then amortized over the term of the contract. There is a risk that the net book value of a given pass is impaired, due to sport performance below expectations, injuries to athletes and other circumstances.	"We evaluated the assumptions defined by the Board of Directors in calculating the value of impairment losses of players passes. In addition, we carried out the following procedures: - Reading of all contracts related to the acquisition of players passes; - We analyzed whether the contracts were registered in the correct financial year; - We analyzed the information available on the sports performance (minutes played in competition) of the main players; - We tested the calculation of amortization and financial updating factors considered at the time of initial recognition of the asset; and - We validated the information on sports agents included in Note 8. We also checked the adequacy of the applicable disclosures, namely those included in Notes 2.5, 2.8, 28 and 34.3."

Source: Adapted from R&C Futebol Clube do Porto (2019, p.109)

Studies on Key Audit Matters

Based on the literature review, it may be highlighted that the introduction of KAM in audit reports, despite still being recent, has been the subject of previous studies, and the conclusions drawn from these studies are fundamental in the formulation of hypotheses, to answer the questions raised in this chapter.

According to Velt and Issa (2019) KAM regulations may affect in a positive or in a negative way the reputation of companies. The inclusion of the KAM in the audit report has caused an expectation for companies, auditors, and investors, regarding a greater transparency and communication in audit reports, however, there is still no consensus whether its inclusion has brought positive effects for users of financial statements' (Colares et al., 2020). Ciger et al. (2019) stated that the implementation of this point, in addition to having the objective of making the audit report more transparent and improve communication between the auditors and users of the financial statements, also aims to eliminate the difference in expectations, giving the users a more accurate, informative, and detailed report. Nevertheless, Sirois et al. (2018), have concluded that the inclusion of KAM in audit report implies a lower audit quality perception being perceived that the assurance provided by the auditor is different within the financial statements components.

Studies carried out on KAM focused mainly on their impact on investment decision changes, audit quality and market reactions (Pereira, 2019). However, the study of the present chapter is a little different from the more usual studies on the subject, essentially focusing on the evolution of the reporting of

KAM in audit reports since 2016, and the impact of the rotation of the audit firm on the reporting of relevant matters. The way in which the KAM were communicated by the auditors in the reports, both qualitatively (form and content) and quantitatively (the number), is of general interest to users of financial statements (Fülöp, 2018).

Regarding the quantitative evolution, that is, the number of KAM reported by the auditors, according to Pereira (2019), who analyzed the KAM reported in 2016 and 2017 of companies listed on the Euronext Lisbon Stock Exchange, there was a positive evolution in the number of KAM reported, with their average number increasing from 2016 to 2017. For Levanti (2019), only considering the years 2016 and 2017, it is expected that, based on the experience acquired by the auditors in relation to the audited company, the auditors will make changes with the objective of improving the reporting of the main KAM.

Regarding the qualitative evolution of KAM reported by auditors, according to the literature review by Lennox et al. (2019), several authors have shown that about 75% of KAM reported each year are reported again next year. These authors carried out a study on the repetition rate on the KAM reported, having arrived at an approximate rate of their literature review, concluding that most of the KAM reported are repeated in subsequent years. Colares et al. (2020), also carried out a study on the qualitative evolution of the KAM reported, concluding that more than half of the KAM reported in a year were repeated in the following years. According to Pereira (2019), the issue of a relevant audit matter being repeated in the vast majority of times in the following year, may be related to the fact that, the removal of a relevant matter from an audit, entails greater responsibility for the auditor, when compared to the inclusion of a new material audit matter.

In relation to the rotation of auditors, Geiger and Raghunandan (2002), when studying and analyzing companies that went bankrupt, found that there were more errors in audit reports in the first years, which leads to the conclusion that in longer-term relationships, the auditor's knowledge of the audited entity is also larger, which provides a better quality of audit reports. For Nagy (2005) long periods of relationship between auditors and their clients are associated with the improvement of audit quality and not with its decrease. Regarding the impact of the rotation of the audit company on the reporting of KAM, according to The Financial Reporting Council (FRC) (2015) the number and types of KAM differ depending on the company that provides the audit services. Lin and Yen (2023) found that it may influence the reporting quality when the auditors make changes on the assessments of major risk, and therefore change the audit conclusions.

Colares et al. (2020) in their study also addressed the relationship between the change of audit company and the number of KAM reported, and it was not possible to reach any conclusion, however through the same study it was possible to conclude that when the audit firm is a Big 4, the audit reports include a greater number of relevant matters. This may demonstrate that the type of audit firm affects the number of matters reported. In line with the above-mentioned study, Sierra-Garcia et al. (2019) concluded that the characteristics of the auditor influence the number and type of KAM disclosed in audit reports.

Finally, Vik and Walter (2017) highlighted that differences in the reporting of audit companies are increasingly evident, namely the form and description of KAM. Ciger et al. (2019) through their study, concluded that according to ISA 701, it is expected that the number of KAM, their nature, and the way they will be presented are different, according to the firm and audit.

The next section presents this chapter's objectives, research hypothesis and methodology.

OBJECTIVES, HYPOTESES, AND METHODOLOGY

In pursuit of the objective of analyzing the evolution of the "key Audit Matters Reported" (KAMR), based on the literature review carried out, the following questions were elaborated:

Question 1: In the four years of ISA 701 application, does the number of KAM reported tend to remain constant?

Question 2: In the four years of ISA 701 application, do the KAM reported tend to remain constant, with respect to their nature?

Question 3: Does the number and nature of KAM reported change with the auditor rotation?

To answer to the above questions, the investigation hypotheses were established, which are presented in Table 2.

Table 2. Formulation of research hypotheses

Research hypotheses	
Hypothesis 1 (H_1)	The number of KAM reported has increased over the four years of application of ISA 701.
Hypothesis 2 (H_2)	The KAM reported have been repeated over the four years of application of ISA 701, regarding their nature.
Hypothesis 3 (H_3)	The change in the audit firm has an impact on the number of KAM reported.
Hypothesis 4 (H_4)	The change in the audit firm has an impact on the nature of KAM reported.

To test the hypotheses, the entry into force of ISA 701 in 2016 was considered and companies were counted where the KAMR were systematically registered and to which there was access to the Annual Reports. Based on these assumptions, it naturally falls back on the years 2016 to 2019 and on public interest companies listed on the stock exchange in Portugal, Euronext Lisbon, which constitute the population under study. Therefore, the period for the years 2016, 2017, 2018 and 2019 and the information collected from the Annual Reports of companies listed in Portugal - Euronext Lisbon was considered.

To test the hypotheses raised, with the final objective of answering the starting questions, the variables to be considered in the developed study were defined, as shown in Table 3.

Table 3. Designation and type of variables

Variables	Designation	Category
NKAMR	Number of KAM reported	Numeric
DNKAMR	Different number of KAM reported	Binary
CNKAMR	Changing the nature of KAM reported	Binary
CAF	Change of Audit Firm	Binary

As presented, three of the variables are binary (1: yes, 0: no) and one variable is numerical. For the intended analysis, a mixed methodology was used, qualitative and quantitative, because both approaches complement each other (Morais & Neves, 2017).

As mentioned by Velte and Issa (2019), most of the previous studies on KAM use experimental or archival data, therefore, the reading of the legal certification of accounts (LCA) and subsequent categorization of the KAM reported was carried out according to a qualitative paradigm, with the aim of highlight characteristics that cannot be visualized through a quantitative approach (Raupp & Beuren, 2006). Followed, a quantitative approach was also used, which is characterized by using statistical instruments (Raupp & Beuren, 2006), both in the collection and in the processing of data. This approach was used in the organization of data taken from the legal certification of accounts, and subsequently in the application of descriptive statistics techniques in data processing. This approach has the purpose of summarizing the information that is dispersed in a data set, such as the elaboration of tables and graphs, that allow reaching conclusions based on the results obtained (Martinho, 2009). Based on the conclusions drawn from the mentioned approaches, it was possible to accept or not accept the proposed hypotheses.

The next section presents and discusses the results obtained from the answers to the questions and to the hypotheses identified in the preceding section.

RESULTS AND DISCUSSION

As mentioned, the matters under assessment were analysed by reading the legal certification of accounts and subsequent categorization of the KAM reported. The companies under analysis in the 4 years of study, from 2016 to 2019, as stated, those listed on Euronext Lisbon, are organized by typology, according to the Industry Classification Benchmark (ICB) classifier, as can be seen in table 4.

Table 4. Typology and distribution of Euronext Lisbon companies (2016 to 2019)

Typology (ICB)	2016		2017		2018		2019	
	Number of Companies	%	Number of Companies	%	Number of Companies	%	Number of Companies	%
Consumer goods	3	6.4	3	6.7	2	4.9	2	5.1
Health care	1	2.1	1	2.2	0	0.0	0	0.0
Energy	1	2.1	1	2.2	1	2.4	1	2.6
Real estate	0	0.0	0	0.0	0	0.0	1	2.6
Financial	5	10.6	4	8.9	3	7.3	2	5.1
Industry	10	21.3	9	20.0	8	19.5	8	20.5
Basic Materials	5	10.6	5	11.1	5	12.2	5	12.8
Service to the consumer	**11**	**23.4**	**11**	**24.4**	**11**	**26.8**	**10**	**25.6**
Service public utility	3	6.4	3	6.7	3	7.3	3	7.7
Technology	4	8.5	4	8.9	4	9.8	3	7.7
Telecommunications	4	8.5	4	8.9	4	9.8	4	10.3
Total	**47**		**45**		**41**		**39**	

As can be seen, the companies have different typologies, with the greatest weight, for all the years under analysis, being those that fall under consumer services, followed by companies of industry typology.

It is also possible to verify that over the four years analysed, the number of listed companies did not remain constant, having a decrease been verified. In 2017 the companies *Cimpor* and *Banco Montepio* left; in 2018 the companies *Compal, Luz Saúde, BPI, Santander* and *SDC Investimentos* left; and in 2019 the companies *SAG Gest-Soluções Automóvel Globais* and *Compta-Equip* left. In this last year, the company *Sociedade Comercial Orey Antunes* was not considered because, at the time of preparation of this research, its accounts were not yet available. On the other hand, these four years saw the entry of *Flexedeal* in 2018 and Merlin in 2019.

In a first analysis of the data, the number of companies listed (39) on Euronext Lisbon in 2019 is 17% lower than the number of companies listed (47) in 2016.

From the consultation carried out to the legal certifications of the accounts of the companies listed on Euronext Lisbon, it was possible to verify that the "Number of Key Audit Matters Reported" (NKAMR) per year presented fluctuations by type of company, having in total presented a slight increase from 2016 to 2017 and a sharp decrease in subsequent years, as can be seen in table 5.

Table 5. NKAMR of companies on Euronext Lisbon (2016 to 2019)

Typology (ICB)	2016	2017	2018	2019
	NKAMR	NKAMR	NKAMR	NKAMR
Consumer goods	12	13	9	10
Health care	3	3	NA	NA
Energy	4	3	4	5
Real estate	25	21	13	7
Financial	NA	NA	NA	2
Industry	**36**	**40**	**34**	**33**
Basic Materials	17	18	13	11
Service to the consumer	26	24	22	21
Service public utility	11	16	12	12
Technology	14	13	12	9
Telecommunications	16	16	14	15
Total	**164**	**167**	**133**	**125**

As can be seen, the largest number of KAM reported refer to companies in the industry area, followed by consumer service companies and companies in the financial sector. This order does not remain constant over the years. It appears for the year 2019 that the number of KAM reported referring to public utility service companies is higher than that of companies in the financial sector.

It is now important to understand the number of KAM reported in relation to the number of listed companies in each year under review, as shown in Figure 2.

Figure 2. NKAMR and number of companies on Euronext Lisbon (2016 to 2019)

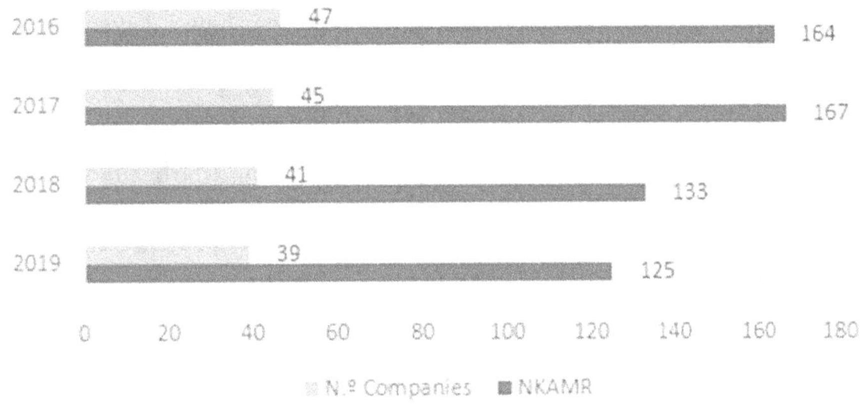

By observing the figure, it may be seen a decrease in the number of KAM reported from 164 to 125 from the first to the last year under study, which translates into a decrease of 31.2%.

As illustrated, the number of listed companies is not constant, showing a decrease in the last two years, so it is considered relevant to understand what happens in each of the sectors of activity in relation to the average number of KAM reported. To this end, Figure 3 was constructed and presented.

Figure 3. Average number of MRARs by type of company

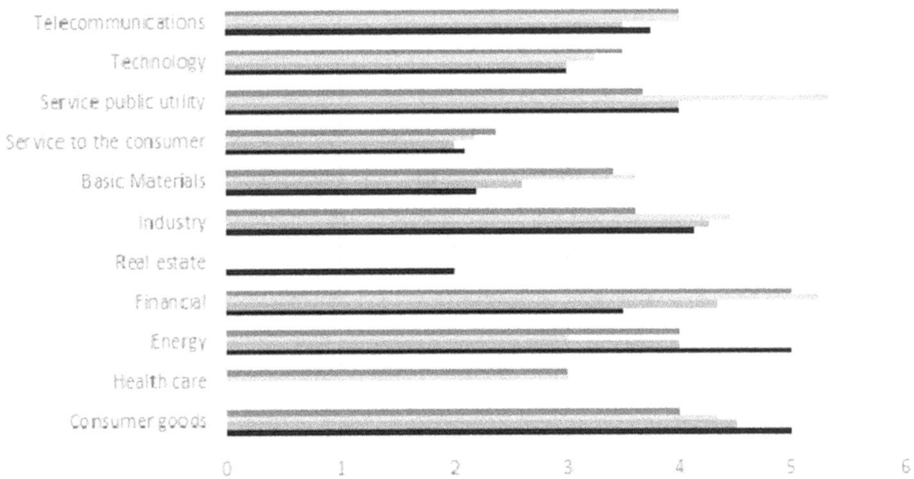

As can be found, only companies in the consumer goods services sector show a growing trend in the four years under study, increasing from 4 to 5 the number of KAM reported. For companies that make up the financial, public utilities, industry and basic materials sectors, there is a significant increase in the number of KAM reported in the years 2016 to 2017, however they show a decrease in the year 2017 for 2018. In the case of companies in the financial sector, industry and basic materials, this decrease is also maintained for the year 2019, thus accompanying the absolute trend seen in Figure 3. On the other hand, only the energy, consumer services and technology sectors show a decrease from 2016 to 2017, contrary to the absolute trend in the number of KAM reported. Regarding the health sector composed of only one entity, there was no variation from 2016 to 2017, with the company delisting from the Lisbon stock exchange in 2018.

Thus, the evolution of the average number of KAM reported in the four years analyzed is presented jointly, by year, in Figure 4.

Figure 4. Annual average of KAMR (2016 to 2019)

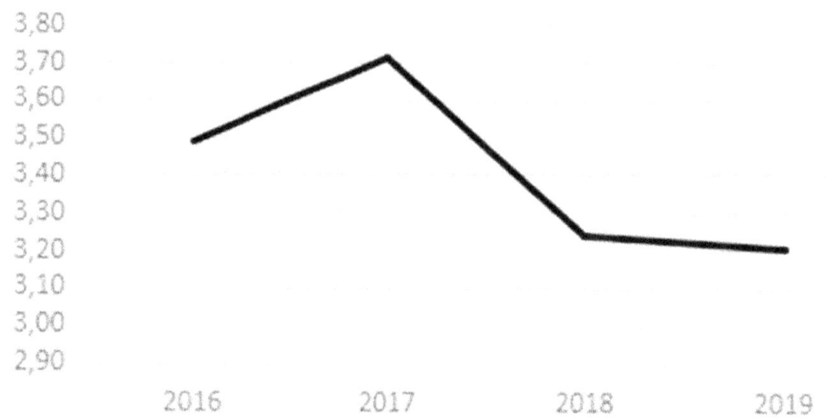

As regarding the content presented in Figure 4, the average evolution in the number of KAM reported increased from 2016 to 2017, showing an increase of 6.7%. On the other hand, in subsequent years the variation was the opposite, showing a decrease from 2017 to 2018 of 12.6% and 1.2% from 2018 to 2019.

Comparing the average trend and the absolute trend in the number of KAM reported, shown in Graphs 2 and 3, it is possible to observe that the evolutionary trend is identical, verifying an increase in the number of KAM reported from 2016 to 2017 and a decrease in subsequent years. In short, in the four years analyzed, there was a decrease of 8.2% in the average number of KAM reported in the legal certifications of the accounts of companies listed on Euronext Lisbon.

As mentioned earlier, during the period under analysis, there were exits and entries of some companies from the Lisbon stock exchange, and these situations may have some impact on the number of KAM reported and thus influence the analysis carried out on the evolution of the number of KAM reported in the four years application of ISA 701. Table 6 presents the number of KAM reported only referring to companies that remained on the Lisbon stock exchange during the four years analyzed.

Table 6. NKAMR in companies listed on Euronext Lisbon from 2016 to 2019

Typology (ICB)	Number of Companies	2016	2017	2018	2019
Consumer goods	2	10	10	9	10
Health care	1	4	3	4	5
Energy	1	5	5	5	5
Real estate	8	31	38	34	33
Financial	5	17	18	13	11
Industry	10	24	22	20	21
Basic Materials	3	11	16	12	12
Service to the consumer	3	11	10	10	9
Service public utility	4	16	16	14	15
Technology	**37**	**129**	**138**	**121**	**121**

Observing Table 6, it is possible to verify that the largest number of KAM reported refer to companies in the industry and consumer services area, driven by the weight that this type of companies has in the total of companies under analysis. Based on this information, it is possible to verify a 7% increase in the number of KAM reported (138/129) between 2016 and 2017, and that, on the other hand, there was a 12% decrease in the number of KAM reported between 2018 and 2017 (121/138), and in 2019 there was no change compared to 2018 (121/121). In this way, it is possible to show that the growth in the number of KAM reported in 2017 compared to 2016, and the decrease verified in 2018 compared to 2017, is consistent with the trend verified in the number of KAM reported by all companies that make up the population.

According to the studies by Lennox et al. (2019), and Colares et al. (2020), another of the factors considered relevant in relation to the KAM reported is their nature. Therefore, an analysis was carried out in relation to the companies under study.

Table 7 presents the nature of the KAM reported from publicly traded companies for the four years analysed.

Table 7. KAM nature reported for Euronext Lisbon companies (2016-2019)

Nature KAM	2016	2017	2018	2019
Goodwill	20	19	16	15
Biological Assets	3	3	3	3
Provisions, contingent assets, and liabilities	16	17	13	11
Bills to receive	12	11	8	7
Tax matters	11	10	7	8
Employee benefits	8	6	4	3
Non-current assets held for sale	4	3	2	1
Resolution background	4	3	1	1
Investments in other companies	14	14	12	10
Financial instruments	4	4	3	4
Tangible/intangible fixed assets	24	25	19	19
Financing obtained	2	2	2	1
Inventories	5	5	4	3
Revenue	16	16	14	14
Specificities	9	12	12	5
Investment properties	5	5	5	6
Opening balances	1	2	0	1
Expense recognition	1	1	2	1
Commercial discounts	4	4	3	2
Audit components	1	2	2	1
Liquidity risk	0	2	0	0
Locations	0	0	0	7
Credit to customers	0	1	1	2
Total	**164**	**167**	**133**	**125**

Based on Table 7, it is possible to verify that the KAM most reported in all years analyzed in this investigation are those concerning Tangible and Intangible Fixed Assets, followed by matters referring to Goodwill and Revenue. On the other hand, the least reported KAM is related to Liquidity Risk followed by Opening Balances and Customer Loans.

The report of a key audit matter includes the nature, description of the associated risks and the associated audit procedures to respond to the identified risks. To understand the evolution of the reporting of KAM, that is, if the KAM reported in a given year had already been reported in the previous year, their repetition rate was calculated, based on their nature.

The number of KAMRs per year, by nature and for each company, was the result of reading the legal certification of accounts, originating the database to support this work.

For each year, the total NKAMR by nature was calculated, called the total:

$NKAMR_{a,n}$:

$$\sum_{e=1}^{k} NKAMR_{a,n,e}$$

where k is the number of companies audited per year, a is the year under study, n is the nature of the relevant audit matter reported and e is the company in question.

The number of KAMRs repeated per year, by nature and for each company was calculated as follows:

$$NKAMRrep_{a,n;e} = \min\left(NKAMR_{a,e}; NKAMR_{a-1,e}\right)$$

The year is fixed and the repeated NKAMR is calculated by nature based on the NKAMR for that year (a) and for the immediately previous year (a-1), this calculation is carried out for all companies listed in both years.

Once the NKAMRrep has been calculated for all companies each year, by nature, it is important to know their total in that year (total $NKAMRrep_{a,n}$), which is obtained by adding all the NKAMRrep previously calculated:

$$\sum_{e=1}^{k} NKAMRrep_{a,n,e}$$

Thus, the repetition rate of KAMRs for each year by nature is given by the expression:

$$TxrepKAM_{a;n} = \frac{\sum_{e=1}^{k} NKAMRrep_{a,n,e}}{\sum_{e=1}^{k} NKAMR_{a-1,n,e}}$$

For the calculation of this rate, only the nature of the KAM was considered, with neither the risks nor the audit procedures being considered due to the fact that on some occasions the way in which they are reported differs from year to year and from audit firm to audit firm, however the relevant audit matter reported refers to the same matter as in the previous year, so only the nature of the KAM was considered.

Figure 5 represents the repetition rate of KAM reported during the four years analyzed.

Figure 5. KAMR repetition rate

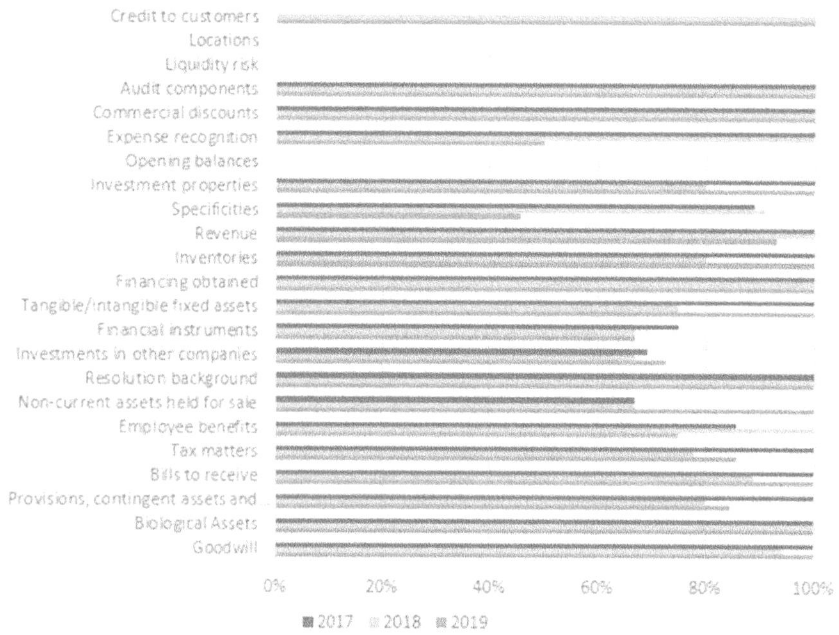

Based on Figure 5, in general the repetition rates of different types and in the different years are quite high, and in most cases a repetition rate of 100% is reached. In the KAM relating to Biological Assets, Resolution Fund, Obtained Financing, Commercial Discounts and Audit of Components, the repetition rate in the three years is 100%, thus making it possible to state, in these cases, all matters that are reported each year are also reported in the following year. In the case of KAM relating to Credit to Customers, it also has a repetition rate of 100% in 2018 and 2019, and in 2017 the repetition rate was not calculated given that in 2016 no relevant matter was reported of this nature. Regarding KAM relating to Investments in Other Companies, Financial Instruments and Specifics, matters relating to these natures were reported in all years, however in none of the years was a repetition rate of 100% achieved.

The lowest repetition rate verified in these cases was 45% in the year 2019 in the relevant matters concerning Specificities, with the remaining rates between 67% and 91%, rates that still reflect a high repetition of the matters reported in subsequent years. On the other hand, it is possible to verify that in the relevant matters related to Opening Balances and Liquidity Risk, there was no repetition rate, however this situation was already expected in relation to Opening Balances given that this type of matter is only reported when it is the first audit year of a given audit firm, and audit firms generally have terms longer than one year. In the case of key matters relating to Liquidity Risk, matters of this nature were only reported in 2017. In relation to KAM relating to Leases, the repetition rate was not calculated, as matters of this nature were only reported in 2019.

To better understand the overall repetition rate, the average repetition rate for the three years was calculated. As previously mentioned, during the four years under analysis there were companies that did not remain constant. So that this situation does not bias the results obtained, it was decided to recalculate the average repetition rate, now considering the companies that remained constant in the period under study (2016 -2019).

Figure 6 shows the average repetition rate of KAM reported by companies listed on Euronext Lisbon in at least one of the years under review and the average repetition rate of KAM reported by companies listed on Euronext Lisbon from 2016 to 2019.

Figure 6. KAMR average repetition rate

Through the observation of Figure 6, it appears that in 2017 the average rate of repetition of KAM reported by all companies that were present on Euronext Lisbon in at least one of the years of the period under review (89.3%) is 1.6 higher percentage points compared to the repetition rate of KAM reported by companies listed on Euronext Lisbon from 2016 to 2019 (87.7%). In 2018, there was a decrease in both rates compared to 2017, and it was in that year that the average repetition rates of KAM reported showed the lowest value, around 79.7% considering the companies listed on Euronext Lisbon from 2016 to 2019 and 80.3% considering all companies that were present in at least one of the years in the analyzed period. Even so, it is possible to state that the rates verified in 2018 are quite indicative that there is a high repetition in the KAM reported over the four years analyzed. In 2019 there was an increase compared to 2018, being in line with the rates verified in 2017, and in this year the repetition rate of the KAM reported was higher when considering only the companies listed on Euronext Lisbon from 2016 to 2019, the opposite of what happened in 2017. Comparing the average repetition rates of KAM in the period under review, it is possible to state that both rates are high in all years and that the differences between them are insignificant.

After analyzing the evolution that occurred in the first four years of application of ISA 701 through the number and repetition rate of KAM reported, it is also important to understand possible factors that may influence this evolution. Thus, according to the literature review, one of the factors to be considered is the audit firm responsible for the legal certification of accounts and consequently responsible for reporting this type of matter. Thus, a survey of audit firm changes was carried out in the various companies under study. Table 8 shows the number of companies that changed the audit firm and the number of companies that did not change the audit firm between 2016 and 2019.

Table 8. Audit firm (AF) changes occurred between 2016 and 2019

	2017		2018		2019	
	Number	%	Number	%	Number	%
Companies that changed AF	10	22.2	10	24.4	2	5.1
Companies that did not change AF	35	77.8	31	75.6	37	94.9
Total	**45**		**41**		**39**	

Through Table 8, it is possible to verify that there was a change of audit firm in 10 companies in the years 2017 and 2018 and in 2 companies in the year 2019. These changes occurred in 22.2% of the companies in 2017, 25% in 2018 and 5 .3% in 2019. The decrease seen in 2019 was predictable since in previous years there had been a change in audit firm in several companies. It is not expected that a company changes its audit firm more than once in a four-year period. In the present investigation, a different number of KAM was considered whenever the number of KAM reported by a given company is lower or higher than the previous one. Regarding the nature of the KAM, it was considered as a change in the nature of the KAM reported the replacement of a certain relevant audit matter reported by another of a different nature.

To better understand the impact that the change in audit firm may have on changing the number and nature of KAM reported, Table 9 presents the survey of these data carried out based on the analysis of the legal certifications of accounts for companies that presented audit firm change.

Table 9. Different Nº and KAM changes nature

Companies	2017			2018			2019		
	Nº	DNKAMR	ANKAMR	Nº	DNKAMR	ANKAMR	Nº	DNKAMR	ANKAMR
AF change	10	7	0	10	7	2	2	0	0
No AF change	35	11	2	30	11	3	37	14	8
Total	**45**	**18**	**2**	**40**	**18**	**5**	**39**	**14**	**8**

As seen in Table 9, in the three years analyzed there were more changes in the number of KAM reported than in their nature. About the number of KAM reported, it appears that in 2017 and 2018 there were changes in 18 companies, which is equivalent to 40% (18/45) and 45% (18/40) of the number of companies that were quoted in those years and in the immediately preceding years.

In 2019, the audit firm of the 14 companies reported a different number of KAM compared to the previous year, representing around 36.8% (14/38) of the total number of companies listed in 2019 and which were already listed on the last year. Regarding changes in the nature of KAM, it appears that in 2017 the change in these was 4.4% (2/45), in 2018 it was 12.5% (5/40) and in 2019 was 21.1% (8/38).

Having analyzed the results obtained through the legal certification of accounts, to better understand the impact that a change in the audit firm may have on the different number (DNKAMR) and on the "Change in the Nature of the Key Audit Matters Reported" (CNKAMR), it is important to relate these variables with the audit firm change variable. Thus, these dimensions were analyzed in percentage terms in cases for both situations: with audit firm change and without audit firm change.

Figure 7 presents the rates of change that occurred in the number and nature of KAM reported, when there is a change in the audit firm and when there is no change in the audit firm.

Figure 7. DNKAMR and ANKAMR with and without audit firm change

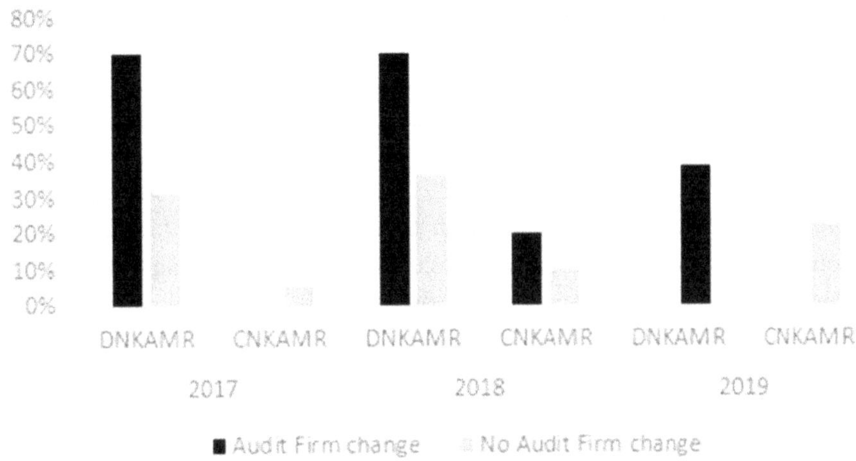

Observing Figure 7, it is possible to verify that regarding the differences in the number of KAM reported, the proportion in the first two years in companies that changed the audit firm is 70%, above the proportions referring to companies that did not change the audit firm (31.4% in 2017 and 36.7% in 2018). In 2019, given that there were no changes in the number of KAM reported in companies that changed the audit firm, the proportion of these is lower when compared to companies that did not change the audit firm (38.9%). Regarding changes in the nature of the KAM reported, the proportion is, only in 2018, higher in companies that change the audit firm, with a proportion of 20% and companies that have not changed the audit firm have a proportion of 10%. In the remaining years there was no change in the nature of the KAM reported compared to the previous year in the companies that changed the audit firm.

With the aim of generally perceiving the proportions of the different number and the change in the nature of the KAM reported in the three years under analysis, the respective average proportions were calculated. Based on the three years under analysis, Figure 8 presents the average proportion of the different number and change in nature of KAM reported both in companies that changed the audit firm and companies that did not change the audit firm.

Figure 8. Mean DNKAMR and CNKAMR with and without audit change

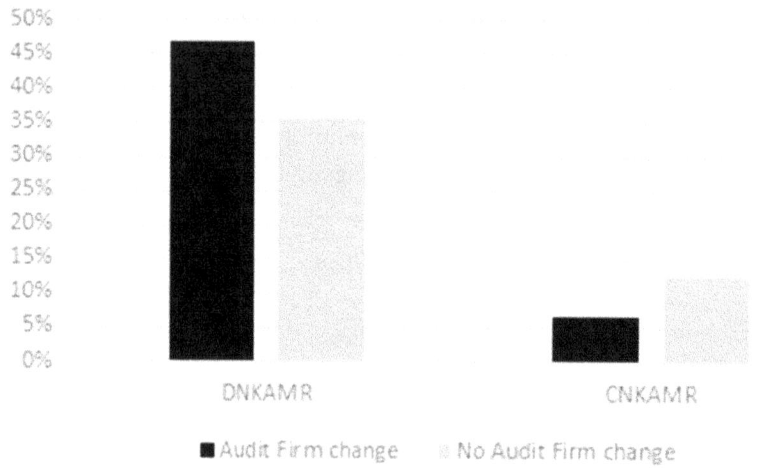

Based on Figure 8, it is possible to verify that in relation to the number of KAM reported, in the analyzed period, on average, there were more changes in companies that changed the audit firm (46.7%) compared to companies that did not change the audit firm (35.7%), verifying a difference of 11 percentage points. About the average rate of change in the nature of KAM reported, it appears to be higher in companies that did not change the audit firm, given that they have an average rate of 12.7% compared to 6.7% referring to companies that changed the audit firm, thus existing a difference of 6 percentage points.

The next section presents a summary of the main conclusions obtained during the development of this analysis and limitations of the present study, as well as some suggestions for future investigations.

CONCLUSION

This chapter aims to analyse the evolution of the reporting of KAM in companies listed on Euronext Lisbon, since the beginning of the adoption of ISA 701, and the impact of auditor rotation on KAM reporting. Data for this study were taken from the financial report between 2016 and 2019, of companies listed on Euronext Lisbon. For this purpose, a mixed methodology was used, resulting in complementarity between qualitative and quantitative research.

The importance of auditing in society and the problems that have occurred related to it, led to the need to reform some auditing procedures, namely those related to the auditor's report. In this sense, the starting point of this chapter arises, where its focus was on the evolution of the reporting of KAM, one of the measures that emerged within the scope of the European audit reform, with the objective of providing greater transparency in the auditor's reports. For this new measure, it was expressed through ISA 701 in 2016, the mandatory application for public interest companies. The present study focused on the evolution of the number of KAM reported over the first four years of application of ISA 701, the maintenance of KAM reported based on their nature and the impact that auditor rotation can have in reporting KAM. To answer the starting questions, hypotheses were defined based on the literature review, which are now answered:

Regarding (H1): *The number of relevant matters reported has increased over the four years of application of ISA 701*, **this hypothesis is not accepted** from the tests carried out. To test this hypothesis, the evolution of the number of KAM reported, in the first four years of application of ISA 701, of all the companies that make up the Euronext Lisbon stock exchange in the various years, was analyzed. Additionally, the evolution of only the companies that remained on the stock exchange was analyzed from 2016 to 2019. In both analyzes it was found that there is an increase in the number of relevant matters reported in 2017 compared to 2016, however in the following years the values decreased. In fact, it was verified that the number of KAM reported in 2019 was lower than the number reported in 2016.

About (H2): *The KAM have been repeated over the four years of application of ISA 701 regarding their nature*, the repetition rate of the KAM reported by all the companies that were listed on Euronext Lisbon in at least one of the years under study and the repetition rate of KAM reported only by companies that remained constant on Euronext Lisbon from 2016 to 2019. Regarding repetition rates of the KAM reported by all companies that were listed on Euronext Lisbon in at least one of the years, they amounted to 89.3% in 2017, 80.3% in 2018 and 88.7% in 2019. Regarding the repetition rate of KAM reported by companies that were listed on Euronext Lisbon throughout the period under review, the rates rose to 87.7% in 2017, 79.7% in 2018 and 88.7% in 2019. It was thus verified that the lowest repetition rates correspond to the year 2018, having been close to 80%. Through these results, it is possible to state that the repetition rate of the KAM reported is quite high, and to conclude that most of the KAM reported each year, are reported again in the following year about their nature. As such, **it is possible to** accept **H2**.

As for (H3): *The change in audit firm has an impact on the number of KAM reported*, through the investigation carried out it was possible to verify that proportionally in the years 2017 and 2018 there are more changes in the number of KAM reported compared to the previous year when there is a change in audit firm, 70% in both years, than when there is no change in audit firm, 31.4% in 2017 and 36.7% in 2018. In 2019 the trend was reversed, companies that did not change audit firm showed more changes in the number of material audit matters reported (38.9%) than companies that changed audit firm, which did not show any change in the number of material audit matters reported. However, it is important to note that in 2019 only two companies changed audit firm, which may influence this comparison. To be able to generally perceive the years analysed, the average percentage was calculated, and it was verified that the companies that changed their audit firm proportionally showed more changes in the number of KAM reported than the companies that did not change their audit firm by about 11 percentage points. However, due to the proximity of values and the fact that in 2019 there was a change in audit firm in only two entities, the results obtained do not allow accepting this hypothesis, so H3 **is** not accepted.

As for (H4): *The change of audit firm has an impact on the nature of the KAM reported*, through the study carried out it was verified that in the years 2017 and 2019 the companies that changed the audit firm did not present any change in the nature of the relevant matters of audit reports. It is also important to mention, once again, that in 2019 only two companies changed audit firm, a factor that had a significant impact on the results obtained in that year. To be able to perceive the changes that occurred in the nature of the KAM reported in the analyzed period, it has been obtained the average percentage of companies that changed audit firm and that presented changes in the nature of the KAM reported, and the average percentage of companies that did not change audit firm, but which also showed changes in the nature of KAM. By the calculation made, it was found that on average, proportionally more changes occurred when there was no change in audit firm, with a difference of only 6 percentage points. However, due to the proximity of values and due to the fact, that in 2019 only two companies changed their audit firm, the results obtained do not allow accepting this hypothesis, so H4 **is** not accepted.

In summary, it is possible to conclude that there is no growth in the number of KAM over the four years of application of ISA 701 and that most of the KAM that are reported in a given year are reported again in the following years. Regarding the impact that the change in the audit firm has on the reporting of KAM, it is not possible to state that there is a direct relationship, being possible that the reporting of the same KAM may be more associated with other factors such as the type of company and the sector where it operates.

This chapter has some limitations that must be mentioned. One of the limitations identified was the timeframe of this investigation (2016 to 2019). Another of the limitations identified, is the fact that there was a small number of companies that changed their audit firm in this period, which made it difficult to obtain statistical evidence on the impact that these changes may have in reporting KAM. It is also considered as a limitation to the study developed the existing literature, not on the subject of KAM, but on investigations that have fallen into the relationships that we sought to highlight in this chapter. As previously mentioned, the existing studies on the reporting of KAM focused essentially on the impact that such reporting has on changes in investment decisions, on the quality of the audit and on market reactions.

For future investigations, it is suggested to broaden the population, involving other companies, with the aim of identifying more changes in audit firm and thus obtaining significant statistical data, as well as extending the period of analysis, and studying other variables that may have an impact on reporting the KAM both in terms of their number and nature.

REFERENCES

Antle, R. (1982). The auditor as an economic agent. *Journal of Accounting Research*, *20*(2), 503–527. doi:10.2307/2490884

Ciger, A., Vardar, G. Ç., & Kinay, B. (2019). Key audit matters: A research on listed firms in CEE countries and Turkey. *BEH -. Business and Economic Horizons*, *15*(3), 393–422.

Colares, A. C. V., Pinheiro, L. E. T., & Silva, J. N. (2020). Principais Assuntos de Auditoria: A Divulgação ainda é Comunicativa Após Três Anos de Aplicação DA NBC TA 701? *Revista Eletrônica do Departamento de Ciências Contábeis & Departamento de Atuária e Métodos Quantitativos da FEA*, *7*(1), 89–111. doi:10.23925/2446-9513.2020v7i1p89-111

Cooper, B. J., & Grose, R. (2010). Trust Me: I'm An Auditor. *International Review of Business Research Papers*, *6*(5), 160–165.

Cordos, G., & Fülöp, M. (2015). Understanding audit reporting changes: Introduction of Key Audit Matters. *Accounting & Management Information System*, *14*(1), 128–152.

Figueiredo, O. (2015). A nova ISA 701 – Comunicar Matérias Relevantes de Auditoria no Relatório do Auditor Independente e o novo conteúdo do relatório de auditoria. *Revista da Ordem dos Revisores Oficiais de Contas* (71), 8-15.

Fülöp, M. T. (2018). New tendencies in audit reporting, examples of good practices BVB. *Audit Financiar, XVI*, *2*(150), 249–260. doi:10.20869/AUDITF/2018/150/010

Geiger, M. A., & Raghunandan, K. (2002). Auditor Tenure and Audit Reporting Failures. *Auditing*, *21*(1), 67–78. doi:10.2308/aud.2002.21.1.67

Gray, G. L., Turner, J. L., Coram, P. J., & Mock, T. J. (2011). Perceptions and misperceptions regarding the unqualified auditor's report by financial statement preparers, users, and auditors. *Accounting Horizons*, *25*(4), 659–684. doi:10.2308/acch-50060

IAASB. (2009). *ISA 200: Overall objectives of the independent auditor and the conduct of an audit in accordance with international standards on auditing*. IFAC. https://www.ifac.org/system/files/downloads/a008-2010-iaasb-handbook-isa-200.pdf

IAASB. (2015). *ISA 701: Communicating Key Audit Matters in the independent Auditor's Report*. IAASB. https://www.iaasb.org/publications/international-standard-auditing-isa-701-new-communicating-key-audit-matters-independe
nt-auditors-4

Lennox, C. S., Schmidt, J. J., & Thompson, A. M. (2019). Are expanded audit reports informative to investors? Evidence from the UK. SSRN *Electronic Journal*. https://papers.ssrn.com/sol3/papers.cfm?abstract_id=2619785

Levanti, D. A. (2019). Aspects Regarding the Changes to the Independent Auditor"s Report. The Case of Public Interest Entities. *Audit Financiar, XVII*, *3*(155), 486–495. doi:10.20869/AUDITF/2019/155/018

Lin, H. L., & Yen, A. R. (2022). Auditor rotation, key audit matter disclosures, and financial reporting quality. *Advances in Accounting*, *57*, 100594. doi:10.1016/j.adiac.2022.100594

Martinho, C. (2009). *Uma Abordagem Quantitativa Longitudinal do Desempenho dos Alunos do 12º ano (2000-2005)*. Tese de Doutoramento, Faculdade de Ciências e Tecnologia da Universidade Nova de Lisboa.

Mayoral, J. M., & Segura, A. S. (2008). Gobierno corporativo y calidad de la información contable: Evidencia empírica española. *Revista de Contabilidad -. Revista de Contabilidad*, *11*(1), 67–99.

Morais, A. M., & Neves, I. P. (2017). Fazer investigação usando uma abordagem metodológica mista. *Revista Portuguesa de Educação*, *20*(2), 75–104.

Nagy, A. L. (2005). Mandatory Audit firmTurnover, Financial Reporting Quality, and Client Bargaining Power: The Case of Arthur Andersen. *Accounting Horizons*, *19*(2), 51–68. doi:10.2308/acch.2005.19.2.51

OROC. (2017). *Estatuto da Ordem dos Revisores Oficiais de Contas*. OROC. https://www.oroc.pt/a-ordem/estatuto-da-oroc/estatuto-da-oroc/

Pereira, A. C. (2019). *Matérias Relevantes de Auditoria relatadas pelas empresas cotadas na Euronext Lisbon* [Dissertação, Universidade Católica Portuguesa, Lisboa, Portugal]. https://repositorio.ucp.pt/

Pereira, A.C. (2019). Matérias Relevantes de Auditoria relatadas pelas empresas cotadas na Euronext Lisbon. *Revista da Ordem dos Revisores Oficiais de Contas,* (87), 11-23.

PWC. (2015). *Delivering the value of the Audit: New insightful audit reports*. Reino Unido: PWC.

Raupp, F. M., & Beuren, I. M. (2006). Metodologia da pesquisa aplicável às Ciências Sociais. In I. M. Beuren (Ed.), *Como Elaborar Trabalhos Monográficos em Contabilidade: Teoria e Prática* (3rd ed., pp. 76–97). Atlas.

Rocha, M., & Eugénio, T. (2019). Auditoria Financeira- Evolução histórica e conceitos associados. *APOTEC Jornal de Contabilidade*, (471), 188–191.

Sierra-García, L., Gambetta, N., García-Benau, M. A., & Orta-Pérez, M. (2019). Understanding the determinants of the magnitude of entity-level risk and account-level risk key audit matters: The case of the United Kingdom. *The British Accounting Review*, *51*(3), 227–240. doi:10.1016/j.bar.2019.02.004

Simnett, R., & Huggins, A. (2014). Enhancing the Auditor's Report: To What Extent is There Support for the IAASB's Proposed Changes? *Accounting Horizons*, *28*(4), 719–747. doi:10.2308/acch-50791

Sirois, L. P., Bédard, J., & Bera, P. (2018). The informational value of key audit matters in the auditor's report: Evidence from an eye-tracking study. *Accounting Horizons*, *32*(2), 141–162. doi:10.2308/acch-52047

UE (2014). Regulamento (UE) n.º 537/2014. *Jornal Oficial da União Europeia*. L158 (27-05-2014).

UE (2014). Regulamento (UE) n.º 537/2014. Jornal Oficial da União Europeia. L158 (27-05-2014).

Velte, P., & Issa, J. (2019). The impact of key audit matter (KAM) disclosure in audit reports on stakeholders' reactions: A literature review. *Problems and Perspectives in Management*, *17*(3), 323–341. doi:10.21511/ppm.17(3).2019.26

Velte, P., & Issa, J. (2019). The impact of key audit matter (KAM) disclosure in audit reports on stakeholders' reactions: A literature review. *Problems and Perspectives in Management*, *17*(3), 323–341. doi:10.21511/ppm.17(3).2019.26

Vik, C., & Walter, M. C. (2017). *The reporting practices of key audit matters in the big five audit firms in Norway*. [Dissertação de Mestrado, BI Norwegian Business School, Oslo, Noruega]. https://www.semanticscholar.org/paper/The-reporting-practices-of-key-audit-matters-in-the-Vik-Walter/de89523c0fad702da003e642c206337946bafa9d

KEY TERMS AND DEFINITIONS

Auditor rotation: Auditor rotation refers to the rotation of the audit firm and the rotation of the auditor. The mandatory audit firm/auditor rotation entails companies to change the auditor after a certain period of time. It has been defined on the Regulation a period of 10 years as the maximum extent of an audit firm/auditor in a specific audited company.

European audit reform: The European Audit Reform has outcome in 2016, with the adoption of the legislation proposed by the European Commission, the Regulation 537/2014, and the new Directive 2014/56/EU. These proposals were a response to the failings in the European audit system and in the audit function, as a result of the financial crisis. The main purpose was to reinforce confidence in the financial statements reported by companies and to increase audit quality. To accomplish this objective, between the main goals were to strengthen auditor independence, advance auditor supervision, guarantee a higher transparency in the financial information disclosed by companies'.

Key Audit Matters: The Key Audit Matters are those that the auditor as determined to be of most importance and entail more attention in pursuing the audit of financial statements. In order to determine that, the auditor should ponder the areas with higher risk of material misstatement, areas in the financial statements that involved substantial management judgment, the consequence on the audit of important transactions or events that happened on the period.

Chapter 12
The Legal Impact of the Portuguese Whistleblowing System on Financial Reporting

Patrick de Pitta Simões
https://orcid.org/0000-0002-2087-005X
CEDIS, Portugal

ABSTRACT

In an increasingly global information society, public disclosure of corruption cases has been frequent, making us question the conduct of those involved. In order to avoid social alarmism and to safeguard the identification of those involved, a system of reporting channels, also known as the whistleblowing system, has been developed throughout the world. In turn, the evolution in the way financial reports are produced and analysed has caused new demands for social scrutiny to be incorporated such as those relating to the whistleblowing system. This text will address the impact of whistleblowing system on financial reporting, speaking on the recent legal diplomas approved in Portugal, largely influenced by situations that occurred in the USA, within the financial markets, more specifically relating the auditors' work. Compliance, which used to be understood as the best voluntary practices of integrity and organisational transparency, is now legally obligatory and institutionalised in public and private entities, and the content of financial reports is given new prominence.

INTRODUCTION

In the last decades, the public disclosure of situations of serious wrongdoings, wrong governance, illegalities or wrongdoings has been frequently. Such as, as mentioned by Simões (2020, p. 468-469), those disclosed by Julian Assange, founder of WikiLeaks[1]; Edward Snowden, former National Security Agency analyst[2]; and in Portugal, by Rui Pinto, associated to the Football Leaks scandals[3], Malta Files[4] and Luanda Leaks[5] or the so-called Panama Papers[6]. To protect the rights, freedoms and guarantees of the who reports and the reputational value of the organisations involved, the so-called Whistleblowing System has been promoted internationally.

DOI: 10.4018/978-1-6684-7293-4.ch012

This is due to the fact that in the United States of America (USA), after the financial scandal generated by the fraudulent practices of Enron Corporation, in collusion with the auditing company, then one of the top five audit firms (Big 5), Arthur Andersen, but also the problems detected with other entities such as WorldCom or Parmalat[7], the need to pass a law requiring companies to take into consideration on financial reporting a Whistleblowing System.

These events proved to the companies that it is imperative to analyse the transactions that are at the origin of the accounting records, and the best way to do it is through the analysis of the processes and controls instituted in the entity.

The financial world in general was shaken by the publicly disclosed scandals which had repercussions on the credibility of the institutions. Not only the USA, due to its dimension and financial importance, influenced the other countries to adapt the whistleblowing system through the best compliance practices, but they also felt the need to legislate to make this mechanism mandatory so as to avoid further reputational damage and consequently financial losses for stakeholders.

This chapter seeks above all to clarify the rationale behind the legal framework we have in Portugal for the inclusion of whistleblowing in financial reports, necessarily addressing the international environment in an era of globalisation of everything, or practically everything. This chapter will not base on speculative articles, subjective studies or, in our understanding, what Marçal (2014) calls Pseudociência (pseudoscience), but on a more objective analysis as possible because there is a lack of knowledge of the law that now tells for many organisations that it is mandatory to implement the Whistleblowing System.

The European Union, in general, and Portugal, in particular, are no longer in an era that Whistleblowing System is just one best practice of integrity and transparency or based on considerations such as Near, J. P., & Miceli, M. P. (1996) did and which end up being cited by many other authors[8].

This is the methodology that will be used in this chapter, which does not mean that it is merely informative or replicates the law. Writing a chapter on non-objective considerations or with minimal correspondence in law increases the gap between academic ideas and concepts that they are in law (that is the one that gives us rights and obligations).

This doesn't mean that is not good for the academy take into consideration studies such as the 12th edition of the largest global study on occupational fraud, based on 2.110 real cases of occupational fraud, made by The Association of Certified Fraud Examiners (ACFE). This continues to foster what ISO 37002:2021 (Whistleblowing Management System), of 27 July, created by the International Organization for Standardization, also tells: the experience of professionals shows that a large proportion of offences come to the attention of the affected organization through reports from people within or close to the organization.

However, this chapter will be focus on what laws are mandatory. It is structured by a brief legal framework (international and Portuguese), then the whistleblowing system in Portugal (in more detail), a sub-chapter exclusively dedicated to the whistleblowing system in the financial sector, and from the general approach will talk about particularities of the communication of irregularities in management reports. Finally, the conclusions that are drawn are generic guidelines of what the law provides us with, with a kind of clue for future development.

BACKGROUND OF THE LEGAL FRAMEWORK

In this context of financial crisis appears the Sarbanes-Oxley Act (SOX). This Act is founded by senators Paul Sarbanes (Democrat from Maryland) and Michael Oxley (Republican from Ohio), and is probably the most important legislative document in terms of scope, rigour and worldwide impact in this area. With its official name Public Company Accounting Reform and Investor Protection Act, it was approved by the US Congress in July 2002, being applicable to all entities present in the USA stock markets (v.g. NYSE, NASDAQ), with the purpose of establishing very strict requirements in the area of Corporate Governance, namely in the definition of the Internal Control System and its operation, and the responsibility of managers in relation to the reliability of the Financial Statements.

The SOX Act required US Public Companies and their European subsidiaries, as well as foreign companies registered in one of the US stock markets, to create within their audit committee, procedures for the receipt, acceptance and treatment of complaints received in relation to accounting, internal accounting controls or other matters in this area and the confidential and anonymous reporting by employees of concerns in these matters. In addition, section 806 of the SOX Act provides measures to protect against retaliatory actions for employees who make use of the whistleblower system for the purpose of providing evidence of fraud in listed companies.

These provisions are also reflected in the rules of the NASDAQ and the New York Stock Exchange (NYSE). When listed on the NASDAQ and NYSE, companies must submit their certified accounts there in advance. This certification process means that companies are in a position to assess whether or not they comply with a number of rules, including those on whistleblowing. Those that do not comply are subject to heavy sanctions and penalties from the NASDAQ and NYSE or the SEC - Securities and Exchange Commission, the US authority in charge of supervising the application of the SOX law.

In Portugal, the Securities Market Commission issued recommendations on the adoption of Whistleblowing and Law no. 19/2008, of 21 January, amended by Law no. 30/2015, of 22 April, was approved, providing guarantees for whistleblowers.

Progressively, more and more legal obligations have arisen, namely the Commercial Companies Code, the General Regime of Credit Institutions and Financial Companies or the Law establishing measures to Combat Money Laundering and Terrorist Financing, for whistleblowing to take place, within the scope of disclosure of information in financial reports or audits of financial reports.

People who become aware of any serious irregularity related to the administration, accounting organisation and internal supervision of the credit institution or of evidence of breaches of duties provided for in Regulation 575/2013 of the European Parliament and of the Council of 26 June, which is likely to place it in a situation of financial imbalance, have the duty to report them to the supervisory body.

Recently, in Portugal, Law No. 93/2021 of 20 December entered into force, establishing the General Whistleblower Protection and transposing Directive (EU) 2019/1937 of the European Parliament and of the Council of 23 October 2019 on the protection of persons who report breaches of Union law.

The General Whistleblower Protection, has as its scope of application, i.e. it considers as an infringement, the act or omission opposite to rules contained in the European Union acts referred to in the Annex to Directive (EU) 2019/1937 of the European Parliament and of the Council, national rules implementing, transposing or implementing such acts or any other rules laid down in legislative acts implementing or transposing them, including those providing for criminal offences or administrative breaches, concerning the areas of, inter alia, financial services, products and markets, and the prevention of money laundering and terrorist financing the act or omission opposite to and detrimental to the

European Union's financial interests referred to in article 325 of the Treaty on the Functioning of the European Union. The whistleblowing is based on article 325 of the Treaty on the Functioning of the European Union (TFEU), as specified in the applicable Union measures; or the act or omission opposite to internal market rules referred to in article 26(2) of the TFEU, including competition and state aid rules, as well as corporate tax rules.

The General Whistleblower Protection, similarly to ISO 37002:2021, refer that there should be documented information in order to analyse the effectiveness of the implemented systems.

The legal regime, foreseen in the article 17 of the Law No. 93/2021, of 20 December, states that information must be compiled so that the competent authorities may present to the Assembly of the Portuguese Republic (Parliament), by the end of March each year, an annual report containing: (a) the number of external complaints received; (b) the number of proceedings initiated on the basis of those complaints and their outcome; (c) the nature and type of infractions reported; (d) whatever else they consider pertinent to improve the mechanisms for lodging and following up complaints, protection of whistleblowers, related persons and targeted persons, and sanctioning action.

In an era in which, increasingly, everything is known, those who hold information continue to be privileged and those who know how to handle it even more so. Access to information is an essential aspect for stakeholders in companies as well as for the work of any professional, such as an auditor, who wants to perform due diligence on the companies working with him.

In this sense, the task of the stakeholders or of the auditor begins with the collection of documentation (information), focuses on it (if not documented, there is no evidence that it is reliable or auditable) and ends with a final decision, in the case of stakeholders, or with the preparation and approval of a report (documented information) in the case of auditors.

When Compliance, in Portugal, is being institutionalised by the General Regime for the Prevention of Corruption, approved by Decree-Law No. 109-E/2021, of 9 December, the need and concern for reputational damage and the quality of financial reports to include this type of reporting gains greater prominence as civil society becomes more demanding and the business fabric becomes more complex.

The traceability of information is not only important to understand the evolution, history and trends of organisations but also to allow the mitigation of errors (wrongdoings), negligence or the fight against corruption and related infractions. These are the issues we intend to address in the following chapter.

THE WHISTLEBLOWING SYSTEM IN PORTUGAL

In today's world, information is unquestionably abundant, both in the way it is obtained and in the quantity available, which does not necessarily mean that it is trustworthy or worthy of being trusted and, consequently, secure.

In an increasingly global information society, there have been frequent emergence of people entitled Whistleblowers; perhaps the best known are Julian Assange; Edward Snowden and in Portugal, Rui Pinto.

That said, in the USA, after the aftermath of the financial crises generated by companies such as Enron Corporation, then a leading company in energy distribution - electricity and natural gas - and communications, and Arthur Andersen & Co, an auditing company that was its consultant and auditor, which collapsed after being accused of accounting and tax fraud and convicted of collusion and obstruction of justice for having destroyed documents relating to their audits, which ended up negatively influencing the image of Arthur Andersen & Co and consequently the credibility of auditing firms; or even the scandal generated by WorldCom, a company that was accused of distortions to the financial statements and consequently of fraud, on 30th July 2002, as a way to promote Compliance, that is, the legal fulfilment of financial policies that guarantee transparency, responsibility the Sabarnes-Oxley Act (SOX)[9], a system of reporting wrongdoings and/or frauds[10] was established for companies registered in one of its stock markets, including foreign companies, with the provision of sanctions in the event of non-compliance: Whistleblowing System.

As Matias (2022) recalls, SOX aimed to ensure the reliability and credibility of financial information, having, for this purpose, implemented demanding rules, especially in terms of the truthfulness, completeness and timeliness of the financial reporting performed by issuers of securities, the internal compliance control mechanisms, strengthening of the independence of the supervision and certification carried out by the external auditor, of the information provided to the market instead of implementing an aggravated sanctioning regime, with the purpose of ensuring that the cost always exceeds the benefit, as well as the establishment of protection mechanisms for employees who report irregularities or fraud.

Almost three years after the publication of SOX, the European Commission approved a Recommendation[11] encourages companies listed on stock exchanges to set up audit committees to monitor the possibility of employees reporting irregularities allegedly committed within the company and to ensure that a mechanism exists to allow for an independent investigation accompanied by appropriate measures[12].

In Portugal, the Securities Market Commission, also through a Recommendation 10-A, of November 2005, called "Communication of Irregularities", encouraged corporate companies to adopt a policy of reporting irregularities, which mentioned how communications could be made internally, including the persons with legitimacy to receive them, avoiding fear of any abusive or persecutory behaviour.

Less than a year later, the Data Protection Working Party, composed of the data protection authorities of the Member States, also known as the Article 29 Working Party, because it was set up by that same article number of Directive 95/46/EC of the European Parliament and of the Council of 24 October 1995 on the protection of individuals with regard to the processing of personal data and on the free movement of such data, issued Opinion No 1/2006, adopted in February 2006, on the application of European data protection standards to internal whistleblowing schemes in the areas of internal control, accounting, auditing, banking and financial crime and anti-corruption.

According to the remit of the Data Protection Working Party (as set out in article 30 of Directive 95/46/EC) and taking into account cultural differences, historical or social reasons and the specificity of the legal system in each country of the European Union, the opinion was limited to a formal approach to Data Protection rules, excluding Labour Law and Criminal Law, although it sought to reconcile SOX with European data protection standards, avoiding possible attempts to circumvent Directive 95/46/EC under foreign legislation.

Therefore, it remains to be seen to what extent the Whistleblowing System, by fighting and/or preventing irregularities, runs the risk of becoming an internal and private matter of the organisation, generating a sort of "labour soft judgment" or "domestic arbitration", without endangering its goodwill, roughly speaking, the intrinsic value of the organisation's reputation, image or brand, does not constitute a decriminalization, *lato sensu*, of the legal system, such as the disciplinary or criminal rules, such as the mandatory denunciation foreseen in article 242 of the Portuguese Code of Criminal Procedure. In other words, it may be a criminal offence, in the sense of the legal order.

So can it become a perversion of the legal duties to report to a criminal police body or to initiate disciplinary proceedings, due to economic or minimalist vicissitudes that "altruistically" avoid lengthy legal proceedings in general? We do not know how many cases will occur, but it is unlikely that this whistleblowing system will not be misused.

Once again in Portugal, in September 2007, the Securities Market Commission recommended the implementation of a policy for the communication of irregularities allegedly occurred within companies. This time, through its Corporate Governance Code, it provided in point II. 1.4, that the communication policy should adopt the following elements: indication of the means through which communications of irregular practices may be made internally, including the persons with legitimacy to receive communications; indication of the treatment to be given to the communications, including confidential treatment, should it be so intended by the declarant.

In turn, the following year saw the appearance of Law No. 20/2008 of 21 April, which created the criminal regime for corruption in international trade and the private sector[13]; and Law No. 19/2008 of 21 April, which approved measures to combat corruption[14].

The latter established, specifically in article 4, guarantees for employees of the Public Administration and of companies in the business sector of the State, who report the commission of infractions they become aware of while performing their duties.

These whistleblowing workers cannot, in any form, be prejudiced including non-voluntary transfer. They enjoy, under this law, until proven otherwise, the presumption of the application of an abusive disciplinary sanction, when this takes place up to one year after the respective denunciation (the temporal criterion is not understood in detriment of the material one, regardless of the time elapsed). They have the right to anonymity, except for investigators, until charges are brought, and to be transferred at their request, without the possibility of refusal, after charges have been brought.

Initially, the guarantees were for whistleblowers working in the public sector, but since 2015[15], they have also applied to workers in the private sector. It is now expressly guaranteed that workers who report infringements that they become aware of in the course of their duties or because of them cannot, in any way, including non-voluntary transfer or dismissal, be adversely affected. This last situation was already a safeguard provided for in the Labour Code about dismissal without just cause. And a paragraph c) has been introduced, in article 4(3), which strengthens the guarantees for whistleblowers by equating, with the necessary adaptations, the witness protection measures in criminal proceedings provided for in Law No. 93/99, of 14 July, which regulates the application of measures for the protection of witnesses in criminal proceedings, as amended by Laws No. 29/2008, of 4 July and No. 42/2010, of 3 September.

In this chain of compliance policies[16] and soft law normative not so much of the anti-corruption legislation, although it has mentioned Law No. 19/2008 of 21 April, which at the time only applied to public sector workers, the National Commission for Data Protection (the Portuguese Data Protection Authority), in view of the high number of notifications of processing of personal data in Portugal, has also mentioned the Law No. 19/2008 of 21 April. In this chain of compliance policies and soft law normative not so much of the anti-corruption legislation, although it has mentioned Law No. 19/2008, of April 21, which at the time only applied to public sector workers, the National Commission of Data Protection (Portuguese Data Protection Authority), given the high number of notifications of processing of personal data generated by internal communications of acts of irregular financial management in the areas listed by the Data Protection Group[17], deliberated guiding principles (Ethical Guidelines) applicable to this type of processing, in order to safeguard the privacy of the intervenients[18].

This Deliberation established ethical guidelines for the Whistleblowing System and defined it as a system that translates into the creation in the companies of conditions for the reporting of fraudulent or irregular behaviour capable of seriously affecting their activity.

With this Deliberation, we no longer only have guarantees for whistleblowers, provided for in article 4 of Law No. 19/2008, of 21 April, but rules on rights and limits on the processing of personal data in this area.

The National Commission for Data Protection has established specific limits of objective scope (the whistleblowing system is restricted to the aforementioned areas), subjective scope (only persons related to these areas who perform management acts may be subject to whistleblowing), procedural scope (its nature must be subsidiary to the regular activity of the entity) and autonomy of will (the obligation to report only in cases where the criminal and criminal procedural law determines it).

It should be considered that before the General Data Protection Regulation, the National Commission for Data Protection had a power of prior control over this type of data processing, so organisations that wanted to implement Whistleblowing as a system had to ask the National Commission for Data Protection for authorisation to create the mechanism. Currently, the National Commission for Data Protection only supervises compliance with Data Protection rules.

Due to the great influence of the USA, especially commercial and financial; with the emergence of more Leaks (unauthorised communication or disclosure of information, as a rule compromising) involving Europeans; with the growing social awareness[19] and political consciousness[20]; the European Union published on 26 November 2019, in its Official Journal, Directive (EU) 2019/1937 of 23 October of the European Parliament and of the Council on the protection of persons who report breaches of Union law.

This Directive aims to strengthen the application of Union law and policies in specific areas by setting common minimum standards for a high level of protection of whistleblowers, because it is understood that persons who work for a public or private organisation or are in contact with such an organisation in the context of their work-related activities are often the first to know about threats or harm to the public interest which arise in that context.

According to its first whereas of the Directive, by reporting breaches of Union law that are harmful to the public interest, such persons act as 'whistleblowers' and thereby play a key role in exposing and preventing such breaches and in safeguarding the welfare of society. However, potential whistleblowers are often discouraged from reporting their concerns or suspicions for fear of retaliation. In this context, the importance of providing balanced and effective whistleblower protection is increasingly acknowledged at both Union and international level.

However, as Matias (2022) states, the law has not always focused on, or as a relevant element, the privileged position in which some people find themselves, having started to focus on what we may call "rewarded solidarity", i.e., the collaboration of citizens who, having or finding out information about irregularities committed by state agents, could promote their accusation, having, in return, the right to receive part of the fines or penalties that might be applied, the Dodd-Frank Act, which came into force in 2010 increased the protection granted to whistleblowers, in particular by strengthening the preventive and repressive measures in relation to retaliatory actions, introducing the possibility for whistleblowers to seek legal action in view of the retaliation and request the payment of an amount of compensation representing double the amount to which they would be entitled, plus interest as applicable. The Dodd-Frank Act also established the bonus program paid by the U.S. Securities and Exchange Commission (SEC), which has done much to raise the profile of and encourage whistleblowing.

Finally, on 20 December 2021, Law No. 93/2021 was published in the Diário da República, the official gazette of the Portuguese State, establishing the General Regime for the Protection of Whistleblowers, transposing the Directive (EU) 2019/1937 of the European Parliament and of the Council of 23 October 2019.

Under article 5 of Law No. 93/2021, of 20 December, whistleblower is the natural person who denounces or publicly discloses an infringement based on information obtained during their professional activity, regardless of the nature of this activity and the sector in which it is carried out.

Employees in the private, social or public sector; service providers, contractors, subcontractors and suppliers, as well as any persons acting under their supervision and direction; holders of shareholdings and persons belonging to administrative or management bodies or to supervisory or controlling bodies of legal persons, including non-executive members; volunteers and trainees, whether remunerated or not, may also be considered as whistleblowers.

The fact that the complaint or public disclosure of an infringement is based on information obtained in a professional relationship that has ended, as well as during the recruitment process or during another stage of pre-contractual negotiation of an existing or unresolved professional relationship, does not prevent a natural person from being considered as a whistleblower.

In order to benefit from the status of whistleblower, i.e. to have the protection conferred by Law No. 93/2021, of 20 December, the whistleblower must be in good faith and have serious grounds to believe that the information is true when reporting or publicly disclosing it, respecting the rules of precedence of the means of internal and external reporting and public disclosure (provided for in Article 7 of the law).

The protection is also granted, with the necessary adaptations, to the natural person who assists the whistleblower in the whistleblowing procedure and whose assistance must be confidential, including trade union representatives or workers representatives; third parties who are connected to the whistleblower, namely work colleagues or family members, and may be subject to retaliation in a professional context; and legal persons or similar entities that are owned or controlled by the whistleblower, for which the whistleblower works or with which he/she is connected in any way in a professional context.

It should also be noted that for the purposes of the law, the following are considered infringements:

1. The act or omission opposite to rules contained in the European Union acts referred to in the Annex to Directive (EU) 2019/1937 of the European Parliament and of the Council, to national rules implementing, transposing or complying with such acts or to any other rules contained in legislative acts implementing or transposing them, including those providing for criminal offences or administrative offences, concerning the fields of: public procurement; financial services, products and markets and the prevention of money laundering and terrorist financing; product safety and compliance; transport safety; environmental protection; radiation protection and nuclear safety; food and feed safety, animal health and animal welfare; public health; consumer protection; protection of privacy and personal data and network and information systems security.
2. The act or omission against opposite to and detrimental to the financial interests of the European Union referred to in article 325 of the Treaty on the Functioning of the European Union (TFEU), as specified in the applicable Union measures.
3. The act or omission opposite to the internal market rules referred to in article 26(2) TFEU, including competition and state aid rules, as well as corporate tax rules.
4. Violent, especially violent and highly organized crime, as well as the crimes provided for in article 1, no. 1 of Law No. 5/2002, of 11 January, establishing measures to combat organized and economic-financial crime, namely: drug trafficking, in accordance with articles 21 to 23 and 28 of Decree-Law No. 15/93, of 22 January; terrorism, terrorist organizations, international terrorism and financing of terrorism; arms trafficking; influence trafficking; undue receipt of advantage; active and passive corruption, including that practiced in the public and private sectors; corrup-

tion, including that practiced in the public and private sectors. No. 15/93, of 22 January; terrorism, terrorist organizations, international terrorism and terrorism financing; arms trafficking; influence trafficking; undue receipt of advantage; active and passive corruption, including that practiced in the public and private sectors and in international trade, as well as in the sports activity; embezzlement; economic participation in business; money laundering criminal association; child pornography and pimping of minors; counterfeiting, use and acquisition of counterfeit cards or other payment devices and their preparatory acts, acquisition of cards or other payment devices obtained through a computer crime, damage to computer programs or other computer data and computer sabotage, pursuant to articles 3a, 3b and 3c. A, 3b, 3c, 3d, 3e, 4 and 5 of Law 109/2009, of 15 September, and also illegitimate access to a computer system, if it has produced one of the results set out in sub-paragraphs a) and b) of paragraph 5 of article 6 of Law 109/2009, of 15 September. In the areas of national defence and national security, the following acts are also included in the scope of this law: trafficking in persons; counterfeiting of currency and securities equivalent to currency; pimping; smuggling; trafficking in and tampering with stolen vehicles.

In the fields of national defence and security, only the act or omission opposite to the rules of engagement contained in the European Union acts referred to in part i.A of the Annex to Directive (EU) 2019/1937 of the European Parliament and of the Council, or opposite to the purposes of those rules, shall be considered an offence for the purposes of the law.

In addition to crimes against persons in general, there is great concern about the protection of whistleblowers in organised and economic-financial crime because of the negative impact it has on society.

THE WHISTLEBLOWING SYSTEM ON FINANCIAL SECTOR

In the area of financial services, the added value of the protection of whistleblowers has already been recognised by the EU legislator and consequently by individual Member States. In the aftermath of the above-mentioned financial crises, which exposed serious deficiencies in the application of applicable rules, whistleblower protection measures, including the duty to implement internal and external whistleblowing channels as well as the express prohibition of retaliatory acts, have been included in a significant number of legislative acts in the area of financial services (listed in the recitals of Directive (EU) 2019/1937).

The Directive 2009/65/EC of the European Parliament and of the Council of 13 July 2009 on the coordination of laws, regulations and administrative provisions relating to undertakings for collective investment in transferable securities introduced the duty to implement effective and reliable mechanisms to encourage reporting of potential or actual breaches to competent authorities, including secure communication channels.

Such mechanisms should include specific procedures for the receipt of reports on breaches and their follow-up; appropriate protection for employees of investment firms, management companies and depositaries who report breaches committed within those entities, at least against retaliation, discrimination and other types of unfair treatment; protection of personal data relating to persons who report breaches and to natural persons who are allegedly responsible for a breach; clear rules ensuring confidentiality in all cases in relation to persons who report a breach, unless disclosure is required by national law in the context of further investigation or subsequent judicial proceedings.

In this context, a natural person who is an employee or a former employee of an investment company, management company and/or depositary, who reports in a personal capacity and in good faith alleged breaches by those entities of national provisions implementing Directive 2009/65/EC of the European Parliament and of the Council of 13 July 2009.

The Regulation (EC) No Section C of Regulation (EC) No 1060/2009 of the European Parliament and of the Council of 16 September 2009 on credit rating agencies provides that credit rating analysts, employees of the credit rating agency and any other natural person whose services are placed at the disposal or under the control of the credit rating agency and who is directly involved in credit rating activities as well as any person closely associated with them, who considers that any other such person has committed an illegal act, must report that information immediately to the compliance officer, without negative consequences for the whistleblower. This already represents a prohibition on retaliation or the existence of any negative consequence because of the communication that has been made.

In turn, Regulation (EU) No 648/2012 of the European Parliament and of the Council of 4 July 2012 on over-the-counter derivatives, central counterparties and trade repositories states that a natural person or group of natural persons acting jointly, employees (or former employees) of a supervised entity who, acting in their personal capacity and in good faith, provide information to the European Securities and Markets Authority that may serve to detect evidence or relate to a potential infringement.

Under Directive 2013/36/EU of the European Parliament and of the Council of 26 June 2013 relating to the access to the activity of credit institutions and to the prudential supervision of credit institutions, the establishment of effective and reliable mechanisms to encourage reporting of potential or actual breaches of the national legal provisions transposing this Directive and Regulation (EU) No 575/2013 on prudential requirements for credit institutions and investment firms to the competent authorities is imposed.

The mechanisms concerned should include: specific procedures for receiving information on breaches and their follow-up; adequate protection of employees of institutions reporting breaches committed within the institution in relation at least to retaliation, discrimination or other types of unfair treatment; protection of personal data concerning both the person who reports the breaches and any natural person who is allegedly responsible for a breach; and clear rules ensuring confidentiality in any case in relation to the person who reports breaches committed within the institution, unless disclosure is required by national law in the context of further investigation or subsequent judicial proceedings.

Directive 2014/65/EU of the European Parliament and of the Council of 15 May 2014 on markets in financial instruments, using terminology that is far more appropriate to the reality under consideration, stipulates, in respect of reporting breaches, that competent authorities should put in place effective mechanisms to enable potential or actual breaches of the provisions of Regulation (EU) No 600/2014 of the European Parliament and of the Council of 15 May 2014 on markets in financial instruments and amending Regulation (EU) No 648/2012 to be reported to them.

Aligned with mechanisms provided for in other special legislative frameworks within the financial sector, such mechanisms should include, at a minimum specific procedures for the receipt of reports on potential or actual breaches and their follow-up, including the establishment of secure communication channels for such reports; adequate protection for employees of financial institutions who report breaches committed within them from, at a minimum, retaliation, discrimination or other types of unfair treatment; protection of the identity of both the person reporting the breach and the natural person allegedly responsible for it, at all stages of the procedure, unless such disclosure is required by national law in the context of further investigation or subsequent administrative or judicial proceedings.

In this context, it will be required that investment firms, market operators, data reporting services providers, and credit institutions in relation to investment services or activities and ancillary services and branches of third country firms implement appropriate procedures for their employees to report breaches internally through a specific, independent and autonomous channel.

The Regulation (EU) No 909/2014 of the European Parliament and of the Council of 23 July 2014 on improving the settlement of European Union securities and on Central Securities Depositories, which according to Matias (2022) although making use of a terminology that is not coherent or, if we prefer, not harmonised, stipulates the duty to establish effective mechanisms to encourage the reporting of actual or potential breaches of that Regulation.

Again, in line with some of the special regimes referred to above, such mechanisms should include, at a minimum specific procedures for the receipt and investigation of the notification of actual or potential breaches and their follow-up, including the establishment of secure communication channels for such notifications; adequate protection of the staff of institutions who report actual or potential breaches committed within the institution from, at a minimum, retaliation, discrimination or other types of unfair treatment protection of personal data concerning both the person who reports the actual or potential breaches and the natural person who is allegedly responsible for the breach; protection of the identity of both the person who reports the breach and the natural person who is allegedly responsible for the breach, at all stages of the procedure unless such disclosure is required by national law in the context of further investigation or subsequent administrative or judicial proceedings.

In addition, there is also a duty for Central Securities Depositories to have in place appropriate procedures for their staff to report actual or potential breaches internally through a specific, independent and autonomous channel.

In turn, Regulation (EU) No 1286/2014 of the European Parliament and of the Council of 26 November 2014 on key information documents for packaged retail and insurance-based investment products requires the establishment of effective procedures for reporting actual or potential breaches of the Regulation in question.

Again, procedures should include at least: specific procedures for the receipt of reports on actual or potential infringements and their follow-up; adequate protection for employees reporting infringements within their employer, at least from retaliation, discrimination and other types of unfair treatment; and protection of the identity of the persons reporting the infringements and the natural persons who are allegedly responsible for the infringements, at all stages of the procedure unless disclosure is required by national law in the context of further investigation or subsequent judicial proceedings.

In addition, it is also established the prerogative to require employers engaged in activities regulated for financial services purposes to have in place appropriate procedures for their staff to report actual or potential infringements internally through a specific, independent and autonomous channel.

In turn, Regulation (EU) No 596/2014 of the European Parliament and of the Council of 16 April 2014 on market abuse (Market Abuse Regulation) provides for a duty to establish effective mechanisms to enable reporting of actual or potential breaches of this Regulation to competent authorities.

Such mechanisms should include at least specific procedures for the receipt of information on breaches and their follow-up, including the establishment of secure communication channels for such information; appropriate protection within their workplace for persons working under a contract of employment who report breaches or are accused of breaches, with regard to retaliation, discrimination or other types of unfair treatment protection of personal data of both the person who reports the breach and the natural person who is allegedly responsible for the breach, including protection in relation to the confidentiality of the identity of the persons concerned, at all stages of the procedure without prejudice to disclosure of information being required by national law in the context of investigations or subsequent judicial proceedings.

On the other hand, a duty is also established to require employers engaged in regulated financial services activities to have in place appropriate procedures for their employees to report breaches of this Regulation internally.

In addition, and in a novel approach to the (successful) US regime, it establishes the possibility for Member States to provide, in accordance with national law, financial incentives to persons who provide the competent authorities with relevant information about potential breaches of this Regulation, provided that those persons are not subject to a duty to report such information under other pre-existing legal or contractual obligations, and that the information is new, and will result in the imposition of an administrative sanction or criminal sanction or the taking of another administrative measure for a breach of this Regulation.

In this regard to the reporting of infringements, it is important to bear in mind the implementation of the reporting of infringements, as set out in Commission Implementing Directive (EU) No 2015/2392 of 17 December 2015 on Regulation (EU) No 596/2014 of the European Parliament and of the Council as regards the communication to competent authorities of information concerning actual or potential infringements of that Regulation, which regulates the requirement for such communications to be addressed by specialised personnel, their follow-up and applicable procedures, as well as specific communication channels and the duty to keep records of the communications received. In addition to the protection of those communications concerned.

The Regulation (EU) 2015/2365 of the European Parliament and of the Council of 25 November 2015 on the transparency of securities financing transactions and on reuse establishes, with regard to the reporting of infringements, the obligation to establish effective mechanisms so that any infringements of the article referring to the obligation to report and safeguard in respect of securities financing transactions (article 4) or of the article referring to the reporting of securities financing transactions (article 5) can be reported to other authorities. Referring to the reporting obligation and safeguarding in respect of securities financing transactions (article 4) or the article on reuse of financial instruments received under a collateral arrangement (article 15) of the Regulation.

Such mechanisms should include at least: specific procedures for the receipt of notifications of breaches of articles 4 or 15 and their follow-up, including the establishment of secure communication channels for such notifications; adequate protection of persons with a contract of employment who notify breaches of articles 4 or 15, or who are accused of breaching those articles, against retaliation, discrimination or other forms of unfair treatment; protection of personal data of both the person who notifies breaches of articles 4 or 15 and the person who notifies breaches of articles 4 or 15, or who is accused of such breaches, against retaliation, discrimination or other forms of unfair treatment. This includes protection to preserve the confidentiality of their identity at all stages of the procedure, without prejudice to disclosure of any information required by national law in the context of investigations or subsequent judicial proceedings.

Additionally, there is an obligation for counterparties to have in place adequate internal procedures for their employees to report breaches of articles 4 and 15.

The Regulation (EU) 2015/847 of the European Parliament and of the Council of 20 May 2015 on information accompanying transfers of funds establishes the duty to put in place effective mechanisms to encourage reporting of breaches of the provisions of that Regulation to competent authorities.

Such mechanisms should include at least those enshrined in Directive (EU) 2015/849 of the European Parliament and of the Council of 20 May 2015 on the prevention of the use of the financial system for the purpose of money laundering or terrorist financing, namely: adequate protection of employees or persons in a similar position of obliged entities who report breaches committed within the obliged entity; adequate protection of the accused person; protection of personal data relating both to the person reporting the breaches and to any natural person who is allegedly responsible for a breach; and clear rules ensuring confidentiality in any case in relation to the person reporting breaches committed within the obliged entity, unless disclosure is required by national law in the context of further investigation or subsequent judicial proceedings.

In addition, a duty is also established to implement the implementation of internal channels to enable its employees or persons in a similar position to report breaches internally through a secure, independent, dedicated and anonymous channel, proportionate to the nature and size of the payment service provider concerned.

Directive (EU) 2015/849 of the European Parliament and of the Council of 20 May 2015 on the prevention of the use of the financial system for the purpose of money laundering or terrorist financing has established the obligation to put in place effective and reliable mechanisms to encourage reporting to the competent authorities and, where appropriate, to self-regulatory bodies of actual or potential breaches of national provisions transposing that Directive.

It also requires the implementation of one or more secure communication channels for the transmission of actual or potential breaches of the regime set out in that Directive. Those channels ensure that only the competent authorities and, where appropriate, self-regulatory bodies are aware of the identity of the persons providing information.

Such mechanisms should include at least: adequate protection of employees or persons in a similar position within the obliged entities who report breaches committed within the obliged entity; adequate protection of the accused person; protection of personal data relating to both the person who reports the breaches and any natural person who is allegedly responsible for a breach; and clear rules ensuring confidentiality in any case in relation to the person who reports breaches committed within the obliged entity, unless disclosure is required by national law in the context of further investigation or subsequent judicial proceedings.

In addition, duties are also enshrined on the establishment of measures to address possible retaliation as well as effective judicial protection.

Regulation (EU) 2017/1129 of the European Parliament and of the Council of 14 June 2017 on the prospectus to be published when securities are offered to the public or admitted to trading on a regulated market (the Prospectus Regulation) provides for a duty to put in place effective measures to report and encourage reporting of actual or potential breaches of the Regulation in relation to the reporting of infractions.

Such measures should include at least specific procedures for the receipt of reports of actual or potential infringements and their follow-up, including the establishment of secure communication channels for such information; adequate protection for employees reporting infringements, at least with regard to retaliation, discrimination and other types of unfair treatment by their employer or third parties and protection of the identity and personal data of both the person who reports the infringements and the natural persons who are allegedly responsible for the infringements, at all stages of the procedure unless disclosure is required by national law in the context of further investigation or subsequent judicial proceedings.

In addition, similarly to the US regime, Member States will be able to provide, in accordance with national law, financial incentives to persons who provide the competent authorities with relevant information about actual or potential infringements of this Regulation, provided that they are not subject to a duty to disclose such information under other pre-existing legal or contractual obligations, and that the information is new and results in the imposition of an administrative or criminal sanction, or the taking of another administrative measure, for an infringement of this Regulation.

In addition, duties are also established regarding the implementation of specific, independent and autonomous channels for reporting infringements.

The Directive (EU) 2016/97 of the European Parliament and of the Council of 20 January 2016 on insurance distribution, on the reporting of infringements, imposes a duty to establish effective mechanisms to receive reports of potential or actual breaches of the provisions of the Directive's regime.

Such mechanisms should include at least: specific procedures for receiving reports and their follow-up; appropriate protection for employees of insurance or reinsurance distributors and, where possible, other persons who report breaches committed within those entities, at least against retaliation, discrimination or other types of unfair treatment; and protection of the identity of both the person who reports the breaches and the natural person who is allegedly responsible for them, at all stages of the procedure, unless such disclosure is required by national law in the context of further investigation or subsequent administrative or judicial proceedings.

COMMUNICATION OF IRREGULARITIES IN THE MANAGEMENT REPORTS

The entry into force of the General Regime of Prevention of Corruption, on 7 June 2021, means to legalise, in a general way, the institutionalisation of Compliance, that is, to give legal support, through its provision in the law, no longer being only specific to some activities.

Regulatory compliance meant self-regulation (self-accountability) carried out by commercial companies and public corporate entities, with a view to organisational integrity, materialised through the elaboration of prevention, management and risk mitigation mechanisms, which were designed according to the best organisational practices, as a rule, sectorial (by specific areas of activity) and international (by entities that call themselves as such).

It should be clarified that it was not, necessarily and exclusively, the prevention, management and mitigation of risks of fraud, financing of terrorism, money laundering, corruption or related offences. Naturally, it can and should encompass negligence, error, waste and irregularities or, more generally, deviation from good intentions, including ESG - environmental, social & corporate governance.

According to article 5 of the General Regime for the Prevention of Corruption, approved by Decree-Law No. 109-E/2021, of 9 December, applicable to legal persons, public and private, that employ 50 or more employees, these entities adopt and implement a regulatory compliance programme that includes, at least, a plan for the prevention of risks of corruption and related infractions, a code of conduct, a training programme and a channel for denunciations, in order to prevent, detect and sanction acts of corruption and related infractions carried out against or through the entity.

Note that "at least" does not mean that there are not more measures and instruments, such as an internal control system (article 20, number 1, paragraph c)) of the General Regime for the Prevention of Corruption), which may generate a misdemeanour penalty if it does not exist or is poorly implemented.

According to article 20 of Law No. 83/2017, of 18 August, which establishes measures to combat money laundering and terrorist financing, partially transposes Directives 2015/849/EU, of the European Parliament and of the Council, of 20 May 2015, and 2016/2258/EU, of the Council, of 6 December 2016, amends the Criminal Code and the Industrial Property Code and revokes Law No. 25/2008, of 5 June, and Decree-Law No. 125/2008, of July 21[21], obliged entities shall establish specific, independent and anonymous channels that internally ensure, in an appropriate manner, the receipt, processing and filing of reports of irregularities related to possible violations of the law, the regulations that implement it and the policies and procedures and controls defined internally for the prevention of money laundering and terrorist financing.

The channels referred to shall be proportionate to the nature, size and complexity of the activity of the obliged entity; ensure the confidentiality of the communications received and the protection of the personal data of the whistleblower and the suspected offender, in accordance with Regulation (EU) 2016/679 of the European Parliament and of the Council of 27 April 2016 and other data protection legislation.

The persons who, by virtue of the functions they perform in the obliged entity, namely the Compliance Officer, become aware of any serious fact that includes the irregularities referred to above, have the duty to report them to the supervisory body. When no supervisory body has been appointed, the communications shall be addressed to the management body of the obliged entity.

The communications made, as well as the reports to which they give rise, are kept for a period of seven years (as provided for in article 51) and made available at all times to sectoral authorities.

Obliged entities shall refrain from any threats or hostile acts, and in particular any unfavourable or discriminatory labour practices against any person making communications under this Article, and such communications shall not in themselves constitute grounds for the initiation by the obliged entity of any disciplinary, civil or criminal proceedings against the person making the communication, unless such communications are deliberate and manifestly unfounded.

The sectorial authorities may require the respective obliged entities to present a report, under the terms and with the frequency to be defined by those authorities, containing the description of the channels referred to above and a summary indication of the communications received and the respective processing.

Under Article 90 of Law No. 83/2017, of 18 August, without prejudice to legal provisions regarding the supervision of auditors, professional associations are responsible for verifying and adopting the necessary measures to ensure compliance by their members with the duties and obligations set out in this law and in the respective regulatory diplomas.

With the exception of the specificities contained in the sanctionary regime provided for by law, professional associations shall be treated in the same manner as sectorial authorities for the purposes provided for by law, namely as regards the powers conferred upon them and the need to equip themselves with adequate financial, human and technical resources for the performance of such functions.

Without prejudice to the other duties set forth in the law, professional associations shall: create, within their organizational structure, units specifically dedicated to ensuring compliance with this law and the regulations implementing it; prepare and keep updated statistical data on the professions they regulate, so as to enable the identification, assessment and mitigation of money laundering and terrorist financing risks existing in the context of those professions; ensure that the necessary training sessions are provided to ensure compliance by their members with the duty provided for in article 55; ensure that the necessary training sessions are provided to their members, so as to ensure compliance with the duty provided for in article 55.

Professional associations shall prepare a detailed annual report on the activities undertaken to ensure compliance with their obligations under the law, and send it, by 31 March of the following year, to the member of the Government exercising their supervisory powers in accordance with article 45 of Law No. 2/2013 of 10 January.

The annual report shall consider, in particular: the sanctions applied for non-compliance with the obligations arising from this law; the number of irregularity reports received; the number of suspicious transaction reports received; the number of suspicious transaction reports transmitted to the Financial Intelligence Unit; the number and description of the measures undertaken to verify compliance by the obliged entities with their obligations (pursuant to articles 74 and 79).

In the exercise of their supervisory functions, the referred members of the Government supervise compliance with the obligation's incumbent upon professional associations under the law. The professional associations inform the other entities competent for the verification of compliance with the law, through the Coordination Commission, of the annual report foreseen.

In turn, under article 108 of Law No. 83/2017, of 18 August, any person who has knowledge of violations or indications of violations of the law and the respective regulatory diplomas of sectoral application may make a complaint to the relevant sectoral authority.

The protection of the personal data of the whistleblower and of the person concerned shall be guaranteed in accordance with Regulation (EU) 2016/679 of the European Parliament and of the Council of 27 April 2016 and other data protection legislation. Confidentiality about the identity of the whistleblower shall also be always guaranteed or until such time as this information is required to safeguard the rights of defense of those affected by the complaint, in the context of investigations into the complaint or subsequent judicial proceedings.

Obliged entities shall refrain from any threats or hostile acts, and in particular any unfavorable or discriminatory labour practices against those making complaints to the competent sectoral authorities. Reports made shall not in themselves constitute grounds for the initiation of any disciplinary, civil or criminal proceedings against the complainant, unless they are deliberate and manifestly unfounded.

Sectorial authorities must: create specific, independent and anonymous channels that internally ensure, in an appropriate manner, the receipt, processing and filing of complaints; ensure adequate protection to the subject.

According to article 169, paragraph b) of the Law No. 83/2017, of 18 August, it is an administrative offence not to create specific, independent and anonymous channels that internally ensure, in an appropriate manner, the reception, treatment and filing of reports of irregularities, as well as the absence of internal reporting of irregularities or the failure to report to the sectoral authorities, as mentioned above (in violation of numbers 1 to 4 and 7 of article 20.

In a broader sense, we refer that the Portuguese Commercial Companies Code (CSC)[22], which refers in article 1 that commercial companies are those whose object is the practice of commercial acts and which adopt the type of collective name company, limited liability company, public limited company, limited partnership or limited joint stock company, establishes a set of duties to report their management and present their accounts.

Thus, pursuant to article 65 of the CSC, the members of the administration must prepare and submit to the competent bodies of the company the management report, including the non-financial statement or the separate report with this information, both referred to in articles 66-B and 508-G, when applicable, the accounts for the financial year, as well as the other documents of accountability foreseen in the law, relative to each annual financial year.

The preparation of the management report, including the non-financial statement or the separate report, when applicable, and of the accounts for the financial year, as well as the other accounting documents shall comply with the provisions of the law; the memorandum of association may complement, but not derogate from, such legal provisions.

The management report, the separate report with non-financial information, where applicable, and the accounts for the financial year shall be signed by all the members of the administration; any refusal to sign by any of them shall be justified in the document to which it refers and explained by to the competent body for its approval, even if has ceased functions.

The management report, the separate report with non-financial information, where applicable, and the accounts for the financial year shall be drawn up and signed by the managers or directors in office at the time of presentation, but the former members of the administration shall provide all information requested for that purpose concerning the period during which they held office.

The management report, the separate report with non-financial information, if applicable, the accounts for the financial year and other documents of accountability must be submitted to the competent body for consideration, except in special cases envisaged by law, within three months from the closing date of each annual financial year, or within five months from the same date in the case of companies which must present consolidated accounts or which apply the equity method.

In accordance with article 66 of the CSC, the management report must contain, among other aspects mentioned therein, at least a faithful and clear account of the evolution of the business, performance and position of the company, as well as a description of the main risks and uncertainties that it faces. To the extent necessary for an understanding of the company's development, performance or position, the analysis required by the previous paragraph should cover both financial and, where appropriate, non-financial performance references relevant to the company's specific activities, including information on environmental and employee matters. We may include here ESG issues and those arising from the Whistleblowing System, both for targeted employees (whistleblowers) and possible rewards for whistleblowing employees (whistleblowers).

Large companies that are public interest entities, which on the closing date of their balance sheet exceed an average number of 500 employees during the annual financial year, shall include in their management report a non-financial statement, pursuant to article 66-B of the CSC.

The non-financial statement shall contain sufficient information for an understanding of the development, performance, position and impact of its activities, concerning at least environmental, social and employee-related issues, equality between women and men, non-discrimination, respect for human rights, fighting corruption and attempted bribery, including: a brief description of the company's business model; a description of the policies followed by the company in relation to those issues, including the due diligence processes applied; the results of those policies; the main risks associated with those issues (including Badwill), linked to the company's activities, including, if relevant and proportionate, its business relationships, its products or services likely to have negative impacts on those areas and how those risks are managed by the company; and key performance indicators relevant to its specific activity.

Where an undertaking does not have policies in place in respect of one or more of the above issues, the non-financial statement should provide a clear and reasoned explanation as to why this is the case.

The non-financial statement referred to shall also include, where appropriate, a reference to the amounts reported in the annual financial statements and additional explanations relating to those amounts.

In exceptional cases, information concerning imminent facts or matters in the course of negotiation may be omitted, if there is a duly substantiated and signed opinion of the members of the management, direction and supervisory body as provided for numbers 3 and 4 in article 65, considering that the disclosure of such information is likely to seriously harm the commercial position of the company and provided that such omission does not constitute an obstacle to a correct and balanced understanding of the evolution, performance, position and impact of the company's activities. It will be the case to describe those involved in the Whistleblowing System process, in addition to the duty of confidentiality or anonymity provided for in Law No. 93/2021 of 20 December.

According to number 2 of article 70 of the CSC, the company must make available to interested parties, free of charge, on its website, when available, and at its head office, a full copy of the management report, among other documents. The best compliance practices require this, however, as we have seen, the matters that concern the Whistleblowing System may be succinct.

Among other competences, under the terms of article 420 of the CSC, it is the responsibility of the statutory auditor or supervisory board to: supervise the administration of the company; watch over the observance of the law; supervise the efficiency of the risk management system, the internal control system and the internal auditing system, if these exist; and receive the communications of irregularities presented by shareholders, employees of the company or others.

Likewise, it is the responsibility of the Chartered Accountant, under the terms of article 420 of the CSC, to immediately communicate, by registered letter, to the Chairman of the Board of Directors or of the Executive Board of Directors, any facts of which he may have knowledge and that he considers may reveal serious difficulties in the pursuit of the company's object.

Simultaneously, under the terms of article 422 of the CSC, the single auditor, the accounting officer or the members of the auditing board, if there is one, shall have the duty to, among others, exercise conscientious and impartial supervision; shall keep secret any facts and information that they have knowledge of by reason of their functions; shall inform the administration of the verifications, inspections and diligences that they have made and of the results of such verifications, inspections, complaints received and diligences that have been made and of the results of such verifications, inspections, complaints received and diligences.

The single auditor, the auditing officer and the members of the auditing board may not take advantage, except with the express authorisation of the general meeting, of commercial or industrial secrets that have come to their knowledge in the performance of their functions. The single auditor, the auditing officer and the members of the auditing board shall report to the Public Prosecution Service any misconduct of which they have become aware and which constitutes a public crime.

In its turn, it is the Audit Committee's responsibility, under the terms of article 423-F of the CSC, among other duties, to report to the Public Prosecutor's Office any misdemeanours of which it may have become aware and which constitute public crimes. The Audit Committee, under the terms of article 423-F of the CSC, is responsible for, among other duties, supervising the management of the company; supervising compliance with the law; elaborating an annual report on its supervisory action and issuing an opinion on the report, accounts and proposals presented by the management; supervising the efficiency of the risk management system, the internal control system and the internal audit system, if these exist; receiving reports of irregularities presented by shareholders, employees of the company or others; supervising the process of preparation and disclosure of financial information; and supervising the independence of the Chartered Accountant, notably with regard to the provision of additional services.

The members of the audit committee have the duty, among other duties, according to article 423-G of the CSC, to keep secret any facts and information of which they may have knowledge by virtue of their functions; and to record in writing all verifications, inspections, complaints received and steps taken and the results thereof.

However, there is an exception to the situation in which the chairman of the audit committee must inform the Public Prosecutor's Office of any misdemeanours of which becomes aware and which constitute public crimes.

Finally, it should be noted that, under the terms of article 441 of the Portuguese Companies Act, the general and supervisory board is responsible for The general and supervisory board is responsible, among other tasks, for supervising the activities of the executive board of directors; monitoring compliance with the law; issuing an opinion on the management report and accounts for the financial year; supervising the effectiveness of the risk management system, the internal control system and the internal audit system, if any; receiving reports of irregularities submitted by shareholders, company employees or others; supervising the process of preparation and disclosure of financial information; supervising the audit of the company's financial statements; or supervising the independence of the statutory auditor, in particular with regard to the provision of additional services.

The members of the general and supervisory board are obliged to keep secret any facts and information of which they may have knowledge by virtue of their functions (as per article 441-A of the CSC).

CONCLUSION

In the globalised information society, it has been recurrent to make information available in the public sphere (public disclosure) of situations of fraud, corruption, mismanagement or harmful administration, arbitrariness or transgressions in general.

The strategy to combat corruption, fraud and irregularities has become the search for a culture that encourages ethically acceptable conduct on the part of workers and favours responsible and transparent attitudes.

With the objective of ensuring the reliability and credibility of financial information, protecting stakeholders, the Whistleblowing System translates into the creation of conditions for the reporting of irregular behaviour capable of seriously affecting the activity of organisations. In this context, this mechanism (often also synonymous with an ethical decision to act, i.e. to blow the whistle)[23] can make an important contribution to the adoption of an efficient professional conduct (preventive) and an effective internal control (reactive). The Whistleblowing System may be understood as a preventive and internal control mechanism, for the detection of errors and or irregularities (mitigating and or repressing irregularities).

In Portugal, the Whistleblowing System is already a reality, although unknown to many people, either due to the dispersed regulations (recommendations and sectorial laws) that support it, or due to the way in which some irregularities are being reported and which, therefore, generate the need for special protection, beyond the cover of labour legislation, of whistleblowers in a professional context, either with the new legal obligations arising from Law No. 93/2021, of 20 December, which establishes the General Whistleblower Protection Scheme.

The rationale of preventing and fighting poor practices, mitigating coorperative or social (public) judgements in a broad sense, goes beyond the legal and financial dimension and for this reason, in the last decades, an attempt has been made to safeguard the personal data of the individuals involved and the reputation of the organisations, betting heavily on the Whistleblowing System.

As mentioned by Albuquerque and Simões (2021), the existence of a system of qualified reporting of malpractices (whistleblowing) may constitute a criterion of increase, demand and investment interest by stakeholders.

The financial sector, quite exposed to fraud and corruption, has developed legal prerogatives that require the implementation of the Whistleblowing System, leading managers and directors of private companies or public corporate entities to take into consideration management tools, namely whistleblowing channels that protect whistleblowers, as well as management reports that contemplate the impacts of the Whistleblowing System, positive and negative, in a generic way, in their organisations.

As we have seen there are several duties related to the reporting of irregularities and several intervening parties, namely statutory auditors, sole auditors, members of the supervisory board, audit committees and general and supervisory boards who must ensure the possibility and promotion of the communication of irregularities, and therefore the impact of the Whistleblowing System on their activity reports is remarkable.

REFERENCES

Albuquerque, F., & Simões, P. P. (2021). Whistleblowing e goodwill: o que os aproxima para além da terminologia em língua inglesa? In *Compliance y lucha contra la corrupción en España, Portugal e Iberoamérica, da Editora Dykison, Directores Pinto, F. L. C. P., Coutinho, F. P. & Benito, I. L., Coordinadores, García, B. P., de Castro, J. M. G., & Simões*. P. P. Editorial Dykinson. doi:10.2307/j.ctv2gz3vk1.23

Association of Certified Fraud Examiners – ACFE. (2022). *Occupational Fraud 2022: A Report to the Nations*. ACFE: https://legacy.acfe.com/report-to-the-nations/2022/

Barbosa, C. (2012). *Mecanismo de Whistleblowing nas organizações: o caso das empresas cotadas na Euro Next Lisboa*. Instituto Superior de Contabilidade e Administração de Lisboa do Instituto Politécnico de Lisboa (ISCAL).

Carrigy, C. (2005). *Denúncia de Irregularidades no Seio das Empresas (Corporate Wistleblowing)*. Cadernos do Mercado de Valores Mobiliários. https://www.cmvm.pt/pt/EstatisticasEstudosEPublicacoes/CadernosDoMercadoDeValoresMobiliarios/Documents/7c55e782cd6743fbb2320e72021a6335CelinaCarrigy.pdf

Marçal, D. (2014). *Pseudociência*. Fundação Francisco Manuel dos Santos. Relógio D'Água Editores.

Matias, T. S. (2022). Os caminhos cruzados da solidariedade defensiva e da comunicação de irregularidades (whistleblowing) no sector financeiro. In *O Whistleblowing em Portugal – Proteção do Denunciante nas Organizações. Coordenadores Maia, A. J & Simões*. P. P. Editora Almedina.

Near, J. P., & Miceli, M. P. (1996). Whistle-blowing: Myth and reality. *Journal of Management*, *22*(3), 507–526. doi:10.1177/014920639602200306

Schmidt, M. (2005, June). *"Whistle Blowing" Regulation and Accounting Standards Enforcement in Germany and Europe* – an Economic Perspective. *International Review of Law and Economics*, *25*(2), 143–168. doi:10.1016/j.irle.2005.06.001

Simões, P. P. (2019). *O Whistleblowing em Portugal. Será que pode ser praticado pelo auditor?* Revisores Ǝ Auditores, revista da Ordem dos Revisores Oficiais de Contas. http://hdl.handle.net/10400.21/11354

Simões, P. P. (2020). O Whistleblowing é um caso de Polícia(s)? In *Polícias(s) e segurança Pública – História e Perspetivas Contemporâneas. Coordenadores Rollo, M. F., Gomes, P. M., Rodrígues, A. C.* Editor MUP – Museu da Polícia. http://hdl.handle.net/10400.21/12526

Trongmateerut, P., & Sweeney, J. T. (2013). The influence of subjective norms on whistle-blowing: A cross-cultural investigation. *Journal of Business Ethics*, *112*(3), 437–451. doi:10.100710551-012-1270-1

ENDNOTES

1 An international non-profit organisation, which publishes documents, photos and information on sensitive or confidential matters on its website.

2 Who gave the newspapers details of the global surveillance of communications and information traffic, executed by the USA.

3 Electronic platform in which information on football players and clubs was exposed, generating tax lawsuits.

4 Official documents that detail processes developed by the State of Malta to organize tax evasion to the European Union.

5 Name given to the investigation developed by the International Consortium of Investigative Journalists, which disclosed in several media, documents that indicate that, among other people, Isabel dos Santos obtained several favors because of the position of her father, former president of Angola.

6 In which someone calling himself "John Doe" revealed confidential documents in the custody of the Mossack Fonseca law firm.

7 As mentioned by Simões (2019, p. 9) among others such as those entitled: Adecco, Adelphia, Ahold, AOL, Goldman Sachs, Lehman Brothers, Madoff, Nortel, Tyco, Vivendi, the Xerox E, or, even, Operation Lava Jato and the Mensalão Scandal, or the disclosures made through WikiLeaks, the Panama Papers or LuxLeaks.

8 As is the case with Trongmateerut & Sweeney (2013), that use the commonly accepted definition of whistle-blowing offered by Near and Miceli (1985, p. 4): «the disclosure by organization members (former or current) of illegal, immoral, or illegitimate practices under the control of their employers, to persons or organizations that may be able to effect action».

9 Under sections 301 (corporate responsibility of the audit committee in listed companies); 806 (civil counter-retaliation protection in fraud cases); and 1107 (retaliation against whistleblowers). According to Carrigy (2005), whistleblowing by an employee of an institution of alleged illegalities occurring at that same institution was first specifically regulated in the US in an 1863 law, the False Claims Act, established to combat fraud by federal government suppliers during the civil war.

10 According to Article 21 of the Portuguese Civil Code, approved by Decree-Law 47344 of November 25, 1966, as amended, fraud against the law is the de facto or de jure situation created with the intention of avoiding the applicability of the law which, under other circumstances, would be competent.

11 Recommendation 2005/162/EC of 15 February 2005 on the role of non-executive or supervisory directors of listed companies and on the committees of the (supervisory) board. For reasons of limitation of the object and objectives under study, previous documents are not addressed, such as the Communication from the Commission - Completing the reform mandate: progress report and measures to be implemented in 2004 - which in its point 4.4. envisaged the denunciation of irregularities.

12 As per paragraph 8 of point 4.3 of Annex I of the Recommendation.

13 Complying with the Council Framework Decision 2003/568/JAI of 22 July.

14 This Law made the first amendment to Law 5/2002, of 11 January, the seventeenth amendment to the General Tax Law and the third amendment to Law 4/83, of 2 April.

15 With the amendments introduced by Law No. 30/2015 of 24 April, which made the thirty-fifth amendment to the Criminal Code; sixth amendment to Law 34/87 of 16 July; first amendment to Law No. 20/2008 of 21 April; first amendment to Law No. 50/2007 of 31 August; and first amendment to Law 19/2008 of 21 April. No. 19/2008, of April 21, in order to comply with the recommendations addressed to Portugal on corruption by the Council of Europe's Group of States against Corruption, by the United Nations and by the Organisation for Economic Cooperation and Development.

16 Some call it Anti-Fraud Policy, Warning Lines, Irregularity Communication or Reporting Channels. For further developments see Simões (2019).

17 More restrictive than the regime provided for by the Public Interest Disclosure Act in the United Kingdom, or that of SOX in the USA. Schmidt (2005) points out that the legal-labour context of these legal systems is different from continental Europe, where the legal mechanisms for worker protection are more perfected, namely in requiring the dismissal procedure and the application of penalties in the event of non-compliance, or even the existence of trade union associations.

18 Barbosa (2012), despite mentioning in her dissertation the Deliberation of the National Data Protection Commission, with mandatory force under paragraph 3, of article 23 of the then in force Personal Data Protection Act, stated that in Portugal there was only a recommendation from the Securities Market Commission, concerning listed companies, on the adoption of a whistleblowing policy and that the reporting of illegalities within the company by employees or other persons linked to the activity, was not specifically regulated in the Portuguese legislation. One cannot agree with this restrictive interpretation of the legal system as a whole. If there were any doubts about the existence of regulations applicable in Portugal, see for example recitals 7 and 9 of Directive 2019/1937, of 23 October. This last recital refers to an intriguing concept (just culture - protection of workers who report errors committed by them in good faith against acts of retaliation) that is not developed, but its future analysis is noted.

19 Such as WeMoveEurope which organised an international petition for an EU-wide law to protect whistleblowers; or Transparency International (with several affiliates, including the Portuguese Transparency and Integrity Civic Association), an association whose mission is to stop corruption and promote transparency, accountability and integrity at all levels and in all sectors of society.

[20] Encouraged, in the European Union, and especially in Portugal, by the former MEP Dr Ana Gomes.

[21] Amended by Decree-Law No. 144/2019, of 23 September; Law No. 58/2020, of 31 August; Decree-Law No. 9/2021, of 29 January; Decree-Law No. 56/2021, of 30 June and Law No. 99-A/2021, of 31 December.

[22] Approved by Decree-Law 262/86, of 2 September, in its current version.

[23] It should not be seen only and solely as a communication, but rather as a set of operations that involve the analysis and weighing of value judgements on the consequences of the complaint, and the complaint itself.

Compilation of References

Abhayawansa, S., & Adams, S. A. (2022). Towards a conceptual framework for non-financial reporting inclusive of pandemic and climate risk reporting. *Meditari Accountancy Research*, *30*(2), 710–738. doi:10.1108/MEDAR-11-2020-1097

ACCA. (2017). IPSAS implementation: Current status and challenges. *Professional insight report*. ACCA.

ACFE. (2022). *Occupational Fraud 2022: A report to the Nations*. ACFE. https://legacy.acfe.com/report-to-the-nations/2022/

Achenbach, M. (2021). Transparency of Climate-Related Risks and Opportunities: Determinants Influencing the Disclosure in Line with the Task Force on Climate-Related Financial Disclosures. *Globality*, *4*(1), 1–20. doi:10.5334/glo.32

Achleitner, A. K., Günther, N., Kaserer, C., & Siciliano, G. (2014). Real earnings management and accrual-based earnings management in family firms. *European Accounting Review*, *23*(3), 431–461. doi:10.1080/09638180.2014.895620

Adams, C. (2017). Conceptualizing the contemporary corporate value creation process. *Accounting, Auditing & Accountability Journal*, *30*(4), 906–931. https://doi.org/https://doi.org/10.1108/AAAJ-04-2016-2529. doi:10.1108/AAAJ-04-2016-2529

Adams, C. A., & Abhayawansa, S. (2022). Connecting the COVID-19 pandemic, environmental, social, and governance (ESG) investing and calls for 'harmonisation' of sustainability reporting. *Critical Perspectives on Accounting*, *82*, 102309. doi:10.1016/j.cpa.2021.102309

Adm Working Group On Risk Management. (2000). Risk Management for Canada and Canadians: Report of the ADM Working Group on Risk Management. Ottawa: Privy Council Office (PCO), Government of Canada.

AICPA. (2014). *Professional Responsibilities*. AICPA. https://us.aicpa.org/interestareas/personalfinancialplanning/resources/practicecenter/professionalresponsibilities

Ajinkya, B., Bhojraj, S., & Sengupta, P. (2005). The association between outside directors, institutional investors and the properties of management earnings forecasts. *Journal of Accounting Research*, *43*(3), 343–376. doi:10.1111/j.1475-679x.2005.00174.x

Akram, M. U., Ghosh, K., & Sharma, D. (2022). A systematic review of innovation in family firms and future research agenda. *International Journal of Emerging Markets*, *17*(7), 1759–1792. doi:10.1108/IJOEM-06-2021-0936

Al-Adeem, K. R. (2019). Who decides what is publishable? Empirical study on the influence of a journal's editorial board on the observed paradigm shift in US academic accounting research. *The North American Accounting Studies*, *2*(1), 1-21. https://papers.ssrn.com/sol3/papers.cfm?abstract_id=4127109

Albu, O. B., & Flyverbom, M. (2019). Organizational transparency: Conceptualizations, conditions, and consequences. *Business & Society*, *58*(2), 268–297. doi:10.1177/0007650316659851

Albuquerque, F., & Simões, P. P. (2021). Whistleblowing e goodwill: o que os aproxima para além da terminologia em língua inglesa? In *Compliance y lucha contra la corrupción en España, Portugal e Iberoamérica, da Editora Dykison, Directores Pinto, F. L. C. P., Coutinho, F. P. & Benito, I. L., Coordinadores, García, B. P., de Castro, J. M. G., & Simões*. P. P. Editorial Dykinson. doi:10.2307/j.ctv2gz3vk1.23

Ali, A., Chen, T., & Radhakrishnan, S. (2007). Corporate disclosure by family firms. *Journal of Accounting and Economics*, *44*(1–2), 238–286. doi:10.1016/j.jacceco.2007.01.006

Almatrooshi, B., Singh, S. K., & Farouk, S. (2016). Determinants of organizational performance: A proposed framework. *International Journal of Productivity and Performance Management*, *65*(6), 844–859. doi:10.1108/IJPPM-02-2016-0038

Amar, J., Rigot, S., & Demaria, S. (2022). *What are the drivers of Corporates' climate transparency? Evidence from S.* Index.

Amiram, D., Jørgensen, B. N., & Rabetti, D. (2022). Coins for bombs: The predictive ability of on-chain transfers for terrorist attacks. *Journal of Accounting Research*, *60*(2), 427–466. doi:10.1111/1475-679X.12430

Anderson, N. (2019). IFRS Standards and climate-related disclosures. In *Brief Climate-related and other emerging risks disclosures: Assessing financial statement materiality.* https://www.ifrs.org/content/dam/ifrs/news/2019/november/in-brief-climate-change-nick-anderson.pdf

Anderson, R. C., & Reeb, D. M. (2003). Founding family ownership and firm performance: Evidence from the S&P 500. *The Journal of Finance*, *58*(3), 1301–1328. doi:10.1111/1540-6261.00567

Andreaus, M., & Costa, E. (2014). Toward an integrated accountability model for nonprofit organizations. In Costa, E., Parker, D. L., and Andreaus, M. (Eds). Accountability and social accounting for social and nonprofit organizations (pp. 37–106). Howard House: Emerald.

Andreini, D., Bettinelli, C., Pedeliento, G., & Apa, R. (2020). How do consumers see firms' family nature? A review of the literature. *Family Business Review*, *33*(1), 18–37. doi:10.1177/0894486519890229

Ang, J. S., Coles, R. A., & Lin, J. W. (2000). Agency costs and ownership structure. *The Journal of Finance*, *55*(1), 81–106. doi:10.1111/0022-1082.00201

Antle, R. (1982). The auditor as an economic agent. *Journal of Accounting Research*, *20*(2), 503–527. doi:10.2307/2490884

Antosz, D. (2022). The best free invoicing software in 2022. *Zapier.* https://zapier.com/blog/best-free-invoice-software/

Antunes, M. T. P., Grecco, M. C. P., Formigoni, H., & Neto, O. R. D. M. (2012). A adoção no Brasil das normas internacionais de contabilidade IFRS: O processo e seus impactos na qualidade da informação contábil. *Revista de Economia e Relações Internacionais*, *10*(20), 5–19.

Apostolopoulos, N., Newbery, R., & Gkartzios, M. (2019). Social enterprise and community resilience: Examining a Greek response to turbulent times. *Journal of Rural Studies*, *70*, 215–224.

Appelbaum, D., & Nehmer, R. A. (2020). Auditing cloud-based blockchain accounting systems. *Journal of Information Systems*, *34*(2), 5–21. doi:10.2308/isys-52660

Appio, J., Scharmach, Alr, Silva, Akld, Carvalho, Lcd, & Sampaio, Cac. (2009). SWOT analysis as a competitive differential: An exploratory study in Cooperativa Muza Brasil. *Revista Interdisciplinar Científica Aplicada*, *3*(3), 1–18.

Aras, G., Aybars, A., & Kutlu, O. (2010). Managing corporate performance: Investigating the relationship between corporate social responsibility and financial performance in emerging markets. *International Journal of Productivity and Performance Management*, *59*(3), 229–254. doi:10.1108/17410401011023573

Arslanian, H., & Fischer, F. (2019). Blockchain as an enabling technology. In *The Future of Finance* (pp. 113–121). Palgrave Macmillan., doi:10.1007/978-3-030-14533-0_10

Asay, H. S., Elliott, W. B., & Rennekamp, K. (2017). Disclosure readability and the sensitivity of investors' valuation judgments to outside information. *The Accounting Review*, *92*(4), 1–25. doi:10.2308/accr-51570

Ashbaugh-Skaife, H., Collins, D. W., Kinney, W. R. Jr, & Lafond, R. (2009). The effect of SOX internal control deficiencies on firm risk and cost of equity. *Journal of Accounting Research*, *47*(1), 1–43. doi:10.1111/j.1475-679X.2008.00315.x

Aslan, H. (2022). Personal financial distress, limited attention. *Journal of Accounting Research*, *60*(1), 97–128. doi:10.1111/1475-679X.12409

Association of Certified Fraud Examiners – ACFE. (2022). *Occupational Fraud 2022: A Report to the Nations.* ACFE: https://legacy.acfe.com/report-to-the-nations/2022/

Astrachan, J. H., Klein, S. B., & Smyrnios, K. X. (2002). The F-PEC scale of family influence: A proposal for solving the family business definition problem. *Family Business Review*, *15*(1), 45–58. doi:10.1111/j.1741-6248.2002.00045.x

Attig, N., Boubakri, N., Ghoul, S., & Guedhami, O. (2015). The global financial crisis, family control, and dividend policy. *Financial Management*, *45*(2), 291–313. doi:10.1111/fima.12115

Atzori, M. (2017). Blockchain Technology and Decentralized Governance: Is the State Still Necessary? *Journal of Governance and Regulation*, *6*(1), 45–62. doi:10.22495/jgr_v6_i1_p5

Avison, D. E., Davison, R. M., & Malaurent, J. (2018). Information systems action research: Debunking myths and overcoming barriers. *Information & Management*, *55*(2), 177-187. doi:10.1016/j.im.2017.05.004

Avison, D. E., Lau, F., Myers, M., & Nielsen, P. A. (1999). Action research. *Communications of the ACM*, *42*(1), 94–97. doi:10.1145/291469.291479

Baba, H. Ishida, & Y., Aoki, T. (2015). Social Accounting for Nonprofit Organizations: Visualizing the Invisible Value of Social Impacts. Kansai University Review of Business and Commerce, 16, 1–22. Retrieved from: http://baba-hi72.up.seesaa.net/image/KandaiReview2015_baba_etal.pdf

Bae, S. C., Chang, K., & Yi, H. C. (2018). Corporate social responsibility, credit rating, and private debt contracting: New evidence from the syndicated loan market. *Review of Quantitative Finance and Accounting*, *50*(1), 261–299. doi:10.100711156-017-0630-4

Baker, H. E., & Kare, D. D. (1992). Relationship between annual report readability and corporate financial performance. *Management Research News*, *15*(1), 1–4. doi:10.1108/eb028188

Ball, R. (2009). Market and political/regulatory perspectives on the recent accounting scandals. *Journal of Accounting Research*, *47*(2), 277–323. doi:10.1111/j.1475-679X.2009.00325.x

Ball, R., Li, X., & Shivakumar, L. (2015). Contractibility and transparency of financial statement information prepared under IFRS: Evidence from debt contracts around IFRS adoption. *Journal of Accounting Research*, *53*(5), 915–963. doi:10.1111/1475-679X.12095

Balzano, M. (2022). Serendipity in management studies: A literature review and future research directions. *Management Decision*, *60*(13), 130–152. doi:10.1108/MD-02-2022-0245

Bao, Y., Ke, B., Li, B., Yu, Y. J., & Zhang, J. (2020). Detecting accounting fraud in publicly traded U.S. firms using a machine learning approach. *Journal of Accounting Research*, *58*(1), 199–235. doi:10.1111/1475-679X.12292

Baraibar-Díez, E., Odrizola, M. D., & Fernández-Sánchez, J. L. (2017). A survey of transparency: An intrinsic aspect of business strategy. *Business Strategy and the Environment*, *26*(4), 480–489. doi:10.1002/bse.1931

Barbosa, C. (2012). *Mecanismo de Whistleblowing nas organizações: o caso das empresas cotadas na Euro Next Lisboa*. Instituto Superior de Contabilidade e Administração de Lisboa do Instituto Politécnico de Lisboa (ISCAL).

Barrios, J. M., Bianchi, P. A., Isidro, H., & Nanda, D. (2022). Boards of a feather: Homophily in foreign director appointments around the world. *Journal of Accounting Research*, *60*(4), 1293–1335. doi:10.1111/1475-679X.12416

Barth, M. (2018). Accounting in 2036: A learned profession. *The Accounting Review*, *93*(6), 383–385. doi:10.2308/accr-10627

Barth, M. E., Landsman, W. R., & Lang, M. H. (2008). International accounting standards and accounting quality. *Journal of Accounting Research*, *46*(3), 467–498. doi:10.1111/j.1475-679X.2008.00287.x

Basheer, M. F., Gupta, S., Raoof, R., & Waemustafa, W. (2021). Revisiting the agency conflicts in family owned pyramidal business structures: A case of an emerging market. *Cogent Economics & Finance*, *9*(1), 1–18. doi:10.1080/23322039.2021.1926617

Bashkar, K., & Flower, J. (2021). *Disruption in Financial Reporting A Post-pandemic View of the Future of Corporate Reporting*. Routledge.

Baskerville, R., & Grossi, G. (2019). Glocalization of accounting standards: Observations on neo-institutionalism of IPSAS. *Public Money & Management*, *39*(2), 101–110. doi:10.1080/09540962.2019.1580894

Bebbington, J., & Gray, R. (2007). Corporate Accountability and the Physical Environment: Social Responsibility and Accounting Beyond Profit. *Business Strategy and the Environment*, *2*, 1–11. doi:10.1002/bse.3280020201

Bebbington, J., & Unerman, J. (2020, October 20). Advancing research into accounting and the UN Sustainable Development Goals. *Accounting, Auditing & Accountability Journal*, *33*(7), 1657–1670. doi:10.1108/AAAJ-05-2020-4556

Beck, A. C., Campbell, D., & Shrives, P. J. (2010). Content Analysis in Environmental Reporting Research: Enrichment and Rehearsal of the Method in a British-German Context. *The British Accounting Review*, *42*(3), 207–222. doi:10.1016/j.bar.2010.05.002

Ben Amor, D., & Damak Ayadi, S. (2019). The profile of IPSAS-adopters. *Journal of Accounting and Management Information Systems*, *18*(2), 262–282.

Ben-Amar, W., & André, P. (2006). Separation of ownership from control and acquiring firm performance: The case of family ownership in Canada. *Journal of Business Finance & Accounting*, *33*(3-4), 517–543. doi:10.1111/j.1468-5957.2006.00613.x

Ben-Nasr, H., Boubakri, N., & Cosset, J. (2012). The political determinants of the cost of equity: Evidence from newly privatized firms. *Journal of Accounting Research*, *50*(3), 605–646. doi:10.1111/j.1475-679X.2011.00435.x

Berger, P. G., & Lee, H. (2022). Did the Dodd–Frank whistleblower provision deter accounting fraud? *Journal of Accounting Research*, *60*(4), 1337–1378. doi:10.1111/1475-679X.12421

Berrone, P., Cruz, C., & Gómez-Mejía, L. R. (2012). Socioemotional wealth in family firms: Theoretical dimensions, assessment approaches, and agenda for future research. *Family Business Review*, *25*(3), 258–279. doi:10.1177/0894486511435355

Bhatta, G. (2003). Post-NPM issues. In Public Sector Governance, Wellington: State Services Commission. Working Paper no. 17.

Bidabad, B., Amirostovar, A., & Sherafati, M. (2017). Financial transparency, corporate governance and information disclosure of the entrepreneur's corporation in Rastin banking. *International Journal of Law and Management*, *59*(5), 636–651. doi:10.1108/IJLMA-01-2016-0003

Biondi, L., & Lapsley, I. (2014). Accounting, transparency and governance: The heritage assets problem. *Qualitative Research in Accounting & Management*, *11*(2), 146–164. doi:10.1108/QRAM-04-2014-0035

Bischof, J., Daske, H., & Sextroh, C. J. (2020). Why do politicians intervene in accounting regulation? the role of ideology and special interests. *Journal of Accounting Research*, *58*(3), 589–642. doi:10.1111/1475-679X.12300

Bisogno, M., Manes-Rossi, F., & Sicilia, M. (2022). Designing international public sector accounting standards: An analysis of constituents' participation through comment letters. *Financial Accountability & Management*, *38*(4), 661–685. doi:10.1111/faam.12343

Bisogno, M., Santis, S., & Tommasetti, A. (2015). Public-Sector Consolidated Financial Statements: An Analysis of the Comment Letters on IPSASB's Exposure Draft No. 49. *International Journal of Public Administration*, *38*(4), 311–324. doi:10.1080/01900692.2015.999605

Black, C. M. (2013). Accounting for Carbon Emission Allowances in the European Union: In Search of Consistency. Accounting in Europe, 10(2), 223–239. doi:10.1080/17449480.2013.834730

Block, J., & Wagner, M. (2014). The effect of family ownership on different dimensions of corporate social responsibility: Evidence from large US firms. *Business Strategy and the Environment*, *23*(7), 475–492. doi:10.1002/bse.1798

Bonsall, S. B. IV, Leone, A. J., Miller, B. P., & Rennekamp, K. (2017). A plain English measure of financial reporting readability. *Journal of Accounting and Economics*, *63*(2-3), 329–357. doi:10.1016/j.jacceco.2017.03.002

Bonsón, E., & Bednárová, M. (2019). Blockchain and its implications for accounting and auditing. *Meditari Accountancy Research*, *27*(5), 725–740. doi:10.1108/MEDAR-11-2018-0406

Borges, G. F. (2020). *Análise da Legibilidade dos BR_GAAP X Legibilidade das Notas Explicativas de Empresas Brasileiras Abertas*. [Doctoral dissertation, Universidade de São Paulo, São Paulo, SP].

Borralho, J. M., Hernández-Linares, R., Vázquez, D. G., & Paiva, I. (2022). Environmental, social and governance disclosure's impacts on earnings management: Family versus non-family firms. *Journal of Cleaner Production*, *379*, 134603. doi:10.1016/j.jclepro.2022.134603

Borralho, J., Gallardo-Vázquez, D., & Hernández-Linares, R. (2020a). Earnings management in private family versus non-family firms. The moderate effect on family business generation. Spanish Journal of Finance and Accounting / Revista Española de Financiación y Contabilidad, *49*(2), 210–233. doi:10.1080/02102412.2019.1616480

Borralho, J., Gallardo-Vázquez, D., Hernández-Linares, R., & Paiva, I. (2020b). The effect of corporate governance factors on the quality of financial reporting in family and non-family firms. *Revista de Contabilidad/Spanish Accounting Review*, *23*(2), 167–179. doi:10.6018/rcsar.358451

Borzaga, C., & Galera, E. (2014). New Trends in the Nonprofit sector in Europe: The emergence of social enterprises. In E. Costa, D. L. Parker, & M. Andreaus (Eds.), *The Accountability and Social Accounting for Social and Non-profit Organisations* (pp. 107–130). Emerald.

Borzaga, C., & Tortia, E. (2010). The economics of social enterprises. In L. Becchetti & C. Borzaga (Eds.), *The Economics of Social Responsibility, The world of social enterprises* (pp. 15–33). Routledge.

Botosan, C. A., & Plumlee, M. A. (2002). A re-examination of disclosure level and the expected cost of equity capital. *Journal of Accounting Research*, *40*(1), 21–40. doi:10.1111/1475-679X.00037

Boubaker, S., Derouiche, I., & Nguyen, H. (2022). Voluntary disclosure, tax avoidance and family firms. *The Journal of Management and Governance*, *26*(1), 129–158. doi:10.100710997-021-09601-w

Bourveau, T., She, G., & Žaldokas, A. (2020). Corporate disclosure as a tacit coordination mechanism: Evidence from cartel enforcement regulations. *Journal of Accounting Research*, *58*(2), 295–332. doi:10.1111/1475-679X.12301

Bozzolan, S., Fabrizi, M., Mallin, C. A., & Michelon, G. (2015). Corporate social responsibility and earnings quality: International evidence. *The International Journal of Accounting*, *50*(4), 361–396. doi:10.1016/j.intacc.2015.10.003

Brahem, E., Depoers, F., & Lakhal, F. (2022). Corporate social responsibility and earnings quality in family firms. *Journal of Applied Accounting Research*, *23*(5), 1114–1134. doi:10.1108/JAAR-05-2021-0139

Bravo, F. (2015). Forward-looking disclosure and corporate reputation as mechanisms to reduce stock return volatility. *Revista de Contabilidad/Spanish Accounting Review*, *19*(1), 122–131. doi:10.1016/j.rcsar.2015.03.001

Brazil Court of Auditors of the Union. (2014). Referencial Básico de governança aplicável aos órgãos e entidades da administração pública. Brasília: Secretariat of Planning, Governance and Management.

Breijer, R., & Orij, R. P. (2022). The Comparability of Non-Financial Information: An Exploration of the Impact of the Non-Financial Reporting Directive (NFRD, 2014/95/EU). *Accounting in Europe*, *19*(May), 332–361. doi:10.1080/17449480.2022.2065645

Brown, J., & Fraser, M. (2006). Approaches and Perspectives in Social and Environmental Accounting: An Overview of the Conceptual Landscape. *Business Strategy and the Environment*, *15*, 309–321. doi:10.1080/0969160X.2021.1872397

Brown, N. C., Christensen, T. E., Elliott, W. B., & Mergenthaler, R. D. (2012). Investor sentiment and pro forma earnings disclosures. *Journal of Accounting Research*, *50*(1), 1–40. doi:10.1111/j.1475-679X.2011.00427.x

Brown, N. C., Crowley, R. M., & Elliott, W. B. (2020). What are you saying? using topic to detect financial misreporting. *Journal of Accounting Research*, *58*(1), 237–291. doi:10.1111/1475-679X.12294

Buffa, D. W. (2005). *Breach of Trust*. Allen & Unwin.

Bushee, B. J., & Noe, C. F. (2000). Corporate disclosure practices, institutional investors, and stock return volatility. *Journal of Accounting Research*, *38*(SUPPL.), 171–202. doi:10.2307/2672914

Bushman, R. M., Piotroski, J. D., & Smith, A. J. (2004). What determines corporate transparency? *Journal of Accounting Research*, *42*(2), 207–252. doi:10.1111/j.1475-679X.2004.00136.x

BushmanR. M.SmithA. J. (2003). Transparency, financial accounting information, and corporate governance. *Economic Policy Review*, *32*(1-3), 237-333. Available at SSRN: https://ssrn.com/abstract=795547

Byard, D., Li, Y., & Yu, Y. (2011). The effect of mandatory IFRS adoption on financial analysts' information environment. *Journal of Accounting Research*, *49*(1), 69–96. doi:10.1111/j.1475-679X.2010.00390.x

Bychkova, S. M., Karelskaia, S. N., Abdalova, E. B., & Zhidkova, E. A. (2021). Social responsibility as the dominant driver of the evolution of reporting from financial to non-financial: Theory and methodology. *Foods and Raw Materials*, *9*(1), 135–145. doi:10.21603/2308-4057-2021-1-135-145

Cabrera-Suárez, K., De Saa-Pérez, P., & Garcia-Almeida, D. (2001). The succession process from a resource-and knowledge-based view of the family firm. *Family Business Review*, *14*(1), 37–48. doi:10.1111/j.1741-6248.2001.00037.x

Cabrera-Suárez, M. K., Déniz-Déniz, M. C., & Martín-Santana, J. D. (2014). The setting of non-financial goals in the family firm: The influence of family climate and identification. *Journal of Family Business Strategy*, *5*(3), 289–299. doi:10.1016/j.jfbs.2014.05.003

Cai, C. W. (2021). Triple-entry accounting with blockchain: How far have we come? *Accounting and Finance*, *61*(1), 71–93. doi:10.1111/acfi.12556

Call, A. C., Martin, G. S., Sharp, N. Y., & Wilde, J. H. (2018). Whistleblowers and outcomes of financial misrepresentation enforcement actions. *Journal of Accounting Research*, *56*(1), 123–171. doi:10.1111/1475-679X.12177

Callon, M. (1986a). ÉLÉMENTS POUR UNE SOCIOLOGIE DE LA TRADUCTION: La domestication des coquilles Saint-Jacques et des marins-pêcheurs dans la baie de Saint-Brieuc. *L'Année sociologique*, *16*, 169–208.

Callon, M. (1986b). Some elements of a sociology of translation: domestication of the scallops and the fishermen of St Brieuc Bay. In J. Law (Ed.), *Power, action and belief: a new sociology of knowledge?* (pp. 196–223). Routledge.

Campopiano, G., Gabaldón, P., & Giménez-Jiménez, D. (2022). Women directors and corporate social performance: An integrative review of the literature and a future research agenda. *Journal of Business Ethics*. Advance online publication. doi:10.100710551-021-04999-7

Carlin, T. (2018). Blockchain and the journey beyond double entry. *Australian Accounting Review*, *29*(2), 305–311. doi:10.1111/auar.12273

Carnegie, G., Parker, L., & Tsahuridu, E. (2021). It's 2020: What is accounting today? *Australian Accounting Review*, *31*(1), 65–73. doi:10.1111/auar.12325

Carney, M., van Essen, M., Gedajlovic, E. R., & Heugens, P. P. (2015). What do we know about private family firms? A meta-analytical review. *Entrepreneurship Theory and Practice*, *39*(3), 513–544. doi:10.1111/etap.12054

Carrigy, C. (2005). *Denúncia de Irregularidades no Seio das Empresas (Corporate Wistleblowing)*. Cadernos do Mercado de Valores Mobiliários. https://www.cmvm.pt/pt/EstatisticasEstudosEPublicacoes/CadernosDoMercadoDeValoresMobiliarios/Documents/7c55e782cd6743fbb 2320e72021a6335CelinaCarrigy.pdf

Caruana, J. (2019). Shades of governmental financial reporting with a national accounting twist. *Accounting Forum*, *40*(3), 153–165. doi:10.1016/j.accfor.2016.06.002

Cascino, S., Pugliese, A., Mussolino, D., & Sasone, C. (2010). The influence of family ownership on the quality of accounting information. *Family Business Review*, *23*(3), 246–265. doi:10.1177/0894486510374302

Castilhos, S. Pereira. (2016). *Pylinguistics: an open source library for readability assessment of texts written in Portuguese*. [Graduate school dissertation, Universidade Federal do Rio Grande do Sul, Porto Alegre, RS].

Cavalcanti, L. M. R., & Guerra, M. G. G. V. (2019). Institutional diagnosis of the Federal University of Paraíba from SWOT Analysis. *Electronic Journal of Social Development*, (33), 120–137. doi:10.22347/2175-2753v11i33.2270

Cavanagh, J., Flynn, S., & Moretti, D. (2016). *Implementing Accrual Accounting in the Public Sector. Technical Notes and Manuals*. International Monetary Fund - Fiscal Affairs Department.

Cawkwell, S. (2021). *Mandatory Corporate Social Responsibility Reporting; The way forward for more Sustainable Companies? LAWS521: Organisational Law*. Victoria University of Wellington.

Chan, J., & Chan, E. (2010). Social Audits. In: Anheier, K.H., Toepler, S., List, R. (Eds). *International Encyclopedia of Civil Society, 1384-1388*. New York: Springer. https://doi.org/10.1007/978-0-387-93996-4

Chaney, P. K., & Lewis, C. M. (1995). Earnings management and firm valuation under asymmetric information. *Journal of Corporate Finance*, *1*(3-4), 319–345. doi:10.1016/0929-1199(94)00008-I

Chang, J., Cho, Y. J., & Shin, H. H. (2007). The change in corporate transparency of Korean firms after the Asian financial crisis: An analysis using analysts' forecast data. *Corporate Governance*, *15*(6), 1144–1167. doi:10.1111/j.1467-8683.2007.00637.x

Chaudhary, S., Dhir, A., Ferraris, A., & Bertoldi, B. (2021). Trust and reputation in family businesses: A systematic literature review of past achievements and future promises. *Journal of Business Research*, *137*(7-8), 143–161. doi:10.1016/j.jbusres.2021.07.052

Chau, G., & Gray, S. J. (2010). Family ownership, board independence and voluntary disclosure: Evidence from Hong Kong. *Journal of International Accounting, Auditing & Taxation*, *19*(2), 93–109. doi:10.1016/j.intaccaudtax.2010.07.002

Cheng, Q. (2014). Family firm research. A review. *China Journal of Accounting Research*, *7*(3), 146–163. doi:10.1016/j.cjar.2014.03.002

Chen, J. V., Gee, K. H., & Neilson, J. J. (2021). Disclosure prominence and the quality of non-GAAP earnings. *Journal of Accounting Research*, *59*(1), 163–213. doi:10.1111/1475-679X.12344

Chen, J., Chen, N. Y., He, L., & Patel, C. (2022). The effect of ownership structure on disclosure quality and credit ratings in family firms: The moderating role of auditor choice. *Family Business Review*, *35*(2), 140–158. doi:10.1177/08944865211057854

Chen, K. C. W., Chen, T., Han, W., & Yuan, H. (2022). Auditors under fire: The association between audit errors and the career setbacks of individual auditors. *Journal of Accounting Research*, *60*(3), 853–900. doi:10.1111/1475-679X.12399

Chen, S., Chen, X., & Cheng, Q. (2008). Do family firms provide more or less voluntary disclosure? *Journal of Accounting Research*, *46*(3), 499–536. doi:10.1111/j.1475-679X.2008.00288.x

Chen, T. Y., Dasgupta, S., & Yu, Y. (2014). Transparency and financing choices of family firms. *Journal of Financial and Quantitative Analysis*, *49*(2), 381–408. doi:10.1017/S0022109014000313

Chiavenato, I., & Sapiro, A. (2009). *Planejamento estratégico* (2nd ed.). Elsevier.

Cho, S., & Lee, C. (2020). Financial Reporting Conservatism and Voluntary CSR Disclosure. *Accounting Horizons*, *34*(March), 63–82. doi:10.2308/horizons-17-093

Chouaibi, S., Rossi, M., Siggia, D., & Chouaibi, J. (2022). Exploring the moderating role of social and ethical practices in the relationship between environmental disclosure and financial performance: Evidence from esg companies. *Sustainability (Basel)*, *14*(1), 209. doi:10.3390u14010209

Chow, D., & Aggestam Pontoppidan, C. (2019). The United Nations' (UN) decision to adopt International Public Sector Accounting Standards (IPSAS). *Journal of Public Budgeting, Accounting &. Financial Management*, *31*(2), 285–306.

Chrisman, J. J., Chua, J. H., Pearson, A. W., & Barnett, T. (2012). Family involvement, family influence, and family-centered non-economic goals in small firms. *Entrepreneurship Theory and Practice*, *36*(2), 267–293. doi:10.1111/j.1540-6520.2010.00407.x

Christensen, H. B., Floyd, E., Liu, L. Y., & Maffett, M. (2017). The real effects of mandated information on social responsibility in financial reports: Evidence from mine-safety records. *Journal of Accounting and Economics*, *64*(2–3), 284–304. doi:10.1016/j.jacceco.2017.08.001

Christensen, H. B., Lee, E., & Walker, M. (2009). Do IFRS reconciliations convey information? the effect of debt contracting. *Journal of Accounting Research*, *47*(5), 1167–1199. doi:10.1111/j.1475-679X.2009.00345.x

Chua, J. H., Chrisman, J. J., Steier, L. P., & Rau, S. B. (2012). Sources of heterogeneity in family firms: An introduction. *Entrepreneurship Theory and Practice*, *36*(6), 1103–1113. doi:10.1111/j.1540-6520.2012.00540.x

Chytis, E., Georgopoulos, I., Tasios, S., & Vrodou, I. (2020). Accounting Reform and IPSAS Adoption in Greece. *European Research Studies Journal*, *XXIII*(4), 165–184.

Ciger, A., Vardar, G. Ç., & Kinay, B. (2019). Key audit matters: A research on listed firms in CEE countries and Turkey. *BEH -. Business and Economic Horizons*, *15*(3), 393–422.

CIPFA/IFAC. (2021). *International Public Sector Financial Accountability Index: 2020*. IFAC. https://www.ifac.org/what-we-do/global-impact-map/accountability

Claessens, S., Djankov, S., Fan, J. P. H., & Lang, L. H. P. (2002). Disentangling the incentive and entrenchment effects of large shareholdings. *The Journal of Finance*, *57*(6), 2741–2771. doi:10.1111/1540-6261.00511

Clarkson, P. M., Fang, X., Li, Y., & Richardson, G. (2013). The Relevance of Environmental Disclosures: Are Such Disclosures Incrementally Informative? *Journal of Accounting and Public Policy*, *32*(5), 410–431. doi:10.1016/j.jaccpubpol.2013.06.008

Colares, A. C. V., Pinheiro, L. E. T., & Silva, J. N. (2020). Principais Assuntos de Auditoria: A Divulgação ainda é Comunicativa Após Três Anos de Aplicação DA NBC TA 701? *Revista Eletrônica do Departamento de Ciências Contábeis & Departamento de Atuária e Métodos Quantitativos da FEA*, *7*(1), 89–111. doi:10.23925/2446-9513.2020v7i1p89-111

Comitê de Pronunciamentos Contábeis. (2019). CPC 00 R2: *Estrutura Conceitual para Relatório Financeiro*. CPC. http://www.cpc.org.br/Arquivos/Documentos/573_CPC00(R2).pdf

Commerford, B. P., Dennis, S. A., Joe, J. R., & Ulla, J. W. (2022). Man versus machine: Complex estimates and auditor reliance on artificial intelligence. *Journal of Accounting Research*, *60*(1), 171–201. doi:10.1111/1475-679X.12407

Constantinescu, D., Caraianim, C., Lungu, C., & Mititean, P. (2021). Environmental, social and governance disclosure associated with the firm value. Evidence from energy industry. *Accounting and Management Information Systems*, *20*(1), 56–75. doi:10.24818/jamis.2021.01003

Cooper, B. J., & Grose, R. (2010). Trust Me: I'm An Auditor. *International Review of Business Research Papers*, *6*(5), 160–165.

Cordos, G., & Fülöp, M. (2015). Understanding audit reporting changes: Introduction of Key Audit Matters. *Accounting & Management Information System*, *14*(1), 128–152.

Corrales-Villegas, S. A., Ochoa-Jiménez, S., & Jacobo-Hernández, C. A. (2019). Leadership in the family business in relation to the desirable attributes for the successor: Evidence from Mexico. *European Journal of Family Business*, *8*(2), 117–128. doi:10.24310/ejfbejfb.v8i2.5193

Corten, M., Vandekerkhof, P., & Steijvers, T. (2021). The effect of socioemotional wealth diversity within the top management team on earnings management in private family firms: The moderating role of the board of directors. *MDE. Managerial and Decision Economics*, *42*(7), 1886–1896. doi:10.1002/mde.3352

Courtis, J. K. (2004). Colour as visual rhetoric in financial reporting. *Accounting Forum*, *28*(2), 265–281. doi:10.1016/j.accfor.2004.07.003

Cox, P., & Wicks, P. G. (2011). Institutional Interest in Corporate Responsibility: Portfolio Evidence and Ethical Explanation. *Journal of Business Ethics*, *103*(1), 143–165. doi:10.100710551-011-0859-0

Coyne, J., & McMickle, P. (2017). Can Blockchains Serve an Accounting Purpose? *Journal of Emerging Technologies in Accounting*, *14*(2), 101–111. doi:10.2308/jeta-51910

Craig, J., & Moores, K. (2005). Balanced scorecards to drive the strategic planning of family firms. *Family Business Review*, *18*(2), 105–122. doi:10.1111/j.1741-6248.2005.00035.x

Craig, J., & Moores, K. (2010). Strategically aligning family and business systems using the Balanced Scorecard. *Journal of Family Business Strategy*, *1*(2), 78–87. doi:10.1016/j.jfbs.2010.04.003

Cristea, M., Noja, G., Thalassinos, E., Circiumaru, D., Ponea, C., & Duaru, C. (2022). Environmental, Social and Governance Credentials of Agricultural Companies—The Interplay with Company Size. *Resources*, *11*(3), 30. doi:10.3390/resources11030030

Cruz, H., Junior. (2018). *Legibilidade de notas explicativas em empresas de capital aberto no Brasil*. [Undergraduate thesis, Universidade Federal de Uberlândia, Uberlândia, MG].

Cunha, M. P., Soares Leitão, M. J., Clegg, S., Hernández-Linares, R., Moasa, H., Randerson, K., & Rego, A. (2021). Cognition, emotion and action: Persistent sources of parent–offspring paradoxes in the family business. *Journal of Family Business Management*, *12*(4), 729–749. doi:10.1108/JFBM-11-2020-0104

Cunha, R. K. C. (2008). *Análise da facilidade de leitura das demonstrações contábeis das empresas brasileiras: uma investigação do gerenciamento de impressões nas narrativas contábeis*. [Master's thesis, Universidade de Brasília, Brasília, DF].

Cuny, C., Kim, J., & Mehta, M. N. (2020). Politically connected governments. *Journal of Accounting Research*, *58*(4), 915–952. doi:10.1111/1475-679X.12325

Dabbicco, G., & Mattei, G. (2020). The reconciliation of budgeting with financial reporting: A comparative study of Italy and the UK. *Public Money & Management*, *41*(2), 127–137.

Dai, J., & Vasarhelyi, M. A. (2017). Toward Blockchain-Based Accounting and Assurance. *Journal of Information Systems*, *31*(3), 5–21. doi:10.2308/isys-51804

Damodaran, A. (2003). *Investment philosophies: Successful investment philosophies and the greatest investors who made them work*. Wiley and Sons.

Damodaran, A. (2009). *Strategic risk management: reference for enterprise risk taking*. Bookman.

Daske, H., Hail, L., Leuz, C., & Verdi, R. (2008). Mandatory IFRS reporting around the world: Early evidence on the economic consequences. *Journal of Accounting Research*, *46*(5), 1085–1142. doi:10.1111/j.1475-679X.2008.00306.x

Daske, H., Hail, L., Leuz, C., & Verdi, R. (2013). Adopting a label: Heterogeneity in the economic consequences around IAS/IFRS adoptions. *Journal of Accounting Research*, *51*(3), 495–547. doi:10.1111/1475-679X.12005

Davenport, T. H. (1994). *Reengenharia de processos*. Campus.

de Oliveira, D. (2010). *Planejamento estratégico: conceitos, metodologias e prática* (28th ed.). Atlas.

De Villiers, C., Jia, J., & Li, Z. (2022). Corporate social responsibility: A review of empirical research using Thomson Reuters ASSET4 data. *Accounting and Finance*, *00*(4), 1–46. doi:10.1111/acfi.13004

De Wolf, A., & Christiaens, J. (2022): The hurdle model: Analysing the influence of country characteristics on participation in IPSASB's due process. *Public Money & Management*. https://doi.org/10.1080/09540962.2022.2066817

De Wolf, A., & Christiaens, J. (2019). *Stakeholder Participation in the Development of International Public Sector Accounting Standards (IPSAS): A Multi-Issue and Multi-Period Analysis of the Due Process* [Paper presentation]. *International Conference on Public Organization (ICONPO)*, Khon Kaen Province, Thailand. 10.2139srn.3635566

De Wolf, A., Christiaens, J., & Aversano, N. (2021). Heritage assets in the due process of the International Public Sector Accounting Standards Board (IPSASB). *Public Money & Management*, *41*(4), 325–335. doi:10.1080/09540962.2020.1727114

Dechow, P. M., Erhard, R. D., Sloan, R. G., & Soliman, M. T. (2021). Implied equity duration: A measure of pandemic shutdown risk. *Journal of Accounting Research*, *59*(1), 243–281. doi:10.1111/1475-679X.12348

Deephouse, D., & Jaskiewicz, P. (2013). Do family firms have better reputations than non-family firms? An integration of socioemotional wealth and social identity theories. *Journal of Management Studies*, *50*(3), 337–360. doi:10.1111/joms.12015

DeFond, M. L., Raghunandan, K., & Subramanyam, K. R. (2002). Do non-audit service fees impair auditor independence? evidence from going concern audit opinions. *Journal of Accounting Research*, *40*(4), 1247–1274. doi:10.1111/1475-679X.00088

Defourny, J., & Pestoff, V. (2014). Towards a European conceptualization of the third sector. In Costa, E., Parker, D. L., and Andreaus, M. (Eds). Accountability and social accounting for social and nonprofit organizations (pp. 37–106). Howard House: Emerald.

Defourny, J. (2001). Introduction. From third sector to social enterprise. In C. Borzaga & J. Defourny (Eds.), *The Emergence of Social Enterprise* (pp. 1–28). Routledge.

Dello Sbarba, A., & Marelli, A. (2018). Family-controlled businesses and management control: The framing of "shareholder-oriented" practices. *Journal of Management Control*, *28*(4), 417–456. doi:10.100700187-018-0255-3

Deloitte. (2016). *Blockchain: Enigma, Paradox, Opportunity*. DeLoitte. https://www2.deloitte.com/content/dam/Deloitte/nl/Documents/financial-services/deloitte-nl-fsi-blockchain-enigma-paradox-opportunity-report.pdf

Demaria, S., & Rigot, S. (2021). Corporate environmental reporting: Are French firms compliant with the Task Force on Climate Financial Disclosures' recommendations? *Business Strategy and the Environment*, *30*(1), 721–738. doi:10.1002/bse.2651

Desplebin, O., Lux, G., & Petit, N. (2021). To be or not to be: Blockchain and the future of accounting and auditing. *Accounting Perspectives*, *20*(4), 743–769. doi:10.1111/1911-3838.12265

Dey, A., Heese, J., & Pérez-Cavazos, G. (2021). Cash-for-information whistleblower programs: Effects on whistleblowing and consequences for whistleblowers. *Journal of Accounting Research*, 59(5), 1689-1740. doi:10.1111/1475-679X.12370

Dey, C., & Gibbon, J. (2017). Moving on from Scaling Up: Further Progress in Developing Social Impact Measurement in the Third Sector. *Social and Environmental Accountability Journal*, 37(1), 66-72. Doi:10.1080/0969160X.2017.1285712

Dias Filho, J. M., & Machado, L. H. B. (2004). *Abordagens da pesquisa em contabilidade. Teoria avançada da contabilidade*. Atlas.

Directive (EU) 2014/95. *Directive (EU) 2014/95 of the European Parliament and of the Council* Non-financial Reporting Directive. https://eur-lex.europa.eu/legal-content/EN/TXT/PDF/?uri=CELEX:32014L0095&from=EN

Directive (EU) 2022/2464. *Directive (EU) 2022/2464 of the European Parliament and of the Council*. Corporate Sustainability Reporting Directive. EUR-Lex - 32022L2464 - EN - EUR-Lex (europa.eu)

Dube, S., & Zhu, C. (2021). The disciplinary effect of social media: Evidence from firms' responses to Glassdoor reviews. *Journal of Accounting Research*, *59*(5), 1783–1825. doi:10.1111/1475-679X.12393

Duque-Grisales, E., & Aguilera-Caracuel, J. (2021). Environmental, Social and Governance (ESG) Scores and Financial Performance of Multilatinas: Moderating Efects of Geographic International Diversifcation and Financial Slack. *Journal of Business Ethics*, *168*(2), 315–334. doi:10.100710551-019-04177-w

Duréndez, A., & Madrid-Guijarro, A. (2018). The impact of family influence on financial reporting quality in small and medium family firms. *Journal of Family Business Strategy*, *9*(3), 205–218. doi:10.1016/j.jfbs.2018.08.002

Dyreng, S. D., Hoopes, J. L., & Wilde, J. H. (2016). Public pressure and corporate tax behavior. *Journal of Accounting Research*, *54*(1), 147–186. doi:10.1111/1475-679X.12101

Eccles, G. R., & Mirchandani, B. (2022). We need universal ESG Accounting Standards. *Harvard Business Review*. Retrieved from https://hbr.org/2022/02/we-need-universal-esg-accounting-standards

Eccles, R. G., & Krzus, M. P. (2018). Why Companies Should Report Financial Risks From Climate Change. *MIT Sloan Management Review*, *9*(3), 1–6.

Eccles, R. G., & Krzus, M. P. (2019). Implementing the Task Force on Climate-related Financial Disclosures Recommendations: An Assessment of Corporate Readiness. *Schmalenbach Business Review*, *71*(2), 287–293. doi:10.100741464-018-0060-4

Eccles, R. G., & Serafeim, G. (2015). Corporate and integrated reporting: A functional perspective. In E. Lawler, S. Mohrman, & J. O'Toole (Eds.), *Corporate Stewardship: Achieving Sustainable Effectiveness* (pp. 156–171). Greenleaf. doi:10.9774/GLEAF.9781783532605_10

Efimova, O.V., & Rozhnova, O.V. (2020). The Strategy for Harmonizing Financial and Non-financial Reporting on Climate Risk Disclosures. *Accounting. Analysis. Auditing.* *7*(3):18-25. (In Russ.) doi:10.26794/2408-9303-2020-7-3-18-25

EFRAG [European Financial Reporting Advisory Group] (2020). How to improve climate-related reporting. *Project Task Force on Climate-related Reporting*. European Reporting Lab. https://www.efrag.org/Lab1

Elshandidy, T., Shrives, P. J., Bamber, M., & Abraham, S. (2018). Risk Reporting : A Review of the Literature and Implications for Future Research. *Journal of Accounting Literature*, *40*(1), 54–82. doi:10.1016/j.acclit.2017.12.001

Englisch, P., Hall, C., Burgess, I., Macoto, H., Astrachan, J., & Pieper, T. M. (2015). Women in leadership: Family business advantage. *Special report based on a global survey of the World's largest family businesses*. EY. https://familybusiness.ey-vx.com/pdfs/ey-women-in-leadership-the-family-business-advantage.pdf

Erkens, M., Paugam, L., & Stolowy, H. (2015). Non-financial information: State of the art and research perspectives based on a bibliometric study. In Accounting Auditing Control, 21(3), 15–92. doi:10.3917/cca.213.0015

Espíndula, R. P., & Costa, P. S. (2008). Análise da influência da publicação e da legibilidade dos atos ou fatos relevantes no preço da ação das empresas brasileiras de capital aberto no período de 2002 a 2006. Horizonte Científico, Uberlândia, 2(1).

Espino, G. (2014) Fundamentos de Auditoria. Grupo Patria Editorial (Hachette Livre Group).

Ethereum. (n.d.). *Introduction to Smart Contracts*. Ethereum. https://ethereum.org/pt-br/smart-contracts/#introduction-to-smart-contracts. (Retrieved in May 2022).

Etzioni, A. (2010). Is transparency the best disinfectant? *Journal of Political Philosophy*, *18*(4), 389–404. doi:10.1111/j.1467-9760.2010.00366.x

European Commission (EC). (2013). Towards implementing harmonised public sector accounting standards in Member States. Report from the Commission to the Council and the European Parliament. EC.

European Commission. (2021). *Investment Building an economy that works for people: an action plan for the social economy*. COM(2021)778 final. Retrieved from https://eur-lex.europa.eu/legal-content/EN/TXT/PDF/?uri=CELEX:52021DC0778

European Commission. (2021). Proposal for a directive of the European Parliament and of the Council amending Directive 2013/34/EU, Directive 2004/109/EC, Directive 2006/43/EC and Regulation (EU) No 537/2014, as regards corporate sustainability reporting. https://eur-lex.europa.eu/legal-content/EN/TXT/?uri=CELEX:52021PC0189

European Commission. (2022). *Investment Support for Ecosystems Proximity and Social Economy*. Retrieved from https://ec.europa.eu/docsroom/documents/ 51115/attachments/2/translations/en/renditions/native

European Commission. (n.d.). The European Blockchain Services Infrastructure [EBSI] - European Blockchain. https://ec.europa.eu/digital-building-blocks/wikis/display/EBSI/About+us (retrieved in September 2022)

European Financial Reporting Advisory Group. (2021). *Proposals for a Relevant and Dynamic EU Sustainability Reporting Standard-Setting*, 228. EFRAG. https://www.efrag.org/Assets/Download?assetUrl=%2Fsites%2Fwebpublishing%2FSiteAssets%2FEFRAG%2520PTF-NFRS_MAIN_REPORT.pdf

European Parliament. (2022). Proposal for a Directive of the European Parliament and of the Council amending Directive 2013/34/EU, Directive 2004/109/EC, Directive 2006/43/EC and Regulation (EU) No 537/2014, as corporate sustainability reporting. https://www.consilium.europa.eu/media/57644/st10835-xx22.pdf

Eurostat, (2013). *European Systems of Account (ESA 2010)*. Retrieved from https://ec.europa.eu/eurostat/web/esa-2010

Eurostat, a. *Statistics explained*. Retrieved from https://ec.europa.eu/eurostat/statistics-explained/index.php?title=Glossary:Satellite_account

EY. (2016). *Approach for narrowing down of options within IPSAS*. EYGM.

Facci, L. (2010). The provision of welfare and general-interest services. In L. Becchetti & C. Borzaga (Eds.), *The Economics of Social Responsibility, The world of social enterprises* (pp. 88–104). Routledge.

Fan, J. P. H., & Wong, T. J. (2005). Do external auditors perform a corporate governance role in emerging markets? evidence from east Asia. *Journal of Accounting Research*, *43*(1), 35–72. doi:10.1111/j.1475-679x.2004.00162.x

Fanning, K., & Centers, D. (2016). Blockchain and Its Coming Impact on Financial Services. *Journal of Corporate Accounting & Finance*, *27*(5), 53–57. doi:10.1002/jcaf.22179

Fan, P. H. J., & Wong, T. J. (2002). Corporate ownership structure and the informativeness of accounting earnings in East Asia. *Journal of Accounting and Economics*, *33*(3), 401–425. doi:10.1016/S0165-4101(02)00047-2

Ferramosca, S., & Allegrini, M. (2018). The complex role of family involvement in earnings management. *Journal of Family Business Strategy*, *9*(2), 128–141. doi:10.1016/j.jfbs.2018.01.001

Figueiredo, O. (2015). A nova ISA 701 – Comunicar Matérias Relevantes de Auditoria no Relatório do Auditor Independente e o novo conteúdo do relatório de auditoria. *Revista da Ordem dos Revisores Oficiais de Contas* (71), 8-15.

Filios, R. (1991). Non-monetary accounting: A Necessary Development for Better managerial decisions. *Business Int. J. Value-Based Management*, *4*(2), 133–143.

FIPECAFI. (2019). Blockchain e o futuro da contabilidade como fonte informacional. Fipecafi. https://blog.fipecafi.org/blockchain-e-o-futuro-da-contabilidade-como-fonte-informacional/

Flamholz, G. E. (1999). *Human Resource Accounting Advances in Concepts, Methods and Applications*. Springer.

Flesch, R. F. (1979). *How to write plain English: A book for lawyers and consumers*. Harpercollins.

Fombrun, C., & Rindova, V. (2000). The road to transparency: Reputation management at Royal Dutch/Shell. In M. Schultz, M. J. Hatch, & M. H. Larsen (Eds.), *The expressive organization: Linking identity, reputation and the corporate brand* (pp. 77–97). Oxford University Press.

Francis, J., Nanda, D., & Olsson, P. (2008). Voluntary disclosure, earnings quality, and cost of capital. *Journal of Accounting Research*, *46*(1), 53–99. doi:10.1111/j.1475-679X.2008.00267.x

Frezatti, F. (2021). *Calls for paper*. FEA. http://rcf.fea.usp.br/index.php/news/

Fülöp, M. T. (2014). Why do we need effective corporate governance? *International Advances in Economic Research*, *20*(2), 227–228. doi:10.100711294-013-9430-3

Fülöp, M. T. (2018). New tendencies in audit reporting, examples of good practices BVB. *Audit Financiar, XVI*, *2*(150), 249–260. doi:10.20869/AUDITF/2018/150/010

Galant, A., & Cadez, S. (2017). Corporate social responsibility and financial performance relationship: A review of measurement approaches. *Ekonomska Istrazivanja*, *30*(1), 676–693. doi:10.1080/1331677X.2017.1313122

Gantz, F. (2014). External Auditing. *Science Direct*. https://www.sciencedirect.com/topics/computer-science/external-auditing

Gao, F., Wu, J. S., & Zimmerman, J. (2009). Unintended consequences of granting small firms exemptions from securities regulation: Evidence from the Sarbanes Oxley act. *Journal of Accounting Research*, *47*(2), 459–506. doi:10.1111/j.1475-679X.2009.00319.x

Garcia, M. (2019). Roles & Responsibilities of External Audit Firms. *Small Business*. https://smallbusiness.chron.com/roles-responsibilities-external-audit-firms-73924.html

Gaspar, R., Rohde, P., & Giger, J. C. (2019). Unconventional settings and uses of human enhancement technologies: A non-systematic review of public and experts' views on self-enhancement and DIY biology/biohacking risks. *Human Behavior and Emerging Technologies*, *1*(4), 295–305. doi:10.1002/hbe2.175

Gebhardt, W. R., Lee, C. M. C., & Swaminathan, B. (2001). Toward an implied cost of capital. *Journal of Accounting Research*, *39*(1), 135–176. doi:10.1111/1475-679X.00007

Geiger, M. A., & Raghunandan, K. (2002). Auditor Tenure and Audit Reporting Failures. *Auditing*, *21*(1), 67–78. doi:10.2308/aud.2002.21.1.67

Gelbcke, E. R. (2018). Manual de contabilidade societária: aplicável a todas as sociedades de acordo com as normas internacionais e do CPC.

Gerakos, I. (2021). *Dimosio Logistiko me vasi to PD 54/2018*. OTS.

Gerakos, I. (in press). *To plaisio gia to Neo Dimosio Logistiko (Proedriko Diatagma 54/2018)*. Athens. *Benos.*

Giannarakis, G. (2014). Corporate governance and financial characteristic effects the extent of corporate social responsibility disclosures. *Social Responsibility Journal*, *10*(4), 569–590. doi:10.1108/SRJ-02-2013-0008

Gibbon, J., & Affleck, A. (2008). Social enterprise resisting social accounting: Reflecting on lived experiences. *Social Enterprise Journal*, *4*(1), 41–56. doi:10.1108/17508610810877722

Gillette, J. R., Samuels, D., & Zhou, F. S. (2020). The effect of credit ratings on disclosure: Evidence from the recalibration of Moody's municipal ratings. *Journal of Accounting Research*, *58*(3), 693–739. doi:10.1111/1475-679X.12307

Gjergji, R., Vena, L., Sciascia, S., & Cortesi, A. (2021). The effects of environmental, social and governance disclosure on the cost of capital in small and medium enterprises: The role of family business status. *Business Strategy and the Environment*, *30*(1), 683–693. doi:10.1002/bse.2647

Goldsack, J. C., Dowling, A. V., Samuelson, D., Patrick-Lake, B., & Clay, I. (2021). Evaluation, Acceptance, and Qualification of Digital Measures: From Proof of Concept to Endpoint. *Digital Biomarkers*, *5*(1), 53–64. doi:10.1159/000514730 PMID:33977218

Goldstein, M. A., Hotchkiss, E. S., & Sirri, E. R. (2007). Transparency and liquidity: A controlled experiment on corporate bonds. *Review of Financial Studies*, *20*(2), 235–273. doi:10.1093/rfs/hhl020

Gómez-Mejía, L. R., Haynes, K. T., Núnez-Nickel, M., Jacobson, K. J., & Moyano-Fuentes, J. (2007). Socioemotional wealth and business risks in family-controlled firms: Evidence from Spanish olive oil mills. *Administrative Science Quarterly*, *52*(1), 106–137. doi:10.2189/asqu.52.1.106

González, M., Guzmán, A., Pombo, C., & Trujillo, M. A. (2014). Family involvement and dividend policy in closely held firms. *Family Business Review*, *27*(4), 365–385. doi:10.1177/0894486514538448

Grant, S. M. (2020). How does using a mobile device change investors' reactions to firm disclosures? *Journal of Accounting Research*, *58*(3), 741–775. doi:10.1111/1475-679X.12299

Gray, G. L., Turner, J. L., Coram, P. J., & Mock, T. J. (2011). Perceptions and misperceptions regarding the unqualified auditor's report by financial statement preparers, users, and auditors. *Accounting Horizons*, *25*(4), 659–684. doi:10.2308/acch-50060

Gray, R. (2001). Thirty years of social accounting, reporting and auditing: What (if anything) have we learnt? *Business Ethics (Oxford, England)*, *10*(1), 9–15.

Grigg, I. (2005). Triple entry accounting. *Systemics Inc*. Iang. https://iang.org/papers/triple_entry.html

Gromoff, A., & Stavenko, J. (2012). An attempt at a systems approach to operational risk management. *Far East Journal of Psychology and Business*, *8*(3), 38–49.

Guedhami, O., Pittman, J. A., & Saffar, W. (2014). Auditor choice in politically connected firms. *Journal of Accounting Research*, *52*(1), 107–162. doi:10.1111/1475-679X.12032

Guggenmos, R. D., Rennekamp, K., Rupar, K., & Wang, S. (2022). The relationship between non-GAAP earnings and aggressive estimates in reported GAAP numbers. *Journal of Accounting Research*, *60*(5), 1915–1945. doi:10.1111/1475-679X.12434

Gu, L., & Hackbarth, D. (2013). Governance and equity prices: Does transparency matter? *Review of Finance*, *17*(6), 1989–2033. doi:10.1093/rof/rfs047

Gul, F. A. (2006). Auditors' response to political connections and cronyism in Malaysia. *Journal of Accounting Research*, *44*(5), 931–963. doi:10.1111/j.1475-679X.2006.00220.x

Gull, A. A., Hussain, N., Khan, S. A., Khan, Z., & Saeed, A. (2022). Governing Corporate Social Responsibility Decoupling: The Efect of the Governance Committee on Corporate Social Responsibility Decoupling. *Journal of Business Ethics*. doi:10.100710551-022-05181-3

Guthrie, J., & Abeysekera, I. (2006). Content analysis of social, environmental reporting: What is new? *Journal of Human Resource Costing & Accounting*, *10*(2), 114–126. doi:10.1108/14013380610703120

Habbershon, T. G., & Williams, M. L. (1999). A resource-based framework for assessing the strategic advantages of family firms. *Family Business Review*, *12*(1), 1–25. doi:10.1111/j.1741-6248.1999.00001.x

Habbershon, T. G., Williams, M. L., & MacMillan, I. C. (2003). A unified systems perspective of family firm performance. *Journal of Business Venturing*, *18*(4), 451–465. doi:10.1016/S0883-9026(03)00053-3

Halkos, G., & Nomikos, S. (2021). Corporate social responsibility: Trends in global reporting initiative standards. *Economic Analysis and Policy*, *69*, 106–117. doi:10.1016/j.eap.2020.11.008

Haller, A., Link, M., & Groß, T. (2017). The Term 'Non-financial Information'–A Semantic Analysis of a Key Feature of Current and Future Corporate Reporting. *Accounting in Europe*, *14*(3), 407–429. doi:10.1080/17449480.2017.1374548

Hallman, N. J., Schmidt, J. J., & Thompson, A. M. (2022). Audit implications of non-GAAP reporting. *Journal of Accounting Research*, *60*(5), 1947–1989. doi:10.1111/1475-679X.12433

Han, H., Shiwakoti, R. K., Jarvis, R., Mordi, C., & Botchie, D. (2023). Accounting and auditing with blockchain technology and artificial Intelligence: A literature review. *International Journal of Accounting Information Systems*, *48*, 100598. doi:10.1016/j.accinf.2022.100598

Haniffa, R. M., & Cooke, T. E. (2005). The impact of culture and governance on corporate social reporting. *Journal of Accounting and Public Policy*, *24*(5), 391–430. doi:10.1016/j.jaccpubpol.2005.06.001

Hasan, I., Hoi, C.-S., Wu, Q., & Zhang, H. (2017). Does social capital matter in corporate decisions? evidence from corporate tax avoidance. *Journal of Accounting Research*, *55*(3), 629–668. doi:10.1111/1475-679X.12159

Hasan, M. M. (2020). Readability of narrative disclosures in 10-K reports: Does managerial ability matter? *European Accounting Review*, *29*(1), 147–168. doi:10.1080/09638180.2018.1528169

Hayes, R. M., Jiang, F., & Pan, Y. (2021). Voice of the customers: Local trust culture and consumer complaints to the CFPB. *Journal of Accounting Research*, *59*(3), 1077–1121. doi:10.1111/1475-679X.12364

Heald, D. (2006). Transparency as an instrumental value. In C. Hood & D. Heald (Eds.), *Transparency: The Key to Better Governance?* (pp. 59–74). Oxford University Press. doi:10.5871/bacad/9780197263839.003.0004

Heese, J., & Pérez-Cavazos, G. (2019). Fraud allegations and government contracting. *Journal of Accounting Research*, *57*(3), 675–719. doi:10.1111/1475-679X.12258

Heinberg, M., Liu, Y., Huang, X., & Eisingerich, A. B. (2021). A bad job of doing good: Does corporate transparency on a country and company level moderate corporate social responsibility effectiveness? *Journal of International Marketing*, *29*(2), 45–61. doi:10.1177/1069031X20981870

Hendriksen, E. S., & Van Breda, M. F. (1999). *Teoria da contabilidade* (A. Z. Sanvicente, Trans.). Atlas.

Hernández-Linares, R., & Arias-Abelaira, T. (2022). Adapt or perish! A systematic review of the literature on strategic renewal and the family firm. *European Journal of Family Business*, *12*(2), 137–155. doi:10.24310/ejfbejfb.v12i2.14718

Hernández-Linares, R., & López-Fernández, M. C. (2018). Entrepreneurial orientation and the family firm: Mapping the field and tracing a path for future research. *Family Business Review*, *31*(3), 318–351. doi:10.1177/0894486518781940

Hernández-Linares, R., Sarkar, S., & Cobo, M. J. (2018). Inspecting the Achilles heel: A quantitative analysis of 50 years of family business definitions. *Scientometrics*, *115*(2), 929–951. doi:10.100711192-018-2702-1

Hernández-Linares, R., Sarkar, S., & López-Fernández, M. C. (2017). How has the family firm literature addressed its heterogeneity through classification systems? An integrated analysis. *European Journal of Family Business*, *7*(1-2), 1–13. doi:10.1016/j.ejfb.2017.06.003

Hill, S. (2003). A basis for developing learning strategies for risk management in public service (LMBL de Vasconcelos, Trad.). Brasília: National School of Public Administration - Enap.

Hill, S. (2006). Guide on risk management in the public service (LMBL de Vasconcelos, Trad.). Brasília: National School of Public Administration. (Cadernos Enap, 30).

Hobson, J. L., Mayew, W. J., & Venkatachalam, M. (2012). Analyzing speech to detect financial misreporting. *Journal of Accounting Research*, *50*(2), 349–392. doi:10.1111/j.1475-679X.2011.00433.x

Hochberg, Y. V., Sapienza, P., & Vissing-JØrgensen, A. (2009). A lobbying approach to evaluating the Sarbanes Oxley act of 2002. *Journal of Accounting Research*, *47*(2), 519–583. doi:10.1111/j.1475-679X.2009.00321.x

Hope, O. (2003). Disclosure practices, enforcement of accounting standards, and analysts' forecast accuracy: An international study. *Journal of Accounting Research*, *41*(2), 235–272. doi:10.1111/1475-679X.00102

Hopkins, P. (1996). The effect of financial statement classification of hybrid financial instruments on financial analysts' stock price judgements. *Journal of Accounting Research*, *34*(3), 33–50. doi:10.2307/2491424

Hopwood, A. G. (1987). The archeology of accounting systems. *Accounting, Organizations and Society*, *12*(3), 207–234. doi:10.1016/0361-3682(87)90038-9

Houston, J. F., Jiang, L., Lin, C., & Ma, Y. (2014). Political connections and the cost of bank loans. *Journal of Accounting Research*, *52*(1), 193–243. doi:10.1111/1475-679X.12038

Hribar, P., & Collins, D. W. (2002). Errors in estimating accruals: Implications for empirical research. *Journal of Accounting Research*, *40*(1), 105–134. doi:10.1111/1475-679X.00041

Hribar, P., Mergenthaler, R., Roeschley, A., Young, S., & Zhao, C. X. (2022). Do managers issue more voluntary disclosure when GAAP limits their reporting discretion in financial statements? *Journal of Accounting Research*, *60*(1), 299–351. doi:10.1111/1475-679X.12401

Huang, A., Hui, K. W., & Li, R. Z. (2019). Federal judge ideology: A new measure of ex ante litigation risk. *Journal of Accounting Research*, *57*(2), 431–489. doi:10.1111/1475-679X.12260

Hultman, J., & Axelsson, B. (2007). Towards a typology of transparency for marketing management research. *Industrial Marketing Management*, *36*(5), 627–635. doi:10.1016/j.indmarman.2006.04.001

IAASB. (2009). *ISA 200: Overall objectives of the independent auditor and the conduct of an audit in accordance with international standards on auditing*. IFAC. https://www.ifac.org/system/files/downloads/a008-2010-iaasb-handbook-isa-200.pdf

IAASB. (2015). *ISA 701: Communicating Key Audit Matters in the independent Auditor's Report*. IAASB. https://www.iaasb.org/publications/international-standard-auditing-isa-701-new-communicating-key-audit-matters-independe
nt-auditors-4

Iatridis, G. E. (2013). Environmental Disclosure Quality: Evidence on Environmental Performance, Corporate Governance and Value Relevance. *Emerging Markets Review*, *14*(1), 55–75. doi:10.1016/j.ememar.2012.11.003

IFAC. (2006). *Code of Ethics for Professional Accountants*. IFAC. https://www.ifac.org/system/files/publications/files/ifac-code-of-ethics-for.pdf

IFAC. (2018). . *Final Pronouncement: International Code of Ethics for Professional Accountants (including International Independence Standards)*. International Ethics Standards Board for Accountants. https://www.ifac.org/system/files/publications/files/Final-Pronouncement-The-Restructured-Code_0.pdf

IFAC. (2022). *2022 Handbook of the International Code of Ethics for Professional Accountants*. IFAC. https://www.ethicsboard.org/publications/2022-handbook-international-code-ethics-professional-accountants

IFRS Foundation. (2020). *Effects of climate-related matters on financial statements (November)*, 1–6. IFRS. https://www.ifrs.org/content/dam/ifrs/supporting-implementation/documents/effects-of-climate-related-matters-on-financia
l-statements.pdf

IFRS Foundation. (2021a). *IFRS Foundation announces International Sustainability Standards Board, consolidation with CDSB and VRF, and publication of prototype disclosure requirements*. IFRS. https://www.ifrs.org/news-and-events/news/2021/11/ifrs-foundation-announces-issb-consolidation-with-cdsb-vrf-publication-of-prototypes/

IFRS Foundation. (2021b). *Global sustainability disclosure standards for the financial markets*. IFRS. https://www.ifrs.org/news-and-events/news/2021/11/global-sustainability-disclosure-standards-for-the-financial-markets/

IFRS Foundation. (n.d.). *Who uses IFRS Accounting Standards?* IFRS. https://www.ifrs.org/use-around-the-world/use-of-ifrs-standards-by-jurisdiction/

International Federation of Accountants. (2018). *International Public Sector Financial Accountability Index*. Retrieved from https://www.ifac.org/_flysystem/azure-private/IFAC-CIPFA-Public-Sector-Index-2018-Status.pdf

IPSASB (2016). *Due Process and working procedures*. International Public Sector Accounting Standard Board.

IPSASB. (2020). *Handbook of international public sector accounting pronouncements* (Vol. I). IFAC.

Iqbal, M. O., Obaid, A. J., Agarwal, P., Mufti, T., & Hassan, A. R. (2023). Blockchain Technology and Decentralized Applications Using Blockchain. In M. Tuba, S. Akashe, & A. Joshi (Eds.), *ICT Infrastructure and Computing. Lecture Notes in Networks and Systems* (Vol. 520, pp. 555–563). Springer. doi:10.1007/978-981-19-5331-6_57

Islam, M. A. (2017). *Future of accounting profession: Three major changes and implications for teaching and research*. International Federation of Accountants (IFAC). https://eprints.qut.edu.au/104070/

Islam, A. K. M. N., Mantymaki, M., & Turunen, M. (2019). Why do blockchains split? An actor-network perspective on bitcoin splits. *Technological Forecasting and Social Change*, *148*, 119743. doi:10.1016/j.techfore.2019.119743

Jackson, G., Bartosch, J., Avetisyan, E., Kinderman, D., & Knudsen, J. S. (2020). Mandatory Non-financial Disclosure and Its Influence on CSR: An International Comparison. *Journal of Business Ethics*, *162*(2), 323–342. doi:10.100710551-019-04200-0

Jia, Y., Lent, L. V., & Zeng, Y. (2014). Masculinity, testosterone, and financial misreporting. *Journal of Accounting Research*, *52*(5), 1195–1246. doi:10.1111/1475-679X.12065

Johnson, B., & Kleiner, H. B. (1987). Human Asset Accounting: Where Are We Today? *International Journal of Manpower*, *8*(4), 3–4. doi:10.1108/eb045129

Johnston, A. (2018). Climate-Related Financial Disclosures: What Next for Environmental Sustainability? *Research Paper Series 2018–02*. University of Oslo Faculty of Law Legal Studies.

Jr, S. Cac, S, Am, V. J., & Rabechini, R. (2010). Gerenciamento de riscos em projetos (2a ed.). Rio de Janeiro: Editora FGV.

Kanade, V. (2021). What Is Fraud Detection? Definition, Types, Applications, and Best Practices. *Spiceworks*. https://www.spiceworks.com/it-security/vulnerability-management/articles/what-is-fraud-detection/

Kang, J. K., Stice-Lawrence, L., & Wong, Y. T. F. (2021). The firm next door: Using satellite images to study local information advantage. *Journal of Accounting Research*, *59*(2), 713–750. doi:10.1111/1475-679X.12360

Kang, J.-S., Chiang, C.-F., Huangthanapan, K., & Downing, S. (2015). Corporate social responsibility and sustainability balanced scorecard: The case study of family-owned hotels. *International Journal of Hospitality Management*, *48*, 124–134. doi:10.1016/j.ijhm.2015.05.001

Kaplan, R. S. (2011). Accounting scholarship that advances professional knowledge and practice. *The Accounting Review*, *86*(2), 367–383. doi:10.2308/accr.00000031

Karajovic, M., Kim, H., & Laskowski, M. (2019). Thinking outside the block: Projected phases of blockchain integration in the accounting industry. *Australian Accounting Review*, *29*(2), 319–330. doi:10.1111/auar.12280

Karamanou, I., & Vafeas, N. (2005). The association between corporate boards, audit committees, and management earnings forecasts: An empirical analysis. *Journal of Accounting Research*, *43*(3), 453–486. doi:10.1111/j.1475-679X.2005.00177.x

Katsikas, E., Rossi, M. F., & Orelli, L. R. (2017). *Towards Integrated Reporting Accounting Change in the Public Sector*. Springer.

Kay, A. (2011). *Prove, Improve, Account - The New Guide to Social Accounting and Audit*. Social Audit Network.

Kay, A., & McMullan, L. (2017). Contemporary Challenges Facing Social Enterprises and Community Organisations Seeking to Understand Their Social Value. *Social and Environmental Accountability Journal*, *37*(1), 1–5. doi:10.1080/0969160X.2017.1287583

Kidwell, L., & Lowensohn, S. (2019). Participation in the Process of Setting Public Sector Accounting Standards: The Case of IPSASB. *Accounting in Europe*, *16*(2), 177–194. doi:10.1080/17449480.2019.1632466

Kim, Y., Park, M., & Wier, B. (2012). Is earnings quality associated with corporate social responsibility? *The Accounting Review*, *87*(3), 761–796. doi:10.2308/accr-10209

Kinderman, D. (2020). The challenges of upward regulatory harmonization : The case of sustainability reporting in the European Union. *Regulation & Governance*, *14*(4), 674–697. doi:10.1111/rego.12240

Kitsantas, T., & Chytis, E. (2022). Blockchain Technology as an Ecosystem: Trends and Perspectives in Accounting and Management. *Journal of Theoretical and Applied Electronic Commerce Research*, *17*(3), 1143–1161. doi:10.3390/jtaer17030058

Klassen, K. J., & Laplante, S. K. (2012). Are U.S. multinational corporations becoming more aggressive income shifters? *Journal of Accounting Research*, *50*(5), 1245–1285. doi:10.1111/j.1475-679X.2012.00463.x

Kokina, J., Mancha, R., & Pachamanova, D. (2017). Blockchain: Emergent Industry Adoption and Implications for Accounting. *Journal of Emerging Technologies in Accounting*, *14*(2), 91–100. doi:10.2308/jeta-51911

Kotlar, J., & De Massis, A. (2013). Goal setting in family firms: Goal diversity, social interactions, and collective commitment to family-centered goals. *Entrepreneurship Theory and Practice*, *37*(6), 1263–1288. doi:10.1111/etap.12065

Kozlowski, S. (2018). An Audit Ecosystem to Support Blockchain-based Accounting and Assurance. In D.Y. Chan, V.C. & M.A. Vasarhelyi (Eds.), Continuous Auditing: Theory and Application (299–313). Emerald Publishing. https://doi.org/ doi:10.1108/978-1-78743-413-420181015

Krasodomska, J., Michalak, J., & Świetla, K. (2020). Directive 2014/95/EU: Accountants ' Understanding and Attitude towards Mandatory Non-Financial Disclosures in Corporate Reporting Directive 2014 / 95 / EU Disclosures Incorporate Reporting. *Meditari Account. Res.*, *28*(5), 751–779. doi:10.1108/MEDAR-06-2019-0504

Kubíček, A., & Machek, O. (2020). Intrafamily conflicts in Family businesses: A systematic review of the literature and agenda for future research. *Family Business Review*, *33*(2), 194–227. doi:10.1177/0894486519899573

Kuo, T., Chen, H., & Meng, H. (2021). Do corporate social responsibility practices improve financial performance? A case study of airline companies. *Journal of Cleaner Production*, *310*, 127380. doi:10.1016/j.jclepro.2021.127380

Lambert, R., Leuz, C., & Verrecchia, R. E. (2007). Accounting information, disclosure, and the cost of capital. *Journal of Accounting Research*, *45*(2), 385–420. doi:10.1111/j.1475-679X.2007.00238.x

Landgraf, E., & Riahi-Belkaoui, A. (2003). Corporate disclosure quality and corporate reputation. *Review of Accounting and Finance*, *2*(1), 86–95. doi:10.1108/eb027003

Landrum, N. E., & Ohsowski, B. (2018). Identifying Worldviews on Corporate Sustainability: A Content Analysis of Corporate Sustainability Reports. *Business Strategy and the Environment*, *27*(1), 128–151. doi:10.1002/bse.1989

Lanzana, A. P. (2004). *Relação entre disclosure e governança corporativa das empresas brasileiras.* [Master's thesis, Universidade de São Paulo, São Paulo, SP].

Latour, B. (1987). *Science in action: How to follow scientists and engineers through society.* Harvard University Press.

Latour, B. (2012). Visualisation and cognition: Drawing things together. In H. Kuklick (Ed.), *Knowledge and Society Studies in the Sociology of Culture Past and Present* (Vol. 6, pp. 1–40). Jai Press.

Lazkano, L., & Beraza, A. (2019). Social Accounting for Sustainability: A Study in the Social Economy. *Sustainability*, *11*, 1–5. doi:10.3390u11246894

Lee, C.-C., Kuo, S.-Y., Hsu, H.-H., Mo, T.-L., Chang, E.-Y., & Huang, K.-C. (2022). How does the research community contribute to corporate climate-related risk disclosures? The gap between ideals and reality. In Corporate Social Responsibility and Environmental Management. Wiley. doi:10.1002/csr.2397

Lee, J. (2006). Family firm performance: Further evidence. *Family Business Review*, *19*(2), 103–114. doi:10.1111/j.1741-6248.2006.00060.x

Lee, L. F., Hutton, A. P., & Shu, S. (2015). The role of social media in the capital market: Evidence from consumer product recalls. *Journal of Accounting Research*, *53*(2), 367–404. doi:10.1111/1475-679X.12074

Lee, Y.-J. (2012). The effect of quarterly report readability on information efficiency of stock prices. *Contemporary Accounting Research*, *29*(4), 1137–1170. doi:10.1111/j.1911-3846.2011.01152.x

Lennox, C. S., Schmidt, J. J., & Thompson, A. M. (2019). Are expanded audit reports informative to investors? Evidence from the UK. SSRN *Electronic Journal*. https://papers.ssrn.com/sol3/papers.cfm?abstract_id=2619785

Lennox, C., Lisowsky, P., & Pittman, J. (2013). Tax aggressiveness and accounting fraud. *Journal of Accounting Research, 51*(4), 739–778. doi:10.1111/joar.12002

Leuz, C., & Verrecchia, R. E. (2000). The economic consequences of increased disclosure. *Journal of Accounting Research, 38*(SUPPL.), 91–124. doi:10.2307/2672910

Leuz, C., & Wysocki, P. D. (2016). The economics of disclosure and financial reporting regulation: Evidence and suggestions for future research. *Journal of Accounting Research, 54*(2), 525–622. doi:10.1111/1475-679X.12115

Levanti, D. A. (2019). Aspects Regarding the Changes to the Independent Auditor"s Report. The Case of Public Interest Entities. *Audit Financiar, XVII, 3*(155), 486–495. doi:10.20869/AUDITF/2019/155/018

Li, F. (2008). Annual report readability, current earnings, and earnings persistence. *Journal of Accounting and Economics, 45*(2-3), 221–247. doi:10.1016/j.jacceco.2008.02.003

Li, F. (2010). The information content of forward-looking statements in corporate filings-A naïve bayesian machine learning approach. *Journal of Accounting Research, 48*(5), 1049–1102. doi:10.1111/j.1475-679X.2010.00382.x

Lin, H. L., & Yen, A. R. (2022). Auditor rotation, key audit matter disclosures, and financial reporting quality. *Advances in Accounting, 57*, 100594. doi:10.1016/j.adiac.2022.100594

Li, S., & Zuo, X. (2020). Agency Costs in Family Business: A Review. *Journal of Service Science and Management, 13*(2), 377–387. doi:10.4236/jssm.2020.132025

Lisowsky, P., Robinson, L., & Schmidt, A. (2013). Do publicly disclosed tax reserves tell us about privately disclosed tax shelter activity? *Journal of Accounting Research, 51*(3), 583–629. doi:10.1111/joar.12003

Liu, Y. S., Zhou, X., Yang, J. H., & Hoepner, A. G. F. (2016). Corporate Carbon Emission and Financial Performance: Does Carbon Disclosure Mediate the Relationship in the UK? *Henley Discussion Paper Series*. ICM.

Liu, C., Li, Q., & Lin, Y. E. (2022). (in press). Corporate transparency and firm value: Does market competition play an external governance role? *Journal of Contemporary Accounting & Economics*. Advance online publication. doi:10.1016/j.jcae.2022.100334

Liu, M. (2022). Assessing human information processing in lending decisions: A machine learning approach. *Journal of Accounting Research, 60*(2), 607–651. doi:10.1111/1475-679X.12427

Liu, Y., Valenti, A., & Chen, Y. (2016). Corporate governance and information transparency in Taiwan's public firms. The moderating effect of family ownership. *Journal of Management & Organization, 22*(5), 662–679. doi:10.1017/jmo.2015.56

Li, Y., Gong, M., Zhang, X. Y., & Koh, L. (2018). The impact of environmental, social, and governance disclosure on firm value: The role of CEO power. *The British Accounting Review, 50*(1), 60–75. doi:10.1016/j.bar.2017.09.007

Lo, K., Ramos, F., & Rogo, R. (2017). Earnings management and annual report readability. *Journal of Accounting and Economics, 63*(1), 1–25. doi:10.1016/j.jacceco.2016.09.002

Lombardi, R., Schimperna, F., Paoloni, P., & Galeotti, M. (2022). The climate-related information in the changing EU directive on non-financial reporting and disclosure: First evidence by Italian large companies. *Journal of Applied Accounting Research, 23*(1), 250–273. doi:10.1108/JAAR-04-2021-0117

López-Fernández, M. C., Serrano-Bedia, A. M., Pérez-Pérez, M., Hernández-Linares, R., & Palma-Ruiz, M. (2017). A review of the academic literature on family business in Spanish. In F. W. Kellermanns & F. Hoy (Eds.), *The Routledge Companion to Family Business* (pp. 522–548). Routledge.

Loring, J., & Sinclair, P. (2001). *Breach of the Trust Accounting Rules*. Discipline Case Digest Index. https://lawsociety.mb.ca/wp-content/uploads/2020/01/case_digest_01_05.pdf

Loughran, T., & Mcdonald, B. (2016). Textual analysis in accounting and finance: A survey. *Journal of Accounting Research*, *54*(4), 1187–1230. doi:10.1111/1475-679X.12123

Louie, J., Ahmed, K., & Ji, X. D. (2019). Voluntary disclosures practices of family firms in Australia. *Accounting Research Journal*, *32*(2), 273–294. doi:10.1108/ARJ-04-2016-0042

Lovell, H., de Aguiar, T. S., Bebbington, J., & Larrinaga-Gonzalez, C. (2010). Accounting for Carbon. In *Accounting for Carbon*. Monitoring, Reporting and Verifying Emissions in the Climate Economy. doi:10.1017/CBO9781316162262

Lozano, R., Nummert, B., & Ceulemans, K. (2016). Elucidating the relationship between Sustainability Reporting and Organisational Change Management for Sustainability. *Journal of Cleaner Production*, *125*, 168–188. doi:10.1016/j.jclepro.2016.03.021

Ma, L. (2023). Corporate social responsibility reporting in family firms: Evidence from China. *Journal of Behavioral and Experimental Finance*, *37*, 100730. doi:10.1016/j.jbef.2022.100730

Manchiraju, H., & Rajgopal, S. (2017). Does corporate social responsibility (CSR) create shareholder value? evidence from the Indian companies act 2013. *Journal of Accounting Research*, *55*(5), 1257–1300. doi:10.1111/1475-679X.12174

Manes Rossi, F, & Aversano, N. (2015). Advancing performance measurement: Italian local government vis-à-vis the IPSASB project. *International Journal of Productivity and Performance Management, 64*(1), 76- 93. htpps://doi.org.a0.1108/IJPPM-07-2013-0134

Marçal, D. (2014). *Pseudociência*. Fundação Francisco Manuel dos Santos. Relógio D'Água Editores.

Marsh. (2022). Reporting Climate Change Risk. Preparing for compulsory disclosure. *Marsh*. https://www.marsh.com/tr/en/risks/climate-change-sustainability/insights/reporting-climate-change-risk-preparing-for-compulsory-disclosure.html

Martin, G., Campbell, J., & Gómez-Mejía, L. R. (2016). Family control, socioemotional wealth and earnings management in publicly traded firms. *Journal of Business Ethics*, *133*(3), 435–469. doi:10.100710551-014-2403-5

Martinho, C. (2009). *Uma Abordagem Quantitativa Longitudinal do Desempenho dos Alunos do 12º ano (2000-2005)*. Tese de Doutoramento, Faculdade de Ciências e Tecnologia da Universidade Nova de Lisboa.

Martins, J. J., & André, M. A. (2013). Governance bodies of family business. *European Journal of Family Business*, *3*(1), 47–58. doi:10.24310/ejfbejfb.v3i1.4040

Martins, T. B., Ghiraldelo, C. M., Nunes, M. D. G. V., & de Oliveira, O. N. Junior. (1996). *Readability formulas applied to textbooks in brazilian portuguese*. Icmsc-Usp.

Matias, T. S. (2022). Os caminhos cruzados da solidariedade defensiva e da comunicação de irregularidades (whistleblowing) no sector financeiro. In *O Whistleblowing em Portugal – Proteção do Denunciante nas Organizações. Coordenadores Maia, A. J & Simões*. P. P. Editora Almedina.

Matsumura, E. M., Prakash, R., & Vera-Muñoz, S. C. (2014). Firm-value effects of carbon emissions and carbon disclosures. *The Accounting Review*, *89*(2), 695–724. doi:10.2308/accr-50629

Mayoral, J. M., & Segura, A. S. (2008). Gobierno corporativo y calidad de la información contable: Evidencia empírica española. *Revista de Contabilidad -. Revista de Contabilidad, 11*(1), 67–99.

Mehta, M. N., Srinivasan, S., & Zhao, W. (2020). The politics of M&A antitrust. *Journal of Accounting Research, 58*(1), 5–53. doi:10.1111/1475-679X.12291

Melloni, G., Caglio, A., & Perego, P. (2017). Saying More with Less? Disclosure Conciseness, Completeness and Balance in Integrated Reports. *Journal of Accounting and Public Policy, 36*(3), 220–238. doi:10.1016/j.jaccpubpol.2017.03.001

Melo, M. S. (2000). A Gestão da Qualidade Total e as perspectivas dessa tendência nos serviços públicos [Dissertação de mestrado, Universidade Federal da Paraíba, João Pessoa, PB, Brazil].

Men, L. R., & Hung-Baesecke, C. J. F. (2015). Engaging employees in China: The impact of communication channels, organizational transparency, and authenticity. *Corporate Communications, 20*(4), 448–467. doi:10.1108/CCIJ-11-2014-0079

Miranda, I. A., Reina, D., & Lemes, S. (2018). Grau de legibilidade dos relatórios financeiros em empresas do novo mercado. In *USP International Conference in Accounting* (Vol. 18).

Mitu, I., & Tiron-Tudor, A. (2013). Public Sector Combinations: A New Challenge For IPSASB. [University of Oradea]. *Annals of Faculty of Economics, 1*(2), 540–549.

Mitz, S. (2018). Fraud in Organizations. Fraud in Organizations. *Ethics Sage*. https://www.ethicssage.com/2018/04/fraud-in-organizations-fraud-can-be-defined-as-a-deliberate-misrepresentation-to-gain-an-advantage-over-another-party-fraud.html

Mohammadi, S., & Nezhad, B. M. (2015). The role of disclosure and transparency in financial reporting. *International Journal of Accounting and Economics Studies, 3*(1), 60–62. doi:10.14419/ijaes.v3i1.4549

Moll, J., & Yigitbasioglu, O. (2019). The role of internet-related technologies in shaping the work of accountants: New directions for accounting research. *The British Accounting Review, 51*(6), 100833. doi:10.1016/j.bar.2019.04.002

Montemerlo, D., Minichilli, A., & Corbetta, G. (2013). The determinants of women's involvement in top management teams: Opportunities or obstacles for family-controlled firms? In K. X. Smyrnios, P. Z. Poutziouris, & S. Goel (Eds.), *Handbook of Research in Family Business* (pp. 301–322). Edward Elgar. doi:10.4337/9781781009383.00025

Mook, L. (2014). An integrated social accounting model for nonprofit organizations. In Costa, E., Parker, D. L., and Andreaus, M. (Eds). Accountability and social accounting for social and nonprofit organizations (pp. 220–246). Howard House: Emerald.

Mook, L., & Quarter, J. (2010). Social Accounting for Social Economy Organisations. In: Anheier, K.H., Toepler, S., List, R. (Eds). International Encyclopedia of Civil Society, 1380-1384. New York: Springer. https://doi.org/ doi:10.1007/978-0-387-93996-4

Mook, L., Quarter, J., & Richmond, B. (2007). *What Counts: Social Accounting for Nonprofits and cooperatives*. Sigel Press.

Morais, A. M., & Neves, I. P. (2017). Fazer investigação usando uma abordagem metodológica mista. *Revista Portuguesa de Educação, 20*(2), 75–104.

Morck, R., Schleifer, A., & Vishny, R. W. (1988). Management ownership and market valuation: An empirical analysis. *Journal of Financial Economics, 20*(1-2), 293–315. doi:10.1016/0304-405X(88)90048-7

Moreno, A., & Casasola, A. (2016). A readability evolution of narratives in annual reports: A longitudinal study of two Spanish companies. *Journal of Business and Technical Communication*, *30*(2), 202–235. doi:10.1177/1050651915620233

Murphy, R. (2022). Best Invoicing Software for Small Business. *Nerd Wallet*. https://www.nerdwallet.com/article/small-business/best-invoicing-software-for-small-businesses

Nagy, A. L. (2005). Mandatory Audit firmTurnover, Financial Reporting Quality, and Client Bargaining Power: The Case of Arthur Andersen. *Accounting Horizons*, *19*(2), 51–68. doi:10.2308/acch.2005.19.2.51

Narayanamoorthy, G. (2006). Conservatism and cross-sectional variation in the post-earnings announcement drift. *Journal of Accounting Research*, *44*(4), 763–789. doi:10.1111/j.1475-679X.2006.00218.x

Near, J. P., & Miceli, M. P. (1996). Whistle-blowing: Myth and reality. *Journal of Management*, *22*(3), 507–526. doi:10.1177/014920639602200306

Nicholls, A. (2009). "We do good thigs, don't we?": "Blended Value Accounting" in social entrepreneurship, *Social Accounting. Organizações & Sociedade*, *34*, 755–769. doi:10.1016/j.aos.2009.04.008

Nicholls, A., Paton, R., & Emerson, J. (2015). Social Impact Measurement. In A. Nicholls, R. Paton, & J. Emerson (Eds.), *Social Finance* (pp. 101–102). University Press Scholarship Online., doi:10.1093/acprof:oso/9780198703761.003.0016

Nobes, C. (2020). A half-century of Accounting and Business Research: The impact on the study of international financial reporting. *Accounting and Business Research*, *50*(7), 693–701. https://doi.org/https://doi.org/10.1080/00014788.2020.1742446. doi:10.1080/00014788.2020.1742446

Nobes, C., & Parker, R. (2020). *Comparative International Accounting* (14th ed.). Pearson.

Nordqvist, M., Sharma, P., & Chirico, F. (2014). Family firm heterogeneity and governance: A configuration approach. *Journal of Small Business Management*, *52*(2), 192–209. doi:10.1111/jsbm.12096

O'Dwyer, B., & Unerman, J. (2016). Fostering Rigour in Accounting for Social Sustainability. *Accounting, Organizations and Society*, *49*, 32–40. doi:10.1016/j.aos.2015.11.003

O'Leary, D. (2017). Configuring Blockchain Architectures for Transaction Information in Blockchain Consortiums: The Case of Accounting and Supply Chain Systems. *International Journal of Intelligent Systems in Accounting Finance & Management*, *24*(1), 138–147. doi:10.1002/isaf.1417

O'Leary, D. (2018). Open Information Enterprise Transactions: Business Intelligence and Wash and Spoof Transactions in Blockchain and Social Commerce. *International Journal of Intelligent Systems in Accounting Finance & Management*, *25*(1), 148–158. doi:10.1002/isaf.1438

OECD/IFAC. (2017). *Accrual Practices and Reform Experiences in OECD Countries*. OECD Publishing. doi:10.1787/9789264270572-

Ølnes, S., Ubacht, J., & Hanssen, M. (2017). Blockchain in Government: Benefits and Implications of Distributed Ledger Technology for Information Sharing. *Government Information Quarterly*, *34*(3), 355–364. doi:10.1016/j.giq.2017.09.007

Onken, G. (2022). *Mexico is planning a major e-invoicing update to version 4 of CFDI 4.0 on 1st January 2022*. Product Manager software applications/services electronic business data exchange. https://blog.seeburger.com/mexico-is-planning-a-major-e-invoicing-update-to-version-4-of-cfdi-4-0-on-1st-january-2022/

Orazalin, N., & Baydauletov, M. (2020). Corporate social responsibility strategy and corporate environmental and social performance: The moderating role of board gender diversity. *Corporate Social Responsibility and Environmental Management*, *27*(4), 1664–1676. doi:10.1002/csr.1915

OROC. (2017). *Estatuto da Ordem dos Revisores Oficiais de Contas*. OROC. https://www.oroc.pt/a-ordem/estatuto-da-oroc/estatuto-da-oroc/

Oulasvirta, L. O., & Bailey, S. J. (2016). Evolution of EU public sector financial accounting standardisation: Critical events that opened the window for attempted policy change. *Journal of European Integration, 38*(6), 653–669. doi:10.1080/07036337.2016.1177043

Paiva, I., Lourenço, I., & Branco, M. (2016). Earnings management in family firms: Current state of knowledge and opportunities for future research. *Review of Accounting and Finance, 15*(1), 85–100. doi:10.1108/RAF-06-2014-0065

Paiva, I., Lourenço, I., & Curto, J. (2019). Earnings management in family versus non-family firms: The influence of analyst coverage. *Spanish Journal of Finance and Accounting/Revista Española de Financiación y Contabilidad, 48*(2), 113–133. doi:10.1080/02102412.2018.1463764

Palma, M., Costa, I., & Castelo, M. (2022). Web-based sustainability reporting by family companies: The role of the richest European families. *Accounting Forum, 46*(4), 344–368. doi:10.1080/01559982.2021.1979331

Pascual-Pedreño, E., Gelashvili, V., & Pascual-Nebreda, L. (2021). Blockchain and its application to accounting. *Intangible Capital, 17*(1), 1–16. doi:10.3926/ic.1522

Pazzaglia, F., Mengoli, S., & Sapienza, E. (2013). Earnings quality in acquired and non-acquired family firms: A socioemotional wealth perspective. *Family Business Review, 4*(26), 374–386. doi:10.1177/0894486513486343

Peleias, F. D. 'A. (2017). *Mecanismos linguísticos (des) favoráveis para a readability das demonstrações financeiras: uma análise das empresas listadas no mercado de capitais brasileiro.* [Master's dissertation, Fundação Escola de Comércio Álvares Penteado, São Paulo, SP].

Peng, L., Teoh, S. H., Wang, Y., & Yan, J. (2022). Face value: Trait impressions, performance characteristics, and market outcomes for financial analysts. *Journal of Accounting Research, 60*(2), 653–705. doi:10.1111/1475-679X.12428

Pereira, A. C. (2019). *Matérias Relevantes de Auditoria relatadas pelas empresas cotadas na Euronext Lisbon* [Dissertação, Universidade Católica Portuguesa, Lisboa, Portugal]. https://repositorio.ucp.pt/

Pereira, A.C. (2019). Matérias Relevantes de Auditoria relatadas pelas empresas cotadas na Euronext Lisbon. *Revista da Ordem dos Revisores Oficiais de Contas,* (87), 11-23.

Pereira, M. F. (2010). *Planejamento estratégico: teorias, modelos e processos. São Paulo: Atlas. Matos, J. G. R., Matos, R. M. B., & Almeida, J. R. DE. (2007). Análise do Ambiente Corporativo: do caos organizado ao planejamento.* E-papers.

Petersen, A., Herbert, S., & Daniels, N. (2022). The likely adoption of the IFRS Foundation's proposed sustainability reporting standards. *The Business and Management Review, 13*(2). Advance online publication. doi:10.24052/BMR/V13NU02/ART-03

Peters, G., & Panayi, E. (2016). Understanding Modern Banking Ledgers Through Blockchain Technologies: Future of Transaction Processing and Smart Contracts on the Internet of Money. In P. Tasca, T. Aste, L. Pelizzon, & N. Perony (Eds.), *Banking Beyond Banks and Money* (pp. 239–278). Springer., doi:10.1007/978-3-319-42448-4_13

Petrucelli, J. (2013). *Detecting Fraud in Organizations: Techniques, Tools, and Resources.* John Wiley & Sons, Inc., doi:10.1002/9781118555972

Piazza, F. S. (2017). Bitcoin and the Blockchain as Possible Corporate Governance Tools: Strengths and Weaknesses. *Penn State Journal of Law & International Affairs, 5*(2), 262–301. https://elibrary.law.psu.edu/jlia/vol5/iss2/3

Pieper, T. M., Kellermanns, F. W., & Astrachan, J. H. (2021). *Family businesses' contribution to the US economy*. Washington, DC: Family Enterprise USA.

Pindado, J., & Requejo, I. (2015). Family business performance from a governance perspective: A review of empirical research. *International Journal of Management Reviews*, *17*(3), 279–311. doi:10.1111/ijmr.12040

Piotroski, J. D., & Srinivasan, S. (2008). Regulation and bonding: The sarbanes-oxley act and the flow of international listings. *Journal of Accounting Research*, *46*(2), 383–425. doi:10.1111/j.1475-679X.2008.00279.x

Piotroski, J. D., Wong, T. J., & Zhang, T. (2015). Political incentives to suppress negative information: Evidence from chinese listed firms. *Journal of Accounting Research*, *53*(2), 405–459. doi:10.1111/1475-679X.12071

Pittroff, E. (2021). The legitimacy of global accounting rules: A note on the challenges from path-dependence theory. *The Journal of Management and Governance*, *25*(2), 379–396. doi:10.100710997-020-09546-6

Pivac, S., Vuko, T., & Cular, M. (2017). Analysis of annual report disclosure quality for listed companies in transition countries. *Ekonomska Istrazivanja*, *30*(1), 721–731. doi:10.1080/1331677X.2017.1311231

Plumlee, M., Brown, D., Hayes, R. M., & Marshall, R. S. (2015). Voluntary environmental disclosure quality and firm value: Further evidence. *Journal of Accounting and Public Policy*, *34*(4), 336–361. doi:10.1016/j.jaccpubpol.2015.04.004

Podsakoff, P. M., Mackenzie, S. B., Bachrach, D. G., & Podsakoff, N. P. (2005). The influence of management journals in the 1980s and 1990s. *Strategic Management Journal*, *26*(5), 473–488. doi:10.1002mj.454

Polzer, T., Grossi, G., & Reichard, C. (2022). Implementation of the international public sector accounting standards in Europe. Variations on a global theme. *Accounting Forum*, *46*(1), 57–82. doi:10.1080/01559982.2021.1920277

Prencipe, A., Bar-Yosef, S., & Dekker, H. (2014). Accounting research in family firms: Theoretical and empirical challenges. *European Accounting Review*, *23*(3), 361–385. doi:10.1080/09638180.2014.895621

Prencipe, A., Markarian, G., & Pozza, L. (2008). Earnings management in family firms: Evidence from R&D cost capitalization in Italy. *Family Business Review*, *21*(1), 71–88. doi:10.1111/j.1741-6248.2007.00112.x

PricewaterhouseCoopers. (2016). *What's Next for Blockchain in 2016?* PWC. https://www.pwc.com/us/en/financial-services/publications/viewpoints/assets/pwc-qa-whats-next-for-blockchain.pdf

Primavera. (2022). E Se A Contabilidade Fosse Em Blockchain? *Prima Vera BSS*. https://mz.primaverabss.com/pt/blog/blockchain-na-contabilidade/#:~:text=Com%20a%20blockchain%20na%20contabilidade%2C%20o%20registo%20das,um%20sistema%20interligado%20de%20registos%20de%20contabilidade%20duradouros

Purkayastha, S., Veliyath, R., & George, R. (2022). Type I and type II agency conflicts in family firms: An empirical investigation. *Journal of Business Research*, *153*(3), 285–299. doi:10.1016/j.jbusres.2022.07.054

PWC. (2015). *Delivering the value of the Audit: New insightful audit reports*. Reino Unido: PWC.

PwC. (2019). *Accounting maturity update. 2019 preliminary results*. PricewaterhouseCoopers.

Quain, S. (2018). Importance of an External Audit. https://smallbusiness.chron.com/importance-external-audit-17630.html

Rahman, M. J., & Zheng, X. (2022). Whether family ownership affects the relationship between CSR and EM: Evidence from Chinese listed firms. *Journal of Family Business Management*. doi:10.1108/JFBM-03-2022-0030

Ramanna, K., & Roychowdhury, S. (2010). Elections and discretionary accruals: Evidence from 2004. *Journal of Accounting Research*, *48*(2), 445–475. doi:10.1111/j.1475-679X.2010.00373.x

Ramos, C. (2019). Social Economy Satellite Account (CSES) how to build a Satellite Account *(original article in Spanish), Economia Social Leituras and Debates,* 6. Retrieved from https://knowledgehub.unsse.org/wp-content/uploads/2019/12/Ramos_2019_Social-Economy-Satellite-Account-in-Portugal.pdf

Ramos, V. (2019). A proposal for using risk management for Academic Planning at a Public University. *Journal of Management and Projects*. https://doi.org/ . doi:10.5585/gep.v10i1.14777

Raupp, F. M., & Beuren, I. M. (2006). Metodologia da pesquisa aplicável às Ciências Sociais. In I. M. Beuren (Ed.), *Como Elaborar Trabalhos Monográficos em Contabilidade: Teoria e Prática* (3rd ed., pp. 76–97). Atlas.

Raval, S. (2016). *Decentralized applications: harnessing Bitcoin's blockchain technology*. O'Reilly Media, Inc.

Rawlins, B. (2009). Give the emperor a mirror: Toward developing a stakeholder measurement of organizational transparency. *Journal of Public Relations Research*, *21*(1), 71–99. doi:10.1080/10627260802153421

Refinitiv. (2022). Environmental, Social and Governance (ESG) Scores from Refinitiv. Refinitiv. https://www.refinitiv.com/content/dam/marketing/en_us/documents/methodology/esg-scores-methodology.pdf

Rego, S. O., & Wilson, R. (2012). Equity risk incentives and corporate tax aggressiveness. *Journal of Accounting Research*, *50*(3), 775–810. doi:10.1111/j.1475-679X.2012.00438.x

Regulation of the European Parliament and of the Council of 21 May 2013 on the European system of national and regional accounts in the European Union Text with EEA relevance. No 549/2013 (2013). https://eur-lex.europa.eu/legal-content/EN/ALL/?uri=celex:32013R0549

Reichelt, K. J., & Wang, D. (2010). National and office-specific measures of auditor industry expertise and effects on audit quality. *Journal of Accounting Research*, *48*(3), 647–686. doi:10.1111/j.1475-679X.2009.00363.x

Retolaza, J. L., San-Jose, L., & Ruíz-Roqueñi, M. (2016). *Social Accounting for Sustainability Monetizing the Social Value*. Springer.

Revilla, A. J., Pérez-Luño, A., & Nieto, M. J. (2016). Does family involvement in management reduce the risk of business failure? The moderating role of entrepreneurial orientation. *Family Business Review*, *29*(4), 365–379. doi:10.1177/0894486516671075

Rezende, D. A. (2008). *Planejamento estratégico para organizações: públicas e privadas*. Brasport.

Richardson, A., & Eberlein, B. (2011). Legitimating Transnational Standard-Setting: The Case of the International Accounting Standards Board. *Journal of Business Ethics*, *98*(2), 217–245. doi:10.100710551-010-0543-9

Richardson, R. J. (2008). *Social research: methods and techniques* (3rd ed.). Atlas.

Richmond, J. B., Mook, L., & Quarter, J. (2003). Social Accounting for Nonprofits Two Models. *Nonprofit Management & Leadership*, *13*(4), 308–324.

Rigot, S., Amar, J., & Demaria, S. (2022). Enhancing Financial Transparency to Mitigate Climate Change: Toward a Climate Risks and Opportunities Reporting Index. *Environmental Modeling and Assessment*, *27*(3), 425–439. doi:10.100710666-021-09800-7

Rinaldi, L. (2019). Accounting for Sustainability Governance: The Enabling Role of Social and Environmental Accountability Research. *Social and Environmental Accountability Journal*, *39*(1), 1–22. doi:10.1080/0969160X.2019.1578675

Robson, K. (1991). On the arenas of accounting change: The process of translation. *Accounting, Organizations and Society*, *16*(5-6), 547–570. doi:10.1016/0361-3682(91)90041-C

Robson, K. (1992). Accounting numbers as "inscription": Action at a distance and the development of accounting. *Accounting, Organizations and Society*, *17*(7), 685–708. doi:10.1016/0361-3682(92)90019-O

Rocha, M., & Eugénio, T. (2019). Auditoria Financeira- Evolução histórica e conceitos associados. *APOTEC Jornal de Contabilidade*, (471), 188–191.

Rodhes, R. (1996). The new governance: Governing without government. *Political Studies*, *44*(4), 652–667. doi:10.1111/j.1467-9248.1996.tb01747.x

Rodrigues, F. F. (2012). *Fatores determinantes da evolução das informações divulgadas no relatório da administração das empresas brasileiras de capital aberto.* [Doctoral dissertation, Programa Multi-institucional e Inter-regional de Pós-Graduação em Ciências Contábeis. Brasília, DF].

Rodrigues, J. N., Eiras, R., Nunes, C., & Cardoso, J. F. (2005). 50 gurus for the 21st century. Lisbon: Centro Atlântico.PT.

Rodríguez-Ariza, L., Martínez-Ferrero, J., & Bermejo-Sánchez, M. (2016). Consequences of earnings management for corporate reputation: Evidence from family firms. *Accounting Research Journal*, *29*(4), 457–474. doi:10.1108/ARJ-02-2015-0017

Rooney, H., Aiken, B., & Rooney, M. (2017). Q&A. Is Internal Audit Ready for Blockchain? *Technology Innovation Management Review*, *7*(10), 41–44. doi:10.22215/timreview/1113

Rozario, A. M., & Vasarhelyi, M. A. (2018). Auditing with Smart Contracts. *The International Journal of Digital Accounting Research*, *18*(1), 1–27. doi:10.4192/1577-8517-v18_1

Ruckeshauser, N. (2017). Do We Really Want Blockchain-based Accounting? Decentralized Consensus as Enabler of Management Override of Internal Controls. In Leimeister, J. M. & Brenner, W. (Eds.), Proceedings der 13. Internationalen Tagung Wirtschaftsinformatik (16–30). Institute of Information Management - St. Gallen University.

Santos, A. L., & Rodrigues, L. L. (2021). Banks and climate-related information: The case of Portugal. *Sustainability (Basel)*, *13*(21), 12215. doi:10.3390u132112215

Santos, R., Ribeiro, H. C. M., & Moreira, A. A. A. P. (2018). Swot analysis: A case study in a higher education institution. *Strategy & Development Journal*, *2*(3), 18–34.

Saraiva, H. I. B., Alves, M.-C. G., & Gabriel, V. M. S. (2015). As raízes do processo formal de harmonização contabilística, a sua evolução e influência em Portugal. *De Computis. Spanish Journal of Accounting History*, *12*(22), 172–204. doi:10.26784/issn.1886-1881.v12i22.32

Sarfraz, M., Qun, W., Hui, L., & Abdullah, M. I. (2018). Environmental risk management strategies and the moderating role of corporate social responsibility in project financing decisions. *Sustainability (Basel)*, *10*(8), 2771. Advance online publication. doi:10.3390u10082771

Sarumpaet, S., Nelwan, M. L., & Dewi, D. N. (2017). The value relevance of environmental performance: Evidence from Indonesia. *Social Responsibility Journal*, *13*(4), 817–827. doi:10.1108/SRJ-01-2017-0003

Schmidthuber, L., Hilgers, D., & Hofmann, S. (2020). International Public Sector Accounting Standards (IPSASs): A systematic literature review and future research agenda. *Financial Accountability & Management*, *38*(1), 119–142. https://doi.org/https://doi.org/10.1111/faam.12265. doi:10.1111/faam.12265

Schmidt, M. (2005, June). *"Whistle Blowing" Regulation and Accounting Standards Enforcement in Germany and Europe* – an Economic Perspective. *International Review of Law and Economics*, *25*(2), 143–168. doi:10.1016/j.irle.2005.06.001

Schmitz, J., & Leoni, G. (2019). Accounting and auditing at the time of blockchain technology: A research agenda. *Australian Accounting Review*, *29*(2), 331–342. doi:10.1111/auar.12286

Schnackenberg, A. K., & Tomlinson, E. C. (2016). Organizational transparency: A new perspective on managing trust in organization-stakeholder relationships. *Journal of Management*, *42*(7), 1784–1810. doi:10.1177/0149206314525202

Schulze, W. S., Lubatkin, M. H., Dino, R. N., & Buchholtz, A. K. (2001). Agency relationships in family firms: Theory and evidence. *Organization Science*, *12*(2), 99–116. doi:10.1287/orsc.12.2.99.10114

Scott, J. (2000). Rational choice theory. *Understanding contemporary society: Theories of the present*, *129*, 671-85.

Sdi Unifei. (n.d.). *Risk Management and Controls*. Sdi Unifei. https://sdi.unifei.edu.br/governanca-riscos-e-controles-internos/gestao/

Secinaro, S., Dal Mas, F., Brescia, V., & Calandra, D. (2022). Blockchain in the accounting, auditing and accountability fields: A bibliometric and coding analysis. *Accounting, Auditing & Accountability Journal*, *35*(9), 168–203. doi:10.1108/AAAJ-10-2020-4987

Serra, F., Torres, A., & Torres, M. (2004). *Administração estratégica: conceito, roteiros práticos e casos*. Reichmann & Affonso Editores.

Setia-Atmaja, L., Haman, J., & Tanewski, G. (2011). The role of board independence in mitigating agency problem II in Australian family firms. *The British Accounting Review*, *43*(3), 230–246. doi:10.1016/j.bar.2011.06.006

Seyoum, B. (2009). An empirical analysis of the impact of corporate transparency on foreign direct investment. *Multinational Business Review*, *17*(3), 29–48. doi:10.1108/1525383X200900016

Sharma, P., Chrisman, J. J., & Gersick, K. E. (2012). 25 years of family business review: Reflections on the past and perspectives for the future. *Family Business Review*, *25*(1), 5–15. doi:10.1177/0894486512437626

Shleifer, A., & Vishny, R. (1997). A survey of corporate governance. *The Journal of Finance*, *52*(2), 737–783. doi:10.1111/j.1540-6261.1997.tb04820.x

Sierra-García, L., Gambetta, N., García-Benau, M. A., & Orta-Pérez, M. (2019). Understanding the determinants of the magnitude of entity-level risk and account-level risk key audit matters: The case of the United Kingdom. *The British Accounting Review*, *51*(3), 227–240. doi:10.1016/j.bar.2019.02.004

Silva, B. (2015). *Proposta de modelo de gestão de riscos para uma ifes visando a realização de auditoria baseada em riscos* [Master's thesis, Universidade Federal do Rio Grande do Norte, Natal]

Silva, C. A. T., & Fernandes, J. L. T. (2009). Legibilidade dos fatos relevantes no Brasil. *Revista de Administração Contemporânea - RAC Electronica, 3*(1), 142-159.

Silva, R. B. (2017). *Implicações da OCPC 07 no disclosure e na forma das notas explicativas das demonstrações contábeis*. [Master's dissertation, Universidade Federal do Ceará, Fortaleza, CE].

Simnett, R., & Huggins, A. (2014). Enhancing the Auditor's Report: To What Extent is There Support for the IAASB's Proposed Changes? *Accounting Horizons*, *28*(4), 719–747. doi:10.2308/acch-50791

Simões, P. P. (2019). *O Whistleblowing em Portugal. Será que pode ser praticado pelo auditor?* Revisores ∃ Auditores, revista da Ordem dos Revisores Oficiais de Contas. http://hdl.handle.net/10400.21/11354

Simões, P. P. (2020). O Whistleblowing é um caso de Polícia(s)? In *Polícias(s) e segurança Pública – História e Perspetivas Contemporâneas. Coordenadores Rollo, M. F., Gomes, P. M., Rodrígues, A. C.* Editor MUP – Museu da Polícia. http://hdl.handle.net/10400.21/12526

Sirmon, D. G., & Hitt, M. A. (2003). Managing resources: Linking unique resources, management, and wealth creation in family firms. *Entrepreneurship Theory and Practice*, *27*(4), 339–358. doi:10.1111/1540-8520.t01-1-00013

Sirois, L. P., Bédard, J., & Bera, P. (2018). The informational value of key audit matters in the auditor's report: Evidence from an eye-tracking study. *Accounting Horizons*, *32*(2), 141–162. doi:10.2308/acch-52047

Smith, M., & Taffler, R. (1992). Readability and understandability: Different measures of the textual complexity of accounting narrative. *Accounting, Auditing & Accountability Journal, 5*(4), 0-0.

Sobral, F., & Peci, A. (2008). *Administração: teoria e prática no contexto brasileiro*. Pearson Prentice Hall.

Solomon, J. (2007). *Corporate governance and accountability*. John Wiley & Sons, Ltd.

Soltes, E. (2020). Paper versus practice: A field investigation of integrity hotlines. *Journal of Accounting Research*, *58*(2), 429–472. doi:10.1111/1475-679X.12302

Srinivasan, S., & Richardson, S. A. (2005). Consequences of financial reporting failure for outside directors: Evidence from accounting restatements and audit committee members. *Journal of Accounting Research*, *43*(2), 291–334. doi:10.1111/j.1475-679x.2005.00172.x

Statistics Poland. (2021). *Social Economy Satellite Account for Poland 2018*. Retrieved from https://stat.gov.pl/download/gfx/portalinformacyjny/en/defaultaktualnosci/3681/5/1/1/social_economy_satellite_account_for_poland_2018.pdf

Steenkamp, N., Rahman, A., & Kashyap, V. (2011). Recognition, measurement and disclosure of carbon emission allowances under the EU ETS - An exploratory study. *CSEAR 2011 Australasian Conference*.

Stockmans, A., Lybaert, N., & Voordeckers, W. (2010). Socioemotional wealth and earnings management in private family firms. *Family Business Review*, *23*(3), 280–294. doi:10.1177/0894486510374457

Stockmans, A., Lybaert, N., & Voordeckers, W. (2013). The conditional nature of board characteristics in constraining earnings management in private family firms. *Journal of Family Business Strategy*, *2*(4), 84–92. doi:10.1016/j.jfbs.2013.01.001

Stubben, S. R., & Welch, K. T. (2020). Evidence on the use and efficacy of internal whistleblowing systems. *Journal of Accounting Research*, *58*(2), 473–518. doi:10.1111/1475-679X.12303

Su, E., & Daspit, J. (2021). Knowledge management in family firms: A systematic review, integrated insights and future research opportunities. *Journal of Knowledge Management*, *26*(2), 291–325. doi:10.1108/JKM-08-2020-0658

Swan, M. (2015). *Blockchain: Blueprint for a new economy*. O'Reilly Media, Inc.

Tan, H., Wang, S., & Welker, M. (2011). Analyst following and forecast accuracy after mandated IFRS adoptions. *Journal of Accounting Research*, *49*(5), 1307–1357. doi:10.1111/j.1475-679X.2011.00422.x

Tan, H., Ying Wang, E., & Zhou, B. (2014). When the use of positive language backfires: The joint effect of tone, readability, and investor sophistication on earnings judgments. *Journal of Accounting Research*, *52*(1), 273–302. doi:10.1111/1475-679X.12039

TCFD [Task Force on Climate-related Financial Disclosures]. (2017). *Final Report: Recommendations of the Task Force on Climate-Related Financial Disclosures*. FSB. https://www.fsb-tcfd.org/recommendations/

TCFD [Task Force on Climate-related Financial Disclosures]. (2022). *Task Force on Climate-related Financial Disclosures 2022 Report Status.* FSB. https://www.fsb.org/2022/10/2022-tcfd-status-report-task-force-on-climate-related-financial-disclosures/

Tcu. (n.d.). *Levantamento de governança.* TCU. https://portal.tcu.gov.br/governanca/governancapublica/organizacional/levantamento-de-governanca/levantamento-de-governa nca.htm

Telles, S. V. (2018). *Readability and understandability of notes to the financial statements.* [Doctoral dissertation, Universidade de São Paulo, São Paulo, SP].

The Hartford Business Owners' Playbook. (2022). Growing Safeguards. *Reduce Risk and Safeguard Your Growing Business.* The Hartford. https://www.thehartford.com/business-insurance/strategy/growing/safeguards

Thirlwall, P. A. (1983). *Growth and Development with Special reference to developing economies* (3rd ed.). Macmillan.

Thomson Reuters. (2019). Futuro da Contabilidade: Veja os impactos da tecnologia blockchain na contabilidade. *Domininiosistemas.* https://www.dominiosistemas.com.br/blog/veja-os-impactos-da-tecnologia-blockchain-na-contabilidade/

Toit, E. (2017). *The readability of integrated reports.* Meditari Accountancy Research.

Toudas, K., Poutos, E., & Balios, D. (2013). Concept, regulations and institutional issues of IPSAS: A critical review. *European Journal of Business and Social Sciences, 2*(1), 43–54.

Trongmateerut, P., & Sweeney, J. T. (2013). The influence of subjective norms on whistle-blowing: A cross-cultural investigation. *Journal of Business Ethics, 112*(3), 437–451. doi:10.100710551-012-1270-1

Turzo, T., Marzi, G., Favino, C., & Terzani, S. (2022). Non-financial reporting research and practice : Lessons from the last decade. *Journal of Cleaner Production, 345*, 131–154. doi:10.1016/j.jclepro.2022.131154

Tweedie, D., & Hazelton, J. (2019). Economic inequality: Problems and perspectives for interdisciplinary accounting research. *Accounting, Auditing & Accountability Journal, 32*(7), 1982–2003. doi:10.1108/AAAJ-09-2018-3649

UE (2014). Regulamento (UE) n.º 537/2014. *Jornal Oficial da União Europeia.* L158 (27-05-2014).

UFNS. (n.d.). Risk Management Policy. Ufms. https://www.ufms.br/comite-de-gestao-de-integridade-riscos-e-controle-interno/gestao-de-riscos/

Ufrn achieves 1st place in governance and management. (2022, August 11). UFRN. https://ufrn.br/imprensa/noticias/52219/ufrn-alcanca-1o-lugar-em-governanca-e-gestao

Umans, I., & Corten, M. (2022). Ownership succession intentions affecting earnings management in private family firms. *Small Business Economics*, 1–16. doi:10.100711187-022-00696-5

UNCTAD [United Nations Conference on Trade and Development]. (2021). *Climate-related financial disclosures in mainstream entity reporting: Good practices and key challenges.* UNCTAD. https://unctad.org/system/files/official-document/ciiisard98_en.pdf

United Nations, Department of Economic and Social Affairs. (2018). Satellite Account on Non-profit and Related Institutions and Volunteer Work. Studies in Methods, Handbook of national Accounting, Series F, No. 91, Rev. 1: New York

Vaccaro, A., & Madsen, P. (2009). Corporate dynamic transparency: The new ICT-driven ethics. *Ethics and Information Technology, 11*(2), 113–122. doi:10.100710676-009-9190-1

Velte, P., & Issa, J. (2019). The impact of key audit matter (KAM) disclosure in audit reports on stakeholders' reactions: A literature review. *Problems and Perspectives in Management, 17*(3), 323–341. doi:10.21511/ppm.17(3).2019.26

Vieira, P., & Saraiva, H. (2023). Tokenizing the Portuguese Accounting Standards System. In Prieto, J., Benítez-Martínez, F.L., Ferretti, S., Arroyo Guardeño, D., Tomás Nevado-Batalla, P. (Eds.). *Blockchain and Applications, 4th International Congress. BLOCKCHAIN 2022. Lecture Notes in Networks and Systems*, 595 (324-333). Springer. https://doi.org/10.1007/978-3-031-21229-1_30

Vieira, E. (2016). Earnings management in public family firms. *Australian Accounting Review, 77*(26), 190–207. doi:10.1111/auar.12096

Vik, C., & Walter, M. C. (2017). *The reporting practices of key audit matters in the big five audit firms in Norway.* [Dissertação de Mestrado, BI Norwegian Business School, Oslo, Noruega]. https://www.semanticscholar.org/paper/The-reporting-practices-of-key-audit-matters-in-the-Vik-Walter/de89523c0fad702da00 3e642c206337946bafa9d

Villalonga, B., & Amit, R. (2006). How do family ownership, control and management affect firm value? *Journal of Financial Economics, 80*(2), 385–417. doi:10.1016/j.jfineco.2004.12.005

Villalonga, B., Amit, R., Trujillo, M. A., & Guzmán, A. (2015). Governance of family firms. *Annual Review of Financial Economics, 7*(1), 635–654. doi:10.1146/annurev-financial-110613-034357

von Ravensburg, G. N., Krlev, G., & Mildenberge, G. (2018). *Social Enterprises and their Ecosystems in Europe. Country Report: Germany.* Luxemburg: European Union. https://ec.europa.eu/social/BlobServlet?docId=20563&langId=en

Vural, D. (2018). Disclosure practices by family firms: Evidence from Swedish publicly listed firms. *Accounting in Europe, 15*(3), 347–373. doi:10.1080/17449480.2018.1479531

Wang, D. (2006). Founding family ownership and earnings quality. *Journal of Accounting Research, 44*(3), 619–656. doi:10.1111/j.1475-679X.2006.00213.x

Wang, L., & Juslin, H. (2012). Values and corporate social responsibility perceptions of Chinese university students. *Journal of Academic Ethics, 10*(1), 57–82. doi:10.100710805-012-9148-5

Wang, X., Cao, F., & Ye, K. (2018). Mandatory Corporate Social Responsibility (CSR) Reporting and Financial Reporting Quality: Evidence from a Quasi-Natural Experiment. *Journal of Business Ethics, 152*(1), 253–274. doi:10.100710551-016-3296-2

Wang, Y., & Kogan, A. (2018). Designing Confidentiality-preserving Blockchain-based Transaction Processing Systems. *International Journal of Accounting Information Systems, 30*(1), 1–18. doi:10.1016/j.accinf.2018.06.001

Wan-Hussin, W. N. (2009). The impact of family-firm structure and board composition on corporate transparency: Evidence based on segment disclosures in Malaysia. *The International Journal of Accounting, 44*(4), 313–333. doi:10.1016/j.intacc.2009.09.003

Warwick, P., & Ng, C. (2012). The "Cost" of Climate Change: How Carbon Emissions Allowances are Accounted for Amongst European Union Companies. *Australian Accounting Review, 22*(1), 54–67. doi:10.1111/j.1835-2561.2011.00158.x

Wehmeier, S., & Raaz, O. (2012). Transparency matters: The concept of organizational transparency in the academic discourse. *Public Relations Inquiry, 1*(3), 337–366. doi:10.1177/2046147X12448580

Westerman, G., & Hunter, R. (2008). *O risco de TI: convert ameaças aos negócios em vantagem competitiva.* M. Books do Brasil.

Williams, C. C. (2005). Trust diffusion: The effect of interpersonal trust on structure, function, and organizational transparency. *Business & Society*, *44*(3), 357–368. doi:10.1177/0007650305275299

Wu, D., Li, J., Lu, X., & Li, J. (2018). Journal editorship index for assessing the scholarly impact of academic institutions: An empirical analysis in the field of economics. *Journal of Informetrics*, *12*(2), 448–460. doi:10.1016/j.joi.2018.03.008

Wu, X., Tong, X., & Wang, Y. (2022). Managerial ability and idiosyncratic volatility. *International Journal of Finance & Economics*, *27*(2), 2566–2581. doi:10.1002/ijfe.2287

Xiao, Q., Cooke, F. L., & Chen, L. (2022). Nurses' well-being and implications for human resource management: A systematic literature review. *International Journal of Management Reviews*, *24*(4), 599–624. doi:10.1111/ijmr.12295

Xu, S., & Liu, D. (2018). Do Financial Markets Care about Corporate Social Responsibility Disclosure? Further Evidence from China. *Australian Accounting Review*, *28*(1), 79–103. doi:10.1111/auar.12161

Yermack, D. (2017). Corporate Governance and Blockchains. *Review of Finance*, *21*(1), 7–31. doi:10.1093/rof/rfw074

Yong, J. (2019). *Case Studies on Compliance with the IESBA Code of Ethics*. IFAC. https://www.ifac.org/knowledge-gateway/supporting-international-standards/discussion/case-studies-compliance-iesba-code-ethics

Yuan, X., Li, Z., Xu, J., & Shang, L. (2022). ESG disclosure and corporate financial irregularities – Evidence from Chinese listed firms. *Journal of Cleaner Production*, *332*, 129992. Advance online publication. doi:10.1016/j.jclepro.2021.129992

Zaini, S. M., Sharma, U., Samking, G., & Davey, H. (2019). Impact of ownership structure on the level of voluntary disclosure: A study of listed family-controlled companies in Malaysia. *Accounting Forum*, *44*(1), 1–34. doi:10.1080/01559982.2019.1605874

Zheng, Z., Xie, S., Dai, H.-N., Chen, W., Chen, X., Weng, J., & Imran, M. (2020). An overview on Smart Contracts: Challenges, advances and platforms. *Future Generation Computer Systems*, *105*, 475–491. doi:10.1016/j.future.2019.12.019

Zhong, X., Ren, L., & Wu, X. (2022). Founder domination, industry environment, and family firms' earnings management. *Baltic Journal of Management*, *17*(5), 565–585. doi:10.1108/BJM-09-2021-0360

Zhou, S. (2022). Reporting and Assurance of Climate-Related and Other Sustainability Information: A Review of Research and Practice. *Australian Accounting Review*, *32*(102), 315–333. doi:10.1111/auar.12387

About the Contributors

Fábio Henrique Albuquerque is the Coordinator Professor of accounting and auditing and Director of the master's in accounting at Lisbon Accounting and Business School (ISCAL) of the Politécnico de Lisboa, Portugal. He is a PhD in Financial Economics and Accounting and has a master's degree in Auditing and a bachelor's degree in accounting. Prof. Albuquerque worked for several entities in areas such as accounting, financial reporting, and statistics, in addition to providing business consulting and training on national and international accounting and financial reporting standards. His research has covered accounting, auditing, as well as other related scientific areas such as education and corporate social responsibility. He is a reviewer and member of the editorial boards of several journals in the accounting and reporting areas.

***

João Borralho is an Assistant Professor at the Lusofona University, Lisbon Centre, in the School of Economic Sciences and Organisations (Portugal). He was previously a public auditor at the Inspeção-geral de Finanças (Inspectorate General of Finance). His main research interests include family businesses, earnings management and sustainability. His work has appeared in journals such as Journal of Cleaner Production, Revista de Contabilidad-Spanish Accounting Accounting Review, Spanish Journal of Finance and Accounting Accounting/Revista Española de Financiación y Contabilidad, y European Journal of Family Business (EJFB).

Rômulo Brito Oliveira is a master's student in Accounting from the Universidade Federal de Pernambuco (UFPE), MBA in Public Accounting and Fiscal Responsibility from the Centro Universitário Internacional (UNINTER), Graduated in Accounting from the Universidade Norte do Paraná (UNOPAR),Technologist in Systems Analysis and Development from the Universidade Norte do Paraná (UNOPAR), Technician in School Secretariat by the Instituto Federal de Educação Ciência e Tecnologia da Bahia (IFBA). He currently works as an accounting technician at the Instituto Federal de Educação Ciência e Tecnologia da Bahia (IFBA), Eunápolis campus, where he is responsible for the Accounting, Budget and Finance Sector. His most recent studies are focused on governance and risk management in the public service.

Patrick de Pitta Simões is a Ph.D. student in Law and Security – Nova School of Law Master in Auditing, ISCAL – Lisbon Accounting and Business School Frequency in Public Auditing Postgraduation – Institute for Economic, Financial and Tax Law of University of Lisbon School of Law (IDEFF)

Postgraduate in Water Law. Institute of Legal and Political Sciences of University of Lisbon School of Law Specialist in Administrative Law (postgraduate studies), University of Lisbon School of Law Postgraduate in Environmental Law, Spatial Planning, Urbanism and Tourism. Institute of Legal and Political Sciences of the Faculty of Law of the University of Lisbon Postgraduate in State Extra-Contractual Civil Liability and Other Authorities established under Public Law Regime – Institute of Legal and Political Sciences of University of Lisbon School of Law Bachelor's in Law, University of Lisbon School of Law Postgraduate in Teaching Geography and Regional Planning – Nova School of Social Sciences and Humanities. Level IV postgraduate training course, Specialist in CAD / GIS - Geographic Information Systems, by CESAE – Service and Support Centre for Companies (665h), with professional internship, at Municipia - Cartography and Information Systems Company (160h). Bachelor in Geography and Regional Planning – Major in Regional Planning. Nova School of Social Sciences and Humanities

Jorge Luiz de Santana Junior has a bachelor's degree in Accounting at Federal University of Sergipe (2017) and master's degree in Accounting at Federal University of Bahia (2020). Currently PhD Student in Accounting at University of São Paulo.

Flory Dieck-Assad, PhD in Finance from Tulane University, USA. Author of "Financial Institutions" by McGraw-Hill in 2003 and second edition in 2014. With over 400 publications in refereed journals and magazines of national and international scope, is member of the National System of Researchers since December 2005 to date; "Texas A & M University Press" published in 2005 her second book "Energy and Sustainable Development in Mexico", honored with the Romulo Garza Award 2007 with its second printing in 2008. Awarded with the Prize for Teaching & Research 2007, 2010, 2014, and 2022; the National Ethics Award 2013, the 2015 Distinguished Professor of the Institute of Chartered Accountants of the State of Nuevo Leon, Mexico, and the 2015 National Energy Prize for her contributions to the energy sector. Tenured professor at Tecnologico de Monterrey. fdieck@tec.mx

Sónia Fernandes is a professor of accounting.

John Filos is an Associate Professor in 'Auditing – International Standards' at Public Administration Department in Panteion University, Athens, Greece. He graduated from the Athens Economic University (ASOEE) received his Masters in Business Administration (MBA) at the University of Connenticut, USA majoring in Accounting and Finance and has received his PhD at Panteion University, Athens, Greece. As a professional, he is certified as Certified Internal Auditor - CIA since 2002 and Certified Fraud Examiner – CFE since 2004. He worked in the auditing firm Arthur Andersen for 7 years (left at manager's level)) and as a business consultant for private and public organizations for 10 years, while being internal auditor (part-time) at the Hellenic Deposit & Investment Guarantee Fund (TEKE). By Decisions of Ministers of Finance has been appointed as member to committees for the Public Sector Accounting reforms (2009) and also a member to the Disciplinary Board of the Accounting and Auditing Supervision Board (2012). By Decision of the Ministry of Health has been appointed as president to Drugs Pricing Committee (2015)

Sheizi Freitas is an Associate Professor at the Accounting Department at Federal University of Bahia (UFBA).

Remedios Hernández-Linares is an Associate Professor at the Department of Financial Economy and Accounting at the University of Extremadura (Spain). She is currently serving as an Associated Editor at the European Journal of Family Business (EJFB) and The Bottom Line. Her primary research interests include family businesses, business strategy, entrepreneurship, and higher education learning. Her work has appeared in journals such as Family Business Review, Journal of Small Business Management, Journal of Knowledge Management, Journal of Cleaner Production, Scientometrics, Journal of Family Business Strategy, BRQ Business Research Quarterly, Revista de Contabilidad-Spanish Accounting Review, Spanish Journal of Finance and Accounting/Revista Española de Financiación y Contabilidad, Computer Applications in Engineering Education, and European Journal of Family Business, among others.

María-Pilar Martín-Zamora holds a degree and is a doctor (PhD) in Business Administration from the University of Sevilla (Spain). At present, she is a full professor at the University of Huelva, in the Department of Accounting and Finance. Since 1985, when she started her career in higher education, she has taught different subjects in the field of Financial Accounting. Her basic research is oriented towards Tax Accounting and Business Management. She is the author of some books and articles published in journals and she has presented papers in national and international conferences.

Pedro Pinheiro has a Ph.D. in Management from Universidade Lusíada de Lisboa, a master in Management with a specialization in Finance from Universidade de Évora, Degree in Financial Control and Bachelor in Accounting and Administration from Instituto Superior de Contabilidade e Administração de Lisboa (ISCAL). Professor at ISCAL, belonging to the Accounting and Auditing area. Member of the Representative Assembly Portuguese Chartered Accountants Association and of the Jury of Exams for Access to the Portuguese Chartered Accountants Association. Member of the General Council of Instituto Politécnico de Lisboa. Author of several papers, books, and book chapters in the field of business.

Maria Albertina Barreiro Rodrigues is Chairman of the Audit Committees of entities from the public sector. Professor at Universidade Europeia where she is the Coordinator of the online master's in management and of the online postgraduate studies in auditing and at Lisbon Accounting and Business School, ISCAL – IPL where she is the Vice Director on the Audit master's degree and Vice President of the Pedagogic Council with a PhD in Management. Specialist in Financial Audit. Holds a post-graduation in Strategic Management. The research areas of interest are corporate reporting, sustainability, integrated reporting, audit, ethics, and higher education. Financial and Statutory Auditor and Certified Accountant. Participated in International Conferences and published academic articles in journals and in the proceedings of said conferences. Has a professional career of over 30 years, 10 of which were spent as a Financial Manager in a multinational organisation. Was a member of committees from the Portuguese Institute of Statutory Auditors: Audit - Family and Profession Committee and Code of Ethics Monitoring Committee.

Helena Saraiva is an Adjunct Professor on Accounting and Finance area. Management and Economics Department, in Guarda Polytechnic Institute. Main research areas: Accounting, Accounting History, Balanced Scorecard, Blockchain, Entrepreneurship, Finance, Management Accounting.

Darlene Silva S. Santana has a Master in Letters from the State University of Southwest Bahia – UESB; Graduated in Letters – Portuguese Language and Portuguese Language Literatures from the State University of Bahia – UNEB and specialization in School Management and Pedagogical Practices from the Cândido Mendes University – UCAM. She is currently a language teacher in the municipality of Eunápolis and Secretarial Technician at the Federal Institute of Education, Science and Technology of Bahia – IFBA, Eunápolis campus, where she is responsible for the Planning and Governance Sector. His most recent studies are focused on governance and strategic planning in the public service. In his academic productions, he dealt with the themes: the role of education in the formation of the subject, based on the theory of language, and the constitution of contemporary subjectivity, considering the sign network imposed by technological advances.

Index

G

H

I

J

K

L

M

N

O

P

R

www.ingramcontent.com/pod-product-compliance
Lightning Source LLC
LaVergne TN
LVHW062142300926
849161LV00010B/2603
* 9 7 8 1 6 6 8 4 7 2 9 3 4 *